This volume of specially commissioned essays is a critical introduction to the psychology of Carl Gustav Jung, one of the founders of psychoanalysis. Jung broke with Freud and developed his own theories which he called "analytical psychology." This *Companion* sets Jung in the context of his own time, outlines the current practice and theory of Jungian psychology, and shows how Jungians continue to question and evolve his thinking to fit the post-modern, multi-cultural world of contemporary psychoanalysis.

Andrew Samuels's introduction gives a short appreciation of Jung's work and sets out the three different approaches to contemporary analytical psychology. The book is then divided into three sections: Jung's ideas and their context, which covers Jung's life and discoveries, particularly in relation to Freud; analytical psychology in practice, which deals with issues of clinical practice and includes a case study from the three Jungian approaches (classical, archetypal, and developmental); and analytical psychology in society, which shows how Jung's ideas have been incorporated into gender studies, literature, religion, and political science. The *Companion* includes a full chronology of Jung's life and work, reading lists, and a glossary.

This is an indispensable reference tool for beginning students and general readers, written by an international team of Jungian analysts and scholars from various disciplines. It will also be useful to advanced students and specialists who want to know about recent developments in Jungian thought and practice.

THE CAMBRIDGE
COMPANION TO
# JUNG

# THE CAMBRIDGE
# COMPANION TO
# JUNG

EDITED BY

## POLLY YOUNG-EISENDRATH

*Clinical Associate Professor in Psychiatry, Medical College,*
*University of Vermont*

AND

## TERENCE DAWSON

*Senior Lecturer in English Literature,*
*National University of Singapore*

CAMBRIDGE
UNIVERSITY PRESS

PUBLISHED BY THE PRESS SYNDICATE OF THE UNIVERSITY OF CAMBRIDGE
The Pitt Building, Trumpington Street, Cambridge, United Kingdom

CAMBRIDGE UNIVERSITY PRESS
The Edinburgh Building, Cambridge CB2 2RU, UK
40 West 20th Street, New York, NY 10011-4211, USA
477 Williamstown Road, Port Melbourne, VIC 3207, Australia
Ruiz de Alarcón 13, 28014 Madrid, Spain
Dock House, The Waterfront, Cape Town 8001, South Africa

http://www.cambridge.org

First published 1997
Reprinted 1998, 1999, 2002

Printed in Great Britain by BemroseBooth, Derby

Typeset in Sabon 10/13pt

A catalogue record for this book is available from the British Library

Library of Congress Cataloguing in Publication Data
The Cambridge Companion to Jung / edited by Polly Young-Eisendrath and
Terence Dawson.
p.   cm.
Includes index.
ISBN 0 521 47309 8 (hardback) – ISBN 0 521 47889 8 (paperback)
1. Jung, C. G. (Carl Gustav), 1875-1961. I. Young-Eisendrath,
Polly, 1947-  II. Dawson, Terence.
BF109.J8C36 1996
150.19'54'092-dc20 96-29101 CIP

ISBN 0 521 47309 8 hardback
ISBN 0 521 47889 8 paperback

CE

# CONTENTS

# CONTRIBUTORS

MICHAEL VANNOY ADAMS, D.Phil., C.S.W. is Senior Lecturer in Psycho-analytic Studies at the New School for Social Research in New York City, where he is also a psychotherapist in private practice. He is on the faculty of the Object Relations Institute for Psychotherapy and Psychoanalysis and is an Honorary Research Fellow of the Centre for Psychoanalytic Studies at the University of Kent. He is the author of *The Multicultural Imagination: "Race," Color, and the Unconscious* (1996).

LAWRENCE R. ALSCHULER is Professor of political science at the University of Ottawa, Canada, where he teaches on the political economy of the Third World. He studied for four years at the C. G. Jung Institute in Zurich and is interested in the psychology of oppression and liberation. He has written on multinationals in the Third World, the political thought of Rigoberta Menchu, and on Jung and Taoism.

JOHN BEEBE is a psychiatrist in Jungian analytic practice in San Francisco. He is the US editor of the *Journal of Analytical Psychology* and editor of *The San Francisco Jung Institute Library Journal*. He is also the author of *Integrity in Depth* (1992).

DOUGLAS A. DAVIS, Ph.D. is Professor of Psychology at Haverford College in Pennsylvania. His scholarly interests include the history of psychoanalysis, Freud's biography, and the role of culture in personality development. He is President of the Society for Cross-Cultural Research and co-author, with Susan Schaefer Davis, of *Adolescence in a Moroccan Town: Making Social Sense* (1989).

TERENCE DAWSON lectures in English and European literature at the National University of Singapore. He has published articles on the nineteenth-century novel as well as coedited, with Robert S. Dupree, *Seventeenth-Century English Poetry: The Annotated Anthology* (1994).

CLAIRE DOUGLAS, Ph.D. is a clinical psychologist and a Jungian analyst who practices in Malibu, California, and is a member of the Society of Jungian Analysts of Southern California. She is the author of *The Woman in the Mirror*

(1990) and *Translate this Darkness: The Life of Christiana Morgan* (1993), and the editor of the forthcoming edition of *C. G. Jung: The "Visions Seminars"* (Princeton University Press).

ELIO J. FRATTAROLI, M.D. is a psychiatrist and psychoanalyst in private practice in Philadelphia. He is also a clinical assistant professor of psychiatry at the University of Pennsylvania and a member of the faculty of the Institute of the Philadelphia Association for Psychoanalysis. He has written and lectured on Shakespeare and psychoanalysis, and psychoanalytic philosophy and epistemology. He is currently finishing a book, *Healing the Soul in the Decade of the Brain.*

ROSEMARY GORDON, Ph.D. is a Jungian analyst with a private practice in London. She is also a Training Analyst for the Society of Analytical Psychology and an Honorary Fellow of the Centre for Psychoanalytic Studies at the University of Kent. She was editor of the *Journal of Analytical Psychology* (1986–94). Her publications include *Dying and Creating: A Search for Meaning* (1978) and *Bridges: Metaphor for Psychic Processes* (1993).

DAVID L. HART, Ph.D., is a graduate of the C. G. Jung Institute, Zurich, and has a doctorate in psychology from the University of Zurich. He is a practicing Jungian analyst in the Boston area and has written and lectured widely, particularly on the psychology of fairy-tales.

PAUL KUGLER, Ph.D. is a Jungian psychoanalyst in private practice in East Aurora, New York. He is the author of numerous works ranging from contemporary psychoanalysis to experimental theatre and post-modernism. His most recent publication is *Supervision: Jungian Perspectives on Clinical Supervision* (1995). He is President of the Inter-Regional Society of Jungian Analysts.

DELDON ANNE McNEELY, Ph.D. is a Jungian analyst and body therapist, with a particular interest in dance, practicing in Lynchburg, Virginia. A graduate of the Inter-Regional Society of Jungian Analysts, she is the author of *Touching: Body Therapy and Depth Psychology* (1987), *Animus Aeternus: Exploring the Inner Masculine* (1991), and a forthcoming book on the Trickster Archetype and the Feminine.

CHRISTOPHER PERRY is a Training Analyst of the Society of Analytical Psychology and of the British Association of Psychotherapists and a Full Member of the Group Analytic Society (London). He is author of "Listen to the Voice Within: A Jungian Approach to Pastoral Care" (1991) and of several articles on analytical psychology and group analysis. He is in private practice and teaches on various psychotherapy training courses.

JOSEPH RUSSO is Professor of Classics at Haverford College, Pennsylvania, where he teaches courses on mythology and folklore, as well as Greek and Latin literature and civilization. He has written articles on the Homeric epic, Greek lyric poetry, and proverbs and other wisdom-genres in ancient Greece, and he is a co-author of the Oxford *Commentary to Homer's "Odyssey"* (1988).

SHERRY SALMAN, Ph.D. is a Jungian analyst in New York City and Rhinebeck, N.Y., who teaches, writes, and lectures widely on Jungian psychology. She is a faculty member and supervising analyst at the C. G. Jung Training Institute in New York.

ANDREW SAMUELS is a Training Analyst of the Society of Analytical Psychology, London, where he is in private practice, and a Scientific Associate of the American Academy of Psychoanalysis. His works include *Jung and the Post-Jungians* (1985), *The Father* (1985), *The Plural Psyche* (1989), *Psychopathology* (1989), and *The Political Psyche* (1993). He is the editor of the new edition of Jung's *Essays on Contemporary Events*.

HESTER McFARLAND SOLOMON is a Training Analyst and Supervisor for the Jungian Analytic Section of the British Association of Psychotherapists. She served as Chair of the Association (1992–95), as Chair of the Jungian Training Committee (1988–92), and is currently Chair of the Association's Ethics Committee. She is the author of various papers which examine similarities and differences in theoretical and clinical developments within the field of analytical psychology and psychoanalysis.

ANN BELFORD ULANOV, Ph.D., L.H.D. is the Christiane Brooks Johnson Professor of Psychiatry and Religion at Union Theological Seminary in New York City, where she is also a supervising analyst for the C. G. Jung Institute. Her numerous books include *The Wizards' Gate: Picturing Consciousness* and *The Female Ancestors of Christ*, and, with her husband Barry Ulanov, *Religion and the Unconscious* and *Transforming Sexuality: The Archetypal World of Anima and Animus*.

POLLY YOUNG-EISENDRATH, Ph.D. is a Jungian analyst and psychologist who practices in Burlington, Vermont, where she is clinical associate professor in psychiatry at the University of Vermont. A research psychologist and author, her most recent books are *You're Not What I Expected: Learning to Love the Opposite Sex* (1993), *The Resilient Spirit: Transforming Suffering into Insight and Renewal* (1996), and *Gender and Desire* (1997).

PREFACE

It was inevitable that a volume like this should appear before the end of the twentieth century. For the discoveries of Swiss psychiatrist Carl Jung, who was one of the founders of psychoanalysis, constitute one of the most significant expressions of our time. Many of his ideas anticipate the intellectual and sociocultural concerns of our current "post-modern" period. Decentered selves, multiple realities, the function of symbols, the primacy of human interpretation (as our only means of knowing "reality"), the importance of adult development, spiritual self-discovery, and the necessity of multicultural perspectives are all to be be found in Jung's writings.

And yet, it must be conceded that the enthusiastic accolades for his bold and prescient ideas have been tarnished by wide-ranging allegations against him. At a personal level, he has been accused of cultish mysticism, sexism, racism, anti-Semitism and professional misconduct. With regard to his ideas, his critics have repeatedly insisted that his approach is fuzzy, antiquated, and entrenched in culturally biased categories such as "masculine" and "feminine" and nebulous concepts like the "Shadow" and the "Wise Old Man." They have denounced his theories for their essentialism, elitism, stark individualism, biological reductionism, and naive reasoning about gender, race, and culture.

Even so, analysts and scholars who have taken a professional interest in Jung's ideas have constantly insisted that his basic theories provide one of the most notable and influential contributions to the twentieth century. They firmly believe that his theories provide an invaluable means for deciphering not only the problems but also the challenges that confront us both as individuals and as members of our particular society/societies. They allow us to penetrate the multiple levels both of our own inner reality and of the world around us. And his ideas have had a marked influence on other disciplines, from anthropology and religious studies to literary criticism and cultural studies.

Such radically different assessments of Jung and his work stem in part from the fact that his followers and critics alike have been much too preoccupied with his personal life and presence. It cannot be sufficiently stressed that, whatever his ideas owe to his own psychological make-up, their value – or otherwise – must be established on their own merit. Everyone has failings, and Jung had his fair share of these. It is not the man, but his ideas and contribution that need to be reassessed. In 1916, he began to use the term "analytical psychology" to describe his individual form of psychoanalysis. It is time that the focus shifted to the evaluation of Jung's legacy.

Since Jung's death in 1961, those interested in analytical psychology – including practitioners in clinical, literary, theological, and sociocultural fields – have responded to the charges leveled against him and, in doing so, have radically revised many of his basic ideas. One hears too often the blanket label "Jungian" used to describe any idea whose origins can be traced to him. This is misleading. It is still insufficiently appreciated that "Jungian" studies are not an orthodoxy. The theory of "analytical psychology" has come a long way in the last thirty years.

For some time now, there has been a need for a study that would highlight the originality, complexity, and farsightedness of analytical psychology and that would draw wider attention to the overall promise of some of Jung's major discoveries. At the same time, it would be impossible to do this today without also referring to the achievements of those who have been in the forefront of recent developments in analytical psychology and who have made it the vital and pluralist discipline it now is.

This is the first study specifically designed to serve as a critical introduction to Jung's work and to take into account how he has influenced both psychotherapy and other disciplines. It is divided into three main parts. The first section presents a scholarly account of Jung's own work. The second examines the major trends that have evolved in post-Jungian clinical practice. The third evaluates the influence and contributions of Jung and post-Jungians in a range of contemporary debates. More than anything else, this volume seeks to affirm that analytical psychology is a lively, questioning, pluralist, and continually evolving development within psychoanalysis. It is currently engaged in healthy revisions of Jung's original theories, and in exploring new ideas and methods not only for psychotherapy, but also for the study of a wide range of other disciplines, from mythology to religion, and from gender studies to literature and politics.

We editors asked our contributors the question "How do you evaluate the ideas of Jung and post-Jungians in terms of contemporary preoccupations with post-modernism, with gender, race, culture, and with the current findings in your own field of study or practice?" This volume gives priority to identifying which aspects of analytical psychology should move with us into the next millennium, and why. One of us is a practicing Jungian analyst and psychological researcher (Young-Eisendrath); the other teaches English literature at a university (Dawson). We have both considered seriously the attacks on Jung and responded to them not only as responsible scholars, but also as human beings daily engaged in making use of analytical psychology with real people. Our respect for – and our dedication to – Jung's ideas have not blinded us to the fact that some of what he said and wrote, some of what he theorized clinically and culturally, needs revision. With this orientation and background, we appealed to our contributors to be not only thorough and alive in their topics, but also thoughtfully critical.

## Introduction
In the Introduction, Jungian analyst Andrew Samuels begins with a brief appreciation of Jung's work before delineating the three different "schools" of – or, rather, *emphases* in – contemporary analytical psychology: classical, archetypal, and developmental. He also presents an interpretive model for showing the balance of difference and similarity in the ways in which these schools articulate theory and clinical practice.

## Jung's ideas and their context
This section presents Jung's life and discoveries in the context of his personal and historical influences. It looks in particular at his relationship with Sigmund Freud and at the philosophical debate surrounding the problem of "universals" or originary principles (in Jung's case, archetypes). The section opens with a rich historical account of major influences on Jung's thinking by Jungian analyst Claire Douglas. This is followed by a provocative psychoanalytic interpretation of the relationship between Freud and Jung written by a professor of psychology, Douglas Davis. Jungian analyst Sherry Salman then presents Jung's major contributions to contemporary psychoanalysis and psychotherapy. Showing how and why Jung was prescient, Salman gives a picture of Jung's ideas in relation to current "object relations" theory and other personality and psychodynamic theories. Finally, philosopher and Jungian analyst Paul Kugler puts Jung's major discoveries into the context of the post-modern debate, especially those issues that arise from the tension between deconstruction and essentialism. Kugler traces the evolution of "image" in the development of Western thought, showing how Jung's approach resolves a basic dichotomy operating throughout Western philosophy.

## Analytical psychology in practice

This section focuses especially on issues of clinical practice, particularly in regard to the plurality of analytical psychology in its three strains of classical, archetypal, and developmental. Jungian analyst David Hart, who studied with Jung in Zurich, opens with an engaging review of the major tenets of the classical approach, formerly known as the Zurich school. A director of a graduate program in Psychoanalytic Studies, Michael Vannoy Adams, then presents a historical and phenomenological account of the archetypal approach, showing how it has evolved its focus on the "imaginal." Next, Jungian analyst Hester Solomon provides an in-depth theoretical and clinical analysis of the components of the developmental approach, formerly known as the London school.

These three chapters are followed by a chapter on the clinical understanding of transference and countertransference in Jung's work and in post-Jungian practice, written by Jungian analyst Christopher Perry. A classically trained Freudian analyst, Elio Frattaroli, then examines the differences and common ground between Jungian and Freudian thought. This takes the form of an imaginary dialogue between a Jungian and a Freudian analyst about how the two streams of influence interface and separate in the contemporary practice and experience of psychoanalysis.

The second part of the study concludes with an exciting experiment: the interpretation of a single case through the lenses of each of the three schools of analytical psychology. Jungian analysts John Beebe, Deldon McNeely, and Rosemary Gordon give their respective views on how classical, archetypal, and developmental approaches would understand and work with a woman in her mid-forties who suffers from an eating disorder.

## Analytical psychology in society

This section takes up broader social themes and shows how Jung and other contributors to analytical psychology have advanced understanding and studies in a number of fields. Several of these essays directly establish parameters for revising Jungian theory in the light of useful criticism of its potentially elitist, sexist, or racist nuances. Jungian analyst Polly Young-Eisendrath opens with a chapter on gender and contrasexuality, examining the potential of Jung's theory for analyzing projection and projective identification between the sexes. This is followed by a chapter on mythology in which classics professor Joseph Russo applies a Jungian analysis to the character of Odysseus in order to reveal the nature of the hero as a trickster figure. Terence Dawson, who lectures on English and European literature, then explores the question of how Jung's ideas can contribute to literary debate. He illustrates the importance of identifying a work's effective protagonist and advances a theory of literary history based on Jung's ideas about the withdrawal of projections. Next, a professor of political science, Lawrence Alschuler, addresses the question of whether or not Jung's psychology can produce an astute political analysis. In part, Alschuler answers this question by examining Jung's own political psyche. And finally, Ann Ulanov, a Jungian analyst and professor of Religious Studies, shows in her essay how and why Jung's ideas have been seminal in shaping our contemporary spiritual search, and helping us cope with the breakdown of religious traditions in the West.

These topics are the subject of lively professional debate among the practitioners and consumers of analytical psychology, who include psychotherapists with markedly different backgrounds, and academics from widely different disciplines, as well as their graduate and undergraduate students – indeed, it includes anyone interested in cultural history. Our intention has been to introduce the most recent views in analytical psychology in a sophisticated, engaging, and readily accessible fashion.

This volume presents a fundamentally new framework on analytical psychology. It has been purposely organized to be read in full or in part. Read through from start to finish, it tells a fascinating story of how analytical psychology covers a broad spectrum of activities and critical approaches, revealing multiple insights and layers of meaning. Each section, however, can stand on its own and each essay is also complete in itself, even though some of the later chapters assume an acquaintance with Jungian terms that are thoroughly and historically introduced in the first section. We very much hope that this volume will become a useful resource for future debate and study.

We warmly thank our contributors for sharing with us their original and engaging views, as well as the members of their respective "support groups" within and outside of analytical psychology. We are also grateful to Gustav Bovensiepen, Sonu Shamdasani, and David Tacey, who, for various reasons, were unable to contribute to the volume, and to Susan Ang, for help with preparing the Index. We are very proud to have been a part of this project. The results wholly persuade us that, with its onward movement and revision of Jung's ideas, analytical psychology has a major contribution to make to psychoanalysis in the next century.

## ACKNOWLEDGMENTS

For permission to quote from published sources, grateful acknowledgment is extended to:

Harvard University Press for extracts from: *The Complete Letters of Sigmund Freud to Wilhelm Fliess, 1887–1904*, translated and edited by Jeffrey Moussaieff Masson, Cambridge, Mass.: The Belknap Press of Harvard University Press, © 1985 and under the Bern Convention Sigmund Freud Copyrights Ltd., © 1985 Jeffrey Moussaieff Masson for translated and editorial matter.

Routledge for extracts from: C. G. Jung, *The Collected Works*, 20 volumes, ed. H. Read, G. Adler, M. Fordham, and W. McGuire, 1953–95; Sigmund Freud and C. G. Jung, ed. W. McGuire, *The Freud/Jung Letters*, 1974; C. G. Jung, ed. J. Jarrett, *The Seminars: Volume 2: Nietzsche's "Zarathustra,"* 1988; C. G. Jung, ed. G. Adler, *Letters*, 2 volumes, 1973 and 1975.

Princeton University Press for extracts from: C. G. Jung, *The Collected Works*, 20 volumes, ed. H. Read, G. Adler, M. Fordham, and W. McGuire, 1953–95; Sigmund Freud and C. G. Jung, ed. W. McGuire, *The Freud/Jung Letters*, 1974; C. G. Jung, ed. J. Jarrett, *The Seminars: Volume 2: Nietzsche's "Zarathustra,"* 1988; C. G. Jung, ed. G. Adler, *Letters*, 2 volumes, 1973 and 1975.

Columbia University Press for quotations from Peter L. Rudnytsky, *Freud and Oedipus*, © 1987 Columbia University Press.

Chatto and Windus for extracts from Sigmund Freud and C. G. Jung, ed. W. McGuire, *The Freud/Jung Letters*, 1974.

JUNG'S COLLECTED WORKS


Throughout the book, CW refers to the *Collected Works of C. G. Jung*, 20 vols., ed. H. Read, Michael Fordham, and Gerhard Adler; tr. R. F. C. Hull (London: Routledge & Kegan Paul; Princeton, N.J.: Princeton University Press, 1953–77).

# CHRONOLOGY

Jung was a prolific writer, and the work listed in this chronological outline of his life is highly selective. The majority are articles that first appeared in psychiatric journals. The evolution of his reputation and influence grew from the various "collections" of his articles that began to be published from 1916. Dates are mostly those of original publication, usually in German, but titles are given in English translation.

## 1. Early years

1875    *26 July*    Born in Kesswil, in the Canton of Thurgau, Switzerland. His father, Johann Paul Achilles Jung, is the Protestant clergyman in Kesswil; his mother, Emilie, née Preiswerk, is the daughter of a well-established Basel family

1879    Family move to Klein-Hüningen, near Basel

1884    *17 July*    Birth of sister, Johanna Gertrud (d. 1935)

1886    At the Basel Gymnasium

1888    Jung's father becomes chaplain at the Friedmatt Mental Hospital in Basel

1895    *18 April*    Enters Medical School, Basel University. A month later, becomes a member of the student society, the Zofingiaverein

1896    *28 January*    Death of father
        Between November 1896 and January 1899, gives five lectures to the Zofingia Society (CW A)

1898    Participates in group interested in the mediumistic capabilities of

his fifteen-year-old cousin, Helene Preiswerk. His notes will form
the basis of his subsequent dissertation (see 1902)

1900    Completes his medical studies; decides to become a psychiatrist;
        does his first period of military service

## 2. The young psychiatrist: at the Burghölzli

About two years after assuming his first post, Jung begins his experiments
with "word association tests" (1902–06). Patients are asked to give their
immediate "association" to a stimulus word. The purpose is to reveal that
even slight delays in responding to a particular word reveal an aspect of a
"complex": Jung was the first to use this term in its present sense. He
continues developing his association test until 1909 and, intermittently,
applies it to patients throughout his life. Variants of it are still used today.
His findings draw him toward ideas being developed by Freud.

1900    *11 December*    Assumes duties as Assistant Staff Physician to
        Eugen Bleuler at the Burghölzli, the Psychiatric Hospital for the
        canton of Zurich, which was also the university's research clinic

1902    Publication of his thesis, "On the Psychology and Pathology of
        So-Called Occult Phenomena" (*CW* 1). It anticipates some of his
        later ideas, notably, (a) that the unconscious is more "sensitive"
        than consciousness, (b) that a psychological disturbance has a
        teleological significance, and (c) that the unconscious
        spontaneously produces mythological material
        To Paris, for the Winter Semester 1902–03, to study theoretical
        psychopathology at the Salpêtrière under Pierre Janet

1903    *14 February*    Marries Emma Rauschenbach (1882-1955), the
        daughter of a wealthy industrialist from Schaffhausen

## 3. The psychoanalytic years

Jung's meeting with the Austrian neurologist Sigmund Freud (1856–1939) –
the founder of psychoanalysis – was undoubtedly *the* major event of his
early years. Freud was the author of *Studies in Hysteria* (with Josef Breuer),
which includes an account of the case of "Anna O." (1895), *The Interpretation of Dreams* (1900), *Jokes and their Relation to the Unconscious*,
"Dora" (a case study), and *Three Essays on Sexuality* (all 1905). Psycho-

analysis, a term he coined in 1896, refers to a method of treating patients by letting them talk through their problems and come to terms with them in the light of the analyst's observations. Freud worked mostly with neurotic patients. The question facing Jung, who had quoted from *The Interpretation of Dreams* in his thesis (publ. 1902), was, Could psychoanalysis be used with equal success with the psychotic patients whom he attended at the Burghölzli?

### (a) Years of agreement

1903    Jung and Bleuler begin to seriously interest themselves in the ideas of Sigmund Freud: this represents the first step in the internationalization of psychoanalysis

1904    *17 August*   Sabina Spielrein (1885–1941), a young Russian woman, is interned at the Burghölzli: she is the first patient that Jung treats for hysteria using psychoanalytic techniques
*26 December*   Agatha, his eldest daughter, is born

1905    Promoted to Senior Staff Physician, Burghölzli
Appointed *Privatdozent* (= lecturer) in Psychiatry at the University of Zurich
Sabina Spielrein, still under Jung's supervision, registers as a medical student at the University of Zurich; she graduates in 1911

1906    *8 February*   His second daughter, Anna, is born
"The Psychology of *Dementia Praecox* [i.e. schizophrenia]" (*CW* 3). This represents a major extension of Freud's work
Begins corresponding with Freud, who lives in Vienna
Publication of a young American woman's own account of her vivid fantasies (Miss Frank Miller, "Some Instances of Subconscious Creative Imagination"). Jung's extended analysis of this article eventually brings about his separation from Freud, although whether Jung read the article before 1910, the earliest date he is known to have been working on it, is not known

1907    *1 January*   Freud, in a letter to Jung, describes him as "the ablest helper to have joined me thus far"
*3 March*   Jung visits Freud in Vienna. They quickly develop a close professional friendship. It very soon becomes clear that Freud thinks of Jung as his "heir"

1908   *16 January*   Lecture: "The Content of the Psychoses" (*CW* 3)
Jung analyzes, and is analyzed by, Otto Gross
*27 April*   First Congress for Freudian Psychology (often called
the "First International Psychoanalytic Congress"), in Salzburg
"The Freudian Theory of Hysteria" (*CW* 4)
Jung buys some land in Küsnacht, on the shore of the Lake of
Zurich, and has a large, three-floor house built
*28 November*   Birth of his only son, Franz

1909   *March*   publication of first number of the *Jahrbuch für
psychoanalytische und psychopathologische Forschungen*, the
organ of the psychoanalytic movement: Jung is editor
Jung resigns from his position at the Burghölzli Psychiatric
Hospital and moves to his new house in Küsnacht, where he lives
for the rest of his life. He is now dependent on his private practice
Jung's affair with Sabina Spielrein at its most intense from 1909
to 1910
*6–11 September*   In the US, with Freud, at Clark University,
Worcester, Mass.; on the 11th, they both receive honorary
doctorates
Jung's first recorded experiment with active imagination
*October*   Writes to Freud: "Archeology or rather mythology has
got me in its grip": mythology absorbs him until the end of World
War I
"The Significance of the Father in the Destiny of the Individual"
(rev. 1949, *CW* 4)

1910   *late January*   Jung gives a lecture to science students: possibly his
first public formulation of what later becomes his concept of the
collective unconscious
*30–31 March*   Second International Congress of Psycho-
Analysis, Nuremberg. He is appointed its Permanent President
(resigns 1914)
*Summer*   At the University of Zurich, gives first lecture course on
"Introduction to Psychoanalysis"
"The Association Method" (*CW* 2)
*20 September*   His third daughter, Marianne, born

1911   *August*   Publication of first part of "Symbols and
Transformations of the Libido": there is very little in this that
departs from orthodox psychoanalysis of the time

*August*   In Brussels, lectures on "Psychoanalysis of a Child"
Beginning of relationship with Toni Wolff
*29 November*   Sabina Spielrein reads her chapter "On
Transformation" at Freud's Vienna Society; the whole work,
"Destruction as the Cause of Coming To Be" is published in the
*Jahrbuch* in 1912: it anticipates both Freud's "death wish" *and*
Jung's views on "transformation"; it was undoubtedly a major
influence on both men; she became a Freudian analyst, continued
corresponding with Jung until the early 1920s, returned to Russia
and was probably shot by the Germans in July 1942

### (b) Years of dissent

1912   "New Paths in Psychology" (*CW* 7)
*February*   Jung finishes "The Sacrifice," the final section of part
two of "Symbols and Transformations of the Libido." Freud is
displeased with what Jung tells him of his findings; their
correspondence begins to get more tense
*25 February*   Jung founds The Society for Psychoanalytic
Endeavors, the first forum for debating his own distinct
adaptation of psychoanalysis
"Concerning Psychoanalysis" (*CW* 4)
*September*   Lectures at Fordham University, New York: "The
Theory of Psychoanalysis" sets out Jung's departures from Freud:
(a) the view that repression cannot explain all conditions; (b) that
unconscious images can have a teleological significance; and (c)
libido, which he called psychic energy, is not exclusively sexual
*September*   Publication of part two of "Symbols and
Transformations of the Libido," in which Jung proposes that
fantasies of incest have a symbolic rather than literal meaning

1913   Break with Freud

Freud is shaken by the split; Jung is devastated. The stress it occasions
contributes to an almost complete nervous breakdown which had been
threatening since late 1912, when he had begun to have vivid, catastrophic
dreams and waking visions. He resigns from his post at the University of
Zurich, ostensibly because his private practice had grown so large, but more
probably owing to his state of health. In the midst of these difficulties,
American philanthropists, Edith and Harold McCormick, settle in Zurich.
She has analysis with Jung and is the first of several wealthy and very
generous sponsors.

## 4. Beginnings of analytical psychology

For most of the First World War, Jung was wrestling with his own nervous exhaustion. He turns to Toni Wolff (who had been his patient 1910–13) to help him through this difficult period, which lasts until about 1919 (his close relationship with Toni Wolff continues until her death in 1953). While he produces relatively little new work, he does consolidate some of his findings to date. He had difficulty deciding what to call his brand of psychoanalysis. Between 1913 and 1916, he calls it both "complex psychology" and "hermeneutical psychology" before finally deciding on "analytical psychology."

1913    Publication of "The Theory of Psychoanalysis" (CW 4)
        "General Aspects of Psychoanalysis" (CW 4)

1914    Resigns Presidency of International Congress of Psychoanalysis
        Outbreak of World War I

1916    Founds the Psychological Club, Zurich: the McCormicks donate
        generous property, which gradually becomes a forum for visiting
        speakers from different disciplines as well as the forum for his
        own lecture-seminars
        His international standing is enhanced by two translations:
        Beatrice Hinkle's translation of "Symbols and Transformations of
        the Libido" as Psychology of the Unconscious (CW B), and
        Collected Papers on Analytical Psychology, which includes Jung's
        most important articles to date (CW 8)
        "The Structure of the Unconscious" (CW 7): first use of terms
        "personal unconscious," "collective unconscious," and
        "individuation"
        "The Transcendent Function" (CW 8)
        Begins to develop an interest in Gnostic writings, and, following a
        personal experience with active imagination, produces Seven
        Sermons to the Dead

1917    "On the Psychology of the Unconscious" (CW 7)

1918    Jung first identifies the Self as the goal of psychic development
        "The Role of the Unconscious" (CW 10)
        End of World War I
        Period of military service

1919    "Instinct and the Unconscious" (CW 8): first use of term
        "archetype"

## 5. Analytical psychology and individuation

In 1920, Jung was forty-five. He had come through a difficult "mid-life" crisis with a growing international reputation. During the next few years he traveled widely, mostly in order to visit "primitive" peoples. It was also during this period that he began to retire to Bollingen, a second home that he built for himself (see below).

### (a) Years of travel

1920    Visits Algiers and Tunis

1921    Publication of *Psychological Types* (CW 6), in which he develops
        his ideas about two "attitudes" (extraversion/introversion), and
        four "functions" (thinking/sensation, and feeling/intuition); first
        extensive claim for Self as the goal of psychic development

1922    Buys some isolated land on the shore of the Lake of Zurich, about
        twenty-five miles east of his home in Küsnacht and a mile from a
        hamlet called Bollingen
        "On the Relation of Analytical Psychology to Poetry" (CW 15)

1923    Death of Jung's mother
        Jung learns how to cut and dress stone and, with only occasional
        professional help, sets about building a second home composed of
        a thick-set tower; later he adds a loggia, another tower, and an
        annexe; he does not install electricity or a telephone. He calls it
        simply "Bollingen" and, for the remainder of his life, he retires
        there to seek quiet and renewal. He also takes up carving in stone,
        for therapeutic rather than artistic purposes
        *July*   At Polzeath, Cornwall, to give a seminar, in English, on
        "Human Relationships in Relation to the Process of
        Individuation"
        Richard Wilhelm lectures at the Psychological Club

1924    Visits the United States, and travels with friends to visit Taos
        Pueblo, New Mexico. He is impressed by the simplicity of the
        Pueblo Indians

1925    *23 March – 16 July*   In Zurich, he gives a course of sixteen
lecture-seminars on "Analytical Psychology" (*CW Seminars* 3)
Visits London
*July–August*   At Swanage, England, gives seminar on "Dreams
and Symbolism"
Goes on a safari to Kenya, where he spends several weeks with the
Elgonyi on Mount Elgon
"Marriage as a Psychological Relationship" (*CW* 17)

1926    Returns from Africa via Egypt

(b) Re-formulating the aims of analytical psychology

Four characteristics of this period: (1) the first of several fruitful collabora-
tions with someone working in a different discipline (Richard Wilhelm, who
introduced him to Chinese alchemy); (2) arising from this, a growing interest
in *Western* alchemy; (3) the appearance of the first major study in English
by an analyst influenced by Jung; (4) increasing use of "seminars" as a
vehicle by which to communicate his ideas.

1927    To Darmstadt, Germany, to lecture at Count Hermann
Keyserling's "School of Wisdom"
"The Structure of the Psyche" (*CW* 8)
"Woman in Europe" (*CW* 10)
"Introduction" to Frances Wickes, *The Inner World of Childhood*
(rev. 1965), the first major work by an analyst inspired by Jung

1928    "The Relations between the Ego and the Unconscious" (*CW* 7)
"On Psychic Energy" (*CW* 8)
"The Spiritual Problem of Modern Man" (*CW* 10)
"The Significance of the Unconscious in Individual Education"
(*CW* 17)
*7 November*   Begins seminar on "Dream Analysis," until 25 June
1930 (*CW Seminars* 1)
Publication of two further English translations that advance
Jung's standing in America and England: (1) *Contributions to
Analytical Psychology* (New York and London), which includes a
selection of most important recent articles, and (2) *Two Essays in
Analytical Psychology* (*CW* 7)

1929    "Commentary" on Richard Wilhelm's translation of the Chinese
classic *The Secret of the Golden Flower* (*CW* 13)
"Paracelsus" (*CW* 15), first of his essays on Western alchemy. He

seeks the assistance of Marie-Louise von Franz, then a young
student already fluent in Latin and Greek, and she continues to
help him with his research into alchemy, for the rest of his life

1930    Becomes Vice-President of the General Medical Society for
Psychotherapy
"The Stages of Life" (CW 8)
"Psychology and Literature" (CW 15)
In Zurich, begins two series of seminars: (1) "The Psychology of
Individuation" ("The German Seminar"), from 6 October 1930 to
10 October 1931; and (2) "The Interpretation of Visions" ("The
Visions Seminar"), from 15 October 1930 to 21 March 1934
(CW Seminars 1)

1931    "Basic Postulates of Analytical Psychology" (CW 8)
"The Aims of Psychotherapy" (CW 16)

1932    "Psychotherapists or the Clergy" (CW 11)
"Sigmund Freud in His Historical Setting" (CW 15)
"Ulysses: A Monologue"
"Picasso"
Awarded Literary Prize by the City of Zurich
3–8 October   J. W. Hauer gives a seminar on Kundalini Yoga at
the Psychology Club, Zurich. Hauer had recently founded the
German Faith Movement, which was designed to promote a
religion/religious outlook rooted in "the biological and spiritual
depths of the German nation," as against Christianity, which he
saw as too markedly Semitic
from 12 October   Jung gives four weekly seminars on "A
Psychological Commentary on Kundalini Yoga" (CW Seminars 1)

1933    Begins lecturing at the Eidgenössische Technische Hochschule
(ETH), Zurich
Attends first "Eranos" meeting at Ascona, Switzerland. Delivers
paper on "A Study in the Process of Individuation" (CW 9.i).
Eranos (Gk. = "shared feast") was the name chosen, by Rudolf Otto,
for annual meetings at the home of Frau Olga Froebe-Kapteyn,
whose original purpose was to explore links between Western and
Eastern thinking. From 1933, these meetings offered Jung an
opportunity to discuss new ideas with a wide variety of other
thinkers, including Heinrich Zimmer, Martin Buber, and others

Made President of the General Medical Society for Psychotherapy, which, soon after, comes under Nazi supervision
Becomes editor of its journal, the *Zentralblatt für Psychotherapie und ihre Grenzgebiete*, Leipzig (resigns 1939)
*Modern Man in Search of a Soul* (New York and London), another collection of recent articles: quickly becomes standard "introduction" to Jung's ideas

## 6. Further ideas on archetypal images

Jung was fifty-eight in July 1933, the year the Nazis came to power. He was seventy when the war ended. These were tense and difficult times, even in neutral Switzerland. Jung chose to retain his post as President of the International General Medical Society for Psychotherapy after the Nazis had seized power and excluded Jewish members from the German chapter. Although he claimed that he made the decision in order to ensure that Jews were able to remain members of other chapters, and so continue to participate in professional debates, many have questioned his judgment in failing to resign. Charges of anti-Semitism began to be leveled at him, even though his Jewish colleagues, friends, and students defended him. The rise of Nazism and the ensuing war form the background to the gradual elaboration of his theory of archetypal images.

### (a) While Europe drifts toward war

1933    *20 October*   Begins seminar on "Modern Psychology," to 12 July 1935

1934    Founds and becomes first President of International General Medical Society for Psychotherapy
*2 May*   Begins seminar on "Nietzsche's *Zarathustra*": eighty-six sessions, lasting until 15 February 1939 (*CW Seminars 2*)
2nd Eranos meeting: "Archetypes of the Collective Unconscious" (*CW* 9.i)
"A Review of the Complex Theory" (*CW* 8)
"The State of Psychotherapy Today" (*CW* 10)
"The Practical Use of Dream Analysis" (*CW* 16)
"The Development of the Personality" (*CW* 17)

1935    Appointed Professor at the ETH
Founds the Swiss Society for Practical Psychology
3rd Eranos meeting: "Dream Symbols of the Individuation

Process" (revised as "Individual Dream Symbolism in Relation to Alchemy," 1936, CW 12)
To Bad Nauheim, for 8th General Medical Congress for Psychotherapy, Presidential Address (CW 10)
"Psychological Commentary" on W. Y. Evans-Wentz (ed.), *The Tibetan Book of the Dead* (CW 11)
"Principles of Psychotherapy" (CW 16)
In London, gives five lectures for the Institute of Medical Psychology: "Analytical Psychology: Its Theory and Practice" ("The Tavistock Lectures," publ. 1968) (CW 18)

1936    "The Concept of the Collective Unconscious" (CW 9.i)
"Concerning the Archetypes, with Special Reference to the Anima Concept" (CW 9.i)
"Wotan" (CW 10)
"Yoga and the West" (CW 11)
4th Eranos meeting: "Religious Ideas in Alchemy" (CW 12)
To the United States, to lecture at Harvard, where he receives an honorary doctorate, and to give two seminars on "Dream Symbols of the Individuation Process," at Bailey Island, Maine (20–25 September) and in New York city (16–18 and 25–26 October)
Inauguration of the Analytical Psychology Club, New York, presided over by M. Esther Harding, Eleanor Bertine, and Kristine Mann
At ETH, Zurich, winter semester 1936–37: seminar on "The Psychological Interpretation of Children's Dreams" (repeated 1938–39, 1939–40)

1937    5th Eranos meeting: "The Visions of Zozimos" (CW 13)
To United States, to give "Terry Lectures" at Yale University, published as *Psychology and Religion* (CW 11)
To Copenhagen, for 9th International Medical Congress for Psychotherapy: Presidential Address (CW 10)
To India, for fifth anniversary of University of Calcutta, at invitation of British Government of India

1938    *January* Awarded Honorary Doctorates by the Universities of Calcutta, Benares, and Allahabad: Jung unable to attend
6th Eranos meeting: "Psychological Aspects of the Mother Archetype" (CW 9.i)
*29 July – 2 August* In Oxford, England, for 10th International

Medical Congress for Psychotherapy: Presidential Address:
"Views Held in Common by the Different Schools of
Psychotherapy Represented at the Congress" (*CW* 10)
Receives an honorary doctorate from the University of Oxford
*28 October*   Begins seminar on "The Process of Individuation in
Eastern Texts," until 23 June 1939

1939    *15 May*   Elected an Honorary Fellow of the Royal Society of
Medicine, London

(b) During World War II

1939    Outbreak of World War II
Resigns editorship of the *Zentralblatt für Psychotherapie und ihre
Grenzgebiete*
7th Eranos meeting: "Concerning Rebirth" (*CW* 9.i)
Paul and Mary Mellon attend. Paul Mellon (*b.* 1907) was a
wealthy young philanthropist and art-collector; his first wife,
Mary (1904–46), wanted to settle in Zurich to have analysis with
Jung, to see whether it could help her asthma. The subsequent
generosity of the Mellons did much to help disseminate Jung's
ideas (see 1942, 1949)
"What Can India Teach Us?"
"Psychological Commentary" on *The Tibetan Book of the Great
Liberation* (*CW* 11)
"Foreword" to D. T. Suzuki, *Introduction to Zen Buddhism* (*CW* 11)
Begins seminar on "The Process of Individuation: The *Exercitia
Spiritualia* of St. Ignatius of Loyola" (16 June 1939– 8 Mar. 1940)

1940    *The Integration of the Personality* (New York and London),
selection of recent articles.
8th Eranos meeting: "A Psychological Approach to the Trinity"
(*CW* 11)
"The Psychology of the Child Archetype" (*CW* 9.i)
*8 November*   Begins seminar on "The Process of Individuation in
Alchemy: 1," until 28 February 1941

1941    *2 May – 11 July*   Seminar: "The Process of Individuation in
Alchemy: 2"
To Ascona, for the 9th Eranos meeting: "Transformation
Symbolism in the Mass" (*CW* 11)
"The Psychological Aspects of Kore" (*CW* 9.i)

1942    *6 January*   The Bollingen Foundation is established in New York and Washington D.C., with Mary Mellon as President: the editorial board includes Heinrich Zimmer and Edgar Wind
After nine years, resigns post at ETH
10th Eranos meeting: "The Spirit Mercurius" (*CW* 13)
"Paracelsus as a Spiritual Phenomenon" (*CW* 13)

1943    Elected Honorary Member of Swiss Academy of Sciences
"The Psychology of Eastern Meditation" (*CW* 11)
"Psychotherapy and a Philosophy of Life" (*CW* 16)
"The Gifted Child" (*CW* 17)

1944    The University of Basel creates a chair in Medical Psychology for him; illness compels him to resign from the post the following year
Further health problems: suffers a broken foot; has a heart attack; has a series of visions
Edits, and writes introduction, "The Holy Men of India," to Heinrich Zimmer, *The Path to Selfhood* (*CW* 11)
*Psychology and Alchemy* (*CW* 12), based on papers delivered at Eranos meetings of 1935 and 1936

1945    In honor of his seventieth birthday, receives an honorary doctorate from the University of Geneva
13th Eranos meeting: "The Phenomenology of the Spirit in Fairytales" (*CW* 9.i)

(c) After the war
"After the Catastrophe" (*CW* 10)
"The Philosophical Tree" (*CW* 13)

1946    14th Eranos meeting: "The Spirit of Psychology," revised as "On the Nature of the Psyche" (*CW* 8)
*Essays on Contemporary Events* (*CW* 10): collection of recent essays
"The Fight with the Shadow" (*CW* 10)
"The Psychology of the Transference" (*CW* 16)

1947    Begins to spend long periods at Bollingen

1948    *24 April*   Opening of the C. G. Jung Institute of Zurich (cf. *CW* 18)

It serves as a training centre for would-be analysts, as well as a general lecture venue. In time, a great many other Institutes have been founded, notably in the US (e.g. New York, San Francisco, Los Angeles)
To Ascona, for 16th Eranos meeting. Jung's paper: "On the Self" (became ch. 4 of *Aion*, *CW* 9.ii)

1949    The first Bollingen Prize for Poetry is awarded to Ezra Pound

During the war, Pound, who was living in Italy, had broadcast Fascist propaganda. When Italy was liberated, he was detained in a cage near Pisa, where he wrote the first draft of his *Pisan Cantos*, before being repatriated to the US, where he was to stand trial for treason. But in December 1945, he was committed to St. Elizabeth's Hospital for the insane, where he translated Confucius and entertained literary visitors. The award to a traitor and a lunatic created a politico-literary furor, into which Jung's name was dragged as a Fascist sympathizer. The result was that, on 19 August, Congress passed a ruling forbidding its Library to award any more prizes. Yale University Library quickly assumed responsibility for the Prize (which, in 1950, was awarded to Wallace Stevens), but the whole episode did a lot of damage, not least to Jung.

## 7. The late works

Jung was seventy-four at the time of the Bollingen Prize scandal. To his credit, he continued his research for *Aion* (1951) undeterred, and also began revising many of his earlier works.

1950    With K. Kerényi, *Essays on a Science of Mythology* (New York)/ *Introduction to a Science of Mythology* (London): it contains Jung's two articles, on the archetypes of the "Child" (1940) and "Kore" (1941)
"Concerning Mandala Symbolism" (*CW* 9.i)
"Foreword" to the Chinese Classic, *The I Ching, or Book of Changes*, tr. and ed. Richard Wilhelm (*CW* 11)

1951    To Ascona, for 19th Eranos meeting: "On Synchronicity" (*CW* 8)
*Aion: Researches into the Phenomenology of the Self* (*CW* 9.ii)
"Fundamental Questions of Psychotherapy" (*CW* 16)

1952    "Synchronicity: An Acausal Connecting Principle" (CW 8)
Answer to Job (CW 11)
Symbols of Transformation (rev. from 1911–12) (CW 5)

1953    The Bollingen Series begins publishing The Collected Works of
C. G. Jung (until 1976, and Seminars still in course of publication)

1954    "On the Psychology of the Trickster Figure" in Paul Radin, The
Trickster: A Study in American Indian Mythology (CW 9.i)
Von den Wurzeln des Bewusstseins (= From the Roots of
Consciousness), new collection of essays; appears in German, but
not in English

1955    With W. Pauli, The Interpretation of Nature and the Psyche:
Jung's contribution consisted of his essay on "Synchronicity"
(1952)
In honor of his eightieth birthday, receives an honorary doctorate
from the Eidgenössische Technische Hochschule, Zurich
Mysterium Coniunctionis: An Inquiry into the Separation and
Synthesis of Psychic Opposites in Alchemy (CW 14). This is his
final statement on alchemy
27 November   Death of Emma Jung

1956    "Why and How I Wrote my 'Answer to Job' " (CW 11)

1957    The Undiscovered Self (CW 10)
Begins recounting his "memories" to Aniela Jaffé
5–8 August   Jung is filmed in four one-hour interviews with
Richard I. Evans, a Professor of Psychology at the University of
Houston ("The Houston Films")

1958    Memories, Dreams, Reflections, German edition. It is now
realized that this work, which used to be read as autobiography,
is the product of very careful editing both by Jung and Jaffé
Flying Saucers: A Modern Myth (CW 10)

1959    22 October   The "Face to Face" Interview, with John Freeman,
BBC television

1960    Made Honorary Citizen of Küsnacht on his 85th birthday
"Foreword" to Miguel Serrano, The Visits of the Queen of Sheba
(Bombay and London: Asia Publishing House)

1961    *6 June*   After a brief illness, dies at his home in Küsnacht, Zurich

1962    *Memories, Dreams, Reflections,* recorded and edited by Aniela Jaffé (translation published 1963, New York and London).

1964    "Approaching the Unconscious," in *Man and His Symbols,* ed. C. G. Jung and, after his death, by M.-L. von Franz

1973    *Letters: 1: 1906–1950* (Princeton and London)

1974    *The Freud/Jung Letters: The Correspondence between Sigmund Freud and C. G. Jung* (Princeton and London)

1976    *Letters: 2: 1951–1961* (Princeton and London)

ANDREW SAMUELS

# Introduction: Jung and the post-Jungians

Over the past five years, I have spoken on Jungian and post-Jungian psychology and analysis at eighteen universities in seven countries. I have discovered that, in spite of the fact that its core texts are more or less absent from reading lists and curriculum descriptions, there is enormous interest in analytical psychology. When Jung is mentioned, it is primarily as an important schismatic in the history of psychoanalysis. Similarly, in the clinical context, even though most psychoanalysts often pass over his name in silence, many therapists – and not just Jungian analysts – have "discovered" Jung as a major contributor to our thinking about clinical work. These important cultural developments are going on alongside the far better known popular alliance of some aspects of Jungian psychology with "new age" thinking and activity. There are two questions arising from this complicated situation to which, in the course of the chapter, I shall attempt to provide at least a partial answer. First, "Do Jung's ideas merit a place in contemporary debate in the academy?" And second, "Do Jung's ideas merit greater discussion in general clinical training in psychotherapy?"

It is impossible to begin to answer these questions without first exploring the cultural context in which they arise. There is little doubt that Jung has been "banished comprehensively" from academic life (to borrow a phrase used by the distinguished psychologist Liam Hudson [1983] in a review of a collection of Jung's writings). Why is this so?

First, the secret "committee" set up by Freud and Jones in 1912 to defend the cause of "true" psychoanalysis spent a good deal of time and energy on disparaging Jung. The fall-out from this historical moment has taken a very long time to evaporate and has meant that Jung's ideas have been slow to penetrate psychoanalytic circles.

Second, Jung's anti-Semitic writings and misguided involvements in the professional politics of psychotherapy in Germany in the 1930s have, understandably in my view, made it almost impossible for Holocaust-aware psychologists – both Jewish and non-Jewish – to generate a positive attitude to his theories. Some portions of the early Jungian community refused to acknowledge that there was any substance to the charges held against him, and even withheld information that they deemed unsuitable for the public domain. Such evasions only served to prolong a problem which must be faced squarely. Present-day Jungians are now addressing the issue, and assessing it both in the context of the time and in relation to his work as a whole.[1]

Third, Jung's attitudes to women, blacks, so-called "primitive" cultures, and so forth are now outmoded and unacceptable. He converted prejudice into theory, and translated his perception of what was current into something supposed to be eternally valid. Here, too, it is the responsibility of the post-Jungians to discover these mistakes and contradictions and to correct Jung's faulty or amateur methods. When this is done, one can see that Jung had a remarkable capacity to intuit the themes and areas with which late twentieth-century psychology would be concerned: gender; race; nationalism; cultural analysis; the perseverance, reappearance and sociopolitical power of religious mentality in an apparently irreligious epoch; the unending search for meaning – all of these have turned out to be the problematics with which psychology has had to concern itself. Recognizing the soundness of Jung's intuitive vision facilitates a more interested but no less critical return to his texts. This is what is meant by "post-Jungian": correction of Jung's work and also critical distance from it.

In university settings, it is my habit to begin the lecture by asking those present to do a simple association exercise to the word "Jung." I ask them to record the first three things that come to mind. From the (by now) 300+ responses, I have found that the most frequently cited theme, words, concepts, or images have to do with Freud, psychoanalysis, and the Freud–Jung split. The next most frequently cited association concerns Jung's anti-Semitism and alleged Nazi sympathies. Other matters raised include archetypes, mysticism/philosophy/religion, and animus and anima.

Obviously, this is not properly empirical research. But if we "associate to" the associations, we can see the "Jung problem" neatly encapsulated. There *is* a lingering doubt about the ethical viability of taking an interest in Jung. Even so, it is sensed that there is more to the question of Jung and Freud's psychoanalysis than the oft-repeated story of two wrestling men. Considerable interest in Jung and in his work *exists*.

## Jung and Freud

The break in relations between Jung and Freud is usually presented to students as stemming from a father–son power struggle and Jung's inability to come to terms with what is involved in human psychosexuality. On the surface of the Oedipus myth, the father's son-complex is not nearly as easy to access as the son's father-complex. It is tempting to forget Laius's infanticidal impulses.

As far as Jung's angle on sexuality is concerned, the fact that much of the content of his 1912 breakaway book *Wandlungen und Symbole der Libido* – translated as *Psychology of the Unconscious* (CW B) – concerns an interpretation of the incest motif and of incest fantasy is usually overlooked – or is simply not known about. The book is highly pertinent to an understanding of family process and the way in which events in the outer family cohere into what might be called an inner family. In other words, the book now called *Symbols of Transformation* (CW 5) is not an experience-distant text. It asks, How do humans grow, from a psychological point of view? In part, they grow by internalizing – that is, "taking inside themselves" – qualities, attributes and styles of life that they have not yet managed to master on their own. From where does this new stuff come? From the parents or other caretakers. But how does it happen? Here, we can see the usefulness of Jung's theories about incest. It is characteristic of the human sexual drive that it is impossible for anyone to be indifferent to the other who is the recipient of one's sexual fantasy or the source of desire for oneself. A degree of sexualized interest between parents and children that is *not* acted out – and which must remain on the level of incest *fantasy* – is necessary for the two individuals in a situation where each cannot avoid the other. Incest-fueled desire is implicated in the kind of human love that healthy family process cannot do without. What Jung called "kinship libido" is a necessity for internalizing the good experiences of early life.

When I describe Jung's ideas in this way, it challenges the validity of the huge difference that students are encouraged to perceive between Freud and Jung – especially but not exclusively in the area of sexuality – in that Freud is known for his theory of sexuality whereas Jung is thought to have avoided sexuality.

The scene is then set for a linkage of Jungian ideas about sexuality with some critically important psychoanalytic notions, such as Jean Laplanche's (1989) theory of the centrality of seduction in early development. Or, in less abstract vein, a Jungian perspective on child sexual abuse is emerging in which child sexual abuse is seen as a damaging *degeneration* of a healthy and necessary deployment of "incest fantasy." Situating child sexual abuse on a spectrum of human behavior in this way helps to reduce the understandable moral panic that inhibits constructive thinking about the topic and opens the way for its problematics to be addressed.

Often it is pointed out that the whole edifice of modern psychotherapy is unthinkable without Freud's work. In many respects this is the case. However, post-Freudian psychoanalysis has gone on to revise, repudiate, and extend a great many of Freud's seminal ideas – and many of the central issues and features of contemporary psychoanalysis are reminiscent of positions taken by Jung in earlier years. This is not to say that Jung himself is responsible for all the interesting things to be found in contemporary psychoanalysis, or that he worked these things out in as much detail as the psychoanalytic thinkers concerned. But, as Paul Roazen (1976, p. 272) pointed out, "Few responsible figures in psychoanalysis would be disturbed today if an analyst were to present views identical to Jung's in 1913." The point can be made by listing some of the more important issues in which Jung can be seen as a precursor of recent developments more often associated with "post-Freudian" psychoanalysis.

(1) While Freud's Oedipal psychology is father-centered and is not relevant to a period earlier than about the age of four, Jung provided a mother-based psychology in which influence is often traced back much earlier, even to pre-natal events. For this reason, he may be seen as a precursor of the work of Melanie Klein, of the British School of object relations theorists such as Fairbairn, Winnicott, Guntrip, and Balint, and, given the theory of archetypes (of which more in a moment), of Bowlby's ethologically inspired work on attachment.

(2) In Freud's view, the unconscious is created by repression and this is a personal process derived from lived experience. In Jung's view, it has a collective base which means that the unconscious possesses innate structures which greatly affect and perhaps determine its contents. It is not only post-Jungians who are concerned with expanding and modifying the theory of archetypes. If one surveys the work of psychoanalysts such as Klein, Lacan, Spitz, and Bowlby one finds the same emphasis on pre-structuration of the unconscious. That the unconscious is structured like a language (Lacan's view) could easily have been stated by Jung.

(3) Freud's view of human psychology is recognized as a bleak one and, given the history of the century, it seems a reasonable position. But Jung's early insistence that there is a creative, purposive, non-destructive aspect to the human psyche finds echoes and resonances in the work of psycho-analytic writers like Milner and Rycroft and in Winnicott's work on play. Similar links can be made with the great pioneers of humanistic psychology like Rogers and Maslow. To argue that the psyche has knowledge of what is good for it, a capacity to regulate itself, and even to heal itself, takes us to the heart of contemporary expositions of the "true self" such as that found in Bollas's recent work, to give only one example.

(4) Jung's attitude to psychological symptoms was that they should not be

4

looked at exclusively in a causal-reductive manner but also in terms of their hidden meanings for the patient – even in terms of what the symptom is "for."[2] This anticipates the school of existential analysis and the work of some British psychoanalysts such as Rycroft and Home.

(5) In contemporary psychoanalysis, there has been a move away from what often seem like male-dominated, patriarchal, and phallocentric approaches; in psychology and psychotherapy alike, more attention is being paid to the "feminine" (whatever might be meant by this). In the past two decades, feminist psychoanalysis and psychotherapy have come into being. There is little doubt that Jung's "feminine" is still a *man*'s "feminine" but parallels between feminist-influenced psychoanalysis and gender-sensitive Jungian and post-Jungian analytical psychology may be drawn.

(6) As early as 1929, Jung was arguing for the clinical usefulness of what has come to be called the "countertransference" – the analyst's subjective response to the analysand. "You can exert no influence if you are not subject to influence," he wrote, and "the countertransference is an important organ of information" (CW 16, pp. 70–72). Clinician readers of this chapter with a knowledge of psychoanalysis will know how contemporary psychoanalysis has rejected Freud's overharsh assessment in 1910 (Freud, 1910, pp. 139–151) of the countertransference as "the analyst's own complexes and internal resistances" and hence as something to be got rid of. Jung must be seen as one of the pioneers of the clinical use of countertransference, along with Heimann, Little, Winnicott, Sandler, Searles, Langs, and Casement.

(7) The way in which the clinical interaction of analyst and analysand is perceived has changed greatly over the history of psychoanalysis. Analysis is now often regarded as a mutually transforming interaction. The analyst's personality and ethical position are no less involved than his professional technique. The real relationship and the therapeutic alliance weave in and out of the transference/countertransference dynamics. One modern word for this is "intersubjectivity" and Jung's alchemical model for the analytical process is, in a word, an intersubjective one.[3] In this area, Jung's ideas share common ground with the diverse views of Atwood and Stolorow, Greenson, Kohut, Lomas, Mitchell, and Alice Miller.

(8) The ego has been moved away from the center of the theoretical and the therapeutic projects of psychoanalysis. Lacan's decentering of the ego exposes as delusive the fantasy of mastery and unification of the personality, and Kohut's working out of a bipolar self also extends well beyond the confines of rational, orderly ego-hood. The recognition that there are limits to the ego's consciousness, and that there are other kinds of consciousness, are anticipated by Jung's notion of the Self – the totality of psychic

processes, somehow "bigger" than ego and carrying humanity's apparatus of aspiration and imagination.

(9) The deposing of the ego has created a space for what might be called "sub-personalities." Jung's theory of complexes, which he referred to as "splinter psyches," fills out such a theory of dissociation (Samuels, Shorter, and Plaut, 1986, pp. 33–35). We can compare Jung's tendency to personify the inner divisions of the psyche with Winnicott's true and false selves and with the moves made by Eric Berne in transactional analysis wherein ego, id, and superego are seen as relatively autonomous. Guided fantasy, Gestalt work and visualization would be scarcely conceivable without Jung's contribution: "active imagination" describes a temporary suspension of ego control, a "dropping down" into the unconscious, and a careful notation of what one finds, whether by reflection or some kind of artistic self-expression.

(10) Many contemporary psychoanalysts would want to make a distinction between something like "mental health," "sanity," "genitality," and something which could be termed "individuation." That is to say, there is a distinction between norms of adaptation, themselves a microcosm of societal values, and an ethic which prizes individual variation from the norm as highly as, or more highly than, individual adherence to the norm. Although his cultural values have sometimes been criticized as elitist, Jung is *the* great writer on individuation. Psychoanalytic writers on these themes include Winnicott, Milner, and Erikson.

(11) Jung was a psychiatrist and retained an interest in psychosis all his life. From his earliest times in the Burghölzli hospital in Zurich, he argued that schizophrenic phenomena have meanings which a sensitive therapist can elucidate. In this regard, he anticipates Laing and his anti-psychiatry colleagues. Jung's final position in 1958 was that there may be some kind of biochemical "toxin" involved in the serious psychoses which would suggest a genetic element in such illnesses. However, Jung felt that this would do no more than give an individual a predisposition with which life's events would interact leading to a favorable or unfavorable outcome. Here, we see an anticipation of today's psycho-bio-social approach to schizophrenia.

(12) Freud may well have located the start of his psychology at the age of four; Klein started hers at birth. But until recently very few psychoanalysts have tried to create a whole-of-life psychology, one that would include the fulcrum events of mid-life and those of old age and recognition of impending death. Jung did. Writers like Levinson and those who, like Kübler-Ross and Parkes, explore the psychology of death all explicitly acknowledge Jung's very prescient contribution.

(13) Finally, although Jung thought that children have distinct personal-

ities from birth, his idea that problems in childhood may be traced to the "unlived psychological life of the parents" (*CW* 10, p. 25) anticipates many findings of family therapy.

Let me restate the intention of providing this *catalogue raisonnée* of Jung's role as a pioneering figure in contemporary psychotherapy. Recall that he has been openly stated to be a charlatan and a markedly inferior thinker to Freud. I think it is by now reasonable to ask: Why are all the above parallels more or less unrecognized or unacknowledged in the histories of psychoanalysis, in surveys of psychoanalytic thought and in the work of individual psychoanalytic writers?[4] It is clearly time that the profession – and especially the teachers of psychotherapy and psychology – recognized Jung's considerable contribution in all the above fields. A major aim of this volume is to situate his ideas squarely within the mainstream of contemporary psychoanalysis.


## The post-Jungians

Though eschewing psychobiography and the temptation to subsume an emerging discipline in the life story of its founder, up to now my focus has indeed been on Jung's own work and texts. However, as I mentioned earlier, since Jung's death in 1961 there has been an explosion of creative professional activity in analytical psychology. It was in 1985 (Samuels, 1985) that I coined the tag "post-Jungian." This was prompted mainly by my own confusion in a field that seemed utterly chaotic and without any maps or aids as the various groups and individuals fell out, split, and in some cases split again. I intended to indicate some connection to Jung and the traditions of thought and practice that had grown up around his name and also some distance or differentiation. In order to delineate post-Jungian analytical psychology, I adopt a pluralistic methodology in which *dispute* rather than consensus is permitted to define the field. The field is defined by the debates and arguments that threaten to destroy it and not by the core of commonly agreed ideas. A post-Jungian is someone who can plug into, be interested and energized by, and participate in post-Jungian debates whether on the basis of clinical interests, or intellectual exploration, or a combination of these.

For some years, perhaps from 1950 to 1975, it was sufficient to note that there was a "London school" and a "Zurich school" of analytical psychology. The former was said to be "clinical" and the latter "symbolic" in its approach. In the mid 1970s, two things happened to make geography and the supposedly mutually exclusive terms "clinical" and "symbolic" no longer appropriate as descriptions of the field of Jungian analysis. With the spread of its graduates into clinical practice all over the world, the Zurich school found itself at the heart of an international movement of professional analysts. Similarly, the work of the London school, at first highly controversial, began to find acceptance outside London. Another factor that complicated the picture was the emergence in the early 1970s of a third group of analysts and writers who did not seek to call themselves analytical psychologists at all, preferring to label their work "archetypal psychology."

There are by now three main schools of analytical psychology: the classical, developmental, and archetypal schools. The classical school includes what used to be called "Zurich" and the developmental contains what used to be called "London."

The classical school seeks on the whole to work in a way consistent with what is known about Jung's own methods of work. But this should not be understood as implying that the approach has ceased to develop. There can be evolutions and movements within a broadly classical tradition, as we find in many disciplines.

The developmental school has attempted a linkage with several features of contemporary psychoanalysis such as a stress on the importance of early experience and on paying attention to the details of tranference and countertransference in the analytical session.

The archetypal school is perhaps no longer strictly a clinical group. Its principal writers valorize Jung's key concept of the archetype, using it as a base from which to explore and engage with the depth dimensions of all kinds of imaginal experience, whether dream or waking fantasy.

These three schools can be apprehended in a way that respects both their manifest differences and the fact that they have something in common. A way to do this is to imagine a common pool of theoretical concepts and clinical practices. Each school is understood as drawing on the whole pool but privileging and emphasizing certain elements more than others. An advantage of this approach is that it makes space for overlaps between the schools, permits maximal differences within each school, allows for variations between individual practitioners (many of whom do not fit neatly into one school), and provides a relatively rapid and easy access to what is "hot" in analytical psychology for new entrants to the profession or for interested students and practitioners who do not intend to become fully "Jungian."

I suggest that there are six headings which, taken together, constitute the field of post-Jungian analytical psychology. The first three are theoretical:

(1)    the archetype
(2)    the Self
(3)    the development of personality from infancy to old age

The second three derive from clinical practice:

(1) analysis of transference and countertransference
(2) symbolic experiences of the Self in analysis
(3) sticking to highly differentiated imagery as it presents itself

It might be helpful if, at this point, I were to digress so as to define the terms "archetype" and "self." An archetype is, according to Jung, an innate, inherited pattern of psychological performance, linked to instinct. If and when an archetype is activated, it manifests itself in behavior and emotion (e.g. a man who dreams frequently of a "devouring mother" is likely to exhibit character traits related to such an archetype). Jung's theory of the archetypes developed in three stages. In 1912 he wrote of primordial images which he recognized in the unconscious life of his patients as well as by way of his self-analysis. These images were similar to cultural motifs represented everywhere and throughout history. Their main features were their power, depth, and autonomy. Primordial imagery provided for Jung the empirical content for his theory of the collective unconscious. By 1917, he was writing of dominants, nodal points in the psyche which attract energy and hence influence a person's functioning. It was in 1919 that he first made use of the term "archetype" and he did so to avoid any suggestion that it was the content and not the irrepresentable, fundamental structure that was inherited. References are made to the archetype-as-such, to be distinguished clearly from archetypal images, motifs, themes, patterns. The archetype is psychosomatic, linking instinct and image. Jung did not regard psychology and imagery as correlates or reflections of biological drives. His assertion that images evoke the aim of the instincts implies that they deserve equal place. All imagery partakes of the archetypal to some extent.

In Jung's writings, the word "self" (often capitalized in English) was used from 1916 on with certain distinct meanings: (1) the totality of the psyche; (2) the tendency of the psyche to function in an ordered and patterned manner, leading to intimations of purpose and order; (3) the tendency of the psyche to produce images and symbols of something "beyond" the ego – images of God or of heroic personages fulfill this role, referring us to the need and possibility of growth and development; (4) the psychological unity of the human infant at birth. This unity gradually breaks up as life experiences accumulate but serves as the template or blueprint for later experiences of feeling whole and integrated. Sometimes the mother is referred to as "carrying" the infant's self. This is akin to the process that psychoanalysis calls "mirroring."

Returning to the three schools, I want to characterize them by reference to these three theoretical and three clinical foci.

As far as theory goes, I think the classical school weights the options in the following order:
(a) the Self, (b) the archetype, (c) the development of personality.

As far as clinical practice goes, I think the classical school weights the options like this:
(a) symbolic experience of the self, (b) sticking to imagery, (c) analysis of transference and countertransference – although I believe there are some classical analysts who would reverse the order of the last two.

For the developmental school, its theoretical weighting would be:
(a) the development of personality, (b) the Self, (c) the archetype.

The clinical order for the developmental school would be:
(a) analysis of transference and countertransference, (b) symbolic experience of the Self, (c) sticking to imagery – although perhaps some developmental analysts would reverse the last two.

For the archetypal school, in theoretical terms, its prioritizing would be:
(a) the archetype, (b) the Self, (c) the development of personality – but there is not much attention paid to the last two items by the archetypal school.

In clinical contexts, the archetypal school appears to favour the order:
(a) sticking to imagery, (b) symbolic experience of the Self, (c) analysis of transference and countertransference.

My intention here has been to avoid the simplistic polarizing of the kind that claims that the developmental school is uninterested in sticking to imagery or that the classical school has no interest in transference and countertransference. What happens in an analysis conducted by a member of one school when compared to one led by a member of another school is certainly going to vary – but not to the extent that we are justified in claiming that more than one kind of activity is going on, or that we might be contrasting like with unlike.

My arrangement within these six specific groupings arose from a detailed examination of statements and articles written by post-Jungians which have a polemical and self-defining intent. Such polemical articles reveal more clearly than most what the lines of disagreement are within the Jungian and post-Jungian community and I have suggested elsewhere that this is usually the case in psychoanalysis and depth psychology. The literature is polemical, and competitive, and can seem positively desperate for an opponent off whom new ideas can aggressively be bounced.[5] The history of psychoanalysis, particularly the new, revisionist histories that are beginning to emerge, show the tendency rather clearly.

Here are some examples of the polemics to which I am referring. The following comes from Gerhard Adler, whom I would regard as an exponent of the classical school:

> We put the main emphasis on symbolic transformation. I would like to quote what Jung says in a letter to P. W. Martin (20/8/45): ". . .the main interest in my work is with the approach to the numinous. . .but the fact is that the numinous is the real therapy."[6]

Next is an extract from an editorial introduction to a group of papers published in London by members of the developmental school:

> the recognition of transference as such was the first subject to become a central one for clinical preoccupation. . .Then, as anxiety about this began to diminish with the acquisition of increased skill and experience, countertransference became a subject that could be tackled. Finally. . .the transaction involved is most suitably termed transference/countertransference.
>
> (Fordham *et al.*, 1974, p. x)

James Hillman, speaking for the archetypal school of which he may be regarded as the founder, asserts:

> At the most basic level of reality are fantasy images. These images are the primary activity of consciousness. . .*Images are the only reality we apprehend directly.* (Hillman, 1975, p. 174)

And, in the same paper, Hillman goes on to refer to the "primacy of images."

Is it possible to metaphorize the schools and thus to see them as coexisting in the mind of any post-Jungian analyst? We could use the same methodology in which weighting and priority arise out of a process of competition and bargaining. Moreover, we should bear in mind that there are now more than 2,000 Jungian analysts worldwide in twenty-eight countries and probably an additional 10,000 psychotherapists and counselors either Jungian in orientation or heavily influenced by analytical psychology. Debates have been going on explicitly for forty years and implicitly for perhaps sixty. Many practitioners will have by now internalized the debates themselves and feel perfectly capable of functioning as either a classical or a developmental or an archetypal analytical psychologist according to the needs of the individual analysand. Or the analyst may regard his or her orientation as primarily classical, for example, but with a flourishing developmental component, or some other combination.

My hope is that readers, too, will be able to take the model of the schools as a launching point to consider the many issues raised by this volume.

I return to the first of the two questions with which I began – is there any place for Jung in the academy? As I said, in the universities of many Western countries, there is, once again, considerable interest in Jungian studies. Central to this is a historically based reevaluation of the origins of Jung's ideas and practices and of the break with Freud. Literary and art criticism influenced by analytical psychology – even though (it must be said) still often based on somewhat mechanistic and out-of-date applications of Jungian theory – are beginning to flourish. Anthropological, social, and political studies resting not so much on Jung's conclusions as on his intuitions about directions to explore are also being developed. Jung's influence on religious studies has existed for a long time.

As an academic discipline, Psychoanalytic Studies is much more established than Jungian Studies, which is really just getting off the ground. There are advantages to being a generation behind in that it might be possible – and I would stress the word "might" – for analytical psychology to avoid the huge ravines that have tended to separate clinicians and the various kinds of academics within psychoanalysis.

If this separation – surely an unhealthy phenomenon – is to be avoided in Jungian studies, then both the academic and the clinical camps will have to better interact with one another. A struggle between competing groups to "appropriate" analytical psychology is neither desirable nor necessary. Each side can learn from the other. In the last thirty years, analytical psychology has become a healthy, pluralistic discipline. It is time for it to become more consciously inter-disciplinary and to actively claim its proper place in sociocultural debate at tertiary level.

## NOTES

1   See Samuels, 1993 for a full discussion of my views on Jung's anti-Semitism, his alleged collaboration with the Nazis, and the response of the Jungian community to the allegations.
2   See the Introduction to Samuels (ed.), 1989, pp. 1–22 for a fuller account of Jung's ideas about the "teleology" of symptoms and about psychopathology generally.
3   See Samuels, 1989, pp. 175–193 for a fuller account of Jung's alchemical metaphor for the analytical process.
4   One sees this problem in "standard" histories like Gay, 1988.
5   For my theory about pluralism in depth psychology, see Samuels, 1989.
6   Gerhard Adler, unpublished public statement at the time of a major institutional split in the Jungian world in London.

## REFERENCES

Fordham, Michael, *et al.* (eds.) (1974). *Technique in Jungian Analysis*. London: Heinemann.

Freud, Sigmund (1910). "The Future Prospects of Psycho-analytic Therapy." In *The Standard Edition of the Complete Psychological Works of Sigmund Freud*, 24 vols., ed. J. Strachey. London: The Hogarth Press, 1953–74, vol. 11.

Gay, Peter (1988). *Freud: A Life for Our Time*. London: Dent.

Hillman, James (1975). *Loose Ends*. Dallas: Spring Publications.

Hudson, Liam (1983). Review of Storr (ed.), 1983. *Sunday Times*, London, 13 March 1983.

Jung, C. G. (1912). *Psychology of the Unconscious: A Study of the Transformations and Symbolisms of the Libido*, trans. Beatrice Hinkle. CW B. Ed. W. McGuire, 1984.

(1918). "The Role of the Unconscious," CW 10.

(1946). *The Psychology of the Transference*, CW 16.

Laplanche, Jean (1989). *New Foundations for Psychoanalysis*, trans. David Macey. Oxford: Blackwell.

Roazen, Paul (1976). *Freud and His Followers*. London: Penguin.

Samuels, Andrew (1985). *Jung and the Post-Jungians*. London and Boston: Routledge & Kegan Paul.

(1989). *The Plural Psyche: Personality, Morality and the Father*. London and New York: Routledge.

(1993). *The Political Psyche*. London and New York: Routledge.

Samuels, Andrew (ed.) (1989). *Psychopathology: Contemporary Jungian Perspectives*. London: Karnac; New York: Guildford Press, 1990.

Samuels, Andrew, Shorter, Bani, and Plaut, Fred (1986). *A Critical Dictionary of Jungian Analysis*. London and Boston: Routledge & Kegan Paul.

Storr, Anthony (ed.) (1983). *Jung: Selected Writings*. London: Fontana.

# I

## JUNG'S IDEAS AND THEIR CONTEXT

# 1

CLAIRE DOUGLAS

# The historical context of analytical psychology

Considered by many (e.g. Ellenberger, 1970; Rychlak, 1984; Clarke, 1992) the most original, broadly educated, and philosophical of the depth psychologists, Jung inhabited a specific era whose scientific thought and popular culture formed the bedrock out of which analytical psychology developed. It is only recently that analytical psychology has been examined within this historical perspective which reveals Jung's key position as a major figure in psychology and the history of ideas. Henri Ellenberger's (1970) reassessment of Jung stood alone for many years; among the growing number of recent scholars, J. J. Clarke (1992) and B. Ulanov (1992) track the pivotal place Jung's ideas occupied in the philosophical discourse of his time; W. L. Kelley (1991) considers Jung one of the four major contributors to contemporary knowledge of the unconscious; Moacanin (1986), Aziz (1990), Spiegelman (1985, 1987, 1991), and Clarke (1994) explore Jung's relation to Eastern psychology and religious thought; while Hoeller (1989), May (1991), Segal (1992), and Charet (1993) trace Jung's gnostic, alchemical, and European mystical roots.

Jung created his theories at a particular moment in history by synthesizing a wide variety of disciplines through the filter of his own personal psychology. This chapter will briefly look at analytical psychology's heritage in Jung's background and training, and especially focus on his debt to Romantic philosophy and psychiatry, depth psychology, and alchemical, religious, and mystical thought.

Jung believed that all psychological theories reflect the personal history of their creators, declaring "our way of looking at things is conditioned by what we are" (CW 4, p. 335). Jung, himself, grew up in the German-speaking part of Switzerland during the final quarter of the nineteenth century. Though the rest of the world was in upheaval, torn by nationalistic and world wars throughout Jung's life (1875–1961), Switzerland remained a strong, free, democratic, and peaceful federation successfully containing a diversity of languages and ethnic groups. The relevance of Jung's native country to the formation of his character has been pointed out, especially as it came through his father, a frugal, sensually restricted Protestant Baseler (van der Post, 1975; Hannah, 1976; Wolff-Windegg, 1976). Being a Swiss citizen gave Jung a sense of daily order and stability, but the austere, pragmatic, industrious Swiss character contrasts with another side of his character and with Switzerland's flagrantly romantic topography (McPhee, 1984). Switzerland is a turbulent country geographically, with three broad river valleys divided by mountains climbing to 15,000 feet. More than a quarter of the land is under water in the form of glaciers, rivers, lakes, and countless waterfalls; 70 percent of the rest of the land, when Jung was growing up, was forest or productive woodland.

Analytical psychology, as well as Jung's character, unites, or at least forms a confederation analogous to that of the bourgeois Swiss character and its romantic countryside. There is a rational and enlightened side (which Jung, in his 1965 biography, called his Number One character[1]) that carefully maps analytical psychology and presents its empirically grounded psychotherapeutic agenda. The second influence resembles the natural world of Switzerland with its interest in the psyche's heights and depths (which may be compared with what Jung called his Number Two character). This second part is at home with the unconscious, the mysterious, and the hidden whether in hermetic science and religion, in the occult, or in fantasies and dreams. Jung's own combination of these two aspects helped him explore the unconscious and create a visionary psychology while remaining scientifically grounded by his nation's stability. Analytical psychology still struggles to hold the tension of these opposites with different schools, or leanings, or even schisms, veering first to one side of the pole, then to the other (e.g. Samuels, 1985).

Jung's family came from the well-educated and prosperous townspeople. Though Jung's father was a somewhat impoverished rural clergyman, his father's father, a physician in Basel, had been a renowned poet, philosopher, and classical scholar, while Jung's mother came from a Basel family of noted theologians. Jung benefited from an education whose extent and thoroughness is rarely encountered today. It was a comprehensive schooling in the Protestant theological tradition, in classical Greek and Latin literature, and in European history and philosophy.

Jung's university teachers held an almost religious belief in the possibilities of positivistic science and faith in the scientific method. Positivism, as heir to the Enlightenment, was a philosophy deeply congruent with the Swiss national character; it focused on the power of reason, experimental science, and the study of general laws and hard facts. It gave a linear, forwardly progressing, and optimistic slant to history that could be traced back to the classical Aristotelian idea of science espoused by Wilhelm Wundt, the German father of the scientific method. Positivism soon spread throughout contemporary thought, taking such divergent paths as Darwin's theory of evolution, and its application to human behavior by the psychologists of the time, or Marx's use of Positivism in political economics (Boring, 1950).

Positivism gave Jung invaluable training in and respect for empirical science. Jung's medical-psychiatric background is clearly revealed in his empirical research, his careful clinical observation and case histories, his skill in diagnosis, and his formulation of projective tests. This rigorous scientific attitude, key though it is, was not as congenial to him and to many of his fellow students as Romantic philosophy, a contrasting lens which reflected the geography of Switzerland and presented a dramatic, many-layered view of the world. Romanticism, instead of focusing on objective particulars, turned toward the irrational, toward inner, individual reality, and toward the exploration of the unknown and enigmatic whether in myth, ancient realms, exotic countries and peoples, hermetic religions, or altered mental states (Ellenberger, 1970; Gay, 1986). Romantic philosophy eschewed the linear in favor of circumambulation – contemplating an object from many different angles and perspectives. Romanticism preferred Platonic ideals to Aristotelian lists, and focused on unchanging ideal forms behind the rational world rather than worldly movement or the accumulation of data.

Historically, Romanticism can be traced from the pre-Socratic philosophers Pythagoras, Heraclitus, and Parmenides, through Plato, to the Romanticism of the early nineteenth century and its revival at the end of that century. Plato hypothesized that there were certain primordial patterns (that Jung was to later call archetypes) of which humans are more or less defective shadows; among these patterns was an original, complete, and bisexual human being. In Jung's youth, this ideal of original wholeness was echoed in a Romantic belief in the unity of all nature. Yet, at the same time, the Romantics acutely felt their own separation from nature and longed for the ideal. Thus Romanticism gave voice to a transcendental yearning for lost Edens, for the unconscious, and for depth, emotions, and simplicity which, in turn, led to the study of the outer natural world and the soul within.

With the rise of Romanticism, men started not only to explore unknown continents and themselves, but also to look at and revalue what they considered their opposite – women – whom they endowed with the unconsciousness, irrationality, depth, and emotions forbidden to the "masculine" rational self. Claiming the objectivity of Positivist science, many tended to cultivate theories that were based on sexual Romanticism instead. In the scientists' and novelists' imagination, women were the mysterious and fascinating "other," a feminine whose fragile, Romantic vulnerability the masculine could not permit in itself; at the same time, women were also thought to possess mysterious psychic power, a power often reduced to the negative and the erotic. The actual increase in woman's power and her demands for emancipation during the latter half of the nineteenth century served to increase the ambivalence and anxiety of men. Women in Europe and the United States were starting a concerted struggle to obtain education and independence (there were no women students at Swiss universities until the 1890s). As a medical student and as a philosopher, Jung was infected by this particular strain of Romantic imagination and its illusions about women. Like his fellow Romantics, Jung remained deeply drawn to the feminine, yet equally ambivalent about it. He acknowledged his own feminine side, studied it and the women around him through the blurred lens of Romanticism, and formulated his ideas about women accordingly (Ehrenreich and English, 1979; Gilbert and Gubar, 1980; Gay, 1984, 1986; Douglas, 1990, 1993).

Romantic science led to an interest in human psychopathology and the paranormal. It gave rise to explorations of many other unknown areas as well, and helped create new professions such as archeology, anthropology, and linguistics, as well as cross-cultural studies of myths, sagas, and fairy tales. All were viewed from a white, predominantly male, usually Protestant, perspective which looked at other races and cultures with the same Romantic fascination and ambivalence with which it looked at women. This was normal for the culture and time out of which analytical psychology developed but is an area which is being revised today.

Jung considered a career as an archeologist, an Egyptologist, and a zoologist, but turned to medicine as a preferable way of supporting his newly widowed mother and young sister (Bennet, 1962). Jung's reading of Krafft-Ebing's study of psychopathology, with its intriguing case histories, opened the way to Jung's specialization in psychiatry (Jung, 1965). Psychiatry provided a home ground for all the interpenetrating areas of his interests and a creative field for their synthesis. The strains of Positivism and Romanticism warred in Jung's education and training but also produced a dialectical synthesis in which Jung could use the most advanced methods of reason and scientific accuracy to establish the reality of the irrational. Scientists of his time allowed themselves to explore the irrational outside themselves while secure within their own rationality and scientific objectivity. It was Jung's Romantic genius, and Number Two character, that allowed him to understand that humans, himself included, could be at one and the same time "western, modern, secular, civilized and sane – but also primitive, archaic, mythical and mad" (Roscher and Hillman, 1972, p. ix). At the time Jung was formulating his own theories, Positivist methodology joined with the Romantic search for new worlds to bring about an extraordinary flowering in German art and science which has been compared to the Golden Age of Greek philosophy (Dry, 1961). Germany became the center for an eruption of new ideas that fueled the search for human origins in archeology and anthropology; these discoveries were paralleled by the collecting and reinterpreting of Germanic epics and folk tales by people such as Wagner and the brothers Grimm. By the end of the nineteenth century, the mythopoetic, erotic, and dramatic elements of Romanticism became themes for popular literature and further spread the Romantic fascination with the irrational and with altered mental states. More lasting works inspired by Romanticism were written by Hugo, Balzac, Dickens, Poe, Dostoevsky, Maupassant, Nietzsche, Wilde, R. L. Stevenson, George du Maurier, and Proust. As a Swiss student, Jung spoke and read German, French, and English and so had access to these writers as well as to his own nation's popular literature.

The end of the nineteenth century and the beginning of the twentieth brought with them an era of unprecedented creativity. Jung's enthusiasm echoed the ferment reverberating in the philosophy and science he was studying, in the newer psychological texts he found, in the novels he was reading, in discourse with his friends, and in finding himself one of the torchbearers of the synthesis of Empiricism and Romanticism. Jung's brilliance and erudition need to be appreciated for their vital role in the creation of analytical psychology. So much of what was exhilaratingly novel then has since entered the Jungian canon. Perhaps Jung's pioneering virtuosity survives best in the series of seminars he gave between 1925 and 1939, where he regales his audience with news of the new worlds of the psyche he is discovering and starting to map, with the psychological treasures he has found, and the astonishing cross-cultural parallels every-where present (Douglas, forthcoming).

In these seminars and throughout the eighteen volumes of his collected works, Jung delightedly *plays* with ideas in Romantic exuberance. Jung's vigorous and playful creativity is an essential part of analytical psychology that requires an equally vivid and imaginative response. Jung never wanted analytical psychology to become a body of dogma. He warned that his ideas were tentative at best and reflected the era in which he lived: "whatever happens in a given moment has inevitably the quality peculiar to that moment" (*CW* 11, p. 592). A large part of his experimental verve is lost on the less comprehensively educated, contemporary reader but was an essential part of Jung's character and also very much in tune with the spirit of the time. As a true explorer, Jung understood the limits of what he knew; he wrote that as an innovator he had the disadvantages common to all pioneers:

> one stumbles through unknown regions; one is led astray by analogies, forever losing the Ariadne thread; one is overwhelmed by new impressions and new possibilities; and the worst disadvantage of all is that the pioneer only knows afterwards what he should have known before.                    (*CW* 18, p. 521)

Tracing the specific major sources of analytical psychology from the vast body of Jung's learning is a complicated task because it requires a knowledge of philosophy, psychology, history, art, and religion. The following is a brief synopsis of ideas from the Romantic philosophers who played a crucial role in the formation of Jung's theories (see Henri Ellenberger, 1970; B. Ulanov, 1992; and Clarke, 1992 for extensive source studies).

The theories of Kant, Goethe, Schiller, Hegel, and Nietzsche were especially influential in forming Jung's own kind of theoretical model through dialectical logic and the play of opposites. Jung believed that life organized itself into fundamental polarities because "life, being an energic process, needs the opposites, for without opposition there is, as we know, no energy" (*CW* 11, p. 197). He also saw that each polarity contained the seed of its opposite or stood in intimate relation to it. For Jung, both pairs of opposites – the Hegelian thesis and antithesis – are valued as valid points of view as is the synthesis to which they both lead.

There has been much discussion about Jung's debt to Immanuel Kant (1724–1804) and to Georg Wilhelm Hegel (1770–1831). Jung claimed to be a Kantian and wrote that "mentally my greatest adventure had been the study of Kant and Schopenhauer" (*CW* 18, p. 213). Surprisingly, he denied any debt to Hegel. However, Jung made much use of Hegelian dialectics and often wrote of history and psychic development taking place through the play of opposites in which thesis met antithesis, producing a synthesis, a new third. His concept of the new third extended to Jung's formulations about the role of the "transcendent function" in individuation.[2] Jung also was allied to Hegel in their common belief in the divine within the individual self as well as in the reality of evil.

Jung often referred to Immanuel Kant as a precursor. Besides Kant's interest in parapsychology which kindled Jung's own, Jung credited Kant for the development of much of his own archetypal theory. This is because Kant, as a Platonist, felt that our perception of the world conformed to Platonic ideal forms. Kant argued that reality only exists through our apperceptions which structure things according to basic forms. The way to any objective knowledge thus takes place through Kantian categories (Jarrett, 1981). The other side of the argument about Jung's Kantianism is that Jung and Kant are at cross-purposes. This is because Kant's things-in-themselves, his innate categories, start from sensory data which are then structured entirely by human intelligence, with Kant concluding that nothing in the mind is of itself real; Jung, in contrast, starts from archetypes and imagination and does believe in their objectivity as well as in the reality of the psyche (de Voogd, 1977 and 1984). A way through this impasse is to see Jung as a neo-Kantian since he enlarges Kantian thought by adding to it a sense of the reality of history and culture (Clarke, 1992). Archetypes, for example, are ideal forms that can never be known in their entirety, but they *can* be clothed in ways that make them visible and contemporary. Jung believed that: "Eternal truth needs a human language that alters with the spirit of the times. . .only in a new form can [it] be understood anew" (*CW* 16, p. 196).

Jung had much more in common with Johann Wolfgang von Goethe (1749–1832) than with Kant: he had a special affinity with Goethe's ideas and saw him as a predecessor (and even as a possible ancestor). Besides sharing Jung's polaristic way of seeing the world, Goethe pondered the question of evil through images and symbols. Like Jung, he was concerned with the possibility of metamorphosis of self, and with the (masculine) self's relation to the feminine. Jung often referred to Goethe's masterpiece, *Faust*, where Goethe depicted Faust's struggle with evil and his effort to maintain the tension of opposites within himself.

Jung's ideas about the collective unconscious, its archetypes, especially the anima–animus syzygy, were inspired in part by F. W. von Schelling's (1775–1854) impassioned philosophy of nature, his concept of the world-soul which unified spirit and nature, and his idea of the polarity of masculine and feminine attributes as well as our fundamental bisexuality. Von Schelling, like the other Romantic philosophers, stressed the dynamic interplay of the opposites in the evolution of consciousness.

Jung credited many of these philosophers, but claimed Carl Gustav Carus (1789–1869) and Arthur Schopenhauer (1788–1860) as especially important precursors (Jung, 1965). Carus depicted the creative, autonomous, and healing function present in the unconscious. He saw the life of the psyche as a dynamic process in which consciousness and the unconscious are mutually compensatory and where dreams play a restorative role in psychic equilibrium. Carus also outlined a tripartite model of the unconscious – the general absolute, the partial absolute, and the relative – that prefigured Jung's concepts of archetypal, collective, and personal unconscious.

Schopenhauer was the hero of Jung's student days; his pessimistic *angst* reverberated within Jung's own Romanticism (Jung, 1965 and CW A). This Romantic *angst* made both men focus on the irrational in human psychology, as well as the role played by human will, repression and, in a civilized world, the still barbaric force of the instincts. Schopenhauer rejected Cartesian dualism in favor of a Romantic unified world view, though he described this unity as experienced through either of two polarities: blind "will" or "idea." Schopenhauer, following Kant, believed in the absolute reality of evil. He emphasized the importance of the imaginal, of dreams, and of the unconscious in general. Schopenhauer synthesized and clarified the Romantic philosophers' neo-Platonic view of basic primordial patterns which in turn inspired Jung's theory of archetypes. Schopenhauer's idea of the four functions, with thinking and feeling polarized, and introversion revalued, influenced Jung's theory of typology as did their common forefather Friedrich Schiller's (1759–1805) more extensive typology of poets and their poems (*CW* 6). Both Schopenhauer and Jung were deeply involved with ethical and moral issues; both studied Eastern philosophy; both shared a belief in the possibility, and necessity, of individuation.

Jung's fellow townsman Jacob Bachofen (1815–87) was a renowned scholar and historian interested in myths and the meaning of symbols, stressing their great religious and philosophical importance. In Bachofen's monumental work *Das Mutterrecht* (1861; translated as *The Law of Mothers*), he postulated that human history evolved from an undifferentiated and polymorphous hetaeric period, to an ancient matriarchal time, to a time of destabilization, followed by the patriarchy and the repression of all memory of prior eras. Jung also hunted for matriarchal symbolism and accepted matriarchy as, at least, a stage in the development of consciousness. In his foreword to Erich Neumann's *The Origins and History of Consciousness* – which loosely followed Bachofen – Jung wrote that the work grounded analytical psychology on a firm evolutionary base (*CW* 18, pp. 521–522). Jung's ideas about the feminine, especially in his later work on alchemy, often reflect Bachofen's and Neumann's Romantic idealism. Each had a life-long interest in ancient history and the feminine; each also felt that underneath all the vast array of cultural and societal differences there lay certain primordial, ever-repeating patterns.

Friedrich Nietzsche (1844–1900) adopted Bachofen's idea of the primacy of the matriarchy, but redefined the essence of matriarchy and patriarchy into a contrasting Dionysian and Apollonian dualism. Jung utilized both Bachofen and Nietzsche to mold his own sense of history and to elucidate his theory of archetypes. Nietzsche vividly understood life's tragic ambiguity and the simultaneous presence of both good and evil in every human interaction. These apperceptions, in turn, profoundly influenced Jung's ideas about the origin and evolution of civilization. Both men also looked to the future, believing that individual moral conscience was starting to evolve to a critical new point beyond the opposites of good and evil. Jung found inspiration in Nietzsche's stress on the importance of dreams and fantasy as well as in the significance Nietzsche placed on creativity and play in healthy development. Other of Nietzsche's ideas which influenced analytical psychology were Nietzsche's portrayal of the ways sublimation and inhibition work within the psyche; his striking delineation of the power exerted by sexual and self-destructive instincts; and his courageous examination of the dark side of human nature, especially the way negativity and resentment shadowed behavior. Above all, Jung was affected by Nietzsche's deep understanding of and willingness to confront and wrestle with the dark shadows and irrational forces beneath our civilized humanity, forces that Nietzsche described as the Dionysian and Jung as part of the personal and collective shadow (Jung, 1934–39; Frey-Rohn, 1974). Nietzsche's description of the shadow, the persona, the superman, and the wise old man were taken up by Jung as specific archetypal images.

Besides Romantic philosophy, the second major influence in the development of analytical psychology came from Jung's debt to Romantic psychiatry and its historical antecedents. Among the more significant single ideas Jung adopted were J. C. A. Heinroth's (1773–1843) emphasis on the role that guilt (or sin) plays in mental illness and the need for a treatment based on the particular individual rather than on theory; J. Guislain's (1793–1856) belief that anxiety was a root cause of illness; K. W. Ideler's (1795–1860) and Heinrich Neumann's (1814–84) conviction that ungratified sexual impulses contribute to psychopathology. More important, though, is the placing of the analytical psychologist, him- or herself, not only in the neo-Platonic and Romantic camp, but also in the long procession of mental healers who honor, and work by means of, the influence of one psyche on another (the transference/countertransference). This has been traced (e.g. Ellenberger, 1970 and Kelly, 1991) to a chain leading from early (and contemporary) shamanism, to priestly exorcism, through Anton Mesmer's (1734–1815) theory of animal magnetism, and through the use of some sort of magnetic fluid connecting the healer to the healed, to the early nineteenth-century use of hypnosis in therapy. The chain continued in the nineteenth century with Auguste Liebeault's (1823–1904) and Hippolyte Bernheim's (1840–1919) use of hypnotic suggestion and the doctor–patient rapport to bring about a cure.

Liebeault and Bernheim were the founders of the group of psychiatrists who became known as the School of Nancy in France, and whose followers spread the use of hypnotism to Germany, Austria, Russia, England, and the United States. The famous demonstrations of hypnosis that Jean-Martin Charcot (1835–93) conducted at the Salpêtrière in Paris, on indigent women who had been diagnosed as hysterics, continued the chain; the demonstrations also showed how easily hypnosis could become unscientific through manipulation, experimenter bias, and a dramatic relish for well-rehearsed spectacles (Ellenberger, 1970).

As medical students, Freud studied for a term with Charcot while Jung spent a term studying with Pierre Janet (1859–1947). Janet was clearly no Romantic but influenced Jung through his classifications of the basic forms of mental disease, his focus on dual personality and fixed, obsessive, ideas, and his appreciation for neurotic patients' need to let go and sink into their subconscious. Janet also may well be the father of the cathartic method for curing neurosis and he first defined the phenomena of dissociation and complexes (Ellenberger, 1970; Kelly, 1991). Janet's example helped Jung's already strong feeling of dedication and his appreciation for the pivotal importance of the doctor–patient relationship; these were elements which Jung stressed in his writing on psychotherapy and analysis. Janet influenced Jung as a clinician and as a depth psychologist to a much greater extent than did Freud (whose influence on Jung will be discussed in the following chapter).

Much of Jung's reading during his university and medical school years concerned case histories of various forms of multiple personality, trance states, hysteria, and hypnosis – all demonstrating the involvement of one psyche with another and all part of Romantic psychiatry. Jung brought this interest into his course work and his lectures to his fellow students (CW A) as well as to his dissertation on his mediumistic cousin (Douglas, 1990). Soon after Jung finished his dissertation, he started work at the Burghölzli Psychiatric Hospital in Zurich, at the time a famous center for research on mental illness. Auguste Forel (1848–1931) had been its head and had studied hypnosis with Bernheim; Forel taught this process to his successor, Eugen Bleuler (1857–1939), who was in charge of the hospital when Jung joined him as head resident. Jung lived at the Burghölzli from 1902 to 1909, intimately involved with the daily lives of his mentally aberrant patients. Bleuler and Jung both were reading Freud at this time and it was here that Jung's researches first attracted Freud's attention and the two men started a period of alliance and cross-fertilization that lasted from 1907 to 1913.

Jung's book denoting his imminent break with Freud, *Psychology of the Unconscious* (CW B), later revised as *Symbols of Transformation* (CW 5), was influenced by Justinus Kerner's (1786–1862) study of his psychic patient, the Seeress of Prevorst, and her mythopoetic abilities (*Die Seherin von Prevorst*, 1829); it was more directly inspired by Theodore Flournoy's (1854–1920) studies of the mediums of Geneva, especially of a woman to whom he gave the pseudonym Helen Smith; Flournoy described her trance journeys in the book *From India to the Planet Mars* (1900) as examples of unconscious romances. Jung examined and amplified another imaginary saga, the notes sent to Flournoy by a Miss Frank Miller, as an introduction to his own theories of archetypes, complexes, and the unconscious. Although Jung, in a draft of his autobiography, explicitly acknowledges his debt to Flournoy, the latter's influence on analytical psychology is being newly considered (e.g. Kerr, 1993; Shamdasani, work in progress).

Thus the Romantic fascination with studies of possession, multiple personalities, seers, mediums, and trancers, as well as with shamans, exorcists, magnetizers, and hypnotic healers, all contributed to analytical psychology's respect for the mythopoetic imagination and for ways of healing that tapped into the collective unconscious. Whether these healers used spells, psychotropic substances, incantations, prayer, psychic or magnetic power, caves, trees, banquettes, or tables, whether they healed individuals or groups, they all employed altered states of consciousness that linked one psyche to another and made use of the various ways healer and healed enter this vast, omnipresent, yet still mysterious collective world.

Jung's scientific interest in parapsychological phenomena and the occult echoed these interests and was, at the time he was a student, a valid subject for scientific study. In fact much of the original interest in depth psychology came from people involved in parapsychological investigation (Roazen, 1984). It also echoed his mother's life-long interest in and experience with the paranormal. Jung wrote of his own links to this world in his autobiography (Jung, 1965); post-modern science is again taking up this examination, while new scholarship on Jung includes him as one of the pioneers in the serious study of psychic phenomena (e.g. E. Taylor, 1980, 1985, 1991, and in progress). Through his mother's family, Jung was part of a group in Basel involved in spiritism and seances. Much of Jung's outside reading during his student and university years was on the occult and the paranormal. In his autobiography, Jung tells of the psychic happenings he experienced as a boy, and the ghost and folk stories he heard; as a student, he found these phenomena scientifically studied. After finding a book on spiritism during his first year in college, Jung went on to read all of the literature on the occult then available (1965, p. 99). In his autobiography, Jung mentions books on the paranormal in the German Romantic literature of the time as well as specifically alluding to Kerner's, Swedenborg's, Kant's, and Schopenhauer's studies. In an unpublished draft (now in the Jung

Archives at the Countway Library in Boston), Jung writes more extensively of his debt to Flournoy and William James.

Jung brought this interest in psychic phenomena into his course work and his lectures to his fellow students, as well as into his dissertation (Ellenberger, 1970; Hillman, 1976; Charet, 1993). Through Jung's dissertation, his case studies, his seminars, and his articles on synchronicity (see CW 8, pp. 417–531), the paranormal came into analytical psychology as one other form through which the collective unconscious and the personal unconscious may be broached. Yet, during an era when Positivist science has been dominant, and in spite of Jung's training and empirical scrupulosity, this openness to a larger possible world has made analytical psychology problematic and has led to Jung being too often dismissed as an unscientific and mystical thinker. Jung's interest in and knowledge about parapsychology adds a rich though suspect edge to analytical psychology which demands attention congruent with the extended scope of scientific knowledge today.

Jung's mother introduced him not only to the occult, but also to Eastern religions. In his autobiography, Jung recalls that in his early childhood, his mother read him stories about Eastern religions from a richly illustrated children's book, *Orbis Pictus*; its illustrations of Brahma, Siva, and Vishnu greatly attracted him (1965, p. 17). The Romantic philosophers Jung studied in his student years rekindled this interest as they were drawn to all things exotic and Asian. In his early writing, Jung tended to view the East through these philosophers', especially Schopenhauer's, descriptions of it; it is only later, as Jung's knowledge of original sources deepened, that his view becomes more psychological and accurate (Coward, 1985; May, 1991; Clarke, 1994).

As an adult, Jung had three guides and companions for his deepening interest in Eastern philosophy and religion. The first was Toni Wolff; her father had been a Sinologist and she had acquired her interest and knowledge of the East from him and from working with Jung as his library and research associate before she became an analyst herself. During the critical period after Jung's break with Freud, Wolff helped Jung center himself partly through her familiarity with the philosophies of the East. Jung drew comfort from discovering that his own turbulent inner imagery and his attempts to master them through drawing and active imagination directly paralleled some of the religious imagery and meditative techniques of Eastern philosophy. Jung's next book, *Psychological Types* (CW 6, 1921), reveals extensive knowledge of Hindu and Taoist primary and secondary texts and incorporates their understanding about the interplay of opposites. The second influence was Jung's friend Herman Keyserling, who founded the School of Wisdom at Darmstadt where Jung lectured in 1927. From then until Keyserling's death in 1946, the two men kept up an active, though sometimes argumentative, correspondence as well as meeting to talk about religion and the East. Keyserling's main focus was on the need for dialogue between proponents of Eastern and Western thought and the spiritual regeneration that could come from the synthesis of the two systems. The third influence was Jung's friendship and dialogue with Richard Wilhelm, a German scholar and missionary to China who translated classical Chinese texts such as the *I-Ching* and *The Secret of the Golden Flower*. Jung wrote introductory commentaries for each book. These commentaries contain some of Jung's most acute observations of the link between analytical psychology and the Eastern hermetic tradition (Spiegelman, 1985 and 1987; Kerr, 1993; Clarke, 1994).

In his later writing, Jung pointed out the many ways that Eastern philosophy paralleled and informed analytical psychology. He studied the various Hindu yogic systems, especially Vedanta yoga, and the Buddhism of the Japanese Zen masters, the Chinese Taoists, and the Tantric Tibetans. In brief, he found that Eastern philosophy, like analytical psychology, validated the idea of the unconscious and gave further insight into it; it stressed the importance of inner rather than outer life; it tended to value completion rather than perfection; its concept of psychic integration was comparable to, and informed, his idea of individuation. All sought a way beyond the opposites through balance and harmony, and taught paths of self-discipline and self-realization through the withdrawal of projections and through yoga, meditation, and introspection, paths that were similar to a deep analytic process (Faber and Saayman, 1984; Moacanin, 1986; Spiegelman, 1988; Clarke, 1994). Jung used his knowledge of Eastern philosophy to place analytical psychology in a comparable context with the great philosophies of the East. Analytical psychology values many of the same goals and achieves them in a decidedly Western but comparable way. In 1929, Jung wrote:

> I was completely ignorant of Chinese philosophy, and only later did my professional experience show me that in my technique I had been unconsciously following that secret way which for centuries had been the preoccupation of the best minds of the East . . . its content forms a living parallel to what takes place in the psychic development of my patients.    (*CW* 13, p. 11)

Though Jung had known about alchemy since 1914, when Herbert Silberer had used Freudian theory to examine seventeenth-century alchemy, it was only after working on the commentary for *The Secret of the Golden Flower* (1929), a Chinese alchemical text, that Jung then took up the study of Medieval European alchemy; he soon started to collect these rare texts and built up a sizable collection. In his autobiography, Jung writes that alchemy was the precursor of his own psychology:

> I had very soon seen that analytical psychology coincided in a most curious way with alchemy. The experiences of the alchemists were, in a sense, my experiences, and their world was my world. This was, of course, a momentous discovery: I had stumbled upon the historical counterpart of my psychology of the unconscious. The possibility of a comparison with alchemy, and the uninterrupted intellectual chain back to Gnosticism, gave substance to my psychology. When I pored over those old texts everything fell into place: the fantasy-images, the empirical material I had gathered in my practice, and the conclusions I had drawn from it. I now began to understand what these psychic contents meant when seen in historical perspective.          (1965, p. 205)

In the latter part of his life, these alchemical texts and the early Gnostics increasingly interested Jung as he further developed analytical psychology; they took the place of the Romantic philosophers who had once inspired him. Jung believed that alchemy and analytical psychology belonged to the same branch of scholarly inquiry that, since antiquity, had been occupied with the discovery of unconscious processes.

Jung used the alchemists' symbolic formulations as amplifications of his theories of projection and the individuation process. The alchemists worked in pairs, and through their approach to their material transformed it and themselves in much the same way that analysis works. The goal of alchemy was the birth of a new and complete form out of the old, a form which Jung found to be analogous to his concept of the Self (Rollins, 1983; Douglas, 1990).

Jung believed that alchemy was a bridge and link between modern psychology and the mystical Christian and Jewish traditions that led back to Gnosticism (1965, p. 201). He studied the belief systems of the Gnostics and placed analytical psychology firmly within their "hermetic" tradition. This was because of their similar constructs. The Gnostics valued interiority and believed in the direct experience of inner truth and grace, emphasizing individual responsibility and the necessity for individual change. Gnostic theory rested on a vital dualism expressed most clearly in their conviction about the equal reality, power, and struggle between the opposites whether masculine and feminine, good and evil, or conscious and unconscious: both sides of the opposites needed to be reclaimed through the conflict between them. The dualism, in Jung's view, thus contained a pull to restore a lost Platonic unity. Gnostics taught that the opposites can be united through a process of separation and integration at a higher level. Jung used gnostic myths and gnostic terms to further amplify his ideas about the conscious and unconscious psyche (Dry, 1961; Hoeller, 1989; Segal, 1992; Clarke, 1992).

Much of analytical psychology rests on a firm grounding in empirical science. Yet Jung placed his psychology historically, not only within the heritage of the Aristotelian, Enlightenment tradition of the rational scientists who have dominated the scientific world for a large part of the twentieth century, but also within a far more subversive and revolutionary tradition. This is the rich and problematical historical chain that links the shamanic, the religious, and the mystical with modern knowledge about the mind. This tradition has always valued the imaginal; it stresses the continual need for exploration and inner development. It also appreciates the vital connective link between all beings. This tradition of individual responsibility and individual action, but for the benefit of the collective, gives analytical psychology a secure place in the creation of a post-modern science of the mind, body, and soul.

> In the last analysis, the essential thing is the life of the individual. This alone makes history, here alone do the great transformations first take place, and the whole future, the whole history of the world, ultimately spring as a gigantic summation from these hidden sources in individuals. In our most private and most subjective lives we are not only the passive witnesses of our age, and its sufferers, but also its makers. We make our own epoch.
>
> (Jung, CW 10, p. 149)

## NOTES

1 *Erinnerungen, Träume, Gedanken* is the German title of Jung's memoirs "recorded and edited by Aniela Jaffé" (1962, tr. as *Memories, Dreams, Reflections*, 1963/1965). At first regarded as Jung's "autobiography," it is now realized that the printed text was carefully "edited," first by Jung and subsequently by Jaffé.

2 In therapeutic practice, Jung noted that problems often stem from an inability to entertain conflicting viewpoints. The "transcendent function" is the term that he used to describe the "factor" responsible for the (sometimes sudden) change in a person's attitude that results when the opposites *can* be held in balance and which allows the person to see things in a new and more integrated way. Individuation refers to the process by which an individual becomes all that the specific person is responsibly capable of being.

## REFERENCES

Adler, G. (1945). "C. G. Jung's Contribution to Modern Consciousness." *The British Journal of Medical Psychology*, 20/3, pp. 207–220.

Aziz, R. (1990). *C. G. Jung's Psychology of Religion and Synchronicity.* Albany: State University of New York Press.
Bachofen, J. (1861). *Das Mutterrecht.* Stuttgart: Kreis and Hoffman.
Bennet, E. A. (1962). *C. G. Jung.* New York: Dutton.
Boring, E. G. (1950). *A History of Experimental Psychology.* Englewood Cliffs, N.J.: Prentice-Hall.
Charet, F. X. (1993). *Spiritualism and the Foundations of C. G. Jung's Psychology.* Albany: State University of New York Press.
Clarke, J. J. (1992). *In Search of Jung: Historical and Philosophical Enquiries.* New York: Routledge.
(1994). *Jung and Eastern Thought: A Dialogue with the Orient.* New York: Routledge.
Coward, H. (1985). *Jung and Eastern Thought.* Albany: State University of New York Press.
Douglas, C. (1990). *The Woman in the Mirror.* Boston: Sigo.
(1993). *Translate This Darkness: The Life of Christiana Morgan.* New York: Simon & Schuster.
Douglas, C. (ed.) (forthcoming). *The Visions Seminars: Notes of the Seminar Given 1930–1934, by C. G. Jung.* Princeton: Princeton University Press.
Dry, A. M. (1961). *The Psychology of Jung: A Critical Interpretation.* New York: John Wiley & Sons.
Ehrenreich, B. and English, D. (1981). *For Her Own Good: 150 Years of the Experts' Advice to Women.* Garden City, N.Y.: Anchor.
Ellenberger, H. F. (1970). *The Discovery of the Unconscious: The History and Evolution of Dynamic Psychiatry.* New York: Basic Books.
Faber, P. A. and Saayman, G. S. (1984). "On the Relation of the Doctrines of Yoga to Jung's Psychology." In R. Papadopoulos and G. S. Saayman (eds.), *Jung in a Modern Perspective.* London: Wildwood House.
Flournoy, T. (1900). *Des Indes à la planète Mars.* Geneva: Atar.
Frey-Rohn. (1974). *From Freud to Jung: A Comparative Study of the Unconscious.* New York: Putnam.
Gay, P. (1984). "Education of the Senses." *The Bourgeois Experience: Victoria to Freud* vol. I. New York: Oxford University Press.
(1986). "The Tender Passion." *The Bourgeois Experience: Victoria to Freud.* vol. II. New York: Oxford University Press.
Gilbert, S. M. and Gubar, S. (1980). *The Madwoman in the Attic: The Woman Writer and the Nineteenth-Century Literary Imagination.* New Haven: Yale University Press.
Hannah, B. (1976). *Jung, His Life, and His Work: A Biographical Memoir.* New York: Putnam's & Sons.
Hillman, J. (1972). *The Myth of Analysis: Three Essays in Archetypal Psychology.* New York: Harper Colophon.
(1976). "Some Early Background to Jung's Ideas: Notes on C. G. Jung's Medium, by Stefanie Zumstead-Preiswerk." *Spring,* pp. 128–136.
Hoeller, S. (1989). *Jung and the Lost Gospels.* Wheaton, Ill.: Quest.
Jarrett, J. (1981). "Schopenhauer and Jung." *Journal of Analytical Pychology,* 26/1, pp. 193–205.
Jung, C. G. (1902). *The Zofingia Lectures.* CW A. Ed. W. McGuire, 1983.

(1916). *Psychology of the Unconscious*. CW B. Ed. W. McGuire, 1991.
(1921). *Psychological Types*. CW 6.
(1928–30). *Dream Analysis: Notes of the Seminar Given 1928–1930*, ed. W. McGuire, 1984.
(1929a). "Freud and Jung: Contrasts." CW 4, 333–340.
(1929b). Commentary on "The Secret of the Golden Flower." CW 13, pp. 1–56.
(1930–34). *The Visions Seminars: Notes of the Seminar Given 1930–1934*, ed. C. Douglas, in press.
(1933). "The Meaning of Psychology for Modern Man." CW 10, pp. 134–156.
(1934–39). *Nietzsche's "Zarathustra": Notes of the Seminar Given 1934–1939*, ed. J. Jarrett, 1988.
(1940/1948). "A Psychological Approach to the Trinity." CW 11, pp. 107–200.
(1946). "The Psychology of the Transference." CW 16, pp. 163–323.
(1950). Foreword to the *I Ching*. CW 11, pp. 589–608.
(1951). "On Synchronicity." CW 8, pp. 520–531.
(1952). "Synchronicity: An Acausal Connecting Principle." CW 8, pp. 417–519.
(1954). Foreword to Neumann: *The Origins and History of Consciousness*. CW 18, pp. 521–522.
(1961). "Symbols and the Interpretation of Dreams." CW 18, pp. 183–264.
(1965). *Memories, Dreams, Reflections*. New York: Vintage.
(1975). "Psychological Comments on Kundalini Yoga." *Spring*, pp. 1–32.
(1976). "Psychological Comments on Kundalini Yoga (Part Two)." *Spring*, pp. 1–31.
Kelly, W. L. (1991). *Psychology of the Unconscious: Mesmer, Janet, Freud, Jung, and Current Issues*. Buffalo, N.Y.: Prometheus Books.
Kerner, J. (1829). *Die Seherin von Prevorst*, 2 vols. Stuttgart–Tübingen: Cotta.
Kerr, J. (1993). *A Most Dangerous Method: The Story of Jung, Freud, and Sabina Spielrein*. New York: Alfred A. Knopf.
McGuire, W. (ed.) (1962). *The Freud/Jung Letters*. Princeton: Princeton University Press.
McPhee, J. (1984). *La place de la Concorde Suisse*. New York: Farrar, Straus & Giroux.
May, R. M. (1991). *Cosmic Consciousness Revisited: The Modern Origins of a Western Spiritual Psychology*. Rockport, Mass.: John Knox Press.
Moacanin, R. (1986). *Jung's Psychology and Tibetan Buddhism*. Boston: Wisdom Publications.
Neumann, E. (1954). *The Origins and History of Consciousness* [1950]. Princeton: Princeton University Press.
Papadopoulos, R. and Saayman, G. S. (eds.) (1984). *Jung in a Modern Perspective*. London: Wildwood House.
Post, L. van der (1975). *Jung and the Story of Our Time*. New York: Random House.
Roazen, P. (1984). *Freud and His Followers*. New York: New York University Press.
Roscher, W. and Hillman, J. (1972). *Pan and the Nightmare*. Zurich: Spring Publications.
Rychlak (1984). "Jung as Dialectician and Teleologist." In R. Papadopoulos and G. S. Saayman (eds.), *Jung in a Modern Perspective*. London: Wildwood House.
Samuels, A. (1985). *Jung and the Post-Jungians*. London: Routledge & Kegan Paul.

Segal, R. A. (ed.) (1992). *The Gnostic Jung*. Princeton: Princeton University Press.

Spiegelman, J. M. (1976). "Psychology and the Occult." *Spring*, pp. 104–122.

(1985). *Buddhism and Jungian Psychology*. Scottsdale, Ariz.: Falcon Press.

(1987). *Hinduism and Jungian Psychology*. Scottsdale, Ariz.: Falcon Press.

(1991). *Sufism, Islam and Jungian Psychology*. Scottsdale, Ariz.: Falcon Press.

Taylor, E. (1980). "William James and Jung." *Spring*, pp. 157–168.

(1985). "C. G. Jung and the Boston Psychopathologists, 1902–1912." *Voices: The Art and Science of Psychotherapy*, 21, pp. 132–145.

(1991). "Jung and his Intellectual Context: The Swedenborgian Connection." *Studia Swedenborgiana*, 7, pp. 47–69.

Ulanov, B. (1992). *Jung and the Outside World*. Wilmette, Ill.: Chiron.

Voogd, S. de (1977). "C. G. Jung: Psychologist of the Future, Philosopher of the Past." *Spring*, pp. 175–182.

(1984). "Fantasy versus Fiction: Jung's Kantianism Reappraised." In R. Papadopoulos and G. S. Saayman (eds.), *Jung in a Modern Perspective*. London: Wildwood House.

Wolff-Windegg, P. (1976). "C. G. Jung: Bachofen, Burkhardt and Basel." *Spring*, pp. 137–147.

# 2

DOUGLAS A. DAVIS

# Freud, Jung, and psychoanalysis

One repays a teacher badly if one remains only a pupil.
And why, then, should you not pluck at my laurels?
You respect me; but how if one day your respect should tumble?
Take care that a falling statue does not strike you dead!
    You had not yet sought yourselves when you found me.
Thus do all believers –.
Now I bid you lose me and find yourselves;
and only when you have all denied me will I return to you.
(Nietzsche, *Thus Spoke Zarathustra*, quoted Jung to Freud, 1912)

Freudian psychoanalysis, a related body of clinical technique, interpretive strategy, and developmental theory, was articulated piecemeal in dozens of publications by Sigmund Freud, spread over a period of forty-five years. The structure of Freud's monumental twenty-three-volume corpus has been the subject of thousands of critical studies, and Freud is still one of the most popular subjects for biographers. Despite this wealth of writing, however, the effectiveness of Freud's therapeutic methods and the adequacy of his theories remain subjects of animated debate.

This chapter is concerned with the status of Freud's theorizing during his collaboration with Carl Jung, and with the mutual influence of each thinker on the other in the years following their estrangement. Jung's seven-year discipleship with Freud was a turning point in his emergence as a distinctive thinker of world importance (Jung, 1963). At the beginning of his fascination with Freud in 1906, Jung was a thirty-one-year-old psychiatrist of unusual promise, with a gift for psychological research and a prestigious junior appointment at one of Europe's major centers for treatment of psychotic disorders (Kerr, 1993). By the time of his break with Freud in 1913, Jung was internationally known for his original contributions to clinical psychology and for his forceful leadership of the psychoanalytic movement. He was also the author of the seminal work *Transformations and Symbols of the Libido* (CW 5), that would define his independence from that movement.

In another sense, Jung never fully overcame his pivotal friendship with Freud. His subsequent work can be understood in part as an ongoing, if unanswered, discourse with Freud. The tensions in Jung's relationship with Freud are, in retrospect, apparent from the first; and the drama of their intimacy and inevitable mutual antipathy has taken on the character of tragedy, a modern iteration of the Oedipal myth, the prototype of father-son competition.

For his part, Sigmund Freud valued Jung as he did no other member of the psychoanalytic movement, pressed him quickly to assume the role of heir apparent, and revealed his (Freud's) character to Jung in striking ways in years of impassioned friendship. Freud seems also both to have anticipated and to some extent to have precipitated the tensions that would undo the friendship and the professional collaboration. Those tensions concerned the role of sexuality in personality development and neurotic etiology – a topic about which Jung had been cautious from the first and about which Freud was to become increasingly dogmatic in the context of Jung's defection.

The story of Jung and Freud is of crucial importance to an understanding of Freud and psychoanalysis. The theory of erotic and aggressive longings illustrated by the Freud–Jung relationship is, in my view, the key to understanding the importance of each man for the other.

Freud was fifty-one when the friendship began in 1907, Jung thirty-one. Despite the difference in ages, each man was at a turning point in his life. Jung was poised to act on his vaunting ambition, on the brink of developing a distinctive expression of his genius. Freud was in the process of consolidating the insights developed over the preceding decade and eager to foster (but not to manage actively) an international movement. The relationship allowed Freud to free psychoanalysis from his quarrelsome and unsatisfactory Vienna colleagues, to link it to the international reputation of the Burghölzli Psychiatric Clinic (via Bleuler) and to experimental psychology (through Jung's studies of word association), and to articulate for a uniquely qualified interlocutor his ideas about the psychodynamics of culture and religion (Gay, 1988; Jones, 1955; Kerr, 1993). The relationship with Freud allowed Jung to broaden his perspective on the etiology and treatment of both neurosis and psychosis and gave him a satisfying political role to play in the international psychoanalytic movement.

Freud's tendency to interpret the actions (and inactions) of his colleagues in psychoanalytic terms had become well established by the time Jung met him in the year of Freud's fiftieth birthday. In relation to Fliess, Ferenczi, and Jung, Freud played out conflicting elements of his own character in his exaggerated evaluation of each new follower's quality, in overinvestment in the correspondence, in sensitivity to rejection, and finally in bitter anger at disloyalty. The decade of intimate friendship with Fliess in the 1890s displays most fully both the depth of Freud's neurotic needs in friendship and the beauty of his creative intellect as he struggles to define himself (Masson, 1985). It is in relation to Jung, however, that Freud's ambivalences were played out most fully and explicitly in terms of his psychoanalytic theory and practice. Freud wrote for Fliess during the years of his self-creation, and for Jung in the years when his mature theory was being systematized. After Jung there was no equal merging of professional magnanimity and personal investment – and after Jung the core theory of psychoanalysis became reified around a libidinal orthodoxy regarding the role of sexuality in personality development, neurotic etiology, and culture.

Freud developed the theory of transference – the evocative patterns that we all carry with us, as templates for future interpersonal relationships, the residues of the most significant emotional attachments of our childhood. He himself created a profound transferential wake, in which most of those who became his associates found themselves awash. Indeed, the history of psychoanalysis both as a clinical specialty and as a field of scholarship gives ample evidence of the transferential hold Freud continues to exert on each of us. In the therapy Freudians would practice, seduction became the metaphor for the patient–doctor transference. The patient falls for an analyst, whose every move will be assimilated to the erotic and aggressive metaphors of the transference. Understanding the transference is then the key to recovery from the neurosis.

In the light of their personal correspondence and of recent studies of the concurrent clinical and family circumstances of each, it is clear that Freud and Jung were drawn together in part by unresolved personal needs – Freud's for a male intimate to whom he could play out his need for an alter, and Jung's for an idealizable father figure toward whom he could direct his powerful ambitious energy. These personal needs eventually proved deadly to the relationship, as Jung took on increased independence and a distinctive voice of his own and Freud interpreted this growth as Oedipal hostility. After their parting, each man would portray the other as prey to unanalyzed neurotic needs.

At the beginning of the friendship Freud was well known in the psychiatric and psychological communities as the author of an intriguing book on dreams and a controversial theory about the role of sexuality in neurosis. His most recent works – *Three Essays on the Theory of Sexuality* (1905a) and *Fragment of an Analysis of a Case of Hysteria* ("Dora"; 1905b) – had emphatically stated and illustrated in detail his theories of the core role of eroticism in child development and of the sexual metalanguage of neurosis. Freud had claimed in the *Three Essays* that what the "pervert" compulsively does and the neurotic falls ill defending against, every human child both wishes and (within its infantile capacities) does.

Jung's (July 1906) preface to his own publication "The Psychology of *Dementia Praecox*," written just after his correspondence with Freud began, is prescient in its assessment of the points of stress along which the relationship would eventually split:

> I can assure the reader that in the beginning I naturally entertained all the objections that are customarily made against Freud in the literature . . . Fairness to Freud does not imply, as many fear, unqualified submission to a dogma; one can very well maintain an independent judgment. If I, for instance, acknowledge the complex mechanisms of dreams and hysteria, this does not mean that I attribute to the infantile sexual trauma the significance that Freud does. Still less does it mean that I place sexuality so predominantly in the foreground, or that I grant it the psychological universality which Freud, it seems, postulates in view of the admittedly enormous role which sexuality plays in the psyche. As for Freud's therapy, it is at best but one of several possible methods, and perhaps does not always offer in practice what one expects from it in theory (CW 3, pp. 3–4; Kerr, pp. 115–116)

Freud revealed at several points in his correspondence with Jung (a decade after the crucial events of 1897) how he had come to conceptualize himself. On 2 September 1907, he writes of his longing to tell Jung of his "long years of honorable but painful solitude, which began after I cast my first glance into the new world, about the indifference and incomprehension of my closest friends, about the terrifying moments when I myself thought I had gone astray and was wondering how I might still make my misled life useful to my family" (McGuire, 1974, p. 82). Freud's imagery here, as he recalls his self-analysis a decade before and the completion of his dream book, suggests birth as well as a voyage of exploration.

Then on 19 September he sends Jung a portrait and a copy of his fiftieth birthday medallion. In his reply, on 10 October, Jung expresses delight with the photograph and the medallion, then vents his anger with someone who had attacked psychoanalysis in an article. He describes the critic as "a superhysteric, stuffed with complexes from top to bottom" and then likens psychoanalysis to a coin. The man who had written badly of it is its "dismal face," whilst he, in contrast, derives pleasure from the reverse or "under" side. It is a curious metaphor, suggestive that psychoanalysis is a private, even secret, activity. Freud, in his own characterization of his critics, makes an even more revealing slip:

> [W]e know that they are poor devils, who on the one hand are afraid of giving offense, because that might jeopardize their careers, and on the other hand am [*sic*] paralyzed by fear of their own repressed material. (McGuire, p. 87)

He corrected the slip of "am" (*bin*) to "are" (*sind*) before sending, but both men, in their different ways, still tended to project their own "repressed material" onto their critics.

Freud seems to have responded immediately to Jung's intellectual passion, his brilliance, and his originality – all qualities he missed in his Viennese disciples. Jung's reading of Freud's works was incisive, and he knew how to administer a compliment, as in a letter after Freud's four-hour presentation of the "Rat Man" case to the 1908 First International Psychoanalytic Congress in Salzburg:

> As to sentiments, I am still under the reverberating impact of your lecture, which seemed to me perfection itself. All the rest was simply padding, sterile twaddle in the darkness of inanity.          (McGuire, 1974, p. 144)

## Freud and Oedipus

During the late 1890s Freud developed most of the core concepts for his new psychology, as evidenced by his correspondence with Wilhelm Fliess, the Berlin physician who was his closest adult friend and who served as the confidant to whom Freud divulged his struggles to understand neurosis, dreams, traumatic memories, and the emergence of personality (Masson, 1985). Over the course of several years Freud transformed his theorizing about the sources and dynamics of neurotic anxiety from neurophysiological concern with actual predisposing and concurrent causes to interpretive investigation of fantasy and personal psychodynamics. Freud's self-analysis following his father's death in late 1896 led to an increased concern with dream interpretation and to an increasingly rich experience of mutual transferential involvement with patients (Anzieu, 1986; Davis, 1990; Salyard, 1994). At a theoretical level the major change in Freud's thinking during this period involved a movement away from a causal model for the effects of childhood trauma in the formation of adult personality and neurosis – the so-called "seduction theory" – and toward psychoanalysis as a interpretive discipline in which the subjective meaning of experience – whether real or fanciful – is the basis for understanding (Davis, 1994).

In his 1899 paper, "Screen Memories," Freud shows that apparent recall of early experiences may be determined by unconscious links between the memory and repressed wishes, rather than by actual events. Freud (writing as if about a male patient) demonstrates that one of the most poignant and persistent memories of his own childhood was a memory of a fantasied scene. The content of this false memory – playing in a field of flowers with his half-brother Emmanuel's children John and Pauline – permitted Freud to express privately both his felt need for an intimate male friend and the aggression that such a friendship would arouse:

> I greeted my one-year-younger brother (who died after a few months) with adverse wishes and genuine childhood jealousy; and . . . his death left the germ of [self-]reproaches in me. I have also long known the companion of my misdeeds between the ages of one and two years; it is my nephew [John], a year older than myself . . . The two of us seem occasionally to have behaved cruelly to my niece, who was a year younger. This nephew and this younger brother have determined, then, what is neurotic, but also what is intense, in all my friendships. (Masson, 1985, p. 268)

Freud's voluminous correspondence with Fliess (Masson, 1985), with Ferenczi (Brabant and Giampieri-Deutsch, 1993), and with Jung (McGuire, 1974) reveals his longing for a male confidant, his anxious concern that his correspondent respond to his letters quickly and fully, and his readiness to turn on a friend who doubted the core assumptions of Oedipal theory. The false memory Freud analyzed in 1899, of uniting with a boy to take flowers from a girl, is also revealing of the extent to which his relations with males would be mediated by shared interest in a female. Both his rivalry and his interest in a "third" female were to play themselves out in his relationship with Jung.

The degree to which Freud changed his mind about the seduction theory, and his reasons for doing so, have attracted a great deal of attention in recent years (Coleman, 1994; Garcia, 1987; Hartke, 1994; Masson, 1984; Salyard, 1988, 1992, 1994). Most of these discussions have referred to Freud's own stated reasons in a famous letter to Fliess from September 1897, eleven months after the death of his father. In one of the most striking passages from the Fliess correspondence, Freud reported his loss of conviction about his "seduction theory" (the idea that neuroses are based on sexual seduction or abuse by a caregiver) and articulated the reasons for his change of mind. In light of the careful scrutiny this letter has received in recent discussions of Freud (see McGrath, 1986; Krüll, 1986; Balmary, 1982), it is rather surprising that the entire set of reasons Freud gave for abandoning this theory – dubbed his "neurotica" – has received little attention. Freud mentioned several motives for his change of mind, classed in groups.

> The continual disappointment in my efforts to bring a single analysis to a real conclusion; the running away of people who for a period of time had been most gripped [by analysis]; the absence of the complete successes on which I had counted; the possibility of explaining to myself the partial successes in other ways, in the usual fashion – this was the first group. Then the surprise

that in all cases, the father, not excluding my own (*mein eigener nicht ausgeschlossen*), had to be accused of being perverse – [and] the realization of the unexpected frequency of hysteria, with precisely the same conditions prevailing in each, whereas surely such widespread perversions against children are not very probable. The [incidence] of perversion would have to be immeasurably more frequent than the [resulting] hysteria because the illness, after all, occurs only where there has been an accumulation of events and there is a contributory factor that weakens the defense. Then, third, the certain insight that there are no indications of reality in the unconscious, so that one cannot distinguish between truth and fiction that has been cathected with affect. (Accordingly, there would remain the solution that the sexual fantasy invariably seizes upon the theme of the parents.)          (Masson, 1985, p. 264)

Freud's first set of reasons, that perverse acts against children might be common, is epidemiological. The second – that fathers, including Freud's own, stand condemned – is Oedipal/psychoanalytic. The third, having to do with the difficulty of establishing that *any* long-term memory is factual, is the most telling. This theory of memory becomes the argument of his brilliant short paper on "Screen Memories" two years later (Freud, 1899). The practical impossibility of reliably distinguishing *memory* from *wish* in the unconscious points directly to central issues in psychoanalysis: the need for free association and extensive anamnesis in the context of a relationship between analyst and patient that allows continued study of the role of emotional needs in the memories and fantasies of each. In the psycho-analytic transference therapy Freud was beginning to practice by the time he wrote *The Interpretation of Dreams*, no particular memory could be known with certainty. The web of connectedness that gradually emerged from the collaboration of therapist and patient was believed to reveal the salient aspects of the latter's personality.

In a detailed analysis of Freud's overdetermined involvement with the Oedipus myth, Rudnytsky (1987) called attention to Freud's consistent failure to mention the birth and death of his younger brother Julius at seemingly appropriate junctures in his self-analysis. Only in the 1897 letter quoted above, and in a letter dated 24 November 1912, to Ferenczi, in which he explains his several fainting fits in the Park Hotel, does Freud mention that such events must stem from an early experience with death. Freud's reaction to his brother's sudden infant death made Freud himself an instance of his own later theory of "Those Wrecked by Success" (Freud, 1916).

After his brother's death, Freud too was "wrecked by success," and left with an uncanny dread of the omnipotence of his own wishes. His agitation on receiving the medallion on his fiftieth birthday, when he again experienced in reality the fulfillment of a "long-cherished wish," becomes explicable when it is seen as an unconscious reminder of the death of Julius.

By the same token, had it not happened that the death of Julius left in him the germ of "guilt," or, more literally, the "germ of reproaches," Freud would almost certainly not have responded with such "obstinate condolement" to the death of his father. In his unconscious mind, he must have believed that his patricidal wishes had caused his father's death, just as he was responsible for that of Julius. (Rudnytsky, 1987, p. 20)

The pattern of murderous rivalry and uncanny love Freud identified, as a man of forty, in his unconscious memories of Julius, became a template for his relations with male disciples (Colman, 1994; Hartke, 1994; Roustang, 1982).

## Freudian correspondence

Freud was a prolific letter writer throughout his long life, and his rhetorical gifts often found their most vivid expression in his personal correspondence. Each of Freud's relationships with a man in the early period of psycho-analysis is mediated by a woman. In this triangle, Freud's possible homo-erotic feelings for the man can be aroused and sublimated. Freud's adolescent letters to his friend Silberstein, for example, testify to the extent to which his first romantic crush, on the pubescent Gisela Fluss, was in fact motivated in large measure by his fascination with her mother and her older brother (Boehlich, 1990). His later letters repeatedly illustrate this motif.

The recent publication of the first volume of the voluminous correspon-dence between Freud and Sandor Ferenczi, the Hungarian colleague with whom he maintained a twenty-five-year professional and personal relation-ship (Brabant, Falzeder, and Giampieri-Deutsch, 1993), provides new information about Freud's personal and professional concerns during the crucial period of his relations with Jung. Ferenczi offered Freud his admiring friendship in January, 1908 by requesting a meeting in Vienna to discuss ideas for a lecture on Freud's theory of "actual neuroses" (with physical causes) and "psychoneuroses" (with psychological origins). Ferenczi was "eager to approach personally the professor whose teachings have occupied me constantly for over a year" (Brabant, Falzeder, and Giampieri-Deutsch, 1993, p. 1). From the first, Ferenczi's letters display a rather obsequious devotion to Freud's personality and theories. Freud's short note in response to Ferenczi's request expressed regret at not being able on account of the illness of several family members to invite Ferenczi and his colleague Philip Stein to dinner, "as we were able to do in better times with Dr. Jung and Dr. Abraham" (ibid., p. 2). A month later, in his second letter, Ferenczi refers to

Freud as a "paranoid woman," offers to contribute to Freud's joke collection, and expresses his commitment to Freud's psychosexual theory of the neuroses, affirming that it "should no longer be called a theory" (*ibid*., p. 4) and closing with "kindest regards from your most obedient Dr. Ferenczi." Obedient Ferenczi was to prove himself over the long years of Freud's patronage, until the end of his life when he suggested that his transference onto Freud had never been adequately analyzed, prompting Freud's last methodological paper, "Analysis Terminable and Interminable" (Freud, 1937).

In striking contrast to Ferenczi, Jung from the first set limits on the relationship with Freud. Jung also anticipated where the fatal tension would occur – the father–son transference inevitable in discipleship to Freud, and Freud's insistence on acquiescence to his psychosexual theory. Roustang (1982, pp. 36–54 and *passim*) traces Jung's caution on the subject of infantile sexuality from the first correspondence with Freud in 1906 to the crisis in their relationship in 1912 (cf. Gay, 1983, pp. 197–243).

Freud's references to sublimated homosexual feeling as the key to male bonding is ubiquitous in both correspondences, but it is played out more systematically with Jung and more therapeutically with Ferenczi, who regularly attributes his anxieties about communicating with Freud to homoerotic issues. For his part, Jung admits in a remarkable letter early in the friendship in 1907 that his "boundless admiration" for Freud "both as a man and as a researcher" constantly evokes a "self-preservation complex," which he explains as follows:

> [M]y veneration for you has something of the character of a "religious" crush. Though it does not really bother me, I still feel it is disgusting and ridiculous because of its undeniable erotic undertone. This abominable feeling comes from the fact that as a boy I was the victim of a sexual assault by a man I once worshipped. (McGuire, 1974, p. 95)

Freud's next letter, curiously, has been lost. The matter does not seem to have been explicitly raised again. Each time Jung might have felt seductively approached by Freud, however, he withdraws. Each time Freud might have felt attacked by Jung, he panics – in two instances, by fainting.

Freud's relationship with Ferenczi seems to have allowed him to play a more supportive father with the infantile Hungarian than he could with the aggressive Swiss. In one letter, written after Freud and Ferenczi had traveled together to Italy in 1910, Freud complains to Jung about Ferenczi's effeminate dependence:

> My traveling companion is a dear fellow, but dreamy in a disturbing kind of way, and his attitude towards me is infantile. He never stops admiring me,

which I don't like, and is probably sharply critical of me in his unconscious when I am taking it easy. He has been too passive and receptive, letting everything be done for him like a woman, and I really haven't got enough homosexuality in me to accept him as one. These trips arouse a great longing for a real woman. (McGuire, 1974, p. 353)

The three men had traveled together to the US in 1909 so that Freud and Jung could take part in a symposium at Clark University in Worcester, Mass. In the correspondence of Freud with each of the other men about plans for the trip and its aftermath, Jung seems the mature older brother and Ferenczi the dependent younger one. Both Jung's and Freud's remarks were well received by their elite audience of American psychologists, including G. Stanley Hall and William James (Rosenzweig, 1992) but, as we shall see, a return invitation to America was the occasion for the rupture of relations between Freud and Jung.

## The eternal triangle

Throughout his life, Freud experienced competitive feelings for a woman whom he shared with a male intimate companion. The resulting male–female–male triangles usually brought Freud's relationship with the male to a crisis. The prototype, in his own view, was Freud's infantile lust for his mother – threatened when he was displaced from her breast by the birth of baby brother Julius, and eventuating in prototypical guilt when Julius seemed to succumb to Sigmund's hatred by dying (Krüll, 1986). The second instance, recovered by Freud in his analysis of the screen memory of playing in a meadow (Freud, 1899), involved his half-brother Emmanuel's children, John and Pauline Freud. In this memory the aggressive and sexual elements were merged, as three-year-old Sigmund and four-year-old John threw Pauline to the ground and took her dandelions – "deflowered" her.

To illustrate Freud's unconscious sexual fantasies, it is also useful to explore Freud's collaboration with Josef Breuer on *Studies in Hysteria*, published in 1895. This volume produced the first detailed account of a "psychoanalytic" therapy directed at the alleviation of symptoms by recovery of repressed memories. The treatment by Breuer of Bertha Papenheim ("Anna O.") had been conducted by Breuer in the early 1880s and recounted to Freud when the latter was a medical student engaged to his future wife, Martha Bernays. Breuer was reluctant to publish the case fifteen years later, and Freud attributed this reluctance to unanalyzed erotic feelings Breuer had for his young female patient. The details of Breuer's feelings are still in doubt (see Hirschmüller, 1989), but the account Freud gave Ernest

Jones and other psychoanalytic colleagues later suggests a fantasy identification with Breuer. Freud's account, reported in Jones's biography (Jones, 1953), suggested that Breuer's guilt over his erotic feelings for Bertha brought the therapy to a premature close and led to an anxious renewal of the Breuer marriage in the birth of a daughter, Dora (Jones, 1953).

Freud's own choice of the pseudonym "Dora" for his patient Ida Bauer suggests both his identification with Breuer and his obsession with exposing the erotic source of the patient's symptoms, as Breuer had feared to do (Decker, 1982, 1991). Freud's interpretation of his 1895 dream of "Irma's Injection," the exemplar to which he devotes a chapter in the *Interpretation of Dreams* (Freud, 1900), was produced when his friendship with Breuer was under great strain and his devotion to Fliess at its height. The dream casts Breuer ("Dr. M.") as a bungling therapist who has missed the sexual cause of Irma's neurosis, and Freud's interpretation spares Fliess the accusation that the patient's bleeding was caused by careless surgery (Davis, 1990; Masson, 1984).

Rudnytsky sets in apposition three of these Freudian triangles – with John and Pauline, with Wilhelm Fliess and Emma Eckstein (Freud's patient on whose nose Fliess operated in 1895), and with Jung and Sabina Spielrein – and argues that that this configuration affected Freud's treatment of his adolescent patient "Dora" (Freud, 1905). Freud's fantasy alignment of himself with the would-be seducer ("Herr K.") of his adolescent patient was the transition from the second to the third triangle (Rudnytsky, 1987, pp. 37–38). If one aligns Dora, surrounded by her father and "Herr K.," with Sabina flanked by Jung and Freud, and with Emma in the hands of Fliess and Freud, and assimilates them all to Freud and John's "defloration" of Pauline in childhood, the cumulative effect is powerful and disturbing (Rudnytsky, 1987, p. 38).

### Sabina Spielrein

Jung's controversial treatment of his young female patient Sabina Spielrein has been the subject of two books (Carotenuto, 1982; Kerr, 1993). It certainly appears that Jung was personally, and even erotically, involved with his patient both during and after his formal treatment of her. Much of the Freud–Jung–Spielrein correspondence, along with Spielrein's fascinating and disturbing diary, was published in Carotenuto's 1982 *A Secret Symmetry*, but Kerr's book is the first thorough examination of her influence on both Jung and Freud. Spielrein was a severely disturbed young Russian Jewish woman who was treated by Jung in 1904 as a test case in psychoanalysis. She maintained an intimate friendship with Jung for many years, trained in psychoanalysis with Freud, corresponded with both men during the crucial years of their friendship and subsequent alienation, and influenced Russian clinical psychology in the 1920s and 30s. Working from Spielrein's diary, her correspondence with Freud, Jung's correspondence with Freud about her, and her own published papers, Kerr traces in detail Spielrein's influence on both men's theories.

At the time Jung's correspondence with Freud began in 1906, Spielrein's clinical material pertaining to anal eroticism seems to have convinced him of the importance of Freud's assertions on the subject (Freud, 1905a; Kerr, 1993). Spielrein played an especially important role in Jung's theory of the anima and in Freud's theory of a destructive instinct. As he had with Fliess a decade earlier, Freud avoided criticizing Jung's treatment of Spielrein even when there was reason to suspect that the therapy had miscarried badly. Spielrein's diary reveals a fantasy of having a child ("Siegfried") by Jung that Jung seems to have encouraged in therapy sessions even as he denied to Freud that the relationship was sexual (Carotenuto, 1982; McGuire, 1974).

## Oedipus revisited

The last stage of the Freud–Jung friendship was characterized by each man's preoccupation with the role of universal aggressive and erotic forces in childhood personality development. For Freud the result was a renewed commitment to orthodox Oedipal theory, while for Jung the result was his typology of individual differences that allowed him to validate different analytic approaches, encompassing Freud's, Adler's, and Jung's own of sexual and aggressive feelings as they intersect with symbols of a collective unconscious. By 1911 the Freud–Jung correspondence is full of the problem of Adler's and Stekel's defections. Freud notes that he is "becoming steadily more impatient of Adler's paranoia and longing for an occasion to throw him out . . . especially since seeing a performance of *Oedipus Rex* here – the tragedy of the 'arranged libido'" (McGuire, 1974, p. 422). Referring to Adler as "Fliess redivivus," Freud also notes that Stekel's first name is Wilhelm, suggesting that both relationships evoked the ending of his friendship with Wilhelm Fliess in 1901, because of what Freud described as Fliess's paranoia.

Like Ferenczi, Jung had lent a sympathetic ear in 1911 while Freud struggled to explain Schreber's paranoia in terms of repressed homosexuality (Freud, 1911), but the sympathy was not reciprocated. Freud expressed confusion and distress at Jung's attempts to explain his rationale for *Transformations and Symbols of the Libido* the following year. Even in the early days of Oedipal theory in the late 1890s, Freud had suggested to Fliess that our repressed Oedipal complex – universal as it was thought to be – will tend to result in our downplaying or omitting the role of infantile sexuality in later development. Such revisionist accounts will find favor with the public, Freud argued, since they leave each person's repressions intact. Despite frequent assurances from Freud that neither Jung's friendship nor his role in psychoanalysis could be in doubt, there is a growing sense of each man protesting too much. Subsequently, Jung's increasing independence begins to arouse Freud's avuncular concern and finally his hostility in the summer of 1912, as Jung discussed the lectures he was preparing for a second trip to America.

On his return in November, Jung sent Freud a letter, describing the enthusiasm with which his talks on psychoanalysis were received, and added:

> Naturally I made room for those of my views which deviate in places from the hitherto existing conceptions, particularly in regard to the libido theory.
>
> (McGuire, 1974, p. 515)

Freud's reply immediately revealed the chill that was descending on the relationship:

> Dear Dr. Jung:
> I greet you on your return from America, no longer as affectionately as on the last occasion in Nuremberg – you have successfully broken me of that habit – but still with considerable sympathy, interest, and satisfaction at your personal success.
>
> (McGuire, 1974, p. 517)

After repeated exchanges about the now-famous "Kreuzlingen gesture" – Jung's hurt feelings that Freud did not arrange to meet him while visiting his colleague Binswanger in Kreuzlingen, Switzerland, and Freud's hurt feelings that Jung did not show up – a confrontation occurs. Freud gets Jung to admit that he could have inferred the necessary details to appear, and Jung surprisingly recalls that he had been away that weekend. At lunch afterwards, Freud offers hearty and seemingly friendly criticism of Jung and then drops into a faint, in the same room where he had passed out prior to the 1909 trip to Clark University with Jung and Ferenczi. It was also the same room where he had quarreled with Fliess in 1901.

When Freud attempts shortly thereafter to interpret Jung's slip that "even Adler's and Stekel's disciples don't consider me one of theirs/yours," Jung has had enough:

> May I say a few words to you in earnest? I admit the ambivalence of my feelings towards you, but am inclined to take an honest and absolutely

straightforward view of the situation. If you doubt my word, so much the worse for you. I would, however, point out that your technique of treating your pupils like patients is a *blunder*. In that way you produce either slavish sons or impudent puppies (Adler–Stekel and the whole insolent gang now throwing their weight about in Vienna). I am objective enough to see through your little trick. You go about sniffing out all the symptomatic actions in your vicinity, thus reducing everyone to the level of sons and daughters who blushingly admit the existence of their faults. Meanwhile you remain on top as the father, sitting pretty. For sheer obsequiousness nobody dares to pluck the prophet by the beard and inquire for once what you would say to a patient with a tendency to analyze the analyst instead of himself. You would certainly ask him: "who's got the neurosis?" (McGuire, 1974, pp. 534–535)

Jung's assault on Freud's cherished assumptions is frontal. Freud projects his hostility onto his disciples. Freud has never come to terms with his own neurosis. Freud's methods one-sidedly reduce motivation to sexual themes. His self-understanding is flawed, and he is – in the case where it matters most – no therapist. Freud brooded over his response to this letter and sent a draft reply to Ferenczi for comment, speaking of his shame and anger at the personal insult (Brabant, Falzeder, and Giampieri-Deustch, 1993), and finally suggested to Jung that they end their personal relationship. Jung left his positions as head of the movement and editor of its major journal the following year.

In *Totem and Taboo* (Freud, 1912–13), written while the bitterness of the quarrel with Jung was fresh, Freud laid out an anthropological fantasy of primal incest and parricide as justification for a proto-sociobiological theory of the evolution of society. Jung was now, in Freud's view, one of the "primal horde," the brother band (with Adler and Stekel) eager to devour and replace the old man.

Jung's account of Freud in subsequent writings carefully acknowledges the seminal importance of dream interpretation and the role of the unconscious in symptom formation. Jung, however, taking Freud's emphasis on childhood sexuality as evidence of his one-sidedness, suggests the need for concomitant analysis of aggressive strivings (cf. Adler), and treats the Oedipus complex as one among several universal myths in the psyche (CW 5; Jung 1963). Much of Jung's distinctive mission in the decades after Freud was to affirm the creative and prospective, rather than the regressive and reductionistic, role of myth in each lifespan. *Transformations and Symbols of the Libido* was reissued in several editions, and was finally substantially revised in the last years of Jung's life. At that time Jung noted that thirty-seven years had not diminished the book's problematic importance for him:

The whole thing came upon me like a landslide that cannot be stopped. The urgency that lay behind it became clear to me only later: it was the explosion of all those psychic contents that could find no room, no breathing space, in the constricting atmosphere of Freudian psychology and its narrow outlook.

(Jung, 1956, p. xxiii)

When Jung joined psychoanalysis in 1907, it could plausibly claim to be a radical new psychology, devised by Freud and consisting of several related parts: a powerful hermeneutics (Freud, 1900), a revolutionary and partly empirical theory of personality development (Freud, 1905a), a novel therapeutic methodology (Freud, 1905b), and a rudimentary theory of cultural psychology (Freud, 1900). Freud's work on dreams, neurotic etiology, and child development were becoming known beyond Vienna, and a psychoanalytic movement was about to form. When Jung left Freud and the International Psychoanalytic Association, both were players on a world stage and Jung was half-ready to launch a movement of his own. Freud's political leadership of the psychoanalytic movement was vested in an orthodox bodyguard (Grosskurth, 1991) and for most of the next twenty-four years he remained in the background, tinkering with the peripheral concepts of his theories and watching jealously that no variant psycho-analysis abandoned the core premise of childhood sexuality. Freud's ideas remained important to psychology for decades, and his notions regarding cultural evolution had wide influence in other disciplines, but classical psychoanalysis as a therapeutic movement became reified around theories of sexual and aggressive drives, and its most original and fertile new hypoth-eses were developed by practitioners who in one way or another were considered "unorthodox."

Ultimately the professional relationship foundered on arguments over "libido" and its transformations, i.e. on the theory of motivational energy and of the relationship between conscious and unconscious phenomena. Behind this professional squabble lay the aggressive and erotic emotions evident in the letters. Had Freud and Jung sustained their relationship for a few more years, psychoanalytic history would have been very different. There might have been a complete and coherent account of the requirements for psychoanalytic therapy and training – and perhaps a clearer distinction between them (cf. Kerr, 1993). An adequate theory of female eroticism and gender might have had its beginnings (Kofman, 1985). The interplay of sexual *and* aggressive emotions in human development would have been addressed explicitly instead of being deflected into tendentious anthropolo-gical speculation, and the spiritual aspect of life would perhaps have found a place in theory and in therapy.

# REFERENCES

Anzieu, Didier (1986). *Freud's Self-analysis* [1975]. New York: International Universities Press.

Balmary, Marie (1979). *Psychoanalyzing Psychoanalysis: Freud and the Hidden Fault of the Father*. Baltimore: Johns Hopkins University Press.

Boehlich, W. (ed.) (1990). *The Letters of Sigmund Freud to Eduard Silberstein, 1871–1881*, tr. Arnold Pomeranz. Cambridge, Mass.: Harvard University Press.

Brabant, Eva, Falzeder, Ernst, and Giampieri-Deutsch, Patrizia (eds.) (1993). *The Correspondence of Sigmund Freud and Sandor Ferenczi: vol. 1, 1908–1914*, tr. Peter Hoffer. Cambridge, Mass.: Harvard University Press.

Breuer, J., and Freud, S. (1895). *Studies in Hysteria*. In *The Standard Edition of the Complete Psychological Works of Sigmund Freud*, 24 vols., ed. J. Strachey. London: The Hogarth Press, 1953–74 (hereafter *SE*), vol. 2.

Carotenuto, Aldo (1982). *A Secret Symmetry: Sabina Spielrein between Jung and Freud. The Untold Story of the Woman Who Changed the Early History of Psychoanalysis* [1980], tr. A. Pomeranz, J. Shepley, and K. Winston. New York: Pantheon Books.

Colman, W. (1994). "The Scenes Which Lie at the Bottom of the Story: Julius, Circumcision, and the Castration Complex." *Psychoanalytic Review*, 81, pp. 603–625.

Davis, D. A. (1990). "Freud's Unwritten Case." *Psychoanalytic Psychology*, 7, pp. 185–209.

(1994). "A Theory for the 90s: Freud's Seduction Theory in Historical Context." *Psychoanalytic Review*, 81, pp. 627–640.

Decker, Hannah S. (1982). "The Choice of a Name: 'Dora' and Freud's Relationship with Breuer." *Journal of the American Psychoanalytic Association*, 30.

(1991). *Dora, Freud, and Vienna 1900*. New York: The Free Press.

Donn, L. (1988). *Freud and Jung: Years of Friendship, Years of Loss*. New York: Collier.

Ellenberger, H. F. (1970). *The Discovery of the Unconscious: History and Evolution of Dynamic Psychology*. New York: Basic Books.

Freud, S. (1896). "On the Etiology of Hysteria." *SE* 3.

(1899). "Screen Memories." *SE* 3.

(1900). *The Interpretation of Dreams. SE* 4–5.

(1905a). *Three Essays on the Theory of Sexuality. SE* 6.

(1905b). *Fragment of an Analysis of a Case of Hysteria. SE* 7.

(1911). *Psychoanalytic Notes on an Autobiographical Account of a Case of Paranoia. SE* 12, pp. 9–82.

(1912–13). *Totem and Taboo. SE* 13.

(1915). "Papers on Metapsychology." *SE* 14.

(1916). "Those Wrecked by Success." *SE* 14, pp. 316–331.

(1923). *The Ego and the Id. SE* 19.

(1927). *The Future of an Illusion. SE* 21.

(1930). *Civilization and Its Discontents. SE* 21.

(1937). "Analysis Terminable and Interminable." *SE* 23, pp. 216–253.

Garcia, E. E. (1987). "Freud's Seduction Theory." In *Psychoanalytic Study of the Child*, 42, pp. 443–468.

Gay, Peter (1988). *Freud: A Life for Our Time*. New York: Norton.

Grosskurth, P. (1991). *The Secret Ring: Freud's Inner Circle and the Politics of Psychoanalysis*. Reading, Mass.: Addison-Wesley Pub. Co.

Hartke, J. (1994). "Castrating the Phallic Mother: The Influence of Freud's Repressed Developmental Experiences on the Conceptualization of the Castration Complex." *Psychoanalytic Review*, 81, pp. 641–657.

Hirschmüller, A. (1989). *The Life and Work of Josef Breuer: Physiology and Psychoanalysis* [1978]. New York: New York University Press.

Jones, E. (1953, 1955, 1957). *The Life and Work of Sigmund Freud*, 3 vols. New York: Basic Books.

Jung, C. G. (1907). "The Psychology of *Dementia Praecox*." CW 3, pp. 1–15.

(1956). *Symbols of Transformation* (CW 5); translation of original version published as *The Psychology of the Unconscious*, 1912/1916.

(1963). *Memories, Dreams, Reflections*, rec. and ed. Aniela Jaffé. New York: Pantheon.

Kerr, John (1993). *A Most Dangerous Method: The Story of Jung, Freud, and Sabina Spielrein*. New York: Alfred A. Knopf.

Kofman, Sarah (1985). *The Enigma of Woman: Woman in Freud's Writings*. Ithaca: Cornell University Press, 1980.

Krüll, Marianne (1986). *Freud and His Father*. New York: Norton, 1979.

Masson, J. M. (1984). *The Assault on Truth: Freud's Abandonment of the Seduction Theory*. New York: Farrar Straus & Giroux.

Masson, J. M. (ed.) (1985). *The Complete Letters of Sigmund Freud to Wilhelm Fliess, 1887–1904*. Cambridge, Mass.: Harvard University Press.

McGuire, W. (ed.) (1974). *The Freud/Jung Letters: The Correspondence between Sigmund Freud and Carl Jung*, tr. Ralph Manheim and R. F. C. Hall. Princeton: Princeton University Press.

Rosenzweig, Saul (1992). *Freud, Jung, and Hall the Kingmaker: The Historic Expedition to America (1909) with G. Stanley Hall as Host and William James as Guest*. Seattle: Hofgrefe and Huber.

Roustang, François (1982). *Dire Mastery: Discipleship from Freud to Lacan*, 1976, tr. N. Lukacher. Washington: American Psychiatric Press.

Rudnytsky, Peter L. (1987). *Freud and Oedipus*. New York: Columbia University Press.

Salyard, A. (1988). "Freud as Pegasus Yoked to the Plow." *Psychoanalytic Psychology*, 5, pp. 403–429.

(1992). "Freud's Narrow Escape and the Discovery of Transference." *Psychoanalytic Psychology*, 9, pp. 347–367.

(1994). "On Not Knowing What You Know: Object-coercive Doubting and Freud's Theory of Seduction." *Psychoanalytic Review*, 1994, pp. 659–676.

Sulloway, F. J. (1979). *Freud: Biologist of the Mind. Beyond the Psychoanalytic Legend*. New York: Basic Books.

Swales, P. J. (1982). "Freud, Minna Bernays, and the Conquest of Rome: New Light on the Origins of Psychoanalysis." *New American Review*, 1, pp. 1–23.

(1983). *Freud, Martha Bernays, and the Language of Flowers*. Privately published by the author.

Thomas, D. M. (1982). *The White Hotel*. New York: Viking.

Wehr, Gerhard (1988). *Jung: A Biography*, tr. David M. Weeks. Boston: Shambhala.

Young-Bruehl, E. (1988). *Anna Freud: A Biography*. New York: Summit.

# 3

SHERRY SALMAN

# The creative psyche: Jung's major contributions

For Jung, the psyche was a many-splendored thing: fluid, multi-dimensional, alive, and capable of creative development. Having been Assistant Director of a psychiatric hospital, Jung was no stranger to disease, psychosis, and inertia. But he possessed a love for the orderly chaos of the psyche and a trust in its integrity, which both informed his conception of it, and shaped his psychoanalytic vision.

This chapter explores Jung's major discoveries, the bedrock upon which his psychological vision rests, and the ideas which continue to inform contemporary thought and practice: his unique view of psychological process; the subjective, individual path to objective awareness; and the creative use of unconscious material. Although Jung is infamous for having drawn on esoteric sources such as Medieval alchemy, he was actually ahead of his time, prescient in terms of his post-modern view of the psyche.

Disturbed by the trend in which the scientific knowledge of matter was outstripping knowledge of the human psyche, Jung noted that just as chemistry and astronomy had split off from their origins in alchemy and astrology, modern science was distancing itself, but to a dangerous degree, from the study and understanding of the psychological universe. He foresaw the enormity of the discrepancy we face now: while in the process of cracking the genetic code and creating biological life, we remain virtually ignorant regarding the psyche. Jung was drawn to seemingly mystical systems like astrology and alchemy because they were oriented toward a synthetic understanding of matter and psyche. He saw in them unconscious projections of *both* man's inner psychological process *and* his fantasies of the workings of the biological and physical world. In alchemical thinking, the two are not separated, and this is what appealed to Jung.

While rooted in this tradition that believed in the essential interrelatedness of all living matter, Jung's orientation toward the psyche and the world differed from older animistic systems that functioned psychologically by fusion, compulsion, and the baleful eye of fate. But it also diverged from

52

modern rational views oriented toward separation from the unconscious, and ego control over both matter and psyche. Freud's dictum "where id was there ego shall be" (1933, p. 80) could not be further from Jung's concept of the relationship between ego and unconscious. Jung's entire posture toward the psyche was "post-modern": its central metaphor is a *dialogue* between consciousness and the unconscious, which is dependent on self-regulating feedback systems between autonomous unconscious phenomena and the ego's participation, as well as an interplay between subject and object, psyche and matter. The Medieval alchemists said "as above, so below"; contemporary analysts would add "as within, so without," and vice versa. An important element of the Jungian view of psychological process is that it can offer a constructive contribution to the post-modern "deconstruction" of the subject–object dichotomy.

## Jung's view of the psyche

At the heart of Jung's view of the psyche lies his vision of an interplay between intrapsychic, somatic, and interpersonal phenomena, with the world, the analytic process, and last but not least, life. Jung referred to these living and inseparable relationships as deriving from an *unus mundus*, a term borrowed from Medieval philosophy meaning "one unitary world," the original non-differentiated unity, the primordial soup which contains all things.

> Undoubtedly the idea of the *unus mundus* is founded on the assumption that the multiplicity of the empirical world rests on an underlying unity, and not that two or more fundamentally different worlds exist side by side or are mingled with one another. Rather, everything divided and different belongs to one and the same world, which is not the world of sense but a postulate whose probability is vouched for by the fact that until now no one has been able to discover a world in which the known laws of nature are invalid. That even the psychic world, which is so extraordinarily different from the physical world, does not have its roots outside the one cosmos is evident from the undeniable fact that causal connections exist between the psyche and the body which point to their underlying unitary nature . . . The backround of our empirical world thus appears to be in fact a *unus mundus*.          (*CW* 14, p. 538)

Jung's implication is that all levels of existence and experience are intimately linked, and recent discoveries in the technology of DNA echo this theme: all animate life from a blade of grass to a human being is built from the same four components of genetic material, differing only by arrangement. Jung had already found another kind of validation for a "unitary world" in a symbol which exists in every culture throughout history: the mandala, or "magic circle" signifying both undifferentiated unity and integrated wholeness.

In Jung's (CW 14) undifferentiated form of the *unus mundus*, the "potential world outside of time" (p. 505), everything is interconnected, and there is no difference between psychological and physical facts, past, present, or future. This borderline state where time, space, and eternity are united forms the backdrop for Jung's most basic formulation about the structure and dynamics of the psyche: the existence of an objective psyche or collective unconscious, which is the reservoir of human experience both actual and potential, and its components, the archetypes. At this magical, "pre-Oedipal" level of the psyche, which is at odds with rational and causal explanations, certain things just "happen" to occur together (e.g. when I think of my friend, the telephone rings), and psychological significance may be experienced *synchronistically* through meaningful coincidences (Jung, CW 8). Internal and external events are related by their subjective meaning. There are inseparable links between psyche and matter, subject and object; affects, images, and action are virtually identical. One outstanding feature of Jung's approach was the value given to this magical layer of the psyche, and the understanding that it never disappears, but remains the wellspring from which all else flows.

But the ancients also imagined the *unus mundus* as dividing into parts such as subject and object, in order to bring a state of potentiality into actuality. In analytic work, this discrimination process, as in the recognition and integration of projections, constitutes a considerable psychological achievement. Jung also felt that these "parts," once they are separated, have to be reunited into an integrated whole. Although the worlds of subject and object, conscious and unconscious, are necessarily divided for the sake of adaptation, they must be reunited for the sake of health, which for Jung meant wholeness. This potential condition of wholeness he referred to as the *Self* (the entire psyche, not just the ego). Development toward it is part of the psyche's *individuation process*. This emphasis on the synthesis of what had been previously discriminated and divided constitutes another unique feature of the Jungian approach.

Jung's image of psychological process incorporates but moves beyond the subject/object split in which it is usually framed by grounding it in a universal, archetypal symbol, the *unus mundus*. Jung "depathologizes" the archaic level of the psyche in which internal reality and external event are one and the same. He emphasizes that from a psychological standpoint, only in the developmental phase of separation and discrimination is it meaningful and important to refer to subject and object as discrete entities, or to even differentiate between them. At subsequent levels of psychological process the relationship between subject and object, conscious and unconscious, can and should become reintegrated into a subjectively meaningful whole, an experience often referred to as "mystical." This differentiation of the changing relationship between internal reality, external event, subject, object, conscious and unconscious, can make way for a similarly differentiated clinical methodology, which Jung laid ground for but never fully developed (see Salman, 1994).

Contrary to popular opinion, Jung was firmly anchored and innovative in clinical practice. For example, he eschewed the use of an analytic couch in favor of a face-to-face encounter. He took great pains to bring patients to full awareness of their present problems, and sought to help people face the challenges of everyday life. Historically, he was the first to emphasize the fact that development is arrested not only because of past trauma, but also from plain fear of taking necessary developmental steps. He placed major emphasis not on repressed desires, but on current life events as precipitants for the regression experienced in analysis. The material from this regression was used to bring the patient back to reality with a new orientation which could be practically applied.

Just as the reality of relationships and objects cannot be reduced to intrapsychic phenomena, Jung always maintained the fact of the *reality of the psyche per se*. Psychic phenomena are related, but not reducible to other levels of experience such as neurons and synapses. Consequently they should be investigated as they are experienced. For example, the soul, although experienced as something immaterial and transcendent, is nevertheless treated as an objective *psychological fact*, irrespective of scientific proof of its existence. Jung's crucial observation was that psychological phenomena are as "real" in their own right as physical objects. They function autonomously with a life of their own, something which has been "rediscovered" recently in the phenomena of dissociative disorders.

This realization of psychic reality *per se* implies that the unconscious can never be entirely repressed, exhausted, or emptied through reductive analysis. In fact, this would be disastrous for psychic health. Consequently, the dangers of being flooded by it (= "engulfment," "possession") or of identification with it (= "inflation") are always present: thus a kind of madness is always possible. But Jung's solution was a happier one than Freud's: he conceived the optimum relationship between ego and the rest of the psyche to be one of continuous *dialogue*. By definition, this is a never-ending process. What changes is the nature of the conversation.

Jung's own thinking on the nature of this conversation ranged from early formulations of the ego's "fight with the dragon-mother of the unconscious"

(*CW* 5), in which the ego gains a foothold out of its unconscious matrix, to later images of alchemical transformation in which the ego surrenders itself (*CW* 14). But the core issue remains the same: to maintain a dynamic tension and a flexible relationship between the ego and the rest of the psyche. Jungian analysis is not primarily concerned with making the unconscious conscious (an impossibility in Jung's view), or about merely analyzing past difficulties (a potential impasse), although both of these come into play. The object is one of *process*: finding a way to come to terms with the unconscious as well as deal with future difficulties. This process consists of maintaining a continous dialogue with the unconscious that facilitates creative integration of psychological experience.[1]

## The subjective path to objective awareness

Jung was the first analyst to promote the "training analysis" as the *sine qua non* of analytic training. He felt that real knowledge was entirely experiential, what the Gnostics called *gnosis*, an "inner knowing" which was gained through one's own experience and understanding. This "inner knowing" is more than just "consciousness," it includes the experience of *meaning*. Based on his personal and clinical experience of the numinous in psychological life, where he encountered imagery identical to that of different religions, Jung postulated a religious "instinct." When this *instinct* to make meaning is blocked or conflicted, as any instinct can be, disease will result. Jung argued that the archetypal symbols which emerge from the unconscious are part of the psyche's *objective* religious "meaning-making" instinct, but that these symbols will be realized *subjectively* within each individual. For example, there is a human instinct to create an image of a godhead, the function of which is to symbolize our highest values and sense of meaning, but the content of this image varies within cultures and within individuals.

This led Jung to his interest in typology. He saw a need to differentiate the universal components of consciousness in such a way as to delineate how these components work in different ways in different individuals. In the theory of *psychological types* (*CW* 6), Jung described two basic modes of perception: introversion, where the psyche is primarily stimulated by the internal world, and extraversion, where the psychic focus is on the external world. Within these perceptual modes, Jung described four properties of consciousness: thinking, feeling, intuition, and sensation. The modes of perception and the properties of consciousness are found combined in various ways, resulting in sixteen "typologies," basic styles of consciousness, for example the introverted intuitive thinking type, or the extraverted sensate feeling type. The theory implies that there are various ways not only of apprehending but also of functioning in the world, an idea which has been assimilated into couples therapy and business management. The theory also suggests that different clinical "types" of patient may require different treatment modalities.

The understanding of both the objectivity of the psyche and the importance of one's subjective experience of it informs the Jungian view of the analytic process. This process involves the uncovering of one's personal history, unconscious dynamics, and individual limitations, with the attendant suffering and healing of unresolved complexes.[2] But this personal material is considered to have a universal core which derives from the "objective psyche" or "collective unconscious," by which he meant the level and content of the psyche that consists of archetypes. Rather than being an individual matter, the objective psyche is that level of the unconscious which is common to all, and its "discovery" results in knowledge of one's commonality, the universality of experience, and the creation of meaning from this experience.

Since all individual experience has an archetypal core, issues from personal history and archetypal patterns are always interwoven, often needing first to be separated, and then linked back together. Jung envisioned the entire process as parallel to the ancient initiation mythologem of the sun-hero who dies, journeys through the underworld, and is eventually resurrected. Although this model of consciousness has considerable "gender-bias," the mythologem expresses several fundamental themes which hold true: death–rebirth as a psychological process, the healing power of creative introversion, the struggle with regressively charged libido, and the descent through the personal psyche into the wellsprings of psychic energy, the objective psyche.

Jung's way of looking at consciousness was very different from a universal theory applied indiscriminately. Even so, Jung considered all subjective paths of experience, all typologies, all complexes, to lead to the universal objective level of psyche, comprised of the archetypes. Like multi-faceted crystals, archetypes describe the content and behavior of the objective psyche. As psychosomatic "structures," they are our innate capacity to apprehend, organize, and create experience. Archetypes are both biologically based patterns of behavior and the symbolic images of these patterns. As transpersonal structures, they are transcendental "essences" or quintessential distillates of creative power and meaning, revealed to us in symbols.

For example, the archetype of the "Great Mother" symbolizes much more than the experience and reality of one's personal mother (Neumann,

1955). Although "mother" is a personal psychological, emotional and cognitive experience which has cultural determinants, it also has an archetypal instinctual base, in that humans are "wired up" to recognize and participate in mothering and being mothered, as well as an archetypal symbolic base expressed in images such as the Great Goddess, Mother Church, the Fates, and Mother Nature. The experience of "mother" is always heavily influenced by this unconscious template, the Mother archetype, which includes the innate capacity to apprehend and experience nurturance and deprivation, as well as the capacity to symbolize this experience.

The postulate of an archetype helps explain the ubiquitous discrepancy between the child's experience of "mother" and the actual mother. Jungian analysts take great care to differentiate the personal mother from the archetypal image of Mother, which is more than any human mother can incarnate. In many ways, D. W. Winnicott's (1965) formulation of the "good enough mother" (p. 145) relates to Jung's formulation of the maternal archetype: the good enough mother is the one who is able to meet and mediate the child's innate maternal archetypal image. She just has to be "good enough" to do that.

The archetypes delineate how we relate to the world: they manifest as instincts and affects, as the primordial images and symbols in dreams and mythology, and in patterns of behavior and experience. As impersonal, collective and objective elements in the psyche, they reflect universal issues, and serve to bridge the subject/object gap. The recognition of archetypes, including the psyche's personalization of symbolic archetypal motifs (such as the fantasy that one's mother is a witch or an angel) is a vital part of the Jungian process. Of their ubiquity, Jung said:

> Here there are many prejudices that still have to be overcome. Just as it is thought, for instance, that Mexican myths cannot possibly have anything to do with similar ideas found in Europe, so it is held to be a fantastic assumption that an educated modern man should dream of classical myth-motifs which are known only to a specialist. People still think that relationships like this are farfetched and therefore improbable. But they forget that the structure and function of the bodily organs are everywhere more or less the same, including those of the brain. And as the psyche is to a large extent dependent on this organ, presumably it will – at least in principle – everywhere produce the same forms.
>
> (CW 14, p. xix)

Jung (CW 8) imagined the archetypes as spread out over a "spectrum of consciousness" (p. 211) like the light spectrum which ranges from red at one end through the yellows, greens and blues, to violet. At the extreme red and violet ends of the spectrum are the instinctual and spiritual poles, respectively, of the archetype. These aspects of the archetype are unconscious and function powerfully and autonomously. These are the "psychoid" areas of the archetype that function as centers of psychic energy coexisting with consciousness. They manifest in fusion states, like projective identification or mystical illumination, or in psychosomatic conditions, such as the identity between infant and mother. When this magical level of an archetype is activated, there is an intensified energy field felt in the body, which Jung called "numinosity." It can be transmitted by contagion to the whole environment with results as discrepant as mob psychology and faith healing.

The entire character of archetypes, their "all or nothing" affective impact, their impersonality, autonomy, and numinosity, form a rich theoretical backround for many dynamics of the pre-Oedipal field: omnipotence, idealization, fusion, and separation–individuation struggles. This objective psyche is the birthplace and matrix of archetypal images, and the layer at which primary instinct and affect disturbances are healed. It is here that the numinous power of the archetypes is felt, in distinction to rational understanding. The archetypal psyche is the world of the *unus mundus* where nothing is yet separated, but nothing is sequentially connected either. Instead of connections and relationship there is substitution and affect. The part represents the whole, and the whole represents the parts. One's mother's frailties are experienced through the lens of the Terrible Mother, and her graces as the boon of the Great Goddess. Much of analytic work is concerned with differentiating the personal from the archetypal, *while at the same time reintegrating, via symbolization, the personal and archetypal experience.*

Although archetypal images are very different from personal experience they never exist in a void: they are triggered, released, and experienced in an individual. Nature (the archetype) and nurture (the personal experience) are inextricably interwoven. The archetype proper is a skeleton which requires personal experience to flesh it out. The relationship between personal issues and archetypal motifs is paradoxical: although an archetypal image should be analyzed not reductively, but as something symbolic and emergent, it is also true that an archetype is expressed in actual experience. For example, when a patient is in the grip of an idealizing transference (Kohut, 1971) and the analyst is experienced as transcendentally positive and nurturing, the "Good" facet of the Mother archetype is constellated in the patient and projected onto the analyst. In this case the healing agent is transpersonal, but is experienced in personal terms. The archetype compensates for poor personal experience, but the symbol cannot heal without a body and a concrete life. As Jungian analyst Edward Whitmont (1982) puts it,

A lack of relation to the archetypal dimension results in spiritual impoverishment and a sense of meaninglessness in life. But insufficient anchoring and incarnating of the archetypal in the personal realm – that is, speculating about archetypal meaning rather than trying to discover this meaning through living concretely the prosaic and "trivial" problems and difficulties of everyday feelings and relationships, results in mere "head trips" and is the hallmark of narcissistic pathology. Then the symbol fails to heal and may, indeed, insulate analysands from the unconscious, rather than connect them to it.     (p. 344)

In addition to articulating the archetypal dimension of the psyche and one's personal experience of it, Jung had other ideas about psychological development which were prescient. Foremost was the exploration of the feminine archetype in mythology, and the importance accorded it in the psychological development of both sexes. Jung recognized that the "masculine" aspects of the psyche such as autonomy, separateness, and aggressivity were not superior to the "feminine" elements such as nurturance, interrelatedness, and empathy. Rather, they form two halves of a whole, both of which belong to every individual. Jung called the "feminine" archetype within a man the *anima*, and the "masculine" within a woman the *animus*. Jung conceived them as akin to soul-images with their own psychic reality, an "otherness" which needs to be related to as such, thereby connecting the ego to the objective psyche.

By postulating the archetypes of anima/animus Jung enlarged the picture of developmental possibilities for both sexes. Although influenced by gender-based thinking in some of his assumptions about appropriate gender development and behavior, Jung's most stunning accomplishment was to place women and the feminine aspects of the psyche on equal footing with men and the masculine. This, in effect, challenged the entire structure of psychoanalytic and developmental theory, which was based on the ideal of a heroic autonomous individual, separated from the mother at all costs, as its model of psychological health. Qualities such as dependency and empathy had been devalued and pathologized. A woman was *ipso facto* an inferior man. Jung began a revisioning of the feminine archetype, which is resulting in an overhaul of our ideas about mental health by incorporating "feminine" qualities as essential.

Jung also saw psychological development continuing throughout the adult lifespan. He was the first to attempt an outline of the stages of life, based on the myth of the solar hero who rises with the dawn, ascends with the midday sun, and then descends below the horizon into death (CW 8). The idea of life-stages has continued to inspire research, such as the "mid-life crisis" phenomenon. The potential for continuous and qualitative development throughout life adds a necessary compensating factor to genetic theories of development. But because of his belief that many roads lead to Rome, Jung was circumspect about a rigid archetypally based developmental theory. His discovery was of the existence of many subjective paths to objective awareness. And in fact, particular archetypal paradigms may influence individuals somewhat or not at all, and their use may be more relevant to various qualities of psychic function. For example, the hero's fight with the dragon (Neumann, 1954) is illustrative of the adolescent paranoid-schizoid psyche, while Celtic myths with their fluctuating Other-worlds are paradigmatic of the pre-Oedipal psyche (Perera, 1990). In all cases, archetypal material is used to heal, amplify, ground, and give meaning to the personal experience in which it is embedded.

## The Jungian model and its dynamics

While the objectivity of experience is determined by the archetypes, its subjectivity is determined by the nature of one's personal complexes. In many ways Jung was the father of "complex theory." While testing normal subjects using a "word association test" in which subjects responded with associations to stimulus words (CW 2), he found the presence of *internal*, unconscious distractions which interfered with associations to the test words. These internal distractions were called feeling-toned complexes of ideas, *complexes* for short. This work had great bearing on the status of psychoanalysis in the scientific community at that time, yielding empirical indications that an "association" could be disturbed purely from within. Otherwise, critics argued, patients in analysis produced associations, but these were shaped by the analyst's responses (Kerr, 1993). Then Jung provided experimental verification of specific indicators, namely complexes, which he argued were responsible for many associations.

The word association test suggested the presence of many types of complex, contradicting Freud's claim for a core sexual complex. Jung also observed that these complexes were *dissociable*: they functioned as autono-mous split-off contents of the unconscious capable of forming separate personalities. Jung was keenly interested in these split-off contents, which was one reason he was taken with Freud's notion of dissociated traumatic memories. But Jung never believed that dissociations were necessarily caused by sexual trauma, or any trauma at all. For Jung the psyche was inherently dissociable, with complexes and archetypal contents personified and functioning autonomously as complete secondary systems. He con-ceived of there being numerous *secondary selves, not merely unconscious drives* and processes.

This radical view is now being investigated vigorously in contemporary research on trauma, dissociative disorders, and multiple personality disorders, where many of Jung's ideas are being confirmed. And his thinking on the nature of dissociative phenomena was far-reaching: in his doctoral dissertation, Jung (CW 1) first suggested that in some cases the tendency of the psyche to dissociate might be a positive mechanism. He had studied a spirit medium, and found that the personality of the medium's spirit guide was more integrated than that of the medium herself. This "secondary" personality was superior to the primary one. From this observation, Jung began to formulate a most important idea: the *teleological* orientation toward symptomology.

While Freud's psychoanalysis was predominantly archeological, delving into the ruins of the past, Jung's was concerned with the present as it gave rise to future development. Jung saw the ego as prone to errors of misguidedness (inappropriate choices) and one-sidedness (excess). He believed that the material surfacing from the unconscious served to bring light to its fundamental "darkness." He considered unconscious imagery to be symbolic, where a symbol is understood as something that compensates or rectifies the errors of ego consciousness. The symbol has a regulating function. The essence of the teleological position is that (a) all symptoms and complexes have a symbolic archetypal core, and (b) the end result, purpose, or aim of a symptom, complex, or defense mechanism is as important, if not more so, than its causes. A symptom develops not "because of" prior history, but "in order to" express a piece of psyche or accomplish a purpose. The clinical question is not reductive, but synthetic: "what is this symptom for?" In the case of the medium whom Jung (CW 1) studied, her spirit guide was not reduced to a pathological hysterical complex, but considered as "an independent existence as autonomous personality, seeking a middle way between extremes" (p. 132). Jung saw the figure as an attempt to rectify her past and prepare her for adult life; it was a numinous element in the psyche capable of giving meaning to her life. Jung was arguing that a complex, rather than just repeating itself, could also function to regulate current functioning and reorganize the future.

The most serious form of disease is not the existence of complexes *per se*, but the breakdown of the psyche's considerable self-regulating capacities, such as the ability to rectify the current situation by bringing into awareness dissociated complexes and archetypal material. But how are these various dissociated pieces of the psyche organized? The teleological view posits another of Jung's seminal ideas: the existence of the *Self*, by which Jung meant an ideal agency that contains, structures, and directs the development of *the entire psyche*, including the ego.

The ancient and long obsolete idea of man as a microcosm contains a supreme psychological truth that has yet to be discovered. In former times this truth was projected upon the body, just as alchemy projected the unconscious psyche upon chemical substances. But it is altogether different when the microcosm is understood as that interior world whose inward nature is fleetingly glimpsed in the unconscious . . . And just as the cosmos is not a dissolving mass of particles, but rests in the unity of God's embrace, so man must not dissolve into a whirl of warring possibilities and tendencies imposed on him by the unconscious, but must become the unity that embraces them all.

(CW 16, p. 196)

The Self, at the beginning of life, encompasses the potential totality of the personality, but like a seed or genetic blueprint, it also develops over time. Jung elaborated his developmental perspective on the Self in his alchemical amplification of its journey from a chaotic *massa confusa* to the integrated *lapis* or Philosopher's Stone which, by containing all contradictory opposites, symbolizes an ideal condition of wholeness and health (CW 14). Although this condition is never fully realized, the Self functions throughout life as the ordering factor behind development, and as a structuring, prospective force behind symptoms and symbols. A distinguishing feature of Jungian psychology is that all diagnostic, prognostic, and developmental theories are organized from the point of view of the Self, not the ego. Post-Freudian theorists only allude to this notion of a "Self": Masud Khan speaks of the experience of a self which transcends id–ego–superego structure (1974), and Kohut refers to the fundamental and mysterious notion of the self (1971). But in the Jungian model the ego is truly relativized in regard to the Self, and at its best acts as the Self's "executor."

Jung conceived of a psyche having many important structures and centers of gravity, concurrently self-regulating, dissociative, and striving toward order through the Self. Since the psyche is dissociable by nature, its assimilation by the ego is a never-ending process. Jung perceived a yawning gulf between the ego and the unconscious, a gulf that is sometimes bridged but never eradicated, and his formulation included the idea of forever dissociated "irredeemable" pieces of psyche. But within this seemingly chaotic system there is also order: the Self, the structuring, teleological force behind development and symptomology, the destiny and mystery factor in psychological process. The psyche's two regulating mechanisms, *dissociability* and the *Self*, are two "opposites" which together comprise the Jungian model. These opposites have split up in three directions: the classical school, which emphasizes the Self; the archetypal school, which focuses on the psyche's dissociability; and the developmental school on the process of individuation out of unconsciousness. The challenge for the next generation is to move through this plurality into a position which mediates the complexity of a unified vison.

## The creative and symbolic use of unconscious material

In Jungian work, fantasies, dreams, symptomology, defenses, and resistance are all viewed in terms of their creative function and teleology. The assumption is that they reflect the psyche's attempts to overcome obstacles, make meaning, and provide potential options for the future, rather than existing only as maladaptive responses to past history. For example, during a period of depression and anxiety a woman (whose case is discussed in Ch. 10) reported "I'd like to jump in a river." The Jungian approach to this disturbing fantasy works to open up the interpretive field of the patient's suicidal imagery. Its apparent "meaning" and purpose will be seen in the context of its underlying function and symbolism.

Jung's view of most mental illness was that when the natural flow of libido (by which he meant psychic energy *per se*, not only sexual libido) is stopped due to one's inability to meet internal or external difficulties, it regresses. As it regresses, it activates both past internalized images such as those of parents, and archetypal symbols of libido from the objective psyche, such as water. The fantasy of "jumping into a river" is the psyche's image for an impending regression whose quality is "watery." The questions asked as libido regresses and such potent symbols emerge are: what is this for and where is it going? This approach is called the *synthetic and progressive* method of interpretation, to differentiate it from a reductive, retrospective and personalistic approach which analyzes in terms of past history and personal experience. A combination of both methods is used in Jungian treatment.

Regression is a powerful event: it contains both the illness and its potential cure. Libido needs to flow backwards, passing through the phase of parent/child relationships in order to reach deeper wellsprings of psychic energy. This ability to regress, particularly to go through and beyond childhood conflicts and trauma, is another of the psyche's self-regulating mechanisms. Jung considered regression and introversion not only potentially adaptive, but the *sine qua non* of healing if successful. As libido regresses and turns inwards during illness, symbols emerge from the unconscious, such as "jumping into a river." These symbols are not censored or distorted, nor are they merely signs for something else. Freud had considered the function of symbol formation to be protection against unconscious infantile urges. Jung felt that the purpose of a symbol was to *transform libido from one level to another*, pointing the way toward future development. Symbols are like living things, pregnant with meaning and capable of acting like *transformers of psychic energy*.

Symbols speak the language of the archetype *par excellence*. They originate in the archaic magical layer of the psyche, where they are potentially healing, destructive, or prophetic. Symbolic images are genuine transformers of psychic energy because *a symbolic image evokes the totality of the archetype it reflects*. Images evoke the aim and motivation of instincts through the psychoid nature of the archetype. This holds true whether or not they are rationally understood. For example, the fantasy of wanting to "jump into a river" sets into motion a very real psychological process of healing or drowning. The libidinal energy of a complex is "bound" into the image and in this form may be partially assimilated by the ego, resulting in psychic energy being freed for conscious use. Jung was keen on using techniques such as drawing, painting, and active imagination to express symbolic images. This aesthetic expression has its own curative properties, and once the spirit is in the bottle, so to speak, it is easier to begin a dialogue with it. Jung's techniques of drawing, painting, and playing have been adopted by child analysts and numerous other clinicians.

But what eventually happens to the libido during regression? Jung observed the *spontaneous reversal of libido*, which he called *enantiodromia*. This occurrence of a "return to the opposite" characterizes the nature of the libido's flow, and has been depicted in literature and mythology as the sun's return from the belly of the night, the journey back from the center of the earth, or the poet's ascent from Dante's *Inferno*. This crucial self-regulating mechanism may account for the spontaneous remission of depression and psychotic episodes, and puts an end to regression. When it fails, regression becomes a very dangerous event.

When unconscious material is surfacing, the *specificity of the image* is the informing principle in working with it, i.e. a river is a river, not a censored sexual image. The unconscious has its own mythopoetic language and point of view on things, albeit foreign, not derived from verbal language. In fact Jung (*CW* 5) postulated "two kinds of thinking" (p. 7), rational and non-rational, an idea which presaged later scientific discoveries concerning the nature of the two brain hemispheres and different modes of processing information. The symbolizing, imagistic part of the mind works by analogy and correspondence rather than rational explanation. Jung felt that the tenacity and ubiquity of this type of thought indicated its "hard-wired" archetypal origins. The deeper the regression, the more one encountered it. This is why he interpreted modern dreams and phantasies in the light of archaic mythological motifs, a method called *archetypal amplification*.

For example, the image of "jumping into a river" means much more than the dreamer's personal associations to it. It carries with it all the archetypal imagery of moving water: water "solves" by dissolving and moistening obstructed libido. It represents flow vs. fixity, immersion, containment, dissolution and purification. Water relaxes the connections between things, which results in either death or renewal. The sacred rivers of the world, the Nile, the Ganges, the Jordan, are all thought to have healing and regenerative properties, and mythological rivers such as the Styx or the river Lethe are connectors between life and the oblivion of death. In many myths, female deities make a river quest, looking for someone lost, or a part of themselves which must be retrieved: Psyche searches for Eros, Isis for Osiris. Teleologically, the "suicidal" image symbolizes the need to dissolve things back into their constituent parts, to be swept away into the waters of the unconscious and purified, as a prelude to rebirth. Jung believed that from the standpoint of the Self, which sees the "big picture," it is immaterial whether this takes the form of death or a renewed life. In either case one begins anew somewhere else. The ego sees it differently, however. Clinically the crux of the matter is found where archetypal amplification meets the patient's personal experience, capacities, and history. Therapeutically, this image may signal the "reductive" part of analysis: the dissolving waters of tears, grief, mourning, and a deluge of feeling. If the patient's history suggests she can withstand a therapeutic dissolution and survive, the prognosis is excellent. On the other hand, if the patient's traumas have been too overwhelming, and have engendered fear or extreme passivity, her ability to "go with the flow" of libido may be limited, resulting in stagnation, or even potential suicide.

The method of archetypal amplification is very different from traditional free association: it recognizes the limits of free association by placing emphasis on the specificity of the image, i.e. river, as having an objective meaning as a universal symbol. This illumination of true symbols which are beyond rational understanding and capable of imparting meaning to a sense of meaninglessness might be important to a woman who wanted "to jump into a river." In the clinical situation, archetypal amplification and personal experience intermingle to offer information on diagnosis, prognosis, and specific timing which may rectify the dreamer's current situation, including the analytic one. From the Jungian perspective, diagnosis and prognosis are not only concerned with pathology, but with assessing the potential for dialogue and assimilation between ego and unconscious material.

Another way in which Jungian work uses unconscious material in a creative fashion is in its approach to the *experience of opposites* in psychological life. This experience reflects the psychological fact that whatever is in the ego complex has its mirror "opposite" in the unconscious. A controlling ego will constellate disorder in the unconscious: a prince is also a frog, and a frog contains a potential prince. The psyche is not a perfect homogeneous entity; rather, it works to create wholeness. But disorderly frogs are usually pushed into the unconscious, forming a dissociated secondary personality which Jung called the *shadow*. It of paramount importance to bring this, and other "opposites," into conscious awareness; otherwise further dissociation and neurosis will result.

> Since conscious thinking strives for clarity and demands unequivocal decisions, it has constantly to free itself from counter-arguments and contrary tendencies, with the result that especially incompatible contents either remain totally unconscious or are habitually and assiduously overlooked. The more this is so, the more the unconscious will build up its counterposition.
>
> (CW 14, p. xvii)

This notion of contradictory opposites lying side by side, albeit partially repressed, revisions our picture of mental health, and relativizes feelings of inferiority and pathology. Wholeness rather than perfection is the goal. Everyone has a shadow complex; it is "just so," an archetypal given of the psyche. The shadow is never removed or completely assimilated by the ego, rather there is an ethical imperative of acknowledging it, and taking creative responsibility for it, not continuing to project it. Jung was quite definite in his feeling that the way to psychological health and meaning was through the shadow. The demons, robbers, and nasty siblings who pursue us in dreams may be our secondary selves looking for a place at the table.

Although the problem of opposites is perennial, its therapeutic articulation was one of Jung's major contributions. This problem obviously plays itself out in object relations, as the psyche initially projects the shadow and other complexes into interpersonal relationships, i.e. it's the other guy who is a frog. But Jung also turned our attention to the introverted arena: the relationships between the complexes themselves, and the ego's relationship with these complexes. Exploring these relationships is the mature work of psychotherapy, where the important questions become: how will the frog live, if not in projection? How does the prince treat the frog, and the frog the prince? Finding answers is a process of subjective understanding, relativization of the ego, continuous integration of shadow material, and a subjective slant on what constitutes "good and bad" in psychological life.

This struggle is part of the difficult *individuation* process which strives not for perfection, but for wholeness. The "opposites within" are related to both willingness and conscience; adaptation to the collective culture is not the ultimate goal. This movement of libido is different from instinctive growth, adaptation, regression, or general maturation. It is what the alchemists called the "opus contra naturam," the work *against* nature. Although it is dependent on full development of the stages of life, including both an adaptation to society and an attainment of individuality, the crucial shift is from an idealized ego to a truly unique Self-oriented ego. This happens by the differentiation and creative assimilation of psychic opposites, of the shadow and other unconscious material. Its yield is the wisdom of the wholeness of life, and "amor fati": acceptance and love of one's fate.

Jungian psychology emphasizes purposive development, a sense of personal meaning, and creative adaptation as operative factors in the psyche. It is conceived of as a process of continuous psychic integration, always pre-ceded by stages of dissociation, summed up in the alchemical maxim "solve et coagula" (dissolve and coagulate). The purpose of analysis is to help redirect psychic energy toward development with the help of *a symbolic experience of unconscious material*. Jung's major contributions were the insistence on the symbolic and creative function of unconscious material, the healing power of images, and the psyche's prospective tendency toward regression during stress and growth. But he was adamant that there was nothing to be gained, and much to be lost, in the production of regressive material *per se*. In this he was ahead of his time, addressing problems of dependency, regression, and collusion which continue to undermine the value of contemporary psychotherapy.

Jung's work opened up the traditional conceptual and interpretive field of psychoanalysis by exploring the objective field of archetypal dynamics. Issues that are being explored in the field today like "split-object" relations, borderline and pre-Oedipal dynamics, separation individuation struggles, dissociative disorders, and the early holding environment, all have their roots in the archetypal layer of the psyche. Much of what Jung spoke of as "synthetic-constructive" has begun to surface in contemporary psycho-analytic thinking.

But most importantly, Jung "depathologized" the archetypal and trans-personal layer of the psyche by verifying its function as the creative matrix for the entire personality. Repression or denial of it lead to the ills which modern society indeed suffers from: a sense of failure and depression in the face of the unavoidable suffering of life, and a consequent fascination with those who are identified with the archetypal psyche such as religious fanatics and glamorous or power-hungry personalities. Jung's contribution was to point a way toward a more creative relationship with the unconscious, and his personal devotion to this process provides a beautifully rendered illustration of what may be discovered when the psyche meets itself.

## NOTES

1  The dialogue entails loosening the boundaries between conscious and unconscious while maintaining a dynamic tension between them: the psychic energy generated from the tension can produce a symbol which goes beyond both original positions. Jung referred to this process as activation of the *transcendent function* (1916/1969). He considered it the most significant factor in deep psychological work.

2  Jung's view of healing involved stimulating the unconscious to constellate a compensatory archetype, either intrapsychically or via the transference, rather than providing a "corrective emotional experience." Healing can also occur by encountering something in the object world which embodies the particular archetypal pattern which had been unbalanced.

## REFERENCES

Freud, S. (1933). *New Introductory Lectures*. In *The Standard Edition of the Complete Psychological Works of Sigmund Freud*, 24 vols., ed. and tr. J. Strachey. London: Hogarth Press, vol. 22.

Jung, C. G. (1902/1970). "On the Psychology and Pathology of So-called Occult Phenomena." *CW* 1.

(1906/1973). *Experimental Researches*. *CW* 2.

(1912/1956). *Symbols of Transformation*. *CW* 5.

(1921/1971). *Psychological Types*. *CW* 6.

(1916/1969). *The Structure and Dynamics of the Psyche*. *CW* 8.

(1952). "Synchronicity: An Acausal Connecting Principle." In *The Structure and Dynamics of the Psyche*. *CW* 8, pp. 417–519.

(1931). "The Stages of Life." *CW* 8, pp. 387–403.

(1916). "The Transcendent Function." *CW* 8, pp. 67–91.

(1966). *The Practice of Psychotherapy*. *CW* 16.

(1946). "The Psychology of the Transference." *CW* 16, pp. 163–323.

(1956/1970). *Mysterium Coniunctionis*. *CW* 14.

Kerr, J. (1993). *A Most Dangerous Method*. New York: Alfred A. Knopf.

Khan, M. M. R. (1974). *The Privacy of the Self*. New York: International Universities Press.

Kohut, H. (1971). *The Analysis of the Self*. New York: International Universities Press.

Neumann, E. (1954). *The Origins and History of Consciousness*. Princeton: Princeton University Press.

(1955). *The Great Mother: an Analysis of the Archetype*. Princeton: Princeton University Press.

Perera, S. (1990). "Dream Design: Some Operations Underlying Clinical Dream Appreciation." In *Dreams in Analysis*. Wilmette, Ill.: Chiron Publications.

Salman, S. (1994). "Dissociation in the Magical Pre-Oedipal Field." Paper presented at the Conference on Trauma and Dissociation, Center for Depth Psychology and Jungian Studies, Katonah, N.Y.

Samuels, A., Shorter, B., and Plaut, F. (1986). *A Critical Dictionary of Jungian Analysis*. New York: Routledge & Kegan Paul.

Whitmont, E. C. (1982). *Return of the Goddess*. New York: Crossroad.

Winnicott, D. W. (1965). "True and False Self." In *The Maturational Processes and the Facilitating Environment*. New York: International Universities Press.

# 4

PAUL KUGLER

# Psychic imaging: a bridge between subject and object

> The psyche consists essentially of images.
> (Jung, 1926, CW 8, p. 325)

> A psychic entity can be a conscious content, that is it can be represented, only
> if it has the quality of an image.
> (Jung, 1926, CW 8, p. 322)

## Originary principles

Central to all the basic functions of the personality is the process of mental imaging. Without imaging, self-consciousness, speaking, writing, remembering, dreaming, art, culture – essentially what we call the human condition – would be impossible. Depth psychology developed out of the struggle to understand the process of imaging (e.g. dreams, associations, memories, and fantasies) and the role it plays in personality formation and the development of psychopathology. In attempting to account for the structuring of mental images and their effect on the personality, both Freud and Jung opted for some form of "universal." Freud posited the existence of phylogenetic "schemata," the Oedipus complex and its world of desire, whereas Jung opted for "archetypes." While both subscribe to universals, the difference between the two theories resides in the particular *originary principle* each adopted.

Where Freud initiates his theoretical perspective by postulating a world of desire (eros) prior to any kind of experience, Jung's originary principle is the world of images. Image is the world in which experience unfolds. Image constitutes experience. Image is psyche. For Jung the world of psychic reality is not a world of things. Neither is it a world of being. It is a world of image-as-such.

In this chapter, we will situate image and archetype historically, in an attempt to develop a psychological perspective on Jung's foundational concepts and greater understanding of the problem of universals in relation to psychic images. Perhaps nothing in Western thought has appeared more necessary, and yet more problematic to our understanding of mental imaging, than the need for some kind of universal. Beginning with Plato's metaphysical ideals and Aristotle's material forms, to Descartes's *cogito*, up through Kant's categories of pure reason and Jung's archetypes, a long and complicated relationship has evolved between mental images and universals. Western thought has struggled with the question of whether or not there are universal principles upon which to found our concept of human nature. Are there particularly human attributes of the mind, such as reality, truth, self, god, reason, being, or image? And, if so, where are they located? To get some perspective on these questions and how they bear on Jung's foundational concepts, we will turn to the history of imaging in Western thought.

## A brief history of image

He is a thinker; that means, he knows how to make things simpler than they are.                                                      (Nietzsche, 1887/1974, sec. 189)

The idea of image is not something static, fixed, or eternal. Image is a fluid concept that has undergone many transformations over the centuries. To capture some of the subtle shifts and mutations in the concept, we will review its evolution from the early formulations of Greek philosophy, up through Medieval onto-theology and the birth of modernity, to the current debate over the status of image in post-modernism. The background material for this impressionistic history draws primarily from three sources: Frederick Copleston's *A History of Philosophy*, *The Theory of Imagination in Classical and Medieval Thought*, by M. W. Bundy, and especially Richard Kearney's eloquent book *The Wake of the Imagination*.

The history of image in Western thought begins with Plato. In *The Republic*, Plato presents the allegory of the cave, a story that directly addresses the problem of *image and its relation to self and reality*. The allegory portrays humans as living in a cave of ignorance, prisoners trapped in a world of images. The inhabitants of the cave are only able to see the shadows cast on the wall by objects outside. Inevitably, they regard these shadows as real, and have no notions of the objects to which they actually refer. At last someone succeeds in escaping from the cave and rushes out into the light of the sun, into eternity, and for the first time sees real objects. They become aware of having been deceived by the shadows on the wall of the material world.

Briefly, Plato's theory of image and knowledge works from the assumption of an *a priori* ideal (an archetype) located in eternity. While there are many chairs in the material world, there is only one "form" or "archetype" of a chair in eternity. The reflection of a chair in a mirror is only apparent and not "real," and so too are the various particular chairs in the material world only reflections, shadows of the "ideal" in eternity.

Plato views the material temporal world we live in as a copy, a secondary reflection in the mirror of materiality. Image in turn is a copy of the material world, which is itself a copy of its ideal located in eternity. The Platonic theory of images is informed by metaphors of "painting" and "figuring," as, for example, in sculpting or creating an outer figure. Images were not conceived of as interior, but located external to the psyche.

Images, Plato suggests, are like a "drug" (a *pharmakon*) which may serve either as a remedy or a poison. The image functions as a remedy when it records human experience for posterity, preventing it from becoming lost in time. Image may also function as a poison, deceiving us into mistaking the copy for the original. Image poisons by assuming the status of an idol. For Plato, images are exterior reproductions of the material world, which is itself a replica of the eternal world. Images are copies of copies, not first principles.

Plato's student, Aristotle, developed a different theory of image and shifted the area of inquiry from the metaphysical to the psychological. Aristotle locates image within the human and the source of the image is to be found in the material world, not eternity. Images for Aristotle are mental intermediaries between sensation and reason, a bridge between the inner world of the mind and the outer world of material reality. Several of the dominant metaphors Aristotle uses to portray the imaging process are "writing," "draughtsmanship," and "drawing." Today we still use these metaphors when we speak of "drawing" a conclusion or "figuring" something out. Aristotle places primacy, however, not on image, but on sense data. Image is a reflection of sense data, not an origin.

Neither Plato nor Aristotle ever views imaging as an autonomous, originary process. For both, imagining remains largely a *reproductive* activity. Traces of Plato and Aristotle are found at the core of almost all subsequent Western theories of psychology. Either primacy is placed on sensation or primacy is placed on atemporal cognitive structures or a combination of the two as in Piaget's epigenetic model. The common thread for both Plato and Aristotle is their view of psychic images as a second-hand reflection of some more "original" source located beyond the human condition. Imaging is a process of imitation, not creation.

## The Medieval view of imaging

The reproductive view of imaging remained relatively intact throughout the neo-Platonic philosophies of Porphyry, Proclus, and Plotinus, as well as up through the onto-theology of the Middle Ages. The Medieval view of imaging synthesized Hellenic ontology and biblical theology. This onto-theological alliance only served to deepen the distrust of images. From the theological side, there was the biblical condemnation of images as a transgression of the divine order of creation, and from the philosophical side, image was approached as a secondary copy of the original truth of being. Both the Judeo-Christian and the Greek traditions viewed imagining as a reproductive activity, reflecting some more "original" source of meaning beyond the human condition: god, or the forms, whether metaphysical (Plato) or physical (Aristotle).

The Medieval understanding of imaging as represented by Augustine, Bonaventure, and Thomas Aquinas still conformed to the reproductive model of Plato and Aristotle. Throughout Medieval onto-theology, image is treated as a copy, referring to a more original reality beyond itself – to a divine ideal (god) located outside the human condition.

Richard of St. Victor, one of the more interesting writers of this period, portrays images as "borrowed clothing" or "vestments" used to clothe rational ideas. Images are viewed as psychic garments used to suit-up reason so as to make it more presentable to the general population. Especially cautious of images, Richard of St. Victor warns that if reason becomes too pleased with its "dress," then imagination may adhere to reason like a skin. Were this to happen, we may mistake the artificial apparel of images for a natural possession. We are being warned not to confuse our unique nature with our images.

In Richard of St. Victor's fantasy, notice how he fears that we may mistakenly take the image as our skin, our original nature, rather than as an artificial copy. In his fear, we already notice the emergence of a psychic ambivalence as to whether image is only artificial and reproductive, or whether it is an actual part of our genuine nature. The fear that image might be mistakenly experienced as part of our human nature, and not simply a vestment, reflects a growing uneasiness in Western thought as to the rightful place of psychic images in relation to human nature.

As the concept of image evolves in Western thought, it brings a certain instability to the intermediary position it has been forced to occupy for the past 1,000 years. The metaphysical order coming down from Plato and Aristotle has assumed certain primordial dualities: inner/outer, mind/body, reason/sensation, and spirit/matter. Image is always being located *between* these dualities. From the beginning of Greek philosophy these pairs have been laid in concrete, providing the foundation of Western metaphysics, and, unquestionably, have been assumed to support our thought structure.

As Western culture evolves out of Medieval onto-theology, on its course toward the Renaissance and the beginning of the modern world, these metaphysical structures begin to show signs of deterioration. Image, locked in between the fundamental dualities of Western metaphysics, slowly begins to undermine the foundation, endangering the very metaphysical order upon which such oppositions are built. The idea that image is simply a representation of some preexisting original, for example, reason, sensation, god, spirit, matter, form, and so on, is becoming less absolute. As we approach the Renaissance, no longer is it so certain whether the image is a garment we put on – or whether it is in fact our original skin!

## The alchemists: some marginal figures

The Medieval view of image ultimately reflects its dual onto-theological nature, conforming to the fundamentally reproductive model of both its Judeo-Christian and its Hellenic roots. Image is still treated as a re-presentation, a secondary mental image. As we move out of Medieval onto-theology, through the Scholasticism of the thirteenth and fourteenth centuries toward the dawning of Renaissance humanism, a few figures just on the margins of mainstream Western thought begin to radically revise our notion of image. Paracelsus, Ficino, and Bruno develop a new vision of imaging as a creative, transformative, and originary power located *within the human condition.* Just as Copernicus inverted our cosmology in relation to the solar system, so too did the alchemists reverse the traditional theory of knowledge and image. The biblical, Greco-Roman and Medieval systems of thought had located "reality" as a transcendental condition beyond human grasp – Plato's "sun" beyond the temporal confines of the human cave. The alchemists and other hermetic philosophers of this period began to intuit the presence of a "sun" within the human universe, an inner light capable of originary powers. Paracelsus asks: "What else is imagination, if not the inner sun?" (Kearney, 1988).

Bruno, a sixteenth-century hermetic philosopher, dramatically revised the traditional reproductive view of image by going so far as to suggest that human imaging was the source of thought itself! This was, of course, an extremely radical idea at the time. For Bruno, imaging precedes and indeed creates reason. This theoretical formulation located the creative force now properly within the human condition, not in the divine or in eternal forms. These ideas were so radical in relation to the doctrines carried over from

Scholastic and Medieval thought that they were condemned as heresy by the Church. Bruno's punishment for placing imaging at the center of creativity and the human condition was to be burnt at the stake. Several more centuries would need to pass before it would be safe to introduce into the mainstream of Western thought the idea of imaging as central to creativity and the human condition.

The alchemical writings of this period, appearing in the margins of Western thought, subtly begin a move beyond the metaphysics of transcendence, toward a psychology of human creativity. Up to this point, the act of creation had, for the most part, been attributed to an agency beyond the human. The typical Medieval portrait of Christ, for example, was not signed, thereby effacing the individuality of the painter and underscoring the primacy of divine creation. Bruno and other hermetic philosophers of the fifteenth and sixteenth centuries began to develop the heretical idea of locating the agency responsible for the act of creation within the human condition.

## The birth of modernity

The next significant shift in our attitude toward imaging came with René Descartes in the seventeenth century. He was the first modern philosopher to make a decisive break with the dominant ideas of Scholasticism (thirteenth and fourteenth centuries). The ideas developed in his text *Meditations* (1642) are basic to the modern view of the world as being divided into subjects and objects. Working from the proposition "Cogito ergo sum" – I think, therefore I am – Descartes established existence on the basis of the act of a knowing subject, not on a transcendent God, objective Matter or Eternal forms. Descartes's theory of the thinking subject signaled a major change in Western psychological understanding by locating the source of meaning, creativity, and truth *within human subjectivity*. The human mind is given priority over objective being or the divine.

The anthropocentric trend of the sixteenth and seventeenth centuries appears also in the artistic realm with the emergence of "authors" creating novels, and in painting, self-portraiture begins to thrive as an instance of the new aesthetic of subjectivity. The Cartesian theory of the *cogito* (the thinking subject), contains the beginnings of the modern philosophical project to provide an anthropological foundation for metaphysics. No longer are ideal forms (Plato), matter (Aristotle), or god (onto-theology) at the center of our metaphysics. At the center Descartes locates the human subject. Descartes had cut the mind free from its moorings in either transcendental deities, external ideals, or the material world. The human subject was now a first principle capable of *creating* a sense of meaning, certainty, existence, and truth. Although Descartes and his followers opened the way to modern humanism, he continued to subscribe to the view of imaging as a reproductive activity.

### Empiricism: toward an arbitrary fictionalism

The next significant shift in our concept of image came with the empiricism of David Hume (1711–76). Following Descartes, Hume proposed to show that human knowledge could establish its own foundation without appealing to the metaphysical realm of deities or ideals, or to the physical realm of the material world. Once reason is detached from its metaphysical scaffolding, Hume was to discover that the very foundation of positivist rationalism is reduced to an arbitrary fictionalism.

While Hume set out as a supporter of Locke's empiricist description of the mind as a blank slate, a *tabula rasa*, upon which the "faded impression of the senses" is written, he ended up with a radical fictionalism which threatened to destroy the very basis of rationalism. Kearney (1988) suggests that Hume pushed the reproductive view of image to its ultimate limits, declaring that all human knowledge was derived from the association of image-ideas and no longer needed to appeal to any metaphysical laws or transcendent entities.

The act of knowing was reduced by Hume to a series of psychological regularities which governed the associations between images: resemblance, contiguity, identity, and so on. While continuing to subscribe to the reproductive model of image as a mental copy of faded sensations, Hume maintains that this world of representations contained within the human subject, our inner art museum, is the only reality we can know. This troubling conclusion presented Hume with a dilemma: he found himself trapped within his solipsistic museum of mental images. The worlds of reason and of material reality are subjective representations, both fictions. The mental image no longer refers to some transcendent origin or truth, e.g. to an eternal ideal, god, the material world, or even the *cogito*. For Hume, the mental image is the only truth we can know and this means no truth at all, for he still subscribes to the correspondence theory of truth. If we cannot establish a correspondence between the image and a transcendent object, we cannot establish truth. We are left only with an arbitrary fictionalism which we must nevertheless hold on to as if it were real.

Hume, as with Plato earlier, now finds the human condition relating to the world through images. But the critical difference between the two is that Hume has no "transcendent" reality outside the dark cave of shadowy images. For Hume, these shadowy fictions do not refer to any transcendent forms which give them the value of truth and this seriously undermines the metaphysical scaffolding which for the past two thousand years has supported the edifice of reality. Hume's account of psychic images results in the following difficulty: If the "world" we know is a collection of fictions without any transcendent foundations, then all we can use to establish our sense of reality are subjective fictions – foundationless images. The disturbing conclusion that human understanding is dependent upon foundationless fictions led Hume to a philosophical crisis:

> If we embrace this principle [the primacy of imaging] and condemn all refined reasoning, we run into the most manifest absurdities. If we reject it in favour of these reasonings, we subvert entirely the human understanding. We have therefore, no choice but betwixt a false reason and none at all. For my part I know not what ought to be done in the present case.          (Hume, 1976)

It is in this state of unfounded subjectivism and a deep distrust of psychic images that we find Western thought at the end of the Age of Reason. And it is in this skeptical atmosphere that eighteenth-century philosophy prepares for a revolution in the theory of mental images.


## The liberation of imaging

In 1781, Kant stunned his colleagues by proclaiming the process of imaging (*Einbildungskraft*) to be the indispensable precondition of all knowledge. In the first edition of his *Critique of Pure Reason*, he demonstrated that both reason and sensation, the two primary terms in most theories of knowledge up to this point, were *produced, not reproduced, by imaging*. This radical shift was already underway with Hume and his arbitrary fictionalism, but for Hume, images were still reproductive and located within consciousness. Kant's revolution turned on two important points: first, he reconceived of the process of imaging as *productive* as well as reproductive, and secondly, he located the synthetic categories and their process of imagining *transcendent* to reason. Platonic metaphysics had located the transcendental realm in eternity, beyond reach of the human mind. Kant, struggling with the arbitrary fictionalism resulting from dispensing with all transcendent foundations, established a new ground within the human mind, but transcendent to the knowing subject. Two hundred years earlier, a similar view of images had led to Bruno being burnt at the stake. Kant's extraordinary formulation turned the entire hierarchy of traditional epistemology on its head by demonstrating that pure reason could not arrive at the objects of experience except through the finite limits established by imaging. All knowledge is subject to the finitude of human subjectivity. Simply put: *Imaging is the indispensable precondition of all knowledge.*

After Kant, psychic images could no longer be denied a central place in modern theories of knowledge, art, existence, and psychology. With this epistemological shift, mental image ceases to be viewed as a copy, or a copy of a copy, and now assumes the role of ultimate origin and creator of meaning and of our sense of existence and reality. The act of imaging creates our consciousness which then provides the illumination of our world.

The relation between reason and image has come a long way since early Greek thought. As we enter the nineteenth century a more peaceful rapport between the two begins to be established. Kant's liberation of image led in the nineteenth century to the spawning of powerful new movements in art and philosophy. In England, the new Romanticism celebrated the liberation of image from the grip of reason in the works of Blake, Shelley, Byron, Coleridge, and Keats. The celebration continued as well in France through the works of Baudelaire, Hugo, and Nerval. And in philosophy, German idealism developed in the writings of Fichte and Schelling with a focus on our newly found creative powers of imaging. Each movement reemphasized the importance of image in the human condition, but like so many new movements, the emphasis went too far. Confronted with the industrial revolution and its devastation of nature, the mechanization of society through the development of technologies, and the exploitation of the individual by unbridled capitalism, the idealistic vision of Romantic humanism gave way to a more sober, down-to-earth sense of the synthetic powers of imaging in the existential views of Kierkegaard and Nietzsche.

## Image and archetype in depth psychology

I am indeed convinced that creative imagination is the only primordial phenomenon accessible to us, the real Ground of the psyche, the only immediate reality.                    (Jung, a letter, January 1929)

As we enter the twentieth century, one hundred years after Kant, another transformation in our concept of image is about to occur. Freud had already begun to explore the recesses of the human mind through an analysis of psychic images. Dreams, fantasies, and associations were carefully examined in an attempt to understand how psychic images are involved in personality development, psychopathology, and our experience of the past, present, and future. While these were new and puzzling questions for psychiatry and depth psychology, the problem of imaging was by no means new to anyone familiar with the history of Western thought. Freud and Jung took

remarkably different attitudes toward philosophy. Where Freud intentionally avoided reading philosophical texts, Jung immersed himself in the
history of ideas. The first three hundred pages of *Psychological Types*
(1921), a book written by Jung during the period when he was formulating
his concepts of image and archetype, reads like a history of Western
thought. During this period immediately following his theoretical dispute
with Freud over the primacy of desire in psychic life, Jung began to
formulate his own vision of depth psychology. Rather than adopt Freud's
view of mental images as representatives of instincts, Jung opted, instead, to
approach imaging as a primary phenomenon, an *autonomous activity of the
psyche*, capable of both production and reproduction. Earlier, Kant had
revolutionized philosophy, counteracting Hume's arbitrary fictionalism by
establishing imaging as a ground within the human mind, but transcendent
to the knowing subject. Kant's categories (time, space, number, and so on)
provided the *a priori* structures necessary for reason itself. Jung extended
the subtle implications of Kant's *Critique of Pure Reason* to the realm of
depth psychology, positing archetypes as the *a priori* categories of the
human psyche.

> One could also describe these forms as categories analogous to the logical
> categories which are always and everywhere present as the basic postulates of
> reason. Only, in the case of our "forms," we are not dealing with categories of
> reason but categories of the imagination . . . The original structural compo-
> nents of the psyche are of no less surprising a uniformity than are those of the
> body. The archetypes are, so to speak, organs of the prerational psyche. They
> are eternally inherited forms and ideas which have no specific content. Their
> specific content only appears in the course of the individual's life, when
> personal experience is taken up in precisely these forms.
>
> (CW 11, pp. 517–518)

Kant's view of image remained within consciousness, assuming that the
shadowy forms we see in the enigmatic world before us have been created
by the synthetic categories of the knowing subject. Jung, following Freud,
expanded the notion of "the human subject" to also include unconscious
psychic processes and referred to this more inclusive conception of personality as the *psyche*. The human psyche has its own categories analogous to
the logical categories of reason. These structures have to do with particularly human activities associated with mothering, fathering, birth and
rebirth, self-representation, identity, aging, and so on. Contents of personal
experiences are archetypally structured in particularly human ways and
might be compared to the stomach in relation to food. The unconscious is
always empty, the psychic "stomach" to the food (personal experience)

passing through it. The specific content of conscious experience is "metabolized," archetypally structured, according to the categories of the human psyche which makes the experience meaningful for ourselves and others. Without these shared psychic structures, inter-subjective communication through image and word would be, at best, very limited.

## Psychic reality

Jung regarded the psyche, with its capacity to create images, as a mediating agency between the conscious world of the ego and the world of objects (both inner and outer):

> a third, mediating standpoint is needed. *Esse in intellectu* lacks tangible reality, *esse in re* lacks mind. Idea and thing come together, however, in the human psyche, which holds the balance between them. What would the idea amount to if the psyche did not provide its living value? What would the thing be worth if the psyche withheld from it the determining force of the sense-impression? What indeed is reality if it is not a reality in ourselves, an *esse in anima*? Living reality is the product neither of the actual, objective behavior of things nor of the formulated idea exclusively, but rather of the combination of both in the living psychological process, through *esse in anima*.
>
> (*CW* 6, para. 77)

Freud had defined psychic images as mental copies of instincts, while Jung formulated a radically new view of images as the very source of our sense of *psychic reality*. No longer is reality located in god, eternal ideals, or matter, for Jung now places the experience of reality within the human condition as a function of psychic imaging:

> The psyche creates reality every day. The only expression I can use for this activity is *fantasy* . . . Fantasy, therefore, seems to me the clearest expression of the specific activity of the psyche. It is, pre-eminently . . . [a] creative activity.
>
> (*CW* 6, pp. 51–52)

The inner *and* outer worlds of an individual come together in psychic images, giving the person a vital sense of a living connection to both worlds. "Fantasy it was and ever is which fashions the bridge between the irreconcilable claims of subject and object" (*CW* 6, p. 52). The experience of reality is a product of the psyche's capacity to image. It is not an external being (god, ideal forms, or matter), but, rather, the "essence" of being human. Subjectively, reality is experienced as "out there," because its originary principle is located "in the beyond," transcendent to the ego's subjectivity. With this ontological shift, mental image ceases to be viewed as a copy, or a copy of a copy, and now assumes, following Kant, the role of ultimate origin and creator of meaning and of our sense of existence and reality.

## Post-structuralism and the linguistic turn

As we approach the end of the twentieth century, the debate over the role of imaging continues to flourish, but with a new twist. In the past fifty years a revolution has occurred in philosophy with a shift in focus from the role of image to the role of language in human understanding. The new continental philosophers, especially Derrida and Foucault, have developed a radical critique of Western thought focusing on the age-old problem of establishing a ground, an originary principle, for the *act of interpretation*. Historically we have used such metaphysical universals as truth, reality, self, center, unity, origin, archetype, or even author to ground the act of interpretation. The new twist Derrida brings to this old problem revolves around making explicit the language-locked nature of all verbal acts of interpretation. Derrida has attempted to demonstrate that the very metaphysical "universals" that Western thought uses to ground the act of interpretation are not eternal structures (for example, archetypes), but rather linguistic by-products re-sulting from a representational (reproductive) theory of language. Just as the reproductive view of image requires a more primary reality to copy, so does a reproductive theory of language assume a more primary presence beyond the linguistic term. Any such "transcendental" term is a fiction, for no linguistic concept is exempt from the metaphorical status of language. No mode of discourse, not even language, can be literally literal.

This post-modern critique of Western epistemology has led to the conclu-sion that all theories of knowledge are housed in language and work through figures of speech which render them ambiguous and indeterminate. The reader of any *text* is suspended between the literal and metaphoric significances of the text's "root" metaphors, unable to choose between the term's various meanings, and thus thrown into the dizzying semantic indeterminacy of the text.

Derrida's deconstruction of the linguistic foundations of Western theories of knowledge is a logical extension of Hume's empiricist critique of imaging. Just as Hume pushed the reproductive view of image to its ultimate limits by forgoing any appeal to transcendent foundations, so does Derrida push the reproductive theory of language to its ultimate limits. Eliminating any appeal to transcendent entities (universals), Derrida focuses, instead, on linguistic metonymy (the relation between words), rather than referentiality. How words are "curated" becomes the primary point of reference, rather than the word's relation to the author (hence, "the death of the author"), or some other transcendent object of reference. Dismantling the metaphysical scaffolding of language results, for Derrida, in the same troubling dilemma Hume had encountered earlier. Once we dispense with linguistic referentiality (the implicit assumption in the "reproductive" metaphor) we find ourselves trapped in the solipsism of language – unable to transgress the text. The Derridian text no longer refers to some transcendent origin, meaning, or truth, and consequently deconstruction finds itself caught in a post-modern version of Hume's arbitrary fictionalism.

## A bridge to the sublime

If transcendent terms, such as universals, are dispensed with as mere fictions by many of the post-structural approaches, then the "reality" of elements of human nature shared inter-subjectively is called into question. Concern about the "existence" of shared human properties is an old philosophical issue, one that dominated Medieval onto-theology in the form of the debate between nominalism and realism. The nominalist argued that there is no connection between words and things (referents), while the realist treated language as signifying a reality beyond itself. This old debate, which has reemerged as a result of the post-structural critique of referentiality in language, is expressed today in the following terms: "constructionist vs. universalist" coupled with "difference vs. sameness." Advocates of deconstruction, a post-modern form of nominalism, typically appeal to the sociological, the historical, or the inter-subjective categories to demonstrate that universal attributes are constructed through language in time, rather than given as metaphysical realities. But in the process, they frequently, albeit implicitly, universalize their "root" metaphors: "the social," "the historical" or "the inter-subjective." Even if the hallmark of universalizing, *the* definite article, is removed, or singular nouns are pluralized, some degree of universalizing is still involved as the price of linguistic formulation.[1]

Jungian psychology's approach to psychic imaging provides a useful alternative to the current opposing positions of deconstruction and universalism (essentialism). By placing imaging as the mediator between subject and object, Jung opened up a new understanding of imaging and its role in creating our sense of psychic reality. His formulation of psychic image as a bridge between ideas and things comes after an extended discussion of the Medieval debate between nominalism and realism. Jung formulates his view of imaging as a mediating third position, *esse in anima*, between what today would be called deconstruction and universalism. Psychic images point beyond themselves to *both* the "historical particulars" of the world around us and the "essences" and "universals" of the mind and metaphysics.[2] Psychic images signify something that consciousness and its narcissism cannot quite grasp, the as yet unknown depths, transcendent to subjectivity. And this depth is to be found in both the world of objects and the world of ideas, history and eternity. What the image signifies cannot precisely be determined, either by appeal to a difference or universal. While the significance of the image cannot precisely be defined, it does, however, induce consciousness to think beyond itself, not by an appeal to divinities nor to history, but to a knowing that cannot be designated *a priori*. Perhaps the most important function psychic images perform is to aid the individual in transcending conscious knowledge. Psychic images provide a bridge to the sublime, pointing toward something unknown, beyond subjectivity.

## NOTES

1 A closer examination of the universalism/sameness – constructivism/difference opposition reveals that they are not as dichotomous as initially thought. While "universalism" and "sameness" are often grouped together as one pair and "constructivism" and "difference" another, upon closer analysis this *ideal* pairing fails to hold in practice. For example, any specification of a group simultaneously argues for difference from other groups and sameness within the specified group. The grouping "women" requires both *difference* from other groups (e.g. men, animals, etc.), and *sameness* within the group specified (ignoring sexual preference, race, class, and so on). Whether difference or sameness is accentuated seems to be a matter of focus: to predicate some attribute of the category "human being" necessarily foregrounds commonality, whereas to do so with "Asian-Americans" will contrast them (for the moment) both with the white American majority and with other minority groups. How we construe the *markings* of sameness or difference will vary enormously, in part according to our relation to the group being designated and also according to whether we *believe* the markings are constructed or given, i.e. universal (Fuss, 1989).

   The current critique of universals has become so excessive and politicized that many writers have lost sight of the deeper issues being debated. Today in the American academy the skeptical wing of post-modernism, particularly influenced by deconstruction, has tended to homogenize and condemn any universalist position (e.g. humanism) as implying an oppressive metaphysical homogeneity, while treating formulations of constructed heterogeneity as emancipatory. In practice, however, it is very difficult to contain these binary terms and to align them consistently with either progressive or reactionary values. Caution would be advised when employing the opposition constructionist/essentialist as a taxonomic device because it results in deceptive and oversimplified typologies.

2 While we may never be able to eliminate essentialism, it may be psychologically helpful to differentiate forms of essentialism. John Locke made the useful distinction between "real" versus "nominal" essence. The former is equated with

the irreducible and unchanging nature of a thing, while the latter signifies a linguistic convenience, a classificatory fiction used to categorize and to label. Real essences are discovered, while nominal essences are produced. If we translate this distinction into Jungian psychology, we might say that *psychic imaging produces nominal essences.*

## REFERENCES

Aristotle (1952). *Metaphysics*, tr. Richard Hope. Ann Arbor: University of Michigan Press.
Bundy, M. W. (1927). *The Theory of Imagination in Classical and Medieval Thought.* Illinois University Studies in Language and Literature, vol. XII. Urbana, Ill.
Casey, Edward (1976). *Imagining.* Bloomington: Indiana University Press.
Copleston, Frederick (1958). *A History of Philosophy*, vols. I–IV. Westminster, Md.: The Newman Press.
Derrida, J. (1974). *Of Grammatology*, tr. G. C. Spivak. Baltimore: Johns Hopkins University Press.
Descartes, R. (1955). *The Philosophical Works of Descartes*, vols. I and II. New York: Dover Publications.
Fuss, Diana (1989). *Essentially Speaking: Feminism, Nature and Difference.* New York: Routledge.
Heidegger, M. (1962). *Kant and the Problem of Metaphysics.* Bloomington: Indiana University Press.
Hume, David (1963). *Essays Moral, Political and Literary.* London: Oxford University Press.
(1976). *A Treatise of Human Understanding.* London: Oxford University Press.
Jung, C. G. (1916/1926). "Spirit and Life." CW 8, pp. 319–337.
(1921/1971). *Psychological Types.* CW 6.
(1935/1953). Psychological Commentary on "The Tibetan Book of the Dead", CW 11, pp. 509–526.
Kant, Immanuel (1953). *Critique of Pure Reason.* London: Macmillan.
Kearney, Richard (1988). *The Wake of the Imagination: Toward a Postmodern Culture.* Minneapolis: University of Minneapolis Press.
Locke, John (1975). *An Essay Concerning Human Understanding*, ed. Peter Nidditch. Oxford: Clarendon Press.
Nietzsche, F. (1974). *The Complete Works of Friedrich Nietzsche*, tr. Oscar Levy. New York: Gordon Press.
Sartre, J.-P. (1972). *The Psychology of the Imagination.* New York: Citadel Press.
Warnock, Mary (1978). *Imagination.* Berkeley: University of California Press.
Watkins, Mary (1976). *Waking Dreams.* New York: Harper and Row.

# II
# ANALYTICAL PSYCHOLOGY IN PRACTICE

# 5

DAVID L. HART

# The classical Jungian school

## Why classical?

My training at the C. G. Jung Institute in Zurich began in 1948, in the
second semester of its existence. Virtually all of the teachers and analysts
were, or had been, in analysis with Jung himself, so his discoveries and
reflections were coming to us with convincing authority. And beyond this,
Jung's method, such as the attitude of respect, found a deep assent in my
soul. I can label as "classical" a form of Jungian psychoanalysis which sees
the analytic work as one of ongoing mutual discovery, making conscious
the unconscious life and progressively releasing a person from meaninglessness and compulsion. The "classical" approach relies on a spirit of dialogue
between conscious and unconscious, as well as between the two analytic
partners. It therefore also regards the conscious ego as uniquely indispensable to the whole process, in contrast to the "archetypal" school, for which
the ego is one of many autonomous archetypal entities. And in contrast to
the "developmental" school, the "classical" school defines development not
so much by years of age or even by psychological stages, as by an
individual's attainment of that conscious Self which is hers or his alone to
realize. This position will, I hope, become clearer in the course of this
chapter, as will one or two of my own reservations concerning that classical
theory and practice which I encountered, so to speak, in their pristine form.

## The inner world

To be a "classical" Jungian analyst means, not so much to follow and
repeat the terminology of Jung, as to embrace the general method of analysis
which Jung introduced. This involves, above all, respect for what is
encountered; respect for what is unknown, for what is unexpected, for what
is unheard of. When Jung reminded himself, before he began to consider a
patient's dream, "I have no idea what this dream is all about," he was

89

clearing his mind of presuppositions and assumptions which might undermine this essential respect. While I was a student in Zurich, during one of the periodic meetings which were held between Jung and the diploma candidates, I once had the chance to question him about this procedure of his. I asked him, "Professor Jung, when you say you have no idea what a dream is all about – is that apotropaic?" He nodded and said, "Oh, yes." That is, his profession of ignorance was designed to ward off the demons of arrogance and superior knowledge.

The attitude of respect implies that the unconscious, out of which dreams arise, is to be taken seriously, and allowed to emerge just as it is. Thus the dream is not, as Freud maintained, a cover for a repressed wish, disguised so as to find its way into expression; it is a statement of fact, of the way things are in the psychic household. Its tendency is to furnish to consciousness a picture of the psychological state that has been overlooked or disregarded. Hence it is an invaluable tool for understanding and diagnosis.

Jung's view of religion, and of the religious attitude, shows a similar position of respect. Religion is seen as a careful consideration of superior powers and, thus, as a recognition of and respect for what is spiritually and psychologically dominant within individual consciousness. This means, above all, the powers within the unconscious, as revealed and sensed through dreams, imagination, feelings, or intuition. It is this world *within* that needs to be heeded and respected, if the individual is to find a sound and healthy psychological development.

The reason for this emphasis on the inner world is that it is the way to claim or reclaim our true nature. Although we seem to be governed by external powers – beginning with our parents, whose domination of our development is of course enormous – the *true* "dominants" of psychological and spiritual life are centers of energy and imagery working on us from within, and projected onto the world around us. Thus, for instance, the mother acquires her peculiar force and influence on one's life not primarily from a particular woman but from the vast storehouse of inherited human experience of "mother" – that is, from what Jung calls the mother archetype. The archetype, then, is a potential of psychic energy inherent in all the typically human life experiences, and activated in unique focus in each individual life. These forces will be modified according to the infinite varieties of experience – appearing in what Jung calls complexes – but their energy and power derive from the archetype itself.

What is actually going on within the psyche is first met in projected form, as if it were all actually "out there." Projection pulls us into the world, so convincingly that it is easy to think that we are totally shaped by that world. Jung insists, however, that we do not begin life as a *tabula rasa*, a clean slate to be written on by what is outside us. Rather the newborn child emerges from the beginning as a distinct and unique personality with her or his own definite ways of meeting and responding to experience. This view is borne out in Jung's theory of psychological types. The introvert and the extravert are two radically different ways of meeting and judging experience – the one with primary reference to internal reactions and values, the other to those of the external world – yet they are conceived to be directions innate in each individual. So are the so-called functions of consciousness: thinking as against feeling (functions of judgment); and sensation as against intuition (functions of perception). These inherent attitudes and functions can be suppressed and distorted in response to cultural or environmental pressures, but the result then is a less than satisfactory development and flowering of the individual's true nature. The true nature is a given, a definite potential from birth.

## The process of individuation

It follows from this understanding of the personality that the attitude of respect for what appears, as we spoke of it above, must apply to our work as analysts with persons in analysis. We view what emerges in the client – whether in dreams, behavior, or even symptoms – as efforts of this unique personality to come into realization. As the basis and underpinning of this process, Jung assumes the existence of a "Self," that is, of a unified whole of which the conscious ego is only one essential part. The rest is comprised of an unconscious, limitless and unknowable by definition, which makes itself "known" in all kinds of ways – by dreams, hunches, behavior, even accidents and synchronistic events. Since the total personality is seeking to come to realization and consciousness, it may be assumed – and is often borne out by experience – that the Self is the great regulator and promoter of psychological wholeness. For instance, it is clear when one works with dreams that they regularly find a way to provide balance, support, and correction to the particular conscious attitude of the dreamer. This undeniable "compensatory" function provided by the Self proves its role as the central guiding force in an ongoing urge to realize the individual's potential.

What, then, is this wholeness that is the aim of psychological work? It is the fullest possible consciousness of all that comprises one's own personality, and it is approached in the steady, honest, and demanding self-discipline that Jung calls the process of individuation. Since, as we have implied, whatever is unconscious within us is first encountered in projection, the process involves the withdrawal of projection and the assimilation of its content into that conscious being where it belongs – our own. It involves the ever-growing admission of who we really are.

"Admission" is an apt word, for what is involved are its two meanings: both "confessing" and "letting in." What we acknowledge in the course of individuation is first and foremost that unwelcome side of our nature that Jung calls the shadow. This is made up of all of the personal tendencies, motives, and characteristics that we have barred from consciousness, whether deliberately or not. It is, of course, typically projected onto other people; but if we look and listen honestly, we will also learn about it, and thus about ourselves, from our dreams, from self-reflection, and (last but not least) from the responses of others. The admission of the shadow is the *sine qua non* of individuation. It forms the only secure base from which analytical work can proceed, for the shadow is the ground of reality and the counter-balance to illusion and inflation. This is especially so in a Jungian analysis, because of the powerful and compelling nature of the imagery that it requires a patient to confront. Indeed, Jung regards inflation – i.e. unconscious "identification" with an image encountered in one's dreams or other unconscious products – as an inevitable consequence of the conscious ego's initial apprehension of the reality of the Self. Alternately, the opposite may occur. Unless the ego is strong enough to retain its own identity in the face of an experience of the Self, it may not only be "taken over" *by* the Self, but held by it for good. Jung referred to this phenomenon as "possession," i.e. when the ego is, so to speak, invaded by an archetypal figure such as the Self.

For this reason, although in his account of the individuation process Jung makes the shadow the first step of the work, it is clear to me that the acknowledgment of the shadow must be a continuous process throughout one's life. Not only does this help to guarantee stability and even sanity, but, as the work proceeds, repressed or denied shadow elements tend to emerge more and more into the light of day – as if encouraged by the growing conscious attitude of acceptance and honesty. And besides this is the fundamental fact that the psyche *seeks* wholeness: that the unconscious is working constantly to find admission and assimilation into conscious life. The axiom "Truth will out" applies nowhere more vividly than to the life of the psyche.

It is on the basis of a healthy relationship between ego and shadow that the greater "depths" of the psyche can be safely explored. Whereas in typical experience the shadow will be encountered as bearing the same sex as the conscious personality, there exists at another psychic level a contra-sexual archetype, designated by Jung as the anima (in the man) or the animus (in the woman). These "inner" figures are conceived as having a life and distinct personality of their own, derived in part from the archetype of the feminine or the masculine, and in part from the individual's own life experience of woman or man respectively, beginning with mother or father. They inhabit the unconscious depths as a compensation for the attitude of consciousness and a way of rounding out its one-sided experience, whether this be of a man or of a woman.

Naturally, anima and animus are first met in projected form. Their archetypal nature gives them the numinous and fateful quality that accounts for the overwhelming and compelling force that accompanies falling in love. For example, a man who falls in love at first sight might experience a real woman as some kind of goddess and invest her with inhuman power, either positive or negative. A conscious awareness of this inner force can often occur at the same time as the discovery one's own contrasexual image. Jung describes the case of a man, in emotional conflict with his wife, who suddenly turns inward and asks "himself," "Why are you interfering with my relationships?" To his surprise, he gets an answer. A female voice within him begins to tell him about himself and about *her* need to be related to.

This can very often occur during "active imagination," the name Jung gave to a method of experiencing one's own unconscious while awake. The individual deliberately lowers his or her threshold of consciousness, often by concentrating on a scene from a recent dream, until the unconscious spontaneously produces a fantasy (which might or might not be related to the dream in question). In contrast to a day-dream, which is often dictated by conscious wish-fulfillment, active imagination is characterized by its entirely autonomous nature. The contact, in active imagination, with the anima – or, in the case of a woman, with the animus – is a hallmark of Jungian therapy, with its emphasis on withdrawing projections and taking responsibility for one's own psychic life as fully as possible.

Not only are these inner personalities often projected onto others (whether real or imaginary "others"), but they can also "take over" the conscious individual, particularly in moments of stress. A man "possessed" by his anima can become, so to speak, an "inferior woman," that is, moody, sulky, and irrational. In similar fashion, a woman suffering from animus possession can react and behave like an "inferior man," i.e. she can become hard-driving, insistent, and super-logical. It seems to be Jung's typical view that, in a relationship, the man's negative anima is brought into action by the prior eruption of the woman's negative animus – as though in general the conflict of the two were caused by the latter. In my view, this is a serious misreading of the problem, in spite of Jung's pioneering elucidation of it. The anima of the man in this form – passive, sulking, withdrawn, etc. – is just as effective and primary a cause of the conflict as is the animus of the woman, as we know from studies of passive-aggressiveness with all its subtleties and disguises. To claim that the man is the "victim" of the woman's animus is itself a passively aggressive attack. It is felt as such by the woman, and thus serves to fuel the conflict between them. In such cases, the procedure mentioned above, in which a man turns to his *authentic* anima (just as a woman can turn to her *authentic* animus), seems to offer a constructive way out.

Jung regards these vital figures, animus and anima, as mediators to the unconscious world. It is therefore crucial to come to terms with them. For although the anima can be bewitching, deceptive, and frustrating, she leads a man into life in the truest sense – into his emotional and passionate life, into genuine self-discovery, and ultimately into experience of the Self, which is the "sense" beyond all the apparent "nonsense" of her often capricious-appearing influence. But here, as in all the work of individuation, the key is to effect a conscious *relationship* with this life within the psyche – not to be simply at its mercy but to see and acknowledge it for what it is, and to give it its due. Again we have the requirement of respect for the forces that work within us. Jung was fond of saying that we are "not master within our own house": one's conscious ego is not in charge of one's life. Insofar as it believes that it is, it will, in fact, be at the mercy of that unadmitted unconscious with all its archetypal power.

Reinforcing a purely external image of oneself is the "mask" known as the persona – the personality which, wittingly or unwittingly, one presents to the world. This external picture can be, and often is, vastly different from the inner reality of the person, with his or her hidden emotions, attitudes, and conflicts. The persona is an essential and unavoidable means of adapting to and living in the human world; but if the image it presents is too far removed from the person within, there will be a fundamental instability – manifested, for instance, in a man who plays a controlling "masculine" role in his job but gives way to the anima's possession in his intimate relationships. Jung notes, in fact, that persona and anima often stand in a compensatory relation to each other, as if striking a psychological balance of opposites – and bearing out the principle that the psyche finds "wholeness" at any cost. It is important to add, however, that true wholeness is achieved not by any psychic structure which occurs unconsciously, but rather (as we have shown) only in the context of *becoming conscious* of those conflicting elements which make up the psyche.

## The conflict of opposites

For Jung, conflict is not only inherent in the human psychological make-up, but essential to psychological growth. Given the opposing tendencies and directions we have already considered, it is obvious that the work of becoming conscious will mean standing conflict. A simple but major example would be the often experienced conflict between "head" and "heart," or thinking and feeling. Each of these opposite poles may have validity, and the conflict can appear insoluble. In such a situation, the truly life-enhancing way is to endure, as consciously as possible, the tension of these opposites – suppressing neither the one nor the other but holding them unresolved. Out of this painful but honest work, energy will finally recede from the conflict itself and sink into the unconscious and out of that source will emerge a totally unexpected solution, what Jung called a "symbol," which will contribute a new unified direction doing justice to both sides of the original conflict.

The symbol, therefore, is not the product of rational thought, nor can it ever be fully explained. It has the quality of conscious and unconscious worlds together and is a moving force in psychological and spiritual development. Any image or idea can function as a symbol in individual or collective life, as it can also lose its symbolic force and become a mere "sign," standing for something that is fully known. For instance, the Christian Cross is traditionally a genuine symbol, whereas a cross posted at an intersection in the road is simply a sign. The one depicts a reality that cannot be fully explained; the other is immediately understood.

The human psyche not only spontaneously produces images which depict these inherent opposites within (the cross being one of them), but also discovers ways in which apparently conflicting symbolic content can be contained in a single structure. From the East Jung borrowed the term *mandala* to designate such an image, a circle that could contain all sides of psychic life in a *complexio oppositorum*. The reconciliation of opposites was a major concern of Jung's and a frequent theme of his work, since, as we have seen, the primary human tendency is to identify with one psychic quality and project its opposite onto other people – the source of much of the enmity that has always plagued communities and nations. Very few individuals, in Jung's view, take responsibility for their shadow sides or have any real idea of the tragedy and loss that can result from the shadow's projection. And for Jung it is only in the individual that the growth of consciousness can occur, and thus only there that a promise exists of improving the lot of mankind.

The reconciliation of opposites and the transformative power of the symbol find their analogue in another field which deeply occupied Jung: the study of Medieval alchemy. Since the essence of the work of alchemy was the transformation of substances within a hermetic, or closed, vessel, it is easy to see how Jung perceived in the work the very picture of bringing into consciousness the disparate elements of the psyche, holding these within a psychic container and letting the "heat" of this union give rise to a symbolic transformation. Jung actually regarded the work of the alchemists as essentially a depiction of psychic processes, which they understood to be material – that is, as a projection of these inner processes onto matter. The alchemical vessel thus becomes in reality the inner psychic structure enduring the tension of opposites and experiencing the emergence of a wholly new, that is symbolic, resolution, expressed in the imagery of finer, more precious substance distilled from the gross and chaotic material that begins the work.

That the work of wholeness is involved in alchemical symbolism is shown by the constant conjunction of opposites in its imagery: the marriage of sun and moon, of fire and water, of king and queen. This last conjunction forms the basis of Jung's study of the inner processes of the transference, that mysterious and unique relationship that undergirds the work of individuation as it proceeds in analysis. The transference, for Jung, is not a one-sided affair, nor is it merely the projection of parental images from the client onto the analyst. It is not even all that combined with the analyst's projections onto the client. It is, rather, a truly symbolic event in which both persons are changed, an inner "marriage" leading, as one would expect, to a new, third being, comprising both individuals and yet transcending them.

Perhaps it was the very depth and mystery of the transference that led most of us in the early days of Jungian work to ignore it – that is, simply to assume its power and efficacy because we knew that a transformative process was in the works. In any case, in my own training in Zurich, transference was never discussed in any practical or clinical terms; the analytic relationship was assumed to be the very ground from which consciousness, and therefore an emerging transformation into wholeness, could take place. But just so too was the psyche of the individual: at all times, whether in analysis or out of it, through introspection and self-awareness the process of individuation went forward. And any event – "inner" or "outer" – was seen as "grist for the mill" of this process. As if to remind me that all of life was the psychological training ground, my training analyst once said to me as we contemplated a break in our sessions: "The most important things happen on vacation."

## The practical significance of the unexpected

There is a principle here to which I have always adhered, and which could be described as respect for the significance of the unexpected. The principle assumes that life itself has a meaning which needs to be contemplated, and that the rational mind may easily attempt to control and dictate meaning and thereby lose it. Jung was expressing this principle at one of our students' meetings at his home when a student spoke of a certain psychological state and then asked him: "Professor Jung, what is the statistical probability of this state occurring?" Jung's reply was, "Well, you know, as soon as you start talking about statistics, psychology goes out the window."

The unexpected is what gets a chance to emerge in analytic work when a client comes into the session with no "agenda" and announces, "I just have absolutely nothing to talk about today." At this point in my career, I am able to rejoice inwardly at this statement; at one time it would have made me very anxious. I rejoice because I am certain that something unexpectedly meaningful has at least an opportunity to surface. And that, one way or another, is what generally happens.

So the process of individuation could be defined as life lived consciously – not as simple a matter as it sounds. Not only our rational minds, but habits of thought and action contribute to the general unconsciousness in which life can be lived. For Jung, to be unconscious was perhaps the greatest evil, and he meant "unconscious" in a specific sense: unconscious *of our own unconscious*. There is where consciousness needed to focus; otherwise life was lived irresponsibly and even meaninglessly, and Jung felt that a life without meaning was the most unbearable of all.

To illustrate how individuation can proceed in a very individual way and by way of paying heed to the unexpected, I should like to cite a case that I worked with for some years. This was a man of middle age, a writer who had recently, in the course of our work, become aware that he had a serious problem of passive-aggressive behavior. This actually went back to his infancy (as is usually the case), to a combination of abuse and neglect which had left him abnormally compliant while consumed with silent rage. He felt himself to be pretty much the victim of others and took secret revenge, often quite unconsciously.

This man was on vacation far away from home and from analysis, in fact on a trek in the mountains of Nepal, when a decisive event occurred. He was resting on a mountain pass over an abyss when there walked by him a Sherpa carrying an immense load of baggage. My client had a sudden, almost overpowering urge to push this little man off the pass and into the abyss. He struggled with the temptation and the moment passed: the Sherpa went by. But he was left with a shattering realization of what he could actually do to another person, not merely, as before, of what others were always doing to him. That is, in the first place his shadow became a reality to him in a way that he had never experienced before. And in the second place, he had a new and vivid sense of himself as the agent of his life and not merely as a reactive victim. After all, the Sherpa had done nothing to him whatsoever.

His unexpected education did not stop there. A few nights later, while still on the trek, he had a dream. He found himself approaching a square, fenced-in enclosure, perhaps twenty feet on each side, in the center of which was coiled a huge, erect cobra, weaving ominously from side to side. He then discovered, outside the enclosure, a large hunk of raw red meat, such as is fed to the tigers in a zoo. He took a large piece of the meat and threw it in over the cobra's head, so that it had to turn away from him to go after it.

It was only then that the dreamer noticed that within the enclosure, in the rear right corner and hidden from the cobra by a white wooden shield, crouched a man who was closely monitoring the cobra and carefully regulating its feeding. The dreamer knew then that he ought not to have thrown in the meat – that all was being correctly done by this person in charge and that he had interfered too impulsively, thereby upsetting the balance.

For him, the cobra had to do with the unpredictable danger that people often feel within themselves insofar as they have not made peace with their aggressive feelings. The dreamer's first impulse was to avert the danger to himself (by throwing the meat over the cobra's head), that is, to try to pacify his feared aggression while also diverting it somewhere else. This reflected what he would often do in actual life: be as conciliatory as possible while making any aggressive impulse appear to be far removed from himself.

All this, however, was now shown to be unnecessary, for, as the dream revealed, there was actually a superior power in charge of the dangerous cobra. A man was crouched concealed from it but in a state of constant awareness, regulating its feeding and in no way subject to the impulses of the dreamer's frightened and reactive ego. This new figure the dreamer understood to represent the Self, which Jung defines as the center and source of psychic wholeness and regulator of psychic balance. Controlled by the Self, this terrifying creature stayed in its place – not through force, but through careful watching and attention. In fact the role of the hidden man was a true paradigm for the conscious care which is always needed in the work of individuation: not reactive but steadily and persistently active in its attention to whatever goes on in the unconscious life. That kind of regular attention can turn apparent inner chaos into a sense of order and inner relatedness.

The understanding that this man now had, of a superior and reliable power within, gradually relieved him of much of the false burden of responsibility that typically accompanies a severely intimidated ego. For although he had always blamed others' aggression for his problems, he had secretly been terrified of his own and therefore most intent on denying it. Now, having seen it face to face – first in his impulse on the mountainside and then in his dream – he had also been privileged to learn a truly revolutionary fact: there is a power beyond any conscious devising which functions to contain and control psychic life. And this power needs to be known and acknowledged – the ego needs to bow to the Self – as our dreamer was able to do by way of this healing dream.

## The ultimate goal

In a general way the whole development of an individual's life is seen by Jung as a gradual emergence out of the ego's control and into the realm of the Self – out of merely personal values and into those of more impersonal and collective meaning. The first half of life is normally devoted to establishing a secure base in the world: education, profession, family, a personal identity. But at mid-life that crisis threatens whose ubiquity and importance Jung helped to clarify in the public mind. It is at bottom a spiritual crisis, the challenge to seek and to discover the meaning of life. To meet this challenge, none of the tools of the first half of life are adequate. It is not a question of further conquests or acquisitions; it is more a question of exploration of the soul, for its own sake, letting go of the familiar demands of the ego to be fed and gratified. Therefore it is often felt as a loss, and is often powerfully resisted; and yet the psyche, with its own powerful demand to be realized, will persist in confronting consciousness with new and unheard-of views of life's meaning and possibilities. It is here that Jung sees the real work of individuation beginning, for from this point on, everything depends on the broadening of consciousness. Without a real sense that this change carries the true meaning of one's life, and a willingness to take on the inner voyage of discovery, one can fall into despair and a repetitive existence, which in effect only marks time until the end. The challenge of the second half of life is to prepare for death in a questioning, seeking, and *conscious* way, accepting both the pain of disillusionment and the wonder of growth into ever new views of spiritual and psychological reality.

This does not by any means suggest that Jungian analysis or the work of individuation is reserved solely for the second half of life. Many younger people, myself included, have found new meaning and purpose in life through the direct inspiration and guidance of Jung. What it does emphasize is that individuation is a spiritual undertaking. It is the conscious response to an instinct not recognized in biological thought, an innate and powerful drive toward spiritual realization and ultimate meaning. As such, it involves the whole person, who, in the process of emerging into wholeness, is progressively transformed – not into something different, but into the true Self: out of its potential and into its reality. Whoever, in any age or condition, is prepared to heed and respond to this spiritual and fundamentally human drive, is prepared for the process of individuation.

## REFERENCES

Jung, C. G. (1966). *Two Essays on Analytical Psychology. CW* 7 (2nd ed.).
   (1966). "The Psychology of the Transference." In *The Practice of Psychotherapy, CW* 16 (2nd ed.).
   (1967). *Symbols of Transformation. CW* 5 (2nd ed.).
   (1971). *Psychological Types. CW* 6.
Parsons, R. and Wicks, F. (1983). *Passive-Aggressiveness: Theory and Practice.* New York: Brunner/Mazel.

# 6

MICHAEL VANNOY ADAMS

# The archetypal school

## Jung on archetypes and archetypal images

Although Jung named his school of thought "analytical psychology," he might with equal justification have called it "archetypal psychology." For no other term is more basic to Jungian analysis than "archetype"; and yet no other term has been the source of so much definitional confusion. Part of the reason is that Jung defined "archetype" in different ways at different times. Sometimes, he spoke of archetypes as if they were images. Sometimes, he distinguished more precisely between *archetypes* as unconscious forms devoid of any specific content and *archetypal images* as the conscious contents of those forms.

Both Freud and Jung acknowledged the existence of archetypes, which Freud called phylogenetic "schemata" (1918/1955), or phylogenetic "proto-types" (1927/1961). Philosophically, Freud and Jung were neo-Kantian structuralists who believed that hereditary categories of the psyche imaginatively inform the individual human experience of external reality in typical or schematic ways. Freud (1918/1955) alludes to Kant when he says that the phylogenetic schemata are comparable to "the categories of philosophy" because they "are concerned with the business of 'placing' the impressions derived from actual experience." He states that the Oedipus complex is "one of them" – evidently one among many – "the best known" of the schemata. He describes the circumstances under which a schema may exert a dominant influence over external reality:

> Wherever experiences fail to fit in with the hereditary schema, they become remodelled in the imagination – a process which might very profitably be followed out in detail. It is precisely such cases that are calculated to convince us of the independent existence of the schema. We are often able to see the schema triumphing over the experience of the individual. (p. 119)

Jung (CW 10) explicitly says that archetypes are "similar to the Kantian categories" (p. 10). According to him (1976/1977), the Oedipus complex "was the first archetype Freud discovered, the first and only one." He asserts that Freud believed that the Oedipus complex *"was* the archetype," when, in fact, "there are many such archetypes" (pp. 288–289). Jung (*CW* 11) contends that archetypes are *"categories* analogous to the logical categories which are always and everywhere present as the basic postulates of reason," except that they are "categories of the *imagination"* (pp. 517–518).

Many non-Jungians erroneously believe that what Jung means by archetypes are innate ideas. Jung expressly repudiates any such notion. Archetypes are purely formal, categorical, ideational potentialities that must be actualized experientially. According to Jung (*CW* 15), they are only "innate possibilities of ideas." These inherited possibilities "give definite form to contents that have already been acquired" through individual experience. They do not determine the content of experience but constrain the form of it, "within certain categories" (p. 81). Archetypes are a collective inheritance of general, abstract forms that structure the personal acquisition of particular, concrete contents. "It is necessary to point out once more," Jung says (*CW* 9.i), "that archetypes are not determined as regards their content, but only as regards their form and then only to a very limited degree." An archetype "is determined as to its content only when it has become conscious and is therefore filled out with the material of conscious experience" (p. 79). By contents, Jung means images. Archetypes, as forms, are merely possibilities of images. What is consciously experienced – and then imaged – is unconsciously informed by archetypes. A content, or image, has an archetypal, or typical, form. Jung (*CW* 18) says that archetypes appear as both "images and at the same time emotions." It is this emotionality of archetypal images that endows them with dynamic effect. Thus it is an error to regard an archetype "as if it were a mere name, word, or concept," for when it appears as an archetypal image it has not only a formal but also an emotional aspect (p. 257).

A specific example may clarify the distinction between archetypes and archetypal images. If Herman Melville had never been in a position to acquire any direct or indirect experience of a whale, he could never have written *Moby-Dick.* Melville could not have inherited that specific image. He might, however, have written a great American novel about the archetypal, or typical, experience of being (or feeling) psychically engulfed ("swallowed" or "devoured") and then imaged that same form through another, very different content. Jung (*CW* 5) says that the "Jonah-and-the-Whale" complex has "any number of variants, for instance the witch who eats children, the wolf, the ogre, the dragon, and so on" (p. 419). The archetype is an abstract theme (engulfment), and the archetypal images (whale, witch, wolf, ogre, dragon, etc.) are concrete variations on that theme.

## James Hillman and archetypal psychology

What is now known as the school of "archetypal psychology" was founded by James Hillman with a number of other Jungians in Zurich in the late 1960s and early 1970s. The school arose in reaction against what they regarded as unnecessarily metaphysical assumptions in Jung and the complacent, rote application of Jungian tenets. Hillman prefers to regard archetypal psychology not as a "school" but as a "direction" or an "approach" (personal communication, 9 September 1994). Archetypal psychology is a post-Jungian psychology (Samuels, 1985), a critical elaboration of Jungian theory and practice after Jung. Although there are now many archetypal psychologists, Hillman remains the most prominent among them.

The archetypal school rejects the noun "archetype," even as it retains the adjective "archetypal." For Hillman (1983), the distinction between archetypes and archetypal images, which Jung regards as comparable, respectively, to Kantian noumena and phenomena, is untenable. According to him, all that individuals ever encounter psychically are images – that is, phenomena. Hillman is a phenomenologist or an imagist: "I'm simply following the imagistic, the phenomenological way: take a thing for what it is and let it talk" (p. 14). For the archetypal school, there are no *archetypes* as such – no neo-Kantian categories, or noumena. There are only phenomena, or images, that may be *archetypal*.

For Hillman, the archetypal is not a category but simply a consideration – a perspectival operation that an individual may perform on any image. Thus Hillman (1977) says that "any image may be considered archetypal." The archetypal is "a move one makes rather than a thing that is." To *consider* an image archetypal is to regard it as such, from a certain perspective, to endow it operationally with typicality – or, as Hillman prefers to say, with "*value*" (pp. 82–83). Thus, perspectivally, an individual may "archetypalize" any image. Merely considering it so makes it so – or, as Hillman (1975/1979) says, merely *capitalizing* it makes it so – as in the "Sunburnt Girl" (p. 63). In effect, the archetypal school embraces what Jung tries (never, he admits, entirely with success) to avoid – that is, what he (CW 9.i) calls "metaphysical concretism." Jung says that "any attempt at graphic description" of an archetype inevitably succumbs to metaphysical concretism "up to a point," because the qualitative aspect "in which it appears necessarily clings to it, so that it cannot be described at all except in terms of its specific phenomenology" (p. 59). Concrete descriptive qualities cling quite obviously to an archetype like the Great Mother (less evidently to an archetype like the Anima, which is more abstract) – as they also do to the Sunburnt Girl. Most Jungians would be reluctant to dignify the Sunburnt Girl as equal in status to the Great Mother – or even to regard the image as "archetypal" at all. When Hillman capitalizes the Sunburnt Girl, he considers the image archetypal, typical, or valuable. He does not posit or infer the metaphysical existence of archetypes prior to the images. For archetypal psychologists, any and every image, even the most apparently banal, can be considered archetypal.

This post-Jungian, post-structuralist usage of the term "archetypal" is controversial. Most Jungians retain the term "archetype" and continue to define it as Jung did. One Jungian analyst, V. Walter Odajnyk (1984), criticizes Hillman for adopting the name "archetypal psychology." According to Odajnyk, he should simply have called the school "imaginal psychology" or "phenomenal psychology" to avoid unnecessary terminological ambiguity. "Archetypal psychology," Odajnyk says, "sounds as though it were based on the Jungian archetypes, when in fact it isn't" (p. 43). This criticism is cogent to Jungians who remain strict structuralists. It is unpersuasive to archetypal psychologists, for they believe that the archetypal, or the typical, is in the eye of the imaginer – or in the imagination's eye. In a sense, the archetypal is in the eye of the beholder – the subject who beholds an image – but it is also, in another sense, in the eye of the *imagination*, a transcendent dimension that archetypal psychologists regard as ultimately irreducible to any faculty immanent in the subject.

### Re-visioning psychology and sticking to the image

The imagination's eye is a decisive image for Hillman, who would revise – or, as he says, "re-vision" – Jungian analysis: Hillman's Terry Lectures at Yale University in 1972 were published under the title *Re-Visioning Psychology*. For archetypal psychologists, analysis is not only a "talking cure" but also a "seeing cure," which values the visual at least as much as the verbal. Insight has been a dominant image in analysis since Freud (or since the blindness of Oedipus), but Hillman (1975) has emphasized not "seeing in" but "seeing through" (p. 136), by which he means the ability of the imagination's eye to see through the literal to the metaphorical. Re-visioning is deliteralizing (or metaphorizing) reality. According to Hillman, the purpose of analysis is not to make the unconscious conscious, the id ego, or the ego self but to make the literal metaphorical, the real "imaginal." The objective is not to induce individuals to be more realistic (as in the Freudian "reality principle") but to enable them to appreciate that "imagination is reality" (Avens, 1980) and that reality is imagination: that what seems most literally "real" is, in fact, an image with potentially profound metaphorical implications.

Hillman employs "imaginal psychology" as a synonym for "archetypal psychology." Since for Hillman imagination *is* reality, he prefers "imaginal" to "imaginary," which pejoratively connotes "unreal." He adopts the term "imaginal" from Henry Corbin (1972), an eminent scholar of Islam. According to Hillman, the imaginal is just as real as (or even more immediately real than) any external reality. This position is identical to the attitude that Jung stipulated for the practice of "active imagination," the deliberate induction of imaginative activity in the unconscious. To activate the imagination, to imagine actively, requires the individual to regard the images that emerge as if they were autonomous and equal in ontological status to external reality. Hillman applies this method to all images, not only those that arise in active imagination.

The motto of imaginal psychology is "stick to the image," an injunction that Hillman (1975/1979) attributes to Raphael Lopez-Pedraza (p. 194). Evidently, this dictum derives inspiration from Jung (CW 16), who says, "To understand the dream's meaning I must stick as close as possible to the dream images" (p. 149). Sticking to the image is adhering to the phenomenon (rather than, say, freely associating to it, as Freud suggests). For Freud, the image is not what it manifestly appears to be. It is latently something else. For Jung and for Hillman, the image is precisely what it appears to be – and nothing else. To express what it intends, the psyche selects an especially apt image from all of the images available in the experience of the individual in order to serve a quite specific metaphorical purpose. In imaginal psychology, the technique of analysis entails the proliferation of images, strict adherence to these phenomena, and the specification of descriptive qualities and implicit metaphors. The method evokes more and more images and encourages the individual to stick attentively to these phenomena as they emerge, in order to provide qualitative descriptions of them and then elaborate the metaphorical implications in them. As an analyst, an imaginal psychologist must be an imagist, a phenomenologist, and a metaphorician.

## Image, object, subject

Imaginal psychology is not an "object relations" psychology. For Hillman, images are not reducible in any sense to objects in external reality. The imagination is not secondary and derivative but primary and constitutive.

An image does not necessarily derive from, refer to, or correspond accurately or exhaustively with an object in external reality. There may, in fact, be no object at all. As the imaginal psychologist Patricia Berry (1982) says: "With imagination any question of objective referent is irrelevant. The imaginal is quite real in its own way, but never *because* it corresponds to something outer" (p. 57). For imaginal psychologists, the discrepancy between image and object is simply an ineliminable fact of human existence.

Jung (CW 6) advocates a similar position when he discusses psychic images, or "imagos," and what he calls interpretation on the subjective level. Ontologically, he asserts that "the psychic image of an object is never exactly like the object." Epistemologically, he contends that subjective factors condition the image and "render a correct knowledge of the object extraordinarily difficult." As a consequence, he says, "it is essential that the *imago* should not be assumed to be identical with the object." Instead, it is always advisable "to regard it as an image of the subjective relation to the object." The object merely serves as a convenient "vehicle" to convey subjective factors (pp. 472–473). For example, when Jung interprets a dream, he tends to regard the images in the dream not so much as references to objects in external reality but as reflections of aspects of the personality of the subject, the dreamer. According to him, the dream is more reflexive than referential. Hillman differs from Jung in that he grants more autonomy to the imagination. The capacity that Melanie Klein (Isaacs, 1952) attributes to instincts (or drives) in the expression of fantasies independent of objects in external reality, Hillman ascribes to the imagination.

Hillman (1975/1979) also protests against what he considers an inordinate emphasis on subjectivity. He does not believe that the incongruity between image and object is merely a function of subjective factors. Just as imaginal psychologists do not reduce images to objects in external reality, neither do they reduce them to aspects of the personality of the subject. For Hillman, the imagination is truly autonomous, independent of the individual, transcendent to the subject. He supplements the subjective level with a transubjective level. This notion is, of course, also incipient in Jung, who distinguishes the personal unconscious from the collective, or transpersonal, unconscious. Occasionally, Jung (CW 7) employs the expression "transubjective" in just this sense (p. 98). According to Hillman, subjectivity is problematic because it is so possessive. The subject tends naively to believe that all images belong to it because they apparently originate in it. For Hillman (1985), however, these images come to and through the subject from the imagination – from what he calls the "mundus imaginalis," the transubjective dimension of the imagination (pp. 3–4).

## Relativization versus compensation

For Jung, the purpose of analysis is the individuation of the ego in relation to the self (or the Self, as most Jungians prefer to capitalize it in order to stipulate it as an archetype). Fundamental to this process is what Jung (CW 6) calls "compensation." Compensation is a regulatory system that operates to rectify an imbalance between the conscious and the unconscious and to establish psychic equilibrium. According to Jung, the function of the unconscious is to pose alternative perspectives that compensate the biases, the partial or even defective attitudes, of the conscious. In this process, not only what is repressed but also what is ignored or neglected by the conscious is compensated by the unconscious. The unconscious redresses what the conscious either excludes or omits from consideration. Analysis thus provides an opportunity for the integration of the psyche – through the compensation of the conscious by the unconscious and the individuation of the ego in relation to the self.

In contrast to Jung, Hillman considers the purpose of analysis to be the "relativization" of the ego by the imagination. The imagination relativizes, or radically decenters, the ego – demonstrates that the ego, too, is an image, neither the only one nor the most important one but merely one among many equally important ones. For example, when the ego appears as an image in dreams or in active imagination, it tends immodestly, even arrogantly, to presume that it is the whole (or at least the center) of the psyche, when it is actually only one part of it. To demonstrate the relativity of all images is, in effect, to humble (not humiliate) the ego. It is to expose the conceits, or prejudices, of the ego. From this perspective, the objective of analysis is not the integration of the psyche (through the compensation of the conscious by the unconscious and the individuation of the ego in relation to the self) but the relativization of the ego (through the differentiation of the imagination). In this respect, imaginal psychology is most definitely not an ego psychology. According to Hillman (1983), it does not strive to "strengthen" the ego but seeks, in a sense, to "weaken" it – to debunk the pretensions of the ego (p. 17).

## Imagination against interpretation

Many images that appear in dreams or in active imagination are personifica-tions. Jung (1963) recounts how two personifications, whom he named Elijah and Salome, appeared to him in active imagination. According to Jung, the images personified two archetypes: the Wise Old Man (Logos) and the Anima (Eros). He immediately reduces these personifications to *a priori* categories. Then, however, he expresses an important reservation: "One might say that the two figures are personifications of Logos and Eros. But such a definition would be excessively intellectual. It is more meaningful to let the figures be what they were for me at the time – namely, events and experiences" (p. 182). Rather than intellectualize the personifications, Jung says that he prefers to experience them as they are – that is, he regards them as if they were real persons. He engages them in conversation, in the dialogical process that the imaginal psychologist Mary Watkins beautifully describes in *Invisible Guests: The Development of Imaginal Dialogues* (1986). In *Waking Dreams* (1976/1984), Watkins presents a comprehensive history of imaginative techniques – prominent among them active imagination.

There are thus two tendencies in Jung – the one, intellectual; the other, experiential. Hillman consistently emphasizes the latter over the former. He does so because he regards typifications as too general, too abstract, in contrast to personifications, which are particular and concrete. The phenomenological method of imaginal psychology is not an interpretative, or "hermeneutic," method. According to Hillman (1983), hermeneutics is ineluctaby reductionistic. He defines interpretation as a conceptualization of the imagination. That is, interpretation entails the reduction of particular images to general concepts (for example, the reduction of a concrete image of a woman in a dream to the abstract concept of the Anima). For Hillman, interpretation does not stick to the image but interferes with the instrinsic "intelligibility of phenomena" (p. 51). He is by no means alone in this advocacy of phenomenology rather than hermeneutics. For example, the cultural critic Susan Sontag (1967) is also "against interpretation," for exactly the same reason that Hillman is – because it is an intellectualization of experience – what she calls "the revenge of the intellect upon the world" (p. 7). In short, Hillman is not a hermeneut but an imagist, or phenomenologist, who sticks to the image, adheres to the phenomenon, and adamantly refuses to interpret it, or reduce it to a concept.

For example, in contrast to Jung (CW 9.i), who says, "Water is the commonest symbol for the unconscious" (p. 18), Hillman (1975/1979) cautions against the interpretation of "bodies of water in dreams, e.g., bathtubs, swimming pools, oceans, as 'the unconscious'" (p. 18). He urges individuals to attend phenomenologically to "the *kind* of water in a dream" (p. 152) – that is, to the specificity of concrete images. A hermeneutic psychology reduces plural waters, different concrete images (bathtubs, swimming pools, oceans), to a singular "water" and then to an abstract concept, the "unconscious." Imaginal psychology values the particularity of all images over the generality of any concept. In contrast to Freud (1933/

1964), who says that analysis reclaims land (the ego) from the sea (the id), Hillman is no Dutch boy who keeps a finger in the dike but an analyst who prefers to experience the Zuider Zee imaginally rather than intellectualize it conceptually, or interpret it reductionistically. Waters in dreams or in active imagination may be as different as rivers are from puddles. These waters may be deep or shallow; they may be transparent or opaque; they may be clean or dirty; they may flow or stagnate; they may evaporate, condense, precipitate; they may be liquid, solid, or gaseous. The descriptive qualities that they exhibit are so incredibly diverse as to be potentially infinite – as are the metaphorical implications.

## Multiplicity

For Hillman (1975), the most egregious perpetrator of Jungian reductionism is Erich Neumann, who reduces a vast multiplicity of concrete images of females to a unity, the abstract concept of the Great Mother (or the feminine). Such an operation is a grossly arbitrary procedure that reduces significant differences to a specious identity. It is not only Jungians but also Freudians who perpetrate such a facile reduction. Hillman says: "If long things are penises for Freudians, dark things are shadows for Jungians" (p. 8). It is not just that (as Freud might say) a long thing is sometimes just a long thing – or a dark thing sometimes just a dark thing. It is that there are many very different long and dark "things" – that is, many very different images – and they are not reducible to one identical concept. In the philosophical controversy over the one-and-the-many, imaginal psychology values multiplicity over unity. It is Lopez-Pedraza (1971) who most succinctly articulates this position. He reverses the usual formulation that unity contains multiplicity and proposes, instead, that "the many *contains* the unity of the one *without losing* the possibilities of the many" (p. 214).

Imaginal psychologists believe that the personality is fundamentally multiple, rather than unitary. In a sense, there is no personality – only personifications, which, when analysts regard them as if they were real persons, assume the status of autonomous personalities. When Hillman espouses the relativity of all personifications, he might appear irresponsibly to condone multiple personality disorder (or "dissociative identity disorder," as the *Diagnostic and Statistical Manual IV* now renames it). Hillman (1985) does, in fact, say: "Multiple personality is humanity in its natural condition." To regard the multiplicity of personality either as "a psychiatric aberration" or as a failure in the integration of "partial personalities" is simply evidence of a cultural prejudice that erroneously identifies one partial personality, the ego, with the personality as such (pp. 51–52). The definition of multiple personality disorder implies that the personifications have been literalized rather than metaphorized and that the imagination has been dissociated rather than differentiated. It is not only imaginal psychologists who emphasize personifications. The object relations psychologist W. R. D. Fairbairn (1931/1990) presents a case in which an individual dreams five personifications: the "mischievous boy," the "I," and the "critic" (which Fairbairn associates, respectively, with the id, ego, and superego), as well as the "little girl" and the "martyr." Although Fairbairn says that multiple personality disorder is the result of an extreme identification with personifications, he also says, very like Hillman, that such personifications are so prevalent in analysis that they "must be regarded, not only as characteristic, but as compatible with normality" (pp. 217–219).

## Polytheism versus monotheism

Consistent with this emphasis on multiplicity, Hillman (1971/1981) advocates a polytheistic rather than a monotheistic psychology. According to him, religion (or theology) influences psychology. Historically, the three monotheistic religions – Judaism, Christianity, and Islam – have systematically repressed the polytheistic religions. Not only have Judaism and Christianity privileged one god over many gods (and goddesses), which they have disparaged as demons, but they have also privileged an abstract conceptualization of that one god. Islam has been just as intolerant: one god, no images. For Hillman (1983), Christianity has had an especially deleterious impact on psychology. He criticizes fundamentalist Christianity in particular, for it has been most puritanical and iconoclastic. Because fundamentalism has regarded the image literally rather than metaphorically, it has condemned all imagism as idolatry. Among practitioners of imaginal psychology, David L. Miller, a professor of religion, has most cogently elaborated the polytheistic perspective in *Christs: Meditations on Archetypal Images in Christian Theology* (1981a) and in *The New Polytheism: Rebirth of the Gods and Goddesses* (1974/1981b).

From the perspective of imaginal psychology, one reason that ego psychology seems so attractive is because it is so compatible with the tenets of monotheistic religion. It is a monistic psychology that values a unitary, abstract concept, the ego, over multiple, concrete images. In contrast, imaginal psychology is polytheistic (or pluralistic) in orientation. It is not a religion but strictly a psychology. It does not worship the gods and goddesses. It regards them metaphorically, as Jung (*CW* 10) did – as "personifications of psychic forces" (p. 185). According to Jung (*CW* 13), the gods and goddesses appear as "phobias, obsessions and so forth," "neurotic symptoms," or "diseases." As he says, "Zeus no longer rules Olympus but rather the solar plexus, and produces curious specimens for the doctor's consulting room, or disorders the brains of politicians and journalists who unwittingly let loose psychic epidemics on the world" (p. 37). Almost all of the examples that imaginal psychologists cite of gods and goddesses are Greek. They justify, or rationalize, this selectivity on the basis that analysis is historically European in origin and that the Greek gods and goddesses are uniquely dominant in that particular continental context. For imaginal psychology to aspire to a comprehensive multicultural psychology adequate to contemporary concerns about ethnic diversity, however, it will eventually have to include a vast, polytheistic array of gods and goddesses from the entire, global pantheon.

## Mythology

Historically, analysis has had a special interest in mythology. In contrast to Freudian analysis, imaginal psychology does not employ myths simply for confirmatory purposes. For Freud, the Oedipus myth is important because he believes that it independently confirms the discovery – and the theoretical truth – of the Oedipus complex. Freud regards the complex as primary, the myth as secondary. Imaginal psychology reverses this order of priority. For example, Hillman (1975/1979) says that "Narcissism does not account for Narcissus" (p. 221n.) It is a fallacy to reduce the Narcissus myth to a "Narcissus complex" – or to a "narcissistic personality disorder." Nosologically, Hillman (1983) says, narcissism confounds "autoerotic subjectivism with one of the most important and powerful myths of the imagination" (p. 81). Imaginal psychology expresses a definite preference for "literary" over "scientific" modes of discourse. According to Hillman (1975), the very basis of the psyche is "poetic" – or mythopoetic (p. xi).

Hillman is critical, however, of what Jung calls the "hero myth." What is so potentially dangerous about this myth is the tendency of the ego to identify with the hero and thus to act out the hero's role in an aggressive and violent fashion. In contrast to what Hillman (1975/1979) calls the "imaginal ego" (p. 102) – an ego that would modestly acknowledge that it is merely one image among many other equally important images – the "heroic ego" arrogantly assumes the dominant role and relegates all other images to subordinate roles. Other images exist to serve the purposes of the heroic ego, which may then dispense with them or dispose of them through aggression and violence. The heroic ego, Hillman says, "insists on a reality that it can grapple with, aim an arrow at, or bash with a club," because it "literalizes the imaginal" (p. 115). In this account, Hillman is culpable of the same reductionism that he criticizes in others, for "hero" is just an abstract concept, not a concrete image. Different heroes have different styles. They are not all identical. Some are notably non-aggressive and non-violent. As Joseph Campbell (1949) says, the hero has a thousand different faces.

Hillman (1989/1991) is most impressive when he revisits the Oedipus myth in order to re-vision it. According to him, the Oedipus myth unconsciously informs the very method of analysis. There is an "Oedipus method" as well as an Oedipus complex. Hillman is not the only analyst who has criticized the methodological implications of the Oedipus myth. For example, the self psychologist Heinz Kohut (1981/1991) maintains that, to the extent that analysis aspires to be more than merely an abnormal psychology, the Oedipus myth is methodologically inadequate. He wonders what analysis would have been like if it had been founded on another father–son myth – for example, the Odysseus–Telemachus myth – rather than the Laius–Oedipus myth. If Freud had based analysis on a Telemachus complex rather than the Oedipus complex, Kohut argues, the method of analysis would have been radically different. According to Kohut, it is the intergenerational continuity between father and son that "is normal and human, and not intergenerational strife, and mutual wishes to kill and destroy – however frequently and even ubiquitously, we may be able to find traces of those pathological disintegration products of which traditional analysis has made us think as a normal developmental phase, a normal experience of the child" (p. 563).

Hillman (1989/1991), however, is a much more radical critic of the Oedipus myth in traditional psychoanalytic theory and practice than Kohut is. For him, the difficulty is that the Oedipus myth has been the one and only myth, or at least the most important one, that analysts have employed for purposes of interpretation. According to Hillman, the myth demonstrates that blindness results from the literalistic pursuit of insight. Analysis has been a blind-lead-the-blind method. The analyst, a Tiresias who has attained insight after he has been blinded, imparts insight to an Oedipus, the analysand, who is then blinded. This one myth has afforded analysis only one mode of inquiry: the method of heroic insight that leads to blindness. Hillman argues that if analysis were to employ other myths in addition to the Oedipus myth, many different myths with many different motifs – for example, Eros and Psyche ("love"), Zeus and Hera ("generativity and marriage"), Icarus and Dedalus ("flying and crafting"), Ares ("combat, anger and destruction"), Pygmalion ("mimesis where art becomes life through desire"), Hermes, Aphrodite, Persephone, or Dionysos – then the methods of analysis would be very different and much truer to the diversity of human experience (pp. 139–140). The imaginal psychologist Ginette Paris in *Pagan Meditations* (1986) and *Pagan Grace* (1990) is perhaps the most eloquent exponent of this methodological differentiation.

## Soul-in-the-world and soul-making

Imaginal psychology is a "soul" psychology, or depth psychology, rather than an ego psychology. As Hillman (1964) employs the term "soul," it is *"a deliberately ambiguous concept"* that defies denotational definition (p. 46). "Soul," of course, is evocative of numerous religious and cultural contexts. Hillman (1983) notes that African-Americans introduced the word "soul" into popular culture (p. 128). In imaginal psychology, however, the term has a number of quite specific connotations, the most important of which are perhaps vulnerability, melancholy, and profundity. Hillman rejects the strong, manic, superficial ego and advocates a soul that acknowledges the weak, depressive, and deep. "The soul," he says, "isn't given, it has to be made" (p. 18). To that effect, Hillman (1975) quotes Keats: "Call the world if you please, 'The vale of Soul-making.' Then you will find out the use of the world" (p. ix). This is an allusion to the neo-Platonic "world-soul," or *anima mundi*, which Hillman translates as "soul-in-the-world." The making of soul in the world entails a deepening of experience, in which the ego is put down and kept down. Rather than an ego that descends to unconscious depths only in order to be individuated in relation to the self and then ascends to the conscious surface, Hillman advocates an ego that descends to imaginal depths – and stays there – in order to be animated into a soul: like Jung, Hillman emphasizes that "anima" means "soul." In this respect, the purpose of analysis is not individuation but animation. The imaginal psychologist Thomas Moore has popularized this soul psychology in *Care of the Soul* (1992) and *Soul Mates* (1994).

Imaginal psychology emphasizes that not only individuals have souls but that the world has soul – or that material objects in the world have soul. In contrast to the subject–object dualism of Descartes, who asserts that only human "beings" have souls, Hillman (1983) contends – he means it metaphorically, of course – that nonhuman "things" also have souls. In effect, imaginal psychology is an "animistic" psychology. In contrast to the conventional notion that the world is just so much "dead" matter, that material objects (not only natural but also cultural, or artifactual, objects) are inanimate, Hillman insists that they are animate, or "alive." He means that not only individuals but also objects have a certain "subjectivity"

(p. 132), that things have a certain "being." According to Hillman, the world is not dead, but neither is it well: it is alive but sick. It is the deadening (rather than enlivening, ensouling, or animating) attitude of Cartesian subject–object dualism toward the world that has sickened it. Rather than only analyze individuals, Hillman recommends that imaginal psychology analyze the world, or the material objects in it, as if they, too, were subjects. From this perspective, the world needs therapy at least as much as individuals do. Imaginal psychology has thus become an "environmental" or "ecological" psychology. With few exceptions, analysts have tended to ignore or neglect what Harold F. Searles (1960) calls the "nonhuman environment." Imaginal psychologists like Robert Sardello in *Facing the World with Soul* (1992) and Michael Perlman in *The Power of Trees: The Reforesting of the Soul* (1994) have now begun to confront this issue.

## Social and political activism

Imaginal psychology summons individuals to engage the world and to assume social and political responsibility. One of the most important essays that Hillman has written is on an apparently intractable social and political issue: the bias of white supremacy. Hillman (1986) argues that dilemmas presumably due to "ethnic bigotry," although not impossible to alter, are "fundamentally difficult to modify" because the very notion of supremacy is "archetypally inherent in whiteness itself" (p. 29). He cites ethnographic evidence that the anthropologist Victor Turner provides from Africa to demonstrate transculturally that not only whites but also blacks tend to regard the colors "white" and "black" as, respectively, superior (or good) and inferior (or bad). In *On Human Diversity* (1993), the eminent cultural critic Tzvetan Todorov also suggests that racism may persist, in part, "for reasons that have to do with universal symbolism: white–black, light–dark, day–night pairings seem to exist and function in all cultures, with the first term of each pair generally preferred" (p. 95). Both Hillman and Todorov wonder why racism seems so obstinately resistant to serious social and political efforts to eradicate it, and they offer a similar explanation: the unconscious projection of an archetypal, or universal, factor – a valuation about *color* (white–light–day in opposition to black–dark–night) onto *people*. According to Hillman, the problem is that racists are literalists who irrationally confuse physical reality with psychical reality and misapply the white–black color opposition for prejudicial and discriminatory purposes. In order effectively to address this difficulty and to ameliorate racism, he argues that it will be necessary to re-vision (deliteralize, or metaphorize) the spurious oppositional logic that white supremacists employ. From this perspective, racism is a failure of the imagination – an especially pernicious example of the fallacy of literalism. In an interview with Adams (1992b), Robert Bosnak, another imaginal psychologist, discusses blackness in the context of the white–black, light–dark, day–night oppositions. Bosnak distinguishes between what he calls images of "African" blackness and images of "Thanatos" blackness. He states: "The Thanatos blackness has nothing to do with race. Night and fear and death and also romance and love – all the things that are related to night – are transcultural. Something about the night does something to humans, makes us afraid, makes us imagine. That is another kind of black than the racial black. There will be thanatic black figures in the dreams of people from all kinds of different races" (p. 24). Adams directly engages the issue of racism in the white–black sense in *The Multicultural Imagination: "Race," Color, and the Unconscious* (1996).

Bosnak is perhaps the most socially and politically active of the imaginal psychologists. In *Dreaming with an AIDS Patient* (1989), he has interpreted the entire dream journal of a client who suffered and died from the human immunodeficiency virus. He has organized three international conferences on the theme of "Facing Apocalypse" – the first, on nuclear war (Andrews, Bosnak, and Goodwin, 1987); the second, on environmental catastrophe; the third, on charisma and holy war – and he plans a fourth on the millennium. In *The Sacrament of Abortion* (1992), Paris has also applied imaginal psychology to a contemporary social and political issue.

## Post-structuralism, post-modernism

Imaginal psychology is a post-structuralist, post-modernist school that has important affinities with both the semiotic psychology of Jacques Lacan and the deconstructive philosophy of Jacques Derrida. Both Hillman and Lacan abhor ego psychology, and they both radically decenter the ego. The "imaginary" of Lacan is similar (although by no means identical) to the "imaginal" of Hillman. Paul Kugler (1982, 1987) asserts that Lacan's "imaginary" is also similar to Jung's "imago." Adams (1985/1992a) contends that what Hillman means by "re-visioning" is comparable to what Derrida means by "deconstructing." Both Hillman and Derrida criticize the metaphysical logic that opposes image (or signifier) to concept (or signified) and that privileges the latter over the former.

## The institutionalization of archetypal psychology

Although there are Jung Institutes that train and certify analysts to practice professionally, there is no "Hillman Institute." Spring Publications has published many books and, since 1970, *Spring*, a journal of archetypal psychology. The London Convivium for Archetypal Studies publishes *Sphinx: A Journal for Archetypal Psychology and the Arts*. Pacifica Graduate Institute in Santa Barbara features archetypal psychology prominently and has established an archive that contains the private papers of Hillman. The Psychoanalytic Studies Programs at the University of Kent in Canterbury, the New School for Social Research in New York City, and La Trobe University in Melbourne also include archetypal psychology.

Archetypal psychology has been in existence for only a quarter of a century, but in that time it has performed an important service. It has provided a critical "re-visionist" perspective on Jungian analysis. Perhaps the most significant contribution of archetypal psychology is the emphasis on the imagination, both culturally and clinically. In this regard, archetypal psychology has revised the very image of traditional Jungian analysis.

## REFERENCES

Adams, M. V. (1992a). "Deconstructive Philosophy and Imaginal Psychology: Comparative Perspectives on Jacques Derrida and James Hillman [1985]." In R. P. Sugg (ed.), *Jungian Literary Criticism*. Evanston, Ill.: Northwestern University Press, pp. 231–248.

(1992b). "Image, Active Imagination and the Imaginal Level: A *Quadrant* Interview with Robert Bosnak." *Quadrant*, 25/2, pp. 9–29.

(1996). *The Multicultural Imagination: "Race," Color, and the Unconscious*. London and New York: Routledge.

Andrews, V., Bosnak, R., and Goodwin, K. W. (eds.) (1987). *Facing Apocalypse*. Dallas: Spring Publications.

Avens, R. (1980). *Imagination is Reality: Western Nirvana in Jung, Hillman, Barfield, and Cassirer*. Dallas: Spring Publications.

Berry, P. (1982). *Echo's Subtle Body: Contributions to an Archetypal Psychology*. Dallas: Spring Publications.

Bosnak, R. (1989). *Dreaming with an AIDS Patient*. Boston and Shaftesbury: Shambhala.

Campbell, J. (1949). *The Hero with a Thousand Faces*. Princeton: Princeton University Press.

Corbin, H. (1972). "*Mundus imaginalis*, or the Imaginary and the Imaginal." *Spring*, pp. 1–19.

Fairbairn, W. R. D. (1990). "Features in the Analysis of a Patient with a Physical Genital Abnormality [1931]." In *Psychoanalytic Studies of the Personality*. London and New York: Routledge, pp. 197–222.

Freud, S. (1955). "From the History of an Infantile Neurosis [1918]." In *The Standard Edition of the Complete Psychological Works of Sigmund Freud*, 24 vols., ed. and tr. J. Strachey. London: Hogarth Press (hereafter *SE*), vol. 17, pp. 3–122.

(1961). *The Future of an Illusion* [1927]. *SE* 21, pp. 3–56.

(1964). "New Introductory Lectures on Psychoanalysis [1933]." *SE* 22, pp. 3–182.

Hillman, J. (1964). *Suicide and the Soul*. New York: Harper & Row.

(1975). *Re-visioning Psychology*. New York: Harper & Row.

(1977). "An Inquiry into Image." *Spring*, pp. 62–88.

(1979). *The Dream and the Underworld* [1975]. New York: Harper & Row.

(1981). "Psychology: Monotheistic or Polytheistic." In D. L. Miller, *The New Polytheism: Rebirth of the Gods and Goddesses* [1971]. Dallas: Spring Publications, pp. 109–142.

(1983). (with Pozzo, L.) *Inter Views: Conversations with Laura Pozzo on Psychotherapy, Biography, Love, Soul, Dreams, Work, Imagination, and the State of the Culture*. New York: Harper & Row.

(1985). *Archetypal Psychology: A Brief Account*. Dallas: Spring Publications.

(1986). "Notes on White Supremacy: Essaying an Archetypal Account of Historical Events." *Spring*, pp. 29–58.

(1991). "Oedipus Revisited." In K. Kerenyi and J. Hillman, *Oedipus Variations: Studies in Literature and Psychoanalysis* [1989]. Dallas: Spring Publications, pp. 88–169.

Isaacs, S. (1952). "The Nature and Function of Phantasy." In J. Riviere (ed.), *Developments in Psychoanalysis*. London: Hogarth Press, pp. 67–121.

Jung, C. G. (1963). *Memories, Dreams, Reflections* (rev. ed.), rec. & ed. A. Jaffé, tr. R. and C. Winston. New York: Pantheon.

(1966a). "On the Psychology of the Unconscious [1917]." *CW* 7, pp. 3–119.

(1966b). "On the Relation of Analytical Psychology to Poetry [1922]." *CW* 15, pp. 65–83.

(1966c). "The Practical Use of Dream-analysis [1931]." *CW* 16, (2nd ed.), pp. 139–161.

(1967a). "Commentary on *The Secret of the Golden Flower* [1929]." *CW* 13, pp. 3–55.

(1967b). *Symbols of Transformation* [1912]. *CW* 5 (2nd ed.).

(1968a). "Archetypes of the Collective Unconscious [1954]." *CW* 9.i (2nd ed.), pp. 3–41.

(1968b). "Concerning the Archetypes, with Special Reference to the Anima Concept [1936]." *CW* 9.i (2nd ed.), pp. 54–72.

(1968c). "Psychological Aspects of the Mother Archetype [1938]." *CW* 9.i (2nd ed.), pp. 75–110.

(1969). "Psychological Commentary on *The Tibetan Book of the Dead* [1935]." *CW* 11 (2nd ed.), pp. 509–526.

(1970a). "The Role of the Unconscious [1918]." *CW* 10 (2nd ed.), pp. 3–28.

(1970b). "Wotan [1936]." *CW* 10 (2nd ed.), pp. 179–193.

(1971). *Psychological Types* [1921]. *CW* 6.

(1976). "Symbols and the Interpretation of Dreams [1964]." *CW* 18, pp. 185–264.

(1977). "The Houston Films [1976]." In W. McGuire and R. F. C. Hull (eds.), *C. G. Jung Speaking: Interviews and Encounters*. Princeton: Princeton University Press, pp. 277–352.

Kohut, H. (1991). "Introspection, Empathy, and the Semicircle of Mental Health." In P. H. Ornstein (ed.), *The Search for the Self: Selected Writings of Heinz*

*Kohut, 1978–1981* [1981]. Madison, Conn.: International Universities Press, vol. IV, pp. 537–567.

Kugler, P. (1982). *The Alchemy of Discourse: An Archetypal Approach to Language*. Lewisburg, Pa.: Bucknell University Press.

(1987). "Jacques Lacan: Postmodern Depth Psychology and the Birth of the Self-reflexive Subject." In P. Young-Eisendrath and J. A. Hall (eds.), *The Book of the Self: Person, Pretext, and Process*. New York and London: New York University Press, pp. 173–184.

Lopez-Pedraza, R. (1971). "Responses and Contributions." *Spring*, pp. 212–214.

Miller, D. L. (1981a). *Christs: Meditations on Archetypal Images in Christian Theology*. New York: Seabury Press.

(1981b). *The New Polytheism: Rebirth of the Gods and Goddesses* [1974]. Dallas: Spring Publications.

Moore, T. (1992). *Care of the Soul: A Guide for Cultivating Depth and Sacredness in Everyday Life*. New York: Harper Collins.

(1994). *Soul Mates: Honoring the Mysteries of Love and Relationship*. New York: Harper Collins.

Odajnyk, V. W. (1984). "The Psychologist as Artist: The Imaginal World of James Hillman." *Quadrant*, 17/1, pp. 39–48.

Paris, G. (1986). *Pagan Meditations: The Worlds of Aphrodite, Artemis, and Hestia*, tr. G. Moore. Dallas: Spring Publications.

(1990). *Pagan Grace: Dionysos, Hermes, and Goddess Memory in Daily Life*, tr. J. Mott. Dallas: Spring Publications.

(1992). *The Sacrament of Abortion*, tr. J. Mott. Dallas: Spring Publications.

Perlman, M. (1994). *The Power of Trees: The Reforesting of the Soul*. Dallas: Spring Publications.

Samuels, A. (1985). *Jung and the Post-Jungians*. London: Routledge & Kegan Paul.

Sardello, R. (1992). *Facing the World with Soul: The Reimagination of Modern Life*. Hudson, N.Y.: Lindisfarne Press.

Searles, H. F. (1960). *The Nonhuman Environment in Normal Development and in Schizophrenia*. Madison, Conn.: International Universities Press.

Sontag, S. (1967). *Against Interpretation and Other Essays*. New York: Farrar, Straus & Giroux.

Todorov, T. (1993). *On Human Diversity: Nationalism, Racism, and Exoticism in French Thought*, tr. C. Porter. Cambridge, Mass. and London: Harvard University Press.

Watkins, M. (1984). *Waking Dreams* [1976]. Dallas: Spring Publications.

(1986). *Invisible Guests: The Development of Imaginal Dialogues*. Hillsdale, N.J.: Analytic Press.

# 7

## HESTER McFARLAND SOLOMON

# The developmental school

## Introduction

Analytical psychology as elaborated by Jung and his immediate followers did not focus on the depth psychological aspects of early infant and childhood development. Neither was there much attention paid to the usefulness of understanding the varieties of relationship that can occur in the consulting room between patient and analyst. Moreover, whilst Freud and his followers began to make the imaginative leap required to link both areas of investigation – the early stages of development and states of mind on the one hand, and the nature of transference and countertransference on the other – and to include them in psychoanalytic theory, analytical psychology was slow to follow suit despite Jung's early and continued insistence on the importance of the relationship between analyst and patient (for example, CW 16).

These areas of analytic research were not a prime attraction for Jung or the group that had formed around him, who were much more taken up by the rich and attractive field of creative and symbolic activity and collective and cultural pursuits. Nevertheless, in certain respects it could be said that the sources of such activity could be located within exactly these areas, and could be seen rightfully to belong to the examination of the relationship between primary process (that is, the earlier, more primitive mental processes with infantile foundations) and the later secondary mental processes.

The lack of a clinical and theoretical tradition of investigation in these two important areas – i.e. early infantile mental states and the transference and countertransference – with the resultant lack of interest in understanding their interrelationship via the analysis of the infantile transference, left analytical psychology impoverished in an important way. This would need to be rectified if analytical psychology was to go on developing as a creditable professional and clinical endeavor. Jung's considerable contributions to the understanding of the prospective functioning of the psyche, including the self, based on a view of the dialectic of growth and transformation, were in danger of becoming limited because of the lack of a thorough grounding in the historical and genetic understanding of early mental activity.

## The historical context

Although Jung did not focus his researches on the detailed understanding of infantile states of mind, an examination of Jung's model of the psyche will show that this is not a fair representation of his investigations into the foundations of mental activity. Jung did not generally consider that the child had an identity separate from the unconscious of his or her parents. Equally, he was not especially interested in studying the manifestations of early experiences within the transference of the patient to the analyst. He considered these the proper subject of the reductive approach of psychoanalysis, to be used when it was appropriate to locate and address the sources of a patient's present neurotic conflict and symptoms in his early childhood conflicts.

However, Jung was interested in formulating a model of the mind that was concerned with those higher states of mental functioning which included thinking, creativity, and the symbolic attitude, and he focused a large proportion of his psychological inquiry on the second half of life during which, he believed, these aspects were most likely to manifest. He devoted much of his own creative energy to the exploration of some of the most developed cultural and scientific endeavors throughout the centuries. His emphasis on myths, dreams, and artistic creations, as well as his extensive knowledge of alchemical texts and his interest in the new physics, appears to have drawn him away from the study of childhood development, which seemed to fall more within the purview of psychoanalysis with its emphasis on analyzing back to the sources of mental activity. It was almost as if, like the popes of old in face of the globe as it was then, Freud and Jung had divided up the map of the human psyche, with Freud and his followers concentrating on its depths, on the exploration of the early childhood developmental stages, while Jung and his followers focused on its heights, on the functioning of the more mature states of mind, including those creative and artistic states responsible for the invention of the finest cultural, spiritual, and scientific pursuits of mankind, states which Jung studied as aspects and activities of the self.

This notional division of the psyche according to heights and depths could be understood to have arisen because of the different philosophical attitudes that informed Freud's and Jung's approaches to the psyche.

Freud's psychoanalysis was based on the reductive method that sought to provide a detailed account of the development of the personality from its earliest sources in the childhood of the individual. Psychoanalytic understanding of early development was based on a view that a reconstruction of the psyche was possible through a careful decoding of the manifest contents of psychological functioning back to the hidden or latent content. The manifest content was understood as representing a compromise between unconscious pressures arising on the one hand from repressed libidinal (i.e. psychosexually derived) impulses and on the other hand from the demands of the internalized parental superego. The aim of psychoanalysis was to decode the evidence from the manifest level to reveal the latent repressed and hidden contents of the unconscious psyche in order to bring it to light and into consciousness. The psychoanalyst's task was to disclose, via interpretation, the real motives and intentions hidden within the individual's communications, an epistemological approach. This has been called the "hermeneutics of suspicion" by the philosopher Paul Ricoeur (1967), because it does not accept at face value the conscious motivation of any act or intention but proposes instead that embedded within any conscious mental content is an unconscious compromise between the oppositional demands of id and superego.

By contrast, Jung's philosophical approach was based on a teleological understanding of the psyche, whereby all psychological events, including even the most severe symptoms, were considered to have purpose and meaning. Instead of being viewed as solely the repressed and disguised material of unconscious infantile conflict, they could also be the means by which the psyche had achieved the best available solution to date to the problem that had confronted it. At the same time, they could act as the starting point for further growth and development. Furthermore, the meaning of such symptoms was accessible to consciousness through the analytic method of interpretation, association, and amplification. Jung's approach included an understanding of the contribution of early experiences in the development of the personality, based on the historical accumulation of the individual's conscious and unconscious experiences and the interplay of this personal history with the archetypal contents of the collective unconscious. He was interested in the processes of integration and synthesis of these aspects, through the innate resources of the individual for creative and symbolic activity. It was especially the study of these capacities that led Jung to explore those processes that are associated with early mental development.

Jung's exploration of the *bases* of personality took a different tack from that followed early on by Freud in his understanding of the *stages* of personality development. Although Jung always acknowledged the importance of the psychoanalytic understanding of the early *stages* of childhood development, his interest was not in examining them through the regression of the patient in the presence of the analyst, as many psychoanalysts did. Instead, he developed an understanding of the *bases* of human personality via his own inquiry into the deep psychological *structures* of the psyche, which he conceived of as the archetypes of the collective unconscious. He saw that the archetypes were expressed through certain universal images and symbols. These deep structures, laid down through the ages and existing in each individual from birth, were understood by Jung to be directly connected to and an influence on the most developed, sophisticated, and evolved of human artistic and cultural creations. At the same time, he thought of these deep structures as being the source of the crudest, most primitive and violent feelings and behaviors of which human beings were capable.

Jung culled the information for his core clinical inquiry through his main patient group, adult patients with severe psychiatric disorders, including those in psychotic states, and through his own self-analysis. Jung focused his attention on patients whose symptoms and pathologies arose from the most primitive levels of functioning of the combined psyche–soma system. His examination of their disturbed communications was tantamount to an inquiry into the earliest disorders of experiencing, feeling, thinking, and relating. Particularly through his work with mentally ill psychiatric patients, as well as through his own dramatic and disturbing self-analysis, Jung studied the sources and roots of the personality via the various psychopathologies, expressed as they were through the archetypal images of the collective unconscious. These earliest disturbances are now often thought of as the pathologies of the self, belonging to the core of the personality, situated developmentally earlier than the more neurotic disorders that Freud examined when he began the psychoanalytic inquiry.

Increasingly, however, amongst certain Jungian clinicians and theoreticians, there arose a recognition that the treatments of adult patients and children were impeded by the lack of a tradition of understanding and closely analyzing the structure and dynamics of infantile states of mind and how these might be manifested in the transference and the countertransference. There was disquiet lest the Jungian emphasis on the more developed, differentiated, creative, and symbolic states of mind avoided the exploration of the more difficult primitive material that could emerge in those states of regression so often encountered in the consulting room. In some training institutions, the lack of a coherent theoretical understanding of early mental states, including psychotic and psychosexual states, was felt to be a deficit.

The need to develop such an understanding that was also consistent with the broad Jungian *opus* was felt urgently by a number of clinicians.

It was quite natural that this led some Jungians to turn to psychoanalysis to gain a clearer picture of the infantile mind. Jung had always insisted on the importance of locating the roots of the libido in the earliest psychosexual stages. This included Freud's important understanding that the experiences of the infant and toddler were organized chronologically according to the libidinal zones – oral, anal, urethral, phallic, genital. Indeed, this acknowledgment is found as early as 1912 in *Symbols of Transformation*, the work that would herald the cessation of his collaboration with Freud. But, as we have seen, Jung's own interests lay elsewhere, and this meant that the Jungian inquiry tended to bypass the developmental phases of early childhood. Moreover, it did not take into account the understanding gleaned from the later contributions of those psychoanalysts who themselves were making remarkable discoveries amounting to a revision of basic psychoanalytic theory.

It happened that a number of outstanding clinicians and theoreticians, including Melanie Klein, Wilfred Bion, Donald Winnicott, and John Bowlby, were based in London, and published major contributions during the 1940s, 1950s, 1960s, and later. They became central figures in the development of the "object relations school" which grew up within the British Psycho-Analytical Society during those decades and has continued to develop thereafter. There are several diverse theoretical strands within the object relations school, and many other theoreticians and clinicians of note subsequently have made important contributions to the field. However, the main theoretical bifurcation centers around whether the infant or child is driven to gratify basic instinctual impulses which are represented mentally by personifications of body parts, or whether the infant or child is essentially motivated to seek out another, a caregiver in the first instance, with whom to have a relationship in order to fulfill its basic needs, including the need to have human contact and communication in order to learn and grow, as well as to be protected and nurtured.

Whatever the sources of disagreement, the main tenet shared across the various strands of the object relations school is a view of the infant not as primarily driven by instincts, as originally formulated by Freud's economic theory, a kind of "scientific biology of the mind" (Kohon, 1986), but rather as possessing from birth a basic capacity to relate to its important caregivers, or objects, as they were called. The term "object" is a technical one and was used originally in psychoanalysis to denote another person who was the object of an instinctual impulse. It was used by the object relations theorists in two distinct ways:

1. to denote a set of motivations attributed by the infant or child as belonging to the other, usually the caregiver, but in fact defined by and located in the particular libidinal impulses that were active at the moment internally within the infant or child, or

2. to denote the person in the infant or child's environment, again usually the caregiver, with whom the child sought to relate.

Patently, each could overlap and the boundaries between the internal and external experiences of objects would blur. This would be particularly apparent when trying to describe the experience of the patient. Klein was able to bridge the two views by proposing that in the unconscious phantasies of the infant or small child, as well as in the infantile phantasies of adults, there was a dynamic relationship between the self and the other, or the object, which was represented internally as motivated by impulses that in fact reflected the instinctual drives (oral, anal, urethral, etc.) of the self. For example, the object might be experienced by the infant as the mother's breast (and then technically it would be called a "part object," i.e., a part of the mother's body). However, the quality of the experiences with the real person determined whether the infant accumulated overall a more positive or more negative relationship with the important others and their internal counterparts, with direct implications for subsequent emotional and intellectual development.

Klein held the view that the infant was liable to attribute to the other motivations which in fact were experienced internally to the infant, as expressions of instinctual impulses. The question of whether the experience of the object should be viewed as that with a real person in the real caregiving situation, or whether it should be conceived of as solely an internal representation of the infant's own instinctual repertoire, became the focus of heated theoretical debate and controversy.

At the same time, in London, during the decades when object relations theory was being developed, Dr. Michael Fordham and some of his colleagues trained as Jungian analysts and founded the Society of Analytical Psychology, where they established analytic training for those working with adults and, later, for those working with children. They read with interest the innovative psychoanalytic contributions and began researches that sought to elaborate a coherent theory of infantile development consistent with the Jungian tradition, while at the same time able to benefit from and to some extent incorporate the relevant new psychoanalytic findings and techniques, in particular those pertaining to early infantile development and the transference and countertransference. Closer scrutiny of these theoretical developments will allow a greater appreciation of why there was so much interest amongst certain Jungians in these areas of the psychoanalytic inquiry.

## Klein, Winnicott, Bion: London object relations

Certain Jungian clinicians found the Kleinian development the most approachable of the psychoanalytic investigations into early mental life. Klein's conception of body or instinct-based experiences as the root of all psychological contents and processes echoed the findings of Jung concerning the existence of deep psychological structures, which were grounded in instinctual experiences and represented mentally via archetypal images. In this way, Jung's investigations could be linked to the reductive view of the psyche insofar as he examined, as did Klein, the earliest phases of mental life back to its very roots, to the earliest mental representations of instinctual experiences. Jung called these mental images of body-based experiences archetypal images, whereas Klein called them part objects. Despite the difference in language, they both referred to the early relationships of the self with the internal representations of the different functioning capacities of the caregiver. For example, in Jung's language this was expressed as the experience of the dual aspects of the mother, while in Klein's language it was expressed as the experience of the "good" and "bad breast," such that the self was understood to experience the mother/breast (or, indeed, the analyst) as loving, nurturing, available, or poisonous, attacking, withholding, or empty, unexciting, or depressed. Thus, the quality of the experience that the self has in relation to the functioning of the other toward itself was of vital importance.

At the same time, Jung's concept also refers to the spontaneous occurrence and presence of archetypal imagery as a function of the self as it develops over time, throughout the whole life span, thereby able to generate new meanings that can carry the self forward creatively into the future, with the potential to tap into a universal cultural and imaginal reservoir. In this sense, the concept is richer and more complex than Klein's concept of part objects, which essentially refers to the early world of the paranoid/schizoid position, prior to the achievement of whole object constancy in the depressive position.

Jung in his work with psychotic adults and Klein in her work with the pre-Oedipal child investigated essentially that area in the psyche which had not yet reached the later, Oedipal stages of early childhood development in which both good (protective, supportive, or nurturing) and bad (frustrating, aggressive, or limited) aspects of the same person could be held simultaneously in the infant's mind. To indicate the gradual achievement of the capacity to relate to the carer in both their good and bad aspects, Jung's language used such terms as the "integration and synthesis of the opposites." Kleinian language devised the term "whole object" to express this capacity to hold together in mind at the same time both positive and negative experiences and to have knowledge of ambivalent feelings toward the caregiver. For both Jung and Klein, this achievement could never be consistently available, but rather the individual would always vacillate between greater or lesser capacities in these areas.

In whatever language was chosen, both Jung and Klein proposed the existence of deep innate mental structures which directly link to and serve as vehicles for the earliest biological and instinctual experiences of the infant, expressed in terms of archetypal figures (Jung) or parts of objects (Klein). Both understood that the experiences that arise through these deep innate structures are mediated by real experiences of the real environment, via the quality of nurturing and rearing made available by the environmental carers. Klein's particular attraction, especially for those London Jungians who wished to incorporate the analysis of infantile material into their clinical practice, was the solid foundation in work with children that she applied to the understanding of the activity of early mental states in the experiences of adult patients.

Klein had made a pivotal contribution to psychoanalysis through the development of her play technique (1920, 1955), an adaptation and application of traditional psychoanalytic technique to the treatment of very young children. Freer to develop her ideas within the psychoanalytic context of London than she had been while in Vienna or Berlin, Klein evolved methods of analyzing children through observing their play, enabling her to make substantial contributions to the psychoanalytic understanding of early infantile states of mind. She inferred from her analytic work with children states and processes whereby the infant and child organized their perceptions and experiences, both mental and physical, in terms of motivated impulses concerning body areas or parts located either internally or in the caregiver (usually, at first, the mother). She called these *unconscious phantasies*, the "ph" denoting a differentiation from *fantasy* spelt with an "f," which indicated a consciously available mental content, such as daydreams (Isaacs, 1948).

Klein considered that the aim of this early mental organization was to protect the emerging self from the dangers posed by excessive emotional states, such as rage, hatred, anxiety, and other forms of mental disintegration. Klein later thought that these intensely negative states would be directed back at the self if caregivers were incapable or inadequate in responding to them. Klein called these destructive impulses turned against the self expressions of an innate death instinct. To protect itself against the ravages of experiencing the powerful emotions of hatred, aggression, and envy as existing within the self, the child would activate what were called *primitive defenses* (Klein, 1946). Just as the infant or young child is not sufficiently physically developed to carry out by itself complex, integrative, and adaptive activities at the physical level but is dependent for physical survival and protection on the caring capacities of others, so too the mental apparatus of the infant is not sufficiently evolved to manage by itself those mental tasks of thinking, perceiving, and emotional sifting and sorting adequate for its self-protection, without assistance from a caregiver. Klein understood that in order to organize those mental and physical impressions that were so powerful that they could threaten to damage or disintegrate the sense of self, the infant would typically seek to establish by itself a rudimentary mental organization, especially if left by and large with inadequate care. The processes by which this organization took place included such mental activities as splitting, idealization, and identification.

Essentially, because the infant's early mental development is rudimentary and therefore liable to be overwhelmed by overstimulation from outside and inside which could lead to unbearable states of anxiety and disintegration, it needs to find a way to organize its perceptions, whether of its self or its various caregivers and other related conditions, in terms of their good and bad aspects. Jungians were accustomed to conceive of certain unintegrated mental states as the split aspects of the archetype, and used the concept of compensation to denote the psyche's natural tendency to try to hold opposites in relation to each other. Klein's findings through her clinical work with children appealed to some Jungians who sought to bring an understanding of early mental states and processes more directly into their clinical practice. Klein showed that, depending on various factors, the good or bad experiences were felt by the infant to be located either internally or externally, through processes of identification such as projection and introjection. Hence, if the infant felt the source of the good feeling to be within, then the bad would be projected into and identified with the environmental caregiver, or parts of the caregiver, such as the breast. However, the bad feeling could be relocated (or "re-introjected," in Kleinian language) within the self through further identificatory processes. These would be experienced as persecutory feelings, and would result in further splitting of good and bad feelings, leading to ever more projecting and re-introjecting activity. The quality of the environmental responses to these dramatic states, along with the infant's own capacities for self-regulation, would determine his or her tendency towards normal and adaptive or pathological and maladaptive development. In Klein's terms, this meant

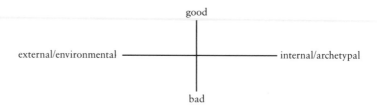

Fig. 1.   Jung/Klein model of split archetypal/environmental objects

greater or lesser control and mastery over the death instinct, the instinct which seeks to destroy the good parts of the self. In the Jungian model, the concept of *enantiodromia* is suggestive of a sudden collapse from one state into its opposite under certain conditions, and the term *shadow* is often used to denote those negative aspects of the self which the self seeks to disavow and therefore will project onto another.

Klein developed the notion of the *paranoid/schizoid position* to describe what happens when the infant is overwhelmed by feelings of possible annihilation of the integrity of the self as a psyche/soma system. The consequent anxiety that the self will be flooded by negative affects results in aggressive impulses towards the source of the bad feeling, wherever it is felt to reside. The death instinct was thus understood as the experience of aggressive impulses directed inwardly. Destructive, envious aspects of the self could become split off from the caring, loving aspects of self with the resultant fear that the source of goodness had been destroyed. The defence against such an overwhelming negative experience was the splitting of the self or the splitting of the caregiver into only good or only bad character-istics, as demonstrated in Figure 1 above.

Klein elaborated a subsequent developmental phase, called the *depressive position*, in which the infant could experience feelings of remorse and concern about the effects of its aggressive attacks upon the internal representation of the caregiver or the real external caregiver. This occurred when the infant achieved the realization that its love and hatred were directed toward the same person. Experiencing the person as a whole brought unconscious feelings of ambivalence and an impulse to repair the damaged other, based on unconscious guilt.

Klein's emphasis on affects as experienced in relation to the important functions of caregivers, or objects, in relation to the self led to her being considered as a founder of the British object relations school. Just as Jung's theory conceived the archetypal images as figures, in personified form, innate to the psyche, giving mental representation to affect-laden instinctual experiences, so Klein thought of the internal representation of important caregivers, or parts of their bodies such as the breast, as the source of affects. The child's experiences of the real caregivers were considered by Klein to be secondary to the innate conceptions and experiences that the child had in relation to that aspect of the caregiver that the child was relating to instinctually at any particular moment in its development. For example, if oral needs were predominant, then the child would have phantasies about the functioning of the breast and the mouth. Despite her recognition of the importance of the quality of the infant's interaction with its caregivers, Klein's emphasis on the instinctual bases of relating to others meant that she was not always included in a list of object relations theorists, since the emphasis of her work lay more in the dynamics of the internal world of the infant rather than with its external relationships.

A basic tenet of Jung's theoretical approach concerned the importance of the quality of environmental mediation of early experience. This had a parallel in the understanding of the importance of the quality of interaction in the consulting room between the patient and the analyst. Jung had written extensively on certain aspects of the transference and counter-transference, both in the clinical context (CW 16) as well as imaginally through the examination of alchemical imagery (CW 14). However, Jung had not studied in depth the infantile content in the relations between patient and analyst. Many London Jungians found Winnicott's clinical approach to the complex and sensitive relationship between infant and mother, and between patient and analyst, particularly compatible with their own analytic practice. Winnicott's vision of a self developing in relation to another found reverberations in the long-standing Jungian view that the development of the self and other archetypal potentials were mediated through interaction with environmental factors, including the important other carers, as well as with the analyst. As Winnicott said:

> "there is no such thing as a baby" meaning that if you set out to describe a baby, you will find you are describing a baby and someone. A baby cannot exist alone, but is essentially part of a relationship ...        (1964, p. 88)

This famous phrase denotes the importance that he gave to what happens at the interface between the self and the other, between the experience of personal creativity and of relatedness, in what he called "the third area." By this he meant that there is an area of experience which is neither internal nor external, but rather a "potential space" between, for example, the infant and mother, in which a shared and meaningful reality is created over time.

Winnicott was especially interested in the crucial role of play and illusion in the development of the self and its capacity for imagination and creativity. He thought that it was through the spontaneous gestures of play that the sense of self developed in relation to another. In a typically paradoxical formulation, Winnicott put forward the view that the true self of the individual, the sense of uniqueness and being real, happened through moments of illusion, where the inner world met and engaged with the outer world, and where the boundaries between the two were blurred. Thus, the quality of the infant's illusion that he or she had created the breast because the breast appeared at the moment when it was hallucinated or, in Jungian language, when the potentiality to experience the archetypal image occurs simultaneously with the real experience of the real object, depended on the match with the environmental provision, the ability of the "good enough" mother to respond to her infant's omnipotent needs. If the infant's spontaneous gesture is not met by an empathic response on the part of the mother because parts of her self supervene (or impinge) inappropriately through, for example, depressive or anxious needs of her own, then it is possible that the infant will experience a disruption in the sense of its developing self. If such negative experiences accumulate disproportionately over time, the infant will erect self-defenses through excessive adaptations to these external pressures. A false self is thereby created to deal with the external world, while the true self is protected from annihilation or fragmentation.

Winnicott shared Jung's teleological view of human nature. His basic premise was that, given a "good enough environment," the infant and child would have every chance to develop, grow and be creative, despite inevitable failures and frustrations in environmental provision. This view recognized that, in large part, the infant's physical and psychological protection was dependent on the capacities of its carers to mediate noxious inner and outer stimuli. These capacities in the adult carers were themselves based upon identificatory processes. However, with an adequate capacity for empathy which would itself be the product of good enough environmental provision, the adult carer would use such subtle techniques of understanding in a way that enabled the infant and child to bear inevitable frustrations in its development and to discover creative solutions to the maturational tasks that they faced.

As theory and clinical practice developed and inter-developed in the middle decades of the century in London, the status of such concepts as internal and external objects became increasingly crucial. The contributions of Wilfred Bion were of particular interest to certain London Jungians who focused much of their clinical attention on issues pertaining to the inter-subjectivity of patient and analyst and to the foundations of thinking and the generation of meaning. Bion showed how early forms of communication based on projective identification could be understood as normal forms of empathic processes between infant and caregiver. Projective identification was a term used especially by Kleinians to denote an aggressive attempt to force a part of the self into another in order to take over or control an aspect of the other's thinking or behaving, particularly in relation to the self. Bion emphasized the importance within the infant–mother dyad whereby the mother could contain often explosive physical or emotional states in the infant through her empathic responses.

Bion's contributions made available new ways of thinking about certain aspects of the transference and countertransference whereby the analyst could experience him- or herself as responding or behaving toward the patient in a manner that reflected the projected content of the patient's inner world. In later formulations, Bion conceived of projective identification in dynamic, intrapsychic terms, where parts of the self were seen as behaving in autonomous ways. For example, unwanted aspects of the self could be projected into external objects, then identified with and re-introjected as persecuting or damaging agents. Just as Jung's work with psychotic patients had led him to formulate the notion of the autonomous complexes, Bion's work (1957) with psychotic processes in his patients led him to devise a theory of internal objects as split-off aspects of the self that acquire a life of their own. Through a process of containment, whereby the caregiver receives and adapts to the mental contents projected by the infant, these elements are made available for further transformations. Such aspects of Bion's work appealed to Jungians interested in psychoanalytic ideas concerning the development of thinking in the infant and child, thereby offering a greater understanding of the processes of meaning making in the young mind.

### Relatedness in the analytic setting: transference and countertransference

The theoretical elaboration of subtle and pre-verbal forms of communication from the earliest days of the infant's life, based on the vicissitudes in the capacity for relatedness of both the infant as much as the caretaker, was increasingly understood to apply to analytic technique itself, and to the clinical role of the analyst's countertransference in response to his patient's primitive, non-verbal communications. Again, this area of psychoanalytic investigation was proximate to the Jungian interest in the states of *participation mystique* and the subtle body, varieties of the analyst's involvement in and availability to the relationship with their patient. Through the variations in states of empathy or negativity, and closeness or separation, in relation to the patient, the analyst was no longer a neutral psychoanalytic mirror whose technique of "free-floating attention" was used to ensure non-involvement in the patient's inner world. Now it was considered an important part of technique that the analyst be available enough to be affected by the patient, but not in an abusive, impinging way. The valuable clinical information gleaned from the availability of both patient and analyst to these channels of communication between them was conceptualized as the various forms of transference and countertransference.

It was as if, in turning to the innovations occurring in psychoanalytic theorizing and clinical practice, those London Jungians interested in developmental understanding found clinical and theoretical corroboration of Jung's dual emphasis on the innate structures represented by the universal archetypal images *and* the central importance of the intensive and ongoing relationship between patient and analyst as it changed over time. At the same time they found in psychoanalytic theory based on careful clinical observation and experience that which they felt to have been missing in the Jungian *opus*, namely an understanding of early infantile states of mind and how this impacts on the analytical relationship.

Winnicott had written convincingly about the link between the understanding of early infantile states of mind and analytic practice with deeply disturbed and regressed adult patients. He stated that adult patients treated intensively on the couch can

> teach the analyst more about early infancy than can be learned from direct observation of infants, and more than can be learned from contact with mothers who are involved with infants. At the same time, clinical contact with the normal and the abnormal experiences of the infant–mother relationship influences the analyst's analytic theory since what happens in the transference (in the regressed phase of some of these patients) is a form of infant–mother relationship. (Winnicott, 1965, p. 141)

Winnicott thought that the blurring of the self–object boundary led to transformations in the development of the self in the transitional space between the infant and mother as well as between the patient and analyst. The infant's experience of the transitional object as both "created and found" is similar to the patient's experience of the well-timed interpretation which happens at the very moment of it being "realized" by the patient. Winnicott called this the mirroring capacity of the analyst, which, like that of the good environmental carer, enables the growth of the sense of self in relation to the object. With the benefit of Daniel Stern's recent (1985) major contribution in respect of infant psychological development, analysts might be more inclined to use the vocabulary of "attunement" to indicate the importance of the quality of the match between both. The studies of Trevarthen (1984) in Scotland and other recent researchers have indicated that, well before speech begins to develop, "pre-speech" exchanges between mother and infant which possess rhythm and pitch form a kind of "pre-music" dialogue between them which ensure interpersonal communication from birth onwards. Similarly, many other research findings indicate how attuned the infant is in many aspects of sense perception, thus allowing it to take in stimulation from and to interact proactively with its caregivers (see A. Alvarez, 1992, for a useful review of this research and its relevance to psychoanalytic theorizing).

The large body of research concerning the capacities of very young children to respond to stimuli from the environment well before the development of any speech facility, and to actively engage in relating to their caregivers in effective ways that do not require speech, indicates the potential extent of the availability of non-verbal material that might be experienced in the consulting room by the adult patient in regressed states. With the current understanding of the breadth and depth of these interactive capacities of the neonate, and possibly also of the foetus (see Piontelli, 1987, for intriguing evidence of the foetus's capacity for learning and interaction within the intrauterine environment), there is every reason to believe that a significant proportion of the interaction in the consulting room which relates to the infancy and childhood of the patient would include pre-verbal and non-verbal experiences, including non-speech-based interactive ex- changes with the caregiver. A new discipline of investigation into this area, that of infant observation, has corroborated this view.

## Infant observation

A tradition grew up in London from the late 1940s onwards at the Tavistock Clinic (from 1948) and the Institute of Psycho-Analysis (from 1960) of infant observational studies (Bick, 1964). These studies provided regular close and detailed observations over a lengthy period of an infant with its mother, from the time of its birth for often more than two years. The one-hour observations take place weekly in the infant's home with mother, and sometimes father and other siblings and caregivers. The observations are followed by weekly small group seminars in which the observations are discussed. The seminar format ensures that a number of infants are closely monitored and discussed by each of the groups. Dr. Michael Fordham, already highly experienced in child analytic work, joined such a group, led by Gianna Henry from the Tavistock Clinic, in the early 1970s (Fordham, 1994). Subsequently, further groups were organized at the Society of Analytical Psychology, and latterly by the Jungian Analytic Training of the British Association of Psychotherapists. These detailed observations and the discussions that take place around them have con- tributed to Fordham's work on a theory of the development of the self.

A culture of careful and non-intrusive observation was developed in which the scientific method of observation and deduction was applied in an atmosphere which accepted that there were inevitable constraints in formulating theories concerning pre-verbal mental states. However, an important aspect to the exercise of observing an infant in a non-active, non-intrusive way was the development within the observer of heightened sensitivity to information contained in non-verbal communications. This was seen to benefit directly the later capacities of the analyst for countertransference responsiveness, which had become recognized as an essential tool in the patient–analyst interaction.

## Fordham's model

Fordham's theory has evolved over time and comprises several different elements which derive from his clinical experience and observational researches. The relevance to Fordham's model of the work of Klein, Winnicott, Bion, and others concerning early object relations and the pathologies of the self, as well as the knowledge gleaned from the growing number of infant observations and concurrent seminars in which to discuss them, allowed an expertise in childhood development to be established within Jungian psychological inquiry. This included the recognition of the importance of the subtle communications between patient and analyst that contribute to an enriched use of the countertransference in understanding early states of mind, and the close scrutiny of the changing transference and countertransference modalities within the treatment of the patient, even within one session and certainly over a long and intensive analytic treatment. To these elements Fordham contributed his own remarkable innovations to clinical and theoretical understanding that formed the foundations of what is now often referred to as the "London developmental school" of analytical psychology (Samuels, 1985). Although Fordham would not separate his developmental theory from other aspects of the Jungian tradition, especially the archetypal, there is no doubt that he introduced a new strand in Jungian theorizing that was grounded in intensive clinical work with very young children and the observation of infants and was influenced by the object relations view of the importance of the earliest interactions with the infant's caregivers.

Fordham's theory has been developed over decades of working psychiatrically and analytically with adults and children, and, since the 1970s, through new insights gleaned from infant observations and infant observation discussions. He has demonstrated the theoretical viability of integrating Jung's interest in the origins and development of the self, including the many archetypal configurations, to his own careful observations of how the young mind develops. In so doing, his achievement has been

> to give Jungians their childhood and a way of thinking about it and analysing it – not as one aspect of the archetypal relationship, but as the basis for the analysis of the transference within archetypal forms . . . [Thereby] he has shown how the psyche oscillates between states of mind – sometimes mature, sometimes immature – which continue with greater or lesser strength throughout the life of the individual. (Astor, 1995)

Fordham has demonstrated, through deductions from his clinical work, that the concept of the self as first described by Jung could be revised and grounded in infant development by positing a primary self, or original integrate. This primary integrate comprises the original psychosomatic unity of the infant, its unique identity. Through a series of encounters with the environment, initiated either from within or from without, called deintegrations, the individual gradually develops a history of experiences which, in successive reintegrations, build up over time to comprise the unique self of that individual. This is a phenomenological view of the self as an active instigator as well as a receiver of experience, which links both biological and psychological experience. The individuation process occurs through the dynamic adaptations that the self makes to its own activities both within itself and within its environment.

Fordham's model describes how the self deintegrates or divides spontaneously into parts. Each part activates or is activated by contact with the environment and subsequently reintegrates the experience through sleep, reflection or other forms of mental digestion in order to develop and grow. Put more concretely, a part of the infant's self is energized from within to meet an external situation, perhaps because it is hungry (it cries) or because the caregiver has come into its field (the mother smiles and talks to the infant). This kind of interchange, which in the early days happens most often between the infant and its mother or other important caregivers, is imbued with a variety of qualitative experiences – for example, there might be a good feed, with a sympathetic or attentive mother, or a disrupted one, or one in which the mother might be emotionally absent. The quality of the experience is reintegrated into the self, with resultant modifications in the structure and repertoire of the self, thus leading to ego development as the ego is the most important deintegrate of the self. Fordham's model ensures that infant development is understood as having physical, mental, and emotional content, where the self is actively engaged in its own formation and the realization of its own potential over time, while adapting itself to what the environment and particularly the caregivers offer in terms of the variety, quality, and content of experience.

Fordham's achievement is to have integrated Jung's pivotal concepts of the self and of the prospective nature and function of the psyche with a view of the psyche–soma development of the infant and child, at the same time demonstrating how this has a direct bearing on the understanding of what happens in the consulting room *between* patient and analyst and *within* each of them. Fordham's approach has been enriched by psychoanalytic contributions concerning the impact of early infantile states of mind on the experience between the adult patient and the analyst in the ever-changing and developing transference and countertransference situation. Astor (1995) has pointed out that Fordham's understanding is linked to Jung's view that

> the instability of the mind gives rise to fierce struggles internally, principally against negative forces of mindlessness, cynicism, and all their derivatives and perverse clothings. Throughout these struggles the beauty of the continuity of the self, of what Jung called the "prospective" nature of the psyche, with its capacity to heal itself, can carry forward the interested enquirer who does not give up the struggle. Fordham's legacy is to have shown us, through his example and published work, that the self in its unifying characteristics can transcend what seem to be opposite forces and that, while it is engaged in this struggle, it is "exceedingly disruptive" both destructively and creatively.
>
> (Astor, 1995)

Jung was not interested in the various modalities of the infantile transference, but he did study the evidence of the early states of mind by inference in his work with adult psychotics. Fordham showed how, in the transference, the energy previously directed into the symptom could be focused on, or transferred to, the person of the analyst (Fordham, 1957). Fordham brought together Jung's emphasis on the "actual situation of the patient," the here-and-now situation, and the clinical understanding of the transference of early childhood material into the analytic relationship, by examining the meaning of the constituent elements of the contemporary neurotic conflict of the patient.

> If, however, the actual situation be defined as the totality of the present causes and the conflicts associated with them, then the genetic (historical) causes are brought into the picture in as much as they are still active in the present as contributing to the conflicts there manifested.
>
> (Fordham, 1957, p. 82, cited in Astor, 1995)

The analysis of the transference is reductive, in the sense of analyzing psychological conflicts found in the here-and-now relationship between patient and analyst back to their childhood causes. The aim is to thereby simplify apparently complex structures back to their basic foundations. Through the Word Association Test, Jung had demonstrated that the complexes, which link the personal and archetypal roots of mental representations, were "affect-laden," that is, they were vehicles for the many varieties of emotional experiences that informed the individual's psychological life. Jung was far more interested in studying the prospective activity of the psyche, as manifested through amplification and active imagination, than in locating the origins of negative mental affectivity, including that which was revealed in the transference, in the history of the individual. Fordham, however, with his long experience of working clinically with children, recognized that children could both receive projections from their parents and project their own affects into their parents, and he equally understood that this process could also happen between patient and analyst. Thus, Fordham and those in London influenced by his work began to place increasing importance on the analysis of the transference through the use of the couch. This enabled greater clarification and elucidation of the contents of complex mental structures and their historical/genetic location within the patient's psyche.

At the same time, Fordham placed great value on Jung's view of the importance of the analyst's availability to the patient's inner world via a state of mutual unconsciousness (Jung, CW 16, para. 364). He therefore increasingly allowed his thinking to be affected by the relationship with the patient. This experience could be thought of as a partial identification, whereby the analyst deintegrates in relation to the patient in order to better understand the patient's inner world. Fordham called this process of heightened availability on the part of the analyst to projective and identificatory processes from the patient's unconscious the syntonic transference/countertransference (1957). It involved

> simply listening to and watching the patient to hear and see what comes out of the self in relation to the patient's activities, and then reacting. This would appear to involve deintegrating; it is as if what is put at the disposal of patients are parts of the analyst which are spontaneously responding to the patient in the way he needs; yet these parts are manifestations of the self.
>
> (Fordham, 1957, p. 97, cited in Astor, 1995)

Naturally, this capacity of the analyst would only be effective and useful if the "affective stability of the analyst is maintained." (*ibid.*) Later he was to understand that what he had termed syntonic countertransference was in fact parts of the patient that he had projectively identified with. As such they belonged to the interaction between patient and analyst and were therefore qualitatively different from countertransference phenomena as usually conceived.

Jung's recognition of the need for the analyst to be influenced by the patient and the reciprocal nature of the treatment relationship is well documented (for example, CW 16, para. 163 and CW 16, para. 285). The danger arose if the analyst was available to the patient in a personal way that impeded the patient's freedom to explore his or her inner world with safety and without undue impingement from the analyst. In grounding analytic treatment in the understanding of the infantile transference, Fordham guarded against the possible disavowal by the analyst of the analytic attitude through emphasis on a certain kind of mutuality in the consulting room, which could run the risk of being an abuse of the patient who was in a dependent relationship to the analyst. The subjective openness of the analyst to unconscious communications from the patient did not imply equality in the analytic relationship. The analytic attitude was fostered by protecting the patient from undue self-revelations on the part of the analyst, thereby leaving the patient's fantasies about the analyst available to be understood and be used as potential material for the patient's inner transformation.

## Conclusion

This chapter has sought to offer an understanding of the theoretical and clinical situation of analytical psychology in England which gave rise to the so-called "London developmental school." It is by necessity an overview which has not included the contributions of many psychoanalysts and analytical psychologists, both in England and elsewhere, who have made advances in the theory of the development of infantile states of mind, and in the theory of the pivotal role of the transference and countertransference in analytic practice.

In London in the decades after World War II, vigorous psychoanalytic investigations were taking place, gleaned from the analyses both of adult patients and of very young children, as well as from conclusions reached through a growing tradition of meticulous infant observations conducted over several years, concerning the development of early infantile states of mind and how these were discernible in the analytical relationship. Equally important were discoveries concerning the crucial role of the analyst's inner responsiveness to the information contained in the patient's often subtle, often powerful, pre-verbal communications.

At the same time as the psychoanalytic understanding of these areas of analytic activity deepened, certain analytical psychologists in London, and in particular Dr. Michael Fordham, became increasingly aware of the necessity of integrating Jung's valued prospective approach to work with the unconscious psyche with a need to ground such work in an understanding of those primitive states of affect and mentation by which the infant and child made its experiences comprehensible to itself. There was a recognition of the need to protect the analytic space by maintaining a boundaried and safe frame within which the exploration of mental contents could be conducted that would ensure that the patient could safely regress, if appropriate, to whatever depth of the psyche he or she was able, or needed, to attain in order for transformation and growth to occur.

Many London Jungians have found Fordham's model helpful in showing how, through a process of deintegration and reintegration, the psyche accrues depth and identity over time. Equally, the model shows how impediments to this process may occur, when either inner or outer impingements interfere with healthy development, such that pathological or maladaptive states of mind result.

It is of course ironic that the great traditions of Freud and Jung have been kept apart by history, personal philosophies, and professional politics. Seen as a whole, the movement of a conjoint analytic tradition comprising psychoanalysis and analytical psychology together might offer, despite whatever real differences may exist, a more inclusive and potentially more creative arena in which fruitful formulations in the broad area of depth psychology in general, and the content and processes of the self in particular, can take place.

## REFERENCES

Alvarez, A. (1992). *Live Company: Psychoanalytic Psychotherapy with Autistic, Borderline, Deprived and Abused Children.* London: Routledge.

Astor, J. (1995). *Michael Fordham: Innovations in Analytical Psychology.* London: Routledge.

Bick, E. (1964). "Notes on Infant Observation in Psycho-Analytic Training." *International Journal of Psychoanalysis,* 45/4, pp. 558–566.

Bion, W. R. (1956). "Development of Schizophrenic Thought." *International Journal of Psychoanalysis,* 37, pp. 344–346; republished (1967) in W. R. Bion, *Second Thoughts.* London: Heinemann, pp. 36–42.

——— (1957). "Differentiation of the Psychotic from Non-psychotic Personalities." *International Journal of Psychoanalysis,* 38, 266–275; republished (1967) in W. R. Bion, *Second Thoughts,* pp. 43–64.

Fordham, M. (1957). *New Developments in Analytical Psychology.* London: Routledge & Kegan Paul.

——— (1993). *The Making of an Analyst: A Memoir.* London: Free Association Books.

Isaacs, S. (1948). "The Nature and Function of Phantasy." *International Journal of Psychoanalysis* 29, pp. 73–97; republished (1952) in M. Klein, P. Heimann, S. Isaacs, and J. Riviere (eds.), *Developments in Psycho-Analysis,* London: Hogarth, pp. 68–121.

Jung, C. G. (1956). "Symbols of Transformation." *CW* 5. (Original work published 1912).

(1963). "Mysterium Coniunctionis." *CW* 14. (Original work published 1955 and 1956).

(1966). "The Practice of Psychotherapy." *CW* 16. (Original work published 1958).

Klein, M. (1920). "The Development of a Child." In *The Writings of Melanie Klein*, vol. I, London: Hogarth, pp. 1–53.

(1946). "Notes on Some Schizoid Mechanisms." *International Journal of Psycho-Analysis* 26; pp. 53–61. Republished (1952) in M. Klein, P. Heimann, S. Isaacs, and J. Riviere (eds.), *Developments in Psycho-Analysis*. London: Hogarth.

(1955). "The Psycho-Analytic Play Technique: its history and significance." In *The Writings of Melanie Klein*, vol. III, London: Hogarth, pp. 122–40.

Kohon, G. (ed.). (1986). *The British School of Psychoanalysis: The Independent Tradition*. London: Free Associations Books.

Piontelli, A. (1987). "Infant Observation from before Birth." *International Journal of Psychoanalysis*, 68.

Ricoeur, P. (1967). *The Symbolism of Evil*. New York: Harper and Row. (Original work published [1960] as *La Symbolique du mal*. Paris: Aubier).

Samuels, A. (1985). *Jung and the Post-Jungians*. London: Routledge & Kegan Paul.

Stern, D. (1985). *The Interpersonal World of the Infant*. New York: Basic Books.

Trevarthen, C. (1984). "Emotions in Infancy: Regulators of Contacts and Relationships with Persons." In K. Scherer and P. Ekman (eds.), *Approaches to Emotion*. Hillsdale, N.J.: Erlbaum.

Winnicott, D. W. (1964). *The Child, the Family and the Outside World*. Harmondsworth: Penguin.

(1965). *The Maturational Process and the Facilitating Environment*. London: Hogarth Press.

# 8

## CHRISTOPHER PERRY

# Transference and countertransference

Jung's writings are peppered by seemingly throwaway comments and assertions that have contributed to Jungian analysis earning the reputation of being a psychodynamic therapy that does not concern itself much with the transference. For example:

> I personally am always glad when there is only a mild transference or when it is practically unnoticeable. (*CW* 16, pp. 172–173)

When taken out of context, such statements can easily undermine the strength of an arc of development in Jung's treatment of the transference which spans fifty years. Already in 1913, alluding to the transference, Jung wrote:

> Thanks to his personal feeling, Freud was able to discover wherein lay the therapeutic effect of psychoanalysis. (*CW* 4, p. 190)

And towards the end of his life he is quite adamant when he states:

> The main problem of medical psychotherapy is the *transference*. In this matter Freud and I were in complete agreement. (Jung 1963, p. 203)

Where Jung and Freud were very much in disagreement was in their views on countertransference, which Freud regarded as an unwelcome interference in the analyst's receptivity to communications from the patient. This interference occurred when the patient activated unconscious conflicts in the analyst which had the effect of making the analyst want to counter the patient, in the sense of warding the patient off. Freud's approach was to insist on the analyst recognizing and overcoming countertransference, a conviction which led him to apologize to his analysand, Ferenczi, for his failure to suppress countertransference intrusions (Freud, 1910).

Jung certainly recognized the dangers of countertransference, which can manifest themselves in "unconscious infection" and "the illness being transferred to the doctor" (*CW* 16, para. 365). It was this recognition that underscored Jung's initiative in pioneering compulsory training analysis for would-be analysts. But whilst being alert to the potentially deleterious effects of countertransference, Jung also characteristically opened himself to the gradual realization that countertransference is "a highly important organ of information" for the analyst. In 1929 he wrote:

> You can exert no influence if you are not susceptible to influence . . . The patient influences [the analyst] unconsciously . . . One of the best known symptoms of this kind is the countertransference evoked by the transference.
>
> (CW 16, p. 176)

This makes clear Jung's view that the analytic relationship is one in which both parties are mutually involved in a dialectical process. Both patients and analysts are partners in a deep, dynamic interchange to which analysts bring their whole personality, training, and experience. Into the empty space that initially exists between the two parties there emerge the phenomena of transference and countertransference, an inextricably linked field of interaction that encompasses two people, two psyches; a field of interaction that becomes a major focus of the therapeutic endeavor.

In this chapter, I shall trace the development of Jung's thinking on transference–countertransference, paying special attention to his amplification of the alchemical metaphor. I shall also describe the diverse developments amongst post-Jungians in the understanding of countertransference.

## Transference

Jung's propositions about transference can be broken down into five basic tenets, which are open to question and research:

1. transference is a fact of life;
2. transference needs to be differentiated from the "real" relationship between patient and analyst;
3. transference is a form of projection;
4. transference has an archetypal as well as a personal (infantile) dimension;
5. transference is in the service of individuation beyond the therapeutic encounter.

### Transference as a fact of life

At the end of a day, it is possible to set aside a time to reflect upon the various meetings/encounters that have taken place over the last few hours. I use the terms "meetings/encounters" advisedly, since I am trying to make the point that there is an area in between in which we are not quite sure which, if either, has happened. The connection breeds doubt, a word which comes from the Latin word *dubium*, meaning "of two minds." The "other" is *the* other, or *another*. We are faced with a paradox. The first generates quite intense feelings, perhaps of longing, love, expectancy, fear, submission, etc.; the second heralds in other possibilities of imagination, fascination, and attraction or repulsion. Both contain within them feelings of familiarity and unfamiliarity; but the one is like stepping into a river in full spate and being carried away by the current; and the other is more like bathing in a still, shallow pool. One is fraught with imaginably unimaginable excitement and dread; the other is a dip into the confines of a well-defined container – like a bath – the effects of which can be dried off as part of continuing with ordinary life.

Recall, if you can, your first experience of falling in love. Along with all the rest of us you will probably have undergone a quite specific process, the sort of process that Jung underwent in relation to his wife, to the "anima," to Toni Wolff, and possibly to others. I can summarize it as follows: one's free-floating attention unconsciously scans the environment in search of a missing part of oneself and/or the other; it alights with unconscious accuracy on a person whose outward appearance seems to fit the internal/external image of the "other"; there is a compelling, often mutual attraction, and an instant feeling of fit; the first separation occurs, and in its wake there is a deep feeling of loss – not only of the other but also of oneself, or a part of oneself; then, over time reconnections are negotiated, and these lead, bit by bit, to disappointment and disillusionment. And one is back at the beginning – that space between "the" other and another where creative interaction can take place. Loss and possibility cohabit. In other words, transference–countertransference at least demands reflection.

You will notice that I am taking transference out of the consulting room because I cannot find any disagreement with Jung when he wrote:

> in reality it is a perfectly natural phenomenon that can happen to [the doctor] just as it can happen to the teacher, the clergyman, the general practitioner, and – last but not least – the husband.   (CW 16, p. 172)

## Transference and the "real" relationship

When analyst and patient first meet each other for a mutual assessment, it is likely that both relate for some of the time in a way that is transference-driven. But for much of the session both relate to each other as adult to adult. The patient scrutinizes the analyst's persona and professionalism; clues about the analyst's personality are sought in the location of the consulting room and more specifically in its layout and contents. And the way the analyst conducts the interview is informative of professionalism, commitment, sensitivity, and empathy.

The analyst is engaged not only in trying to make deep contact with the patient's suffering but is also mapping out the patient's strengths and capacity to meet the practical and emotional demands of analysis. These latter include the willingness of the patient to persevere with the analysis when the going gets rough and feelings of hate, rage, or disappointment fill the analytic space. As Jung says:

> "*Ars requirit totum hominem*," we read in an old treatise. This is in the highest degree true of psychotherapeutic work. (*CW* 16, p. 199)

And it refers to both patient and analyst. This aspect of the relationship has come to be known as the "therapeutic alliance," an alliance made between the conscious, adult parts of both parties principally in the service of the patient's developing field of consciousness and expansion of conscious choice through the analytic process.

### Transference is a form of projection

Whilst the psychoanalysts originally thought of transference as a displacement (Greenson, 1965, p. 152), Jung envisaged it as

> a specific form of the more general process of projection . . . a general psychological mechanism that carries over subjective contents of any kind into the object . . . is never a voluntary act . . . is of an emotional and compulsory nature . . . forms a link, a sort of dynamic relationship between the subject and the object. (*CW* 18, pp. 136–138)

The form is specific because the regularity and constancy of the analytic relationship and the setting tends to evoke and magnify both the process and the contents. An interesting feature of Jung's definition is the phrase "into the object." Projection elsewhere in his writing is thought of as a process of throwing something *onto* someone or something else, just as a projector throws an image onto a blank screen. This definition seems to foreshadow, although it does not make explicit, Klein's notion of projective identification. This idea can be supported by Jung saying a little earlier in the same lecture at the Tavistock Clinic:

> Speaking about the transference . . . One generally means by it an awkward hanging-on, an adhesive sort of relationship . . . the carrying over from one form *into* another. (*CW* 18, p. 136)

Within the transference, any aspect of the patient can be projected onto or into the analyst. Feelings, ideas, impulses, needs, phantasies, and images are all subject to this involuntary act. At first, many of these contents tend to be of an infantile nature. But as the analytic relationship grows and deepens, patients become less concerned with themselves and more preoccupied with the Self. This takes place as the result of working on the personal transference and the withdrawal of projections, of affects, impulses, and other psychic contents that the patient needs for unashamed living.

## Transference has an archetypal dimension

Once these personal contents have been re-owned, Jung noted that

> The personal relationship to me seems to have ceased; the picture shows an impersonal natural process. (CW 9.i, p. 294)

For example, a much unloved and abused man had settled into analysis after a long period of testing his female analyst's commitment and steadiness. A strong negative transference had prevailed featuring intense fear, shame, anger, and hostility. The analyst had patiently and painstakingly worked to understand and interpret her patient's negativistic attitude with the good outcome that the patient was beginning to experience feelings of longing, fondness, and love. These were then distanced through a process of sexualization, which needed further reductive analysis of the relationship with his mother before a more synthetic, teleological approach could be introduced. At that point, the projection of the contrasexual image, the anima, could be reintrojected, enabling the patient to connect at a deeper level to his need for relationship with his Self as an inner source of love and security.

In discussing the archetypal transference Jung wrote:

> It goes without saying that the projection of these impersonal images . . . has to be withdrawn. But you merely dissolve the *act* of projection; you should not, and really cannot dissolve its contents . . . The fact that they are impersonal contents is just the reason for projecting them; one feels they do not belong to one's subjective mind, they must be located somewhere outside one's own ego, and, for lack of a suitable form, a human object is made their receptacle. (CW 18, p. 161)

In terms of technique, then, it becomes clear that ideally the analyst has to use both objective and subjective, as well as reductive and synthetic interpretations. Both are in the service of individuation. Objective/reductive interpretations form the essence of Jung's second and third stages of therapy – elucidation and education; subjective/synthetic interventions constitute the work of the fourth stage, that of transformation. These are not exclusive of one another but rather form a labyrinthine spiral on which the infantile and the archetypal are encountered and reencountered again and again both during and after analysis.

## Transference in the service of individuation

As Fordham has pointed out, the emergence of the archetypal projections can form a watershed in an analysis (Fordham, 1978). Those analysts well versed in mythology and other amplificatory material can take it upon themselves to "educate" the patient, and to work under the illusion that the personal transference has been dissolved. Others may simply take it upon themselves to bear witness to "the impersonal natural process." Yet others, wary of being wafted into lofty spiritual realms at the expense of losing touch with the instinctual, will adhere perhaps too closely to the infantile transference. But there is a middle path, that of thinking of the transference as a bridge to reality (Jung CW 4, pp. 190–191), which entails the patient coming to relate to the analyst as he actually is and the patient discovering that

> his own unique personality has value, that he has been accepted for what he is, and that he has it in him to adapt himself to the demands of life.
>
> (CW 16, p. 137)

## Jung's understanding of the transference

In 1913, Jung was already acknowledging the infantile, personal transference and the process whereby the imagos of the parents were projected onto the analyst. He positively connoted this process seeing in it a potential for the patient to separate from the family of origin, however erroneous the analyst, amongst others, might consider the chosen path. He soon realized that the analyst's maturity and personality were of great importance and, with this in mind, began to advocate training analysis (CW 16, p. 137).

At about the same time, Jung was in correspondence with Dr. Loy. These letters stress the importance of sexualized transference acting as a means of achieving deeper empathy as a means toward greater "individualization"; Jung also, at this time, saw the seeds of growth in the negative as well as the positive transference.

Then there is a gap of eight years, during which Jung's thinking seems to have developed along important lines. In "The Therapeutic Value of Abreaction" (CW 16), Jung proposed that the intensity of the transference is inversely related to the degree of understanding between analyst and patient. Jung attacks the exclusive use of reductive analysis and suggests the

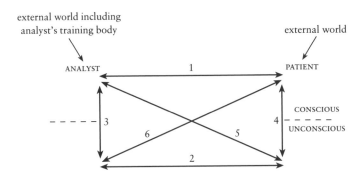

Fig. 2.   The analytic or "marriage" quaternio

addition of a teleological point of view. The transference is goal-seeking, the goal being the withdrawal of projections by both parties, particularly the patient. And great emphasis is laid on the personality of the analyst.

By 1926, in *Two Essays on Analytical Psychology* (CW 7), Jung was exploring the question of what happens to psychic energy when it is freed from the personal transference. He concluded that it reappeared as a

> transpersonal control point ... I cannot call it anything else – a *guiding function* and step by step gathered to itself all the former personal over-valuations.                                                          (CW 7, p. 131)

This is a clear statement that he saw transference as a dynamic with its own in-built propulsion toward individuation.

It was in an alchemical text, *Rosarium Philosophorum*, that Jung found a visual amplification of transference, individuation and the unfolding of the dialectic between the unconscious of the analyst and that of the patient. Jung's commentary on the text and the ten woodcuts is extremely complex and difficult, drawing as it does on alchemy, mythology, anthropology, etc. I shall attempt to condense it. Before doing so, I shall briefly examine Jung's diagram, which I have modified for the sake of simplicity. The diagram depicts what Jung calls the "counter-crossing transference relationships . . . the marriage *quaternio*" (CW 16, p. 222).

Line 1 refers to the conscious real relationship between analyst and patient and represents the therapeutic alliance. Line 2 is the unconscious relationship, which is characterized by projective and introjective identification. Line 3 is the analyst's relationship with his/her unconscious, an internal communication channel that should, because of the training analysis and experience, be less blocked than that of the patient, represented by line 4. Line 5 signifies the patient's need for the analyst's ego, and a channel for the patient's projection; and the analyst's conscious attempt to understand the unconscious of the patient. Line 6 is the analyst's line for projection onto the patient, and the patient's conscious access to the unconscious of the analyst.

In the woodcuts of the *Rosarium Philosophorum*, Jung saw illustrated a love story, the incestuous relationship between king and queen, brother and sister, conscious and unconscious, masculine and feminine. For Jung, the woodcuts illustrated developments within and beyond the transference of the individuation process. It is perhaps no accident that he chose the *Rosarium* to elucidate his thesis, since it is one of the few alchemical texts in which projection is made onto another person rather than onto chemical substances alone.

Of central importance throughout the woodcuts is the depiction of the *vas mirabile*, the "miraculous [i.e. alchemical] retort" within which the process of mutual transformation takes place.

> The *vas bene clausum* (well-sealed vessel) is a precautionary measure very frequently mentioned in alchemy, and is the equivalent of the magic circle. In both cases the idea is to protect what is within from the intrusion and admixture of what is without, as well as to prevent it from escaping.
>
> (*CW* 12, p. 167)

The *vas* appears mainly as a bath containing the water of the unconscious, and represents the container in which the *prima materia* (= "first matter," in sense of "essential being") of analyst and patient, masculine and feminine, conscious and unconscious are transformed so as to produce the goal of individuation – the *lapis philosophorum* ("philosophical stone") – i.e. self-realization or individuation. The container refers to the analytic setting and to the analyst's interventions which are required to keep the heat at a level of anxiety optimal to the patient's self-discovery and the analyst's development both as an analyst and as a human being.

At this point, the interested reader is referred to "The Psychology of the Transference" (*CW* 16), in which the woodcuts are reproduced. Their abstruse nature invites contemplation over years, partly because we are summoned directly into the realms of symbolic incest, which so often feels *as if* it could become actual; but the very agent of transformation lies in the capacity and the necessity within both parties of the analytic endeavor to live through and come to symbolize the sexuality of the erotic (Eros) and the compassion of charity (the ancient Greek for which is *agape*).

In Picture 1, the "Mercurial Fountain," we see a fountain fed from below and above – the conscious and unconscious aspects of the relationship between analyst and patient, who in terms of analysis, are relatively impersonal. Both may think of each other as virginal, dangerous, and life-giving. And all three contain some truth. Both are embarking on an unknown journey, and both have their resistances. The two parties can be transformed by Mercurius, the tricky one, he who abides at the threshold (of change); but there is a warning of which all analysts will take note in their assessment:

> No fountain and no water has my like
> I make both rich and poor men whole or sick
> For deadly can I be and poisonous.

The fountain, the source, can therefore be the wellspring of psychic life, but Jung also likens it to the *foetus spagyricus* ("alchemical foetus"): i.e. in developmental terms, to a neonatal state from which a new insight will grow. In this first woodcut, we also see the masculine and feminine portrayed as sun and moon, leitmotifs which permeate the series. This has often caused confusion, particularly in cases where the analyst and patient are of the same sex. We cannot take Jung concretely here. Rather we are left to explicate for ourselves the complexities arising from the admixture of different biological and psychological contra-sexual combinations, as well as different attitude and function types. We, like him, have to struggle with the greatest possible confusion. Hetero/homo-sexual feelings, impulses and phantasies need to blossom: i.e. to be symbolized so as to be lived through.

In Picture 2, we are introduced to the protagonist and antagonist of the narrative: the king and queen, who are now more clearly related to sun and moon, brother and sister. They are in touch, but in a sinister (lefthanded) way, a pathway often associated with the unconscious and, hence, with the beginnings of projective/introjective identification implied by line 2 of our diagram. I am referring to the dangers of boundarylessness, and the point at which the relationship can take off into lofty spirituality or the enactment of incest. Guarding against these dual dangers is the figure of the dove, that creature which returned to Noah with evidence that the flooding of the unconscious was now over. Here the *mundus imaginalis* (a "world of images") is constellated (Samuels, 1989), where the tension between actual and symbolic incest is held, worked through, and transformed. Analyst and patient fall "in love" with each other; but there is no symmetry. In the analyst is evoked the image of the child-within-the-patient, who has therapeutic *needs*. The patient is put into a more difficult position because s/he is beginning to know about the analyst's deficits. And it is these, when insisted upon by the patient, that help the analyst to review and reflect upon mistakes.

These begin to appear in Picture 3, the "Naked Truth," which symbolizes both analyst and patient denuded of their personae. For example, the analyst might give the "wrong" bill to a patient or double-book an appointment. The patient may get "lost" on the journey to the session. Shadow elements from both parties creep in, and Sol and Luna grasp each other indirectly through and across the two branches, already depicted in Picture 2 where one end of each is left in mid air. Analyst and patient are cornered at one time or another; essentially this is the beginning of total honesty in trying to discover, acknowledge, and work toward forgiveness (a long-term aim) of the shortcomings that both parties bring to the analytic quest, and towards self-forgiveness.

Picture 3 is a challenge to both parties to continue through the process of mutual transformation, watched over and impregnated by the dove, the Holy Spirit which unifies (possibly a reference to the Christian doctrine of the Trinity). Here we are into the realm of faith in the third that issues from the two – faith in the analytic relationship. From the analyst's side, this comes from the training analysis; the patient, on the other hand, is beginning to reside with discomfort in the area between the actual and the symbolic – between actual touching and feeling touched by the analyst's symbolic touch. The union must therefore be symbolic rather than actual despite the passionate intensity of the affect between the two parties. Jung offers a reminder:

> Incest symbolizes union with one's own being, it means individuation or becoming a self . . . it exerts an unholy fascination. (CW 16, p. 218)

The alchemists were, in part, in revolt against the sexual asceticism of the Christian Middle Ages. They seem to have known about the age-old longing of lovers to immerse naked with one another in water – to fuse. And so, in Picture 4, "Immersion in the Bath," the couple sit rather demurely, still joined together symbolically. Sol looks quite relaxed (a false position for the analyst) and Luna looks shyly towards her partner's genital area. The ends of both wands are limp, but the potentially erotic nature of the *coniunctio* ("union") is immanent. And it is generally thought that the water in the bath represents the unconscious – a state of fusion, known nowadays as projective identification. But Jung adds an interesting note:

> I do not, of course, mean the synthesis or identification of two individuals, but the conscious union of the ego with everything that has been projected *into* the "you." (CW 16, p. 245, n. 16; my italics)

And the Holy Spirit maintains his vigilance – presumably a function projected onto or into the analyst but, sometimes, alas, the patient. Imagine this scenario: the patient comes out for a session, and talks. Apparently

Picture 3:   The naked truth

disjointed fragments of narrative, like a news broadcast, ensue. The analyst is lost and disturbed by "unknowingness." Feeling that no meaningful contact has been made in the session, the analyst pats the shoulder of the patient as the latter leaves the consulting room and says: "See you tomorrow." The patient instantly "knows" that the symbolic attitude has been lost and is filled with despair and longing. The initiation of baptism into symbolism has been lost, and the patient has been left with tantalization.

Any thought that Picture 5, the "Coniunctio Sive Coitus" ("love-making or sex"), is an invitation to sexual enactment is dispelled by Picture 5a, in which the incestuous couple are seen with wings despite the fact that the

Picture 5a:   The conjunction

water refers "to the boiling solution in which the two substances unite" (*CW* 16, p. 250). The tension between spirit and instinct is held throughout the series, although it takes different forms. Notice also that the left hand reappears, Sol's tentatively exploring Luna's breast, and Luna's travelling toward her lover's penis. Whilst he looks at her, she is looking out, beyond the couple. For what? I wonder, and Jung answers:

> let no day pass without humbly remembering that everything has still to be learned.
> (*CW* 16, p. 255)

What Jung says exactly portrays the states of mind of the couple who are deeply in love and (I would add in the therapeutic relationship) in hate. The honeymoon of idealization is at an end; the frustration of the longing to be connected is at its height. Analyst and patient seethe under the guise of fermentation: a loving, loathing concoction that leads to a temporary state of death.

Death, Picture 6: it is stated that

Here King and Queen are lying dead
In great distress the soul is sped.

The *vas mirabile* has become a sort of sarcophagus, a word which means "flesh-devouring," a projection of the death-dealing aspects of the Great Mother, and an image conjured up to us by the coffin. The flow of the Mercurial fountain of Picture 1 is at a standstill. And yet, the picture's title suggests conception through rotting – putrefaction. This is the darkest time, the time of despair, disillusionment, envious attacks; the time when Eros and Superego are at daggers drawn, and there seems no way forward. This, in alchemical treatises, is called the *nigredo*, the blackening. One has to have faith in the regenerative capacities of compost through long periods of apparent inertia, inactivity, and, most importantly, despair. Faith in the process, faith in the relationship, the analyst's faith in method/technique have to be counterbalanced, to my mind, at this stage by an absorption into total doubt, which, clinically, is usually enunciated by the patient as abandonment or psychotic relating, the latter of which is sometimes of the analyst's making. There occurs empathic failing, which ultimately can be therapeutic; but its therapeutic efficacy rests upon the analyst's persistent self-analysis, aided by the patient's cues.

Picture 7, not surprisingly, is a paradox. The "Ascent of the Soul" is juxtaposed with being impregnated. The longed-for deathly state of fusion veils the realization that projective identification leads inevitably to loss of soul, not ego-lessness but a loss of the experience of I–Thou, Ego–Self, conscious–unconscious relatedness. There are one body, two heads, and a *homunculus* up in the clouds. This may lead either to a continuation along the path of individuation or to psychotic disintegration/dissociation/splitting. The *vas mirabile* has been swiveled slightly to the *left*, and its right extremities are shaded – at a deeply unconscious level. We can think of this as denial of difference – and the projection of hope and separation, split off into an analytic child – such as an idea, or a Messianic interpretation.

Picture 8 is subtitled "Mundificatio" (the "making of the world") – a profound allusion to the primal scene. We could call it "coming back to earth," but this is a process which is beyond and outside the conscious egos of both participants. What was black now slowly becomes white; the *nigredo* of despair and loss of soul are now followed by the falling of the heavenly dew, which prepares the soil of the analytic relationship for the return of soul, transformed. To get in touch with this process bodily, take a walk through the mist, and dwell in the sensation of being soaked to the skin without immediate realization.

The feet of the couple have been transferred from the extreme left of the *vas* (its sinister, dark side) to a more centrally positioned place. The legs are in a position to open equilaterally; and whilst Luna continues to look outside and beyond the *vas*, Sol looks up at the falling dew, the divine, the numinous. At this stage, the analyst relies even more on the powers of Logos (interpretation) and Agapaic Eros (compassion). The two were never disjoined, but they can now be put together in a statement from the analyst which conveys an understanding of the need to suffer through relinquished enchantment, with its deepest joys, sadnesses, and intense frustrations.

"Animae jubilatio" means "the joy of the soul." It is the title above Picture 9, which is also called "The Return of the Soul." Analysts tend to be more familiar in the early stages of analysis with pain, suffering, and sorrow than with joy. But it is this very feeling that accompanies the patient's gradual process of self-discovery that had as its origins the feeling of tentative enjoyment of immersing in the bath:

> Yet, although the power of the unconscious is feared as something sinister, this feeling is only partially justified by the facts, since we also know that the unconscious is capable of producing beneficial effects. The kind of effect it will have depends to a large extent on the attitude of the conscious mind.
>
> (*CW* 16, p. 293)

But hope has to be balanced. The celestial/chthonic dimensions of Picture 1 are revisited in Picture 9. Notice the two birds (analyst and patient?), apparently addressing one another. One is on *terra firma*; the other, emerging – or sinking – *Materia* and *spiritus*, body and soul. Once again, analyst and patient are caught between the opposites, where the *coincidentia oppositorum* ("meeting of opposites") leads to the growing awareness that it is "the body that gives bounds to the personality" (*CW* 16, p. 294). In clinical practice, for example, we can think of the schizoid personality, who, for so much of the time, tends to oscillate between feeling dis-embodied (depersonalized) or trapped, often with bad feelings, inside the body, or the mother's body. The one is agoraphobic; the other is claustrophobic. Hence the tendency for the schizoid person to dwell at the threshold. The task is to facilitate embodiment.

And so to Picture 10. The *corvex*, the raven, looks upon the scene – the representative of death! In another version, there is a Pelican, an icon of Christ, pecking at itself in order to feed its young. The hermaphrodite, mythically, sexually, and spiritually a sophisticated version of the androgyne, is born from the *unio mystica* ("sacred/secret union"), looking toward right and left (conscious and unconscious), and firmly standing on the moon, the lunatic, which is looking upward and into the genital area, which is enfolded in her crescent. Both patient and analyst have traveled further along the path

Picture 10:   The new birth

of individuation; both have been transformed by the work. The patient hopefully has introjected the analyst as a helpful figure, and has internalized the analytic relationship, which will continue to act as a positive, potent inner resource, particularly during difficult times. The analyst likewise has enlarged and deepened his/her clinical experience and expertise, and has changed primarily as a result of his/her mistakes and failings.

To conclude this section, I can do no better than to quote Jung:

> The transference phenomenon is without doubt one of the most important syndromes in the process of individuation; its wealth of meanings goes far beyond mere personal likes and dislikes. By virtue of its collective contents and symbols it transcends the individual personality. . .        (CW 16, p. 323)

## Post-Jungian developments

In terms of the elucidation of the transference, contemporary Jungians owe much to Michael Fordham, whose work has had as its primary thrust the tracing of the transference to "its roots in infancy and childhood in a way that is congruent with Jung's formulation" (Fordham, 1974a). A further development lies in his pioneering work with the delusional transference, where the "as if" components of the relationship become temporarily lost (Fordham, 1974b), and the patient reverses the analyst–patient relationship in such a way that the analyst feels that s/he is the patient. Confusion reigns, and it becomes vital for the analyst to hang onto the analytic stance as a way of keeping in touch with and relating to the hidden healthy aspects of the patient.

This approach is echoed by Perry in his work with psychotic patients, which illustrates the need for therapists to immerse themselves in the psychotic/delusional transference so that there can be a commingling of personal and collective transference elements, the interpretation of which lead to "a shift from concerns of power and prestige to ones of lovingness and social harmony" (Perry, 1953). This theme is taken up by Ledermann in her work with deeply wounded narcissistic personalities (Ledermann, 1982), and by Redfearn in his work with schizoid and psychotic personalities (Redfearn, 1978).

A middle position between a classical approach and that of those who adhere to the "Jung–Klein" hybrid is taken by Peters (1991), who sees the transference as a libidinal attachment to the analyst and/or to a figure in the patient's external world. He advises that relentless and mechanical interpretation of the transference to the analyst can become an imposition on the patient, and so, by implication, can result in the patient's pathological compliance with the analyst's method. I may be overstating his case if I suggest that this sort of mechanistic approach acts as *a* contributor to interminable and addictive analyses.

Of central importance to the work of the alchemists was a bridged split, that between the *laboratorium* ("work-place"), in which their experiments took place, and the *oratorium* ("place for discourse"), which provided a psychic and physical space for reflection and meditation on the work of transformation. The *oratorium* has come to be the internal or external *temenos* ("sacred space") of supervision, in which the analyst "looks over and overlooks" (*super-videt*) his/her subjective experience of the patient. This subjective experience has come to be called the "countertransference," and it can range from the neurotic countering of the transference by the analyst to the processing of information about the patient through constant self-analysis of the analyst's subjectivity. It is to this reciprocal dimension of the analytic relationship that I now turn.

## Countertransference

Unlike Freud, Jung left us with remarkably few examples of how he actually worked. But he does seem to have been the first analyst to have recognized the therapeutic and anti-therapeutic potential in countertransference. His early insistence on "training analysis" sprang from his belief that analysts could only accompany their patients as far as they had themselves reached in their quest for self-realization. This standpoint, however, seems no longer entirely valid. Its invalidity rests on the supposition that the analyst can potentially empathize and identify with any psychic content within a patient. For example, it is possible to work with victims of catastrophes without having experienced the same actual catastrophe. What is important is that the analyst can be in touch and relate to his/her own internal persecutor/victim complex. What is more likely to limit the analyst is the vertex, or point of view, from which the dialectic is viewed. This is why I included the analyst's external world and training body in the diagram of the transference. Analysts can also act as containers for apparently incomprehensible aspects of their patients whilst the latter gain distance and the advantage of objectivity. Furthermore, analysts can act as companions and witnesses to experiences unknown to themselves, but always waiting in the wings of the theater of life. Nonetheless, Jung was alert to the dangers of blind spots in the analyst, and to the hazards of mutual psychic infection and contagion. And again and again, in different ways, he stresses the importance of the analyst's personality as "one of the main factors in the cure" (CW 4, p. 260).

In contrasting his methods with those of Freud, Jung wrote about the necessity of the patient's illness being transferred into the personality of the analyst, and of the necessity of the analyst being open to this process. The analyst "quite literally 'takes over' the sufferings of [the] patient and shares them" (CW 16, p. 172). It is through this process that the personalities of both parties are transformed. It is, therefore, expected that the analyst will have very strong reactions to the patient, and these might include physical illness as well as exposure to the "overpowering contents of the unconscious" which might become a source of fascination(CW 16, p. 176).

In his later writings on countertransference, Jung draws on the myth of Asklepios, the "wounded healer." It is the analyst's suffering which is the essentially curative factor. And he goes so far as to say: "Unless both doctor and patient become a problem to each other, no solution is found" (Jung,

1963, p. 142). But it has been left to the post-Jungians across the globe to explore and fill in the lacunae left by Jung in his writings on counter-transference. Post-Jungian developments can be summed up in Machtiger's assertion that "It is the analyst's reaction in the countertransference that is the essential therapeutic factor in analysis" (Machtiger, 1982). What she means here is that the analyst must interpret and make use of his or her subjective responses and fantasies in making sense of the analysand's material and experiences. The skill and competence of the analyst in using this countertransference will determine, in large part, the success or failure of the analysis.

In 1955, Robert Moody wrote about his work with a child patient, during which he recognized that his unconscious had been at times activated in a way that he thought merited attention (Moody, 1955). At such times, he found himself relating and behaving in a way that was out of the ordinary in a therapeutic context, whilst simultaneously closely monitoring the interaction that was taking place at an unconscious level between himself and the child. Although wary of the possibility of a censorious reaction from some readers, Moody believed that

> As this material emerges within the reciprocal transference relationship, it can be handled in a way that is decisively – and sometimes rapidly – therapeutic.
>
> (p. 52)

Plaut (1956) sought to differentiate the analyst's responses in the face of personal and archetypal projections. The first, because of their proximity to consciousness, can be fairly readily reintegrated by the patient and will not unduly affect the analyst. But the second, because of their numinosity and powerful affect, pose a risk to the analyst of becoming identified with them and "incarnating" them. It then becomes important to contain the projection until the patient's "ego becomes stronger, so he is able to notice the symbol concealed within the image" (p. 159).

Articles by Strauss (1960), Davidson (1966), Gordon (1968), and Cannon (1968) may be grouped together since all these analysts are concerned from their different vertices with the playful use of transference–countertransference material in an encounter between ego consciousness and the unconscious, not unlike the method of active imagination.

Fordham's thinking on "the reciprocal transference relationship" has spanned some forty years. In an early contribution, Fordham defines countertransference in a fairly classical way as "almost any unconscious behaviour of the analyst" (Fordham, 1957). But later, he prefers to restrict the use of the term "countertransference" to refer to those times in analysis when "the interacting systems become obstructed"; in other words, when the analyst blocks the projections and projective identifications of the patient (Fordham, 1985, p. 150). Early on he distinguished two types of countertransference – the illusory and the syntonic. The first is thought to be neurotic and occurs when unconscious conflicts in relation to a person in the analyst's past have been stirred up and are interfering with the therapeutic space. But the situation can be remedied through supervision and further self-analysis. Syntonic countertransference is a state in which the therapist is empathically closely tuned in to the patient's inner world and therefore could potentially experience aspects of the patient possibly before the patient is conscious of them. Fordham's findings are synchronistic with those of Racker (1968), whose work on complementary and concordant countertransference was further explicated by Lambert (1981).

Three analysts have been concerned with the shadow aspects of counter-transference – Guggenbühl-Craig, Groesbeck, and Lambert. The first two draw on Jung's later references to the Wounded Healer. Guggenbühl-Craig warns of the dangers of inflation and splitting in members of the helping professions, whereby the "wounded" pole of the archetypal image gets projected onto and left with the patient, who in turn projects the "healer" pole onto the analyst (Guggenbühl-Craig, 1971). This theme is developed by Groesbeck, who maintains that both analyst and patient need to with-draw these projections so that the inner healer is activated in the patient (Groesbeck, 1975). Lambert sees the shadow of countertransference in the enactment of the talion law, where the patient's attack is met by counter-attack, which greatly diminishes the patient's trust and acts as a replay of previous damaging relationships. At such times, the analyst has lost empathy with the patient and is under the sway of a complementary countertransference, in which the analyst is identified with and behaving like the patient's negative internal object(s) (Lambert, 1981).

Mario Jacoby's work on transference–countertransference is innovative in that it introduces the notion of a spectrum of countertransference responses rather than a dichotomy of neurotic and non-neurotic. Jacoby has also incorporated Kohut's ideas about "self-objects," merging, mirroring, and idealizing transferences and their counterparts in the analyst; and he makes specific reference to the delusional countertransference, in which the analyst abdicates from his/her symbolic approach to the interactional field (Jacoby, 1984).

This field has been the subject of a research project carried out by Dieckmann and his colleagues, who came up with the startling and yet not so startling conclusion that "the self constellates the synchronicity of fantasies in two persons" (Dieckmann, 1976, p. 28). This was reached by the analysts taking careful note of their own material, associative to that of their patients. This remarkable correspondence had as its shadow the growing realization that resistance is a shared problem between patient and analyst, and not the patient's prerogative.

Dieckmann's emphasis on synchronicity and the extended influence of the Self closely approximates Schwartz-Salant's view that therapy is a process in which two people mutually constellate the unconscious. Schwartz-Salant's approach to countertransference is highly idiosyncratic: it is based on the development in both patient and analyst of a capacity to experience and participate in a shared, imaginal realm, which exists outside of space, time, and any notion of causality, and which manifests itself primarily in *coniunctio* imagery (1989).

Goodheart (1984) has incorporated into Jungian thinking a model devised and refined by the psychoanalyst Robert Langs. The kernel of the Goodheart–Langs hybrid is a model of conscious, continuous internal supervision, whereby the validity of every analytic intervention is tested against the patient's subsequent unconscious communications. These authors maintain that the patient is constantly seeking to correct the analyst, to keep him/her on course, so to speak. So emphasis is laid on the patient's unconscious communication about analyst error, and this is particularly so when the analytic frame – the fee, time, place of meeting, etc. – is altered, a phenomenon which leads to the triggering of unconscious narrative in the patient. This approach, along with others, relies on the analyst carefully processing countertransference information simultaneously with the symbolic meaning of what the patient is unconsciously communicating.

Effectively acting as a bridge between Fordham, Lambert, and Racker on the one hand and Schwartz-Salant on the other, Samuels (1985) has introduced the terms "reflective" and "embodied" countertransference, maintaining that the "analyst's inner world is the *via regia* into the inner world of the patient." Put another way, both analyst and patient contribute to and are part of a shared imaginal realm, in which bodily responses, feelings, and phantasies can be viewed imagistically. Reflective countertransference consists of the analyst's experience of the patient's internal state, such as a feeling of sadness, for example. Embodied countertransference is that state where the analyst experiences him- or herself as if s/he were a particular person or sub-personality from within the patient's psyche. Samuels also pays special attention to the erotic transference–countertransference field, in effect grounding and embodying the lofty image of the "sacred marriage" to the extent that he states: "In order for psychological transformation to result from analytical interaction, that interaction must acquire and radiate something of an erotic nature" (Samuels, 1989, p. 187). His most recent contribution (1993) widens his view of countertransference and takes it into the arena of politics, where "a political valuing of a *citizen's* subjectivity" is envisioned as the *via regia* to *"the culture's social reality"* (p. 28). This is quite revolutionary thinking, the implications of which are beyond this review.

In this section, I have tried to show how post-Jungians have built upon Jung's pioneering work on the countertransference. Many of these developments have taken place alongside and been informed by the very extensive literature that has been contributed by the psychoanalysts, starting with Paula Heimann's seminal work (1950) and continuing up to the present day.

There remains an area of confusion between countertransference and projective identification. There appears to be a general consensus that the latter contributes to countertransference experience, but is not its sole content. Projective identification, which is the developmental precursor of empathy, is a primitive process, primarily a defense against separateness and, in Gordon's view (1993), is "the psychic equivalent of fusion" (p. 216). Its aim is to transmit unassimilable contents of the psyche–soma into someone else, with the unconscious aims of communicating them, of controlling them and the other person, and of creating a state of merger with the other. Its normal variant can be thought of as a mode of communication, and its pathological variant as a mode of evacuation. It is closely related to Jung's *participation mystique*, in which there is no differentiation between subject and object. Part of working through the countertransference lies precisely in achieving differentiation and trying to establish what belongs to whom in the analytic dyad.

The transference–countertransference dynamic is mainly a *mysterium coniunctionis*. And I would stress the word "mystery." Sometimes, it is also a *mysterium* dis*iunctionis* – enshrined in the memories of patients and analysts as some sort of misfit, mismatch, impasse, a deep failure of relationship. Then we can take heed of Jung, once more:

> The psychotherapist learns little or nothing from his successes, for they chiefly confirm him in his mistakes. But failures are priceless experiences, because they not only open the way to a better truth, but force us to modify our views and methods. (CW 16, p. 38)

The persistent and consistent attention paid to the deep exchange between patient and analyst (the transference–countertransference dynamic) over the last third of a century following Jung's death bears testimony, I think, to the shared quest amongst Jungian analysts, of whatever persuasion, of learning to process and understand the complexities and subtleties of the analytic encounter.

# REFERENCES

Cannon, A. (1974). "Transference as Creative Illusion." In M. Fordham *et al.* (eds.), *Technique in Jungian Analysis*. London: Heinemann.

Davidson, D. (1974). "Transference as a Form of Active Imagination." In M. Fordham *et al.* (eds.), *Technique in Jungian Analysis*. London: Heinemann.

Dieckmann, H. (1976). "Transference and Countertransference: Results of a Berlin research group." *Journal of Analytical Psychology*, 21/1.

Fordham, M. (1974a). "Notes on the Transference." In M. Fordham *et al.* (eds.), *Technique in Jungian Analysis*. London: Heinemann.

(1974b). "Jung's Conception of Transference," *Journal of Analytical Psychology*, 19/1.

(1978). *Jungian Psychotherapy*. Chichester: John Wiley & Sons.

(1985). "Countertransference." In M. Fordham, *Explorations into the Self*. London: Academic Press.

Freud, S. (1910b). Letter to Ferenczi of 6 October 1910, quoted in E. Jones, *Sigmund Freud: Life and Work*, vol. II. New York: Basic Books, 1955.

Goodheart, W. B. (1984). "Successful and Unsuccessful Interventions in Jungian Analysis: The Construction and Destruction of the Spellbinding Circle." In N. Schwartz-Salant and M. Stein (eds.), *Transference/Countertransference*. Wilmette, Ill.: Chiron Publications.

Gordon, R. (1974). "Transference as the Fulcrum of Analysis." In M. Fordham *et al.* (eds.), *Technique in Jungian Analysis*. London: Heinemann.

(1993). *Bridges: Metaphor for Psychic Processes*. London: Karnac Books.

Greenson, R. R. (1978). *The Technique and Practice of Psycho-Analysis*. London: The Hogarth Press.

Groesbeck, C. G. (1975). "The Archetypal Image of the Wounded Healer." *Journal of Analytical Psychology*, 20/2.

Guggenbühl-Craig, A. (1971). *Power in the Helping Professions*. Zurich: Spring Publications.

Heimann, P. (1950). "On Countertransference." *International Journal of Psycho-analysis*, 31.

Jacoby, M. (1984). *The Analytic Encounter: Transference and Human Relationship*. Toronto: Inner City Books.

Jung, C. G. (1913). "The Theory of Psychoanalysis." *CW* 4, pp. 83–226.

(1914). "Some Crucial Points of Psychoanalysis." *CW* 4, pp. 252–289.

(1916/1945). "The Relations between the Ego and the Unconscious." *CW* 7, pp. 119–239.

(1921/1928). "The Therapeutic Value of Abreaction." *CW* 16, pp. 129–138.

(1929a). "The Aims of Psychotherapy." *CW* 16, pp. 1–52.

(1929b). "Problems of Modern Psychotherapy." *CW* 16, pp. 53–75.

(1935). "The Tavistock Lectures." *CW* 18, pp. 1–182.

(1944/1968). *Psychology and Alchemy*. *CW* 12.

(1946). "The Psychology of the Transference." *CW* 16, pp. 163–323.

(1950). "A Study in the Process of Individuation." *CW* 9.i.

(1963). *Memories, Dreams, Reflections*. London: Collins and Routledge & Kegan Paul.

Lambert, K. (1981). "Transference, Countertransference and Interpersonal Relations." In K. Lambert, *Analysis, Repair and Individuation*. London: Academic Press.

Ledermann, R. (1982). "Narcissistic Disorder and its Treatment," *Journal of Analytical Psychology*, 27/4.

Machtiger, H. G. (1985). "Countertransference/Transference." In M. Stein (ed.), *Jungian Analysis*. Boston and London: Shambhala, 1985.

Moody, R. (1955). "On the Function of Countertransference." *Journal of Analytical Psychology*, 1/1.

Perry, J. W. (1953). *The Self in Psychotic Process*. Dallas: Spring Publications.

Peters, R. (1991). "The Therapist's Expectation of the Transference." *Journal of Analytical Psychology*, 36/1.

Plaut, A. (1974). "The Transference in Analytical Psychology." In M. Fordham *et al.* (eds.), *Technique in Jungian Analysis*. London: Heinemann.

Racker, H. (1968). *Transference and Countertransference*. New York: International Universities Press.

Redfearn, J. W. T. (1978). "The Energy of Warring and Combining Opposites: Problems for the Psychotic Patient and the Therapist in Achieving the Symbolic Situation." *Journal of Analytical Psychology*, 23/3.

Samuels, A. (1985). "Countertransference, the *Mundus Imaginalis* and a Research Project." *Journal of Analytical Psychology*, 30/1.

(1989). *The Plural Psyche: Personality, Morality and the Father*. London and New York: Routledge.

(1993). *The Political Psyche*. London and New York: Routledge.

Schwartz-Salant, N. (1989). *The Borderline Personality: Vision and Healing*. Wilmette, Ill.: Chiron Publications.

Strauss, R. (1974). "Countertransference." In Fordham, M. *et al.* (eds.), *Technique in Jungian Analysis*. London: Heinemann.

# 9

ELIO J. FRATTAROLI

# Me and my anima: through the dark glass of the Jungian/Freudian interface

The present day shows with appalling clarity how little able people are to let the other man's argument count, although this capacity is a fundamental and indispensable condition for any human community. Everyone who proposes to come to terms with himself must reckon with this basic problem. For, to the degree that he does not admit the validity of the other person, he denies the "other" within himself the right to exist – and vice versa. The capacity for inner dialogue is a touchstone for outer objectivity.
(C. G. Jung, "The Transcendent Function")

Without Contraries is no progression. Attraction and Repulsion, Reason and Energy, Love and Hate, are necessary to Human existence.
(William Blake, *The Marriage of Heaven and Hell*)

When Polly Young-Eisendrath first asked me to write this essay on the interface between analytical psychology and other psychoanalytic schools, it sounded like a daunting task and I doubted that I was qualified to undertake it. I equivocated, asking her what exactly she meant by "other psycho-analytic schools." "Oh, you know," she replied with an ambiguous smile, "hermeneutical approaches, object-relations theory, interpersonal psy-chology, the various 'self'-psychologies, Kleinian theory, *and your personal favorite*, drive theory." I felt an immediate sense of relief, born of a deep inner certitude that I would be utterly incapable of writing such an essay.

Well, to be honest, Polly didn't actually say "*and your personal favorite*," but it's the sort of thing she might have said. We've been discussing such matters for ten years in a weekly study group of psychologists and psychiatrists. It is a fascinatingly, sometimes frustratingly, diverse group, but we all share two beliefs: first, that "the child is father of the man," otherwise known (by academics) as the developmental perspective; and second, that the search for truth requires a dialectic of differing perspectives, otherwise known (by normal people) as the need to argue. True to that need, I'm sure everyone else in the group would groan in dismay at my misapplication of Wordsworth's line. The idea that a child can father himself suggests that an individual is self-contained, has a private line of development, and can be considered in isolation from the interpersonal matrix of family and society. "No, no!" my friends would protest. "An individual is constituted by and develops in an interpersonal context, always in relation to an expanding world of others, starting with mother." They would tendentiously quote Winnicott's (1960) comment that there is no such thing as a baby, and smugly insist that I should have said "the dyad is parent of the person." Especially Polly, who is fond of arguing that an individual private self is a social fiction, the shared construct of a culture dominated by men who are terrified of relatedness.

Of course Polly does acknowledge that Jung's central preoccupation and focus was nothing other than the development of a private self considered in isolation. She calls herself a Jungian, but she is an unorthodox, reconstructed one. And that's the kind of Freudian she accuses me of being. I claim that the psychoanalytic process, in both its Jungian and Freudian evolution, is quintessentially a process of getting in touch with one's private self, in its discernible distinctness from one's socially constructed self. This is not what most Jungians think most Freudians believe or practice. Jung (1975) complained that Freud's was a system of stereotyped reductive interpretations, aimed primarily at improved social adjustment, explaining everything in terms of an innate infantile disposition to perverse hedonism. That's the prejudiced view Polly would have been implying had she actually said "*and your personal favorite*" before she said "drive theory." She didn't. I only imagined it, but once the words came spilling out onto my computer screen, I had to respond to them. Before long, I found that what I had originally intended as a brief personal introduction to the essay was turning into an extended imaginary dialogue between me and my image of Polly – a creative product of my deeply private self, filtered through years of social construction with Polly and my other friends in the study group.

I now had a decision to make. Should I "go with the flow" of my creative impulse and write the entire essay as an imaginary dialogue – a scene from my own inner drama – or should I opt for the more traditional academic presentation that readers would expect to find in a *Cambridge Companion?* I decided to compromise, going with the inner dialogue but adding the brief academic preamble which you are now about to read:

This chapter is intended to be read at two levels: the level of content and that of process, or form. At the level of content it is a discussion of similarities and differences between Jungian and Freudian psychology. At the level of process it is a *dramatic* enactment, in the form of an inner dialogue, of the Jungian concept of the *anima* – more specifically of the relationship between a man (me) and his anima (my *image* of Polly). The *anima* is the unconscious female aspect of a man's personality (the *animus* being the parallel unconscious male aspect of a woman's), with which he is in perpetual conflict but must ultimately come to terms if he is to attain the level of maturity that Jung refers to as individuation.

The anima can be considered as a general form – an *archetype* – or as a particular embodiment of the archetype in an individual, i.e. a personal *complex*. An archetype is a psychological/motivational pattern inherent in the human nature of all men, "a typical basic form, of certain ever-recurring psychic experiences," as Jung defined it (*CW* 6, p. 444). Its universal features are represented in myths (typical anima-myths being those of Eros and Psyche, Pluto and Persephone, Perseus and Medusa), which are distilled cultural expressions of archetypal motifs. But for any archetype, each individual will have his or her own particular version – a complex, that varies from one person to the next, depending on life experiences and constitutional factors. This complex is a stable attitudinal/emotional/motivational pattern within the overall personality of an individual.

In any relationship with a woman, a man will tend to *project* elements of his anima-complex, as an *image*, onto the woman; he will perceive her through filtering lenses that reveal only those aspects of the real woman that conform to the unconscious prototype in his anima. This will lead to a subtle skewing of his attitudes and responses to her, based not on how she actually presents herself but on the anima-image he projects onto her (which affects his *interpretation* of how she presents herself). Thus in relating to a real woman a man is also trying to relate to the disowned female part of himself, dialectically working toward a higher level of integration within his conflicted self-experience. The famous "battle of the sexes" owes its ubiquity to this fact (and to its parallel manifestation in women). It expresses in externalized form the inner conflict from which every man and woman suffers.

When the projection of the anima and subsequent battle with the "anima-bearer" happen in a patient's relationship with his psychoanalyst (as sooner or later they always do, even when the therapist is a man) they constitute the *transference*.[1] They are essential steps in a dialectical process of integration (individuation), that ends when the patient can say – *à la* Walt Kelly's cartoon character Pogo – "We have met the anima, and he is us." This therapeutic process happens more easily when the analyst is relatively silent, refraining from injecting too much of his or her own personality into the dialogue with the patient, thereby leaving the patient free to project onto the analyst (and then protest against) whatever image he needs to, without having to be distracted by superfluous data about what the analyst is really like.

An imaginary dialogue like the one I am about to present between Polly and me will tend to highlight the effects of projection in the same way that analytic transference does. Since the real Polly is not present to counter-balance my projective tendency, I will more readily imagine her half of the dialogue in terms of my projected anima-image, which will then be much more in evidence than it would be in a real conversation. This may strike the reader as too personally revealing a form in which to discuss general psychological principles, but it is also the *only* form – an interpersonal conversation or an interior dialogue – in which we can actually observe the psychological phenomena these principles have been formulated to describe. My purpose therefore is not to write a professional gossip column about the real person, Polly, or my relationship with her (which might be fun for the small group of readers who know us and our theoretical opinions, but would be irrelevant and distracting for everyone else) but to illustrate general principles (the archetype, transference, inner conflict) as they are manifest in the particulars (my own personal anima-projections) of an individual psyche.

I might add that I consider such a form to be more scientific than the usual academic style of presentation. The nature of psychological phe-nomena is such that the observed – inner experience – cannot be clearly distinguished from the observer – the introspective/empathic experiencer. The situation is analogous to that in nuclear physics, where an elementary particle cannot be clearly distinguished from the apparatus – the observa-tional framework – through which it is measured. To achieve scientific objectivity in either realm – or in any realm of experience where the observer constitutes an important part of what is observed – a full description is required both of the observed phenomenon and of the observational frame-work through which the observation is made. In psychology this observa-tional framework is nothing other than the personality of the observer. To achieve an objective scientific description of an inner experience, therefore, it is essential that I describe the personality conflicts, foibles, and prejudices that might have influenced my introspective/empathic observation of that experience. So if I seem to reveal too much of my own personality in what follows, I do so intentionally. My purpose is to describe my own private experience of inner conflict (between me and my anima) in a way that allows the reader to assess for him- or herself the validity of my subjective observations and of the objective conclusions I draw from them. Remember that just because you don't see the subjective determinants of a theory (as in the more usual academic presentation) doesn't mean they aren't there, or that they haven't profoundly influenced, and perhaps distorted, the observa-tions that are then taken as the objective basis for the theory.

"I'm definitely not your man – I mean *person* – Polly," I replied. "I don't know nearly enough about Jung to do a credible job on that kind of essay. And by the way, the only reason you think drive theory is my personal favorite is because it is *your* favorite target for attack. You probably don't even notice yourself attacking because you do it so elegantly and deftly. You only notice me responding to your attack, because I do it clumsily, with passionate intensity. When you put down drive theory, I take it personally (speaking both for me and Freud) and I feel a natural compulsion to defend our honor. Nevertheless, as I have been trying to tell you for ten years, I don't really think about instinctual drives when I think about patients. I think about disowned aspects of the self, or warded-off feelings, trying to push their way into awareness."

"But Elio, that's exactly why you *should* write this essay. [smiling sweetly] That way of thinking is just as Jungian as it is Freudian. So you see, you've already articulated the basis for your essay! And by the way, could you define what you mean by a 'natural compulsion?' It sounds suspiciously like an instinctual drive to me."

"Well, sure it does [off-balance for a moment], and that's my whole point about why drive theory makes sense. [recovering with a flourish] It's very close to lived experience."

"Elio, that is such an outlandish statement. I'm sure you don't really mean it. [still smiling] You couldn't possibly read Freud and come away with a sense that drive theory is experience-near. It is widely recognized that drive theory was Freud's failed attempt to make clinical experience fit the Procrustean bed of nineteenth-century science. I can't believe any analyst of any persuasion would claim that 'libidinal cathexis' is an experience-near concept."

"Well, I don't know about other analysts, but I do know that all I have to do is get into an argument with you, Polly, and I feel very near to my own experience of driven-ness. [warming to the subject even while losing control of it] Remember that 'cathexis' is Strachey's translation, not Freud's term. And whether a concept is experience-near or not depends on how you interpret it. Take the idea of 'dammed-up libido, spilling over into free-floating anxiety.' You could be mean-spirited and call it hydraulic, even naively scientistic, but to me it's a perfectly good way of describing raw unscientific experience. If that's too outlandish a thing to say, it only proves my point that you should get someone else to write the essay."

"Oh no, I'm not falling for that one! [finally dropping that irritating Mona Lisa smile] That's the first time in ten years I've heard you refer to 'dammed-up libido,' even as an unscientific metaphor. Whatever silly male-bonding loyalty you have to drive theory, I'm sure you will soon outgrow it, because you consistently talk in a very different language when you're not trying to taunt me."

"OK, OK. I was being provocative and misleading. The real truth is, no Freudian psychoanalyst nowadays uses the concepts of cathexis, instinctual discharge or even libido, at all. They are history. They belong to Freud's so-called economic theory (hydraulic if you like) of psychic energy which was effectively destroyed through the combined work of Hartmann, Rapaport, and Jacobson in the 1950s (Apfelbaum, 1965)."

"Wait a minute. I thought those three especially used the economic model extensively in their writing."

"Exactly. They elaborated the theory far beyond anything Freud ever would have done, pushing the concepts beyond the limits of their explanatory usefulness, to the point where it became obvious to everyone except themselves that the hydraulic model just didn't work. No one really understood all that cathexis mumbo-jumbo. Of course at the time everyone nodded sagely, but the next generation of analysts, especially Rapaport's students George Klein (1969), Merton Gill (1976), and Robert Holt (1976), began to say loud and clear that this particular emperor had no clothes. I've always considered it ironic that Hartmann, Rapaport, and Jacobson became known as developers of 'ego psychology,' when what they were really doing was taking the ego-concept of Freud's most progressive post-1920 theorizing and twisting it beyond all recognition, as you say, on the Procrustean bed of his most reductionistic pre-1900 theorizing. Their dogmatic elaboration of the weakest element in Freud's thought was a thinly disguised expression of the disciple's repressed death wish against the master: attempted murder by imitation, an unconsciously mocking caricature born of the fear of open disagreement. The real ego psychologists were people like Erikson (1950, 1959) and Waelder (1930, 1967), who didn't go out of their way to announce their disagreement with Freud, but who had almost no use at all for his economic model and its scientistic reductionism. They were loyal to Freud's best thought, which was always experience-near, based on clinical experience, and synthetic, based on the theory of the self implicit in Freud's original terminology for the ego-concept (*das Ich*, properly translated as 'the I,' and *das Über-Ich*, as 'the I that stands above'). The progressive synthetic thrust in Freud's theorizing was present from the beginning but was much more obvious after he replaced the concept of libido with that of Eros."

"Wait a minute, that doesn't sound like the Freud I know. I wasn't aware that either Freud or his followers had ever done much to develop his concept of Eros, yet you're talking about it as if it were the cornerstone of his mature thought. Secondly, I thought you believed passionately in drive theory. Now you're telling me that Robert Waelder, by your account the greatest Freudian thinker after Freud, had no use for it?"

"No, you misunderstand me, but now I see why we always end up arguing about drive theory. You are confusing it with libido theory. True, the two did go together originally. Freud conceptualized libido as the unique form of psychic energy corresponding to the sexual drive. But the concept of a sexual drive never depended on the concept of libido. This became evident in 1920 when Freud introduced his so-called dual-instinct theory. He added the new concept of a destructive/aggressive drive (death instinct) to that of a sexual drive but he didn't add another form of energy to go with it. Although he didn't officially discard the libido concept, the much richer concept of Eros pretty much superseded it. Eros was no longer an energy concept, but rather a force or tendency, like Bergson's *élan vital*. It paved the way for the 1923 structural theory of id–ego–superego (the *It*, the *I*, and the *I that stands above*), and for Freud's revolutionary revision of anxiety theory in 1926. With this new metapsychology based on Eros and the destructive/aggressive drive, it became much more natural to talk about the drives in an experience-near way, as the compelling motivational forces behind the emotions of love and hate."

"OK, that doesn't fully answer my question about Eros, but tell me, what's your actual definition of a drive, and how different is it from Freud's?"

"Well Freud talked about drive as a concept on the border between the psychological and the somatic, but his definition was fuzzy. Waelder (1960) emphasized that the real meaning of 'drive' is contained in the connotations of Freud's original German word, *Trieb*, which suggests a powerfully compelling force, both goal-directed and organically rooted in man's physical nature. I would elaborate on that to say that *a drive is a powerful striving rooted in the psychobiological universals of human nature that expresses itself in the psychobiological particulars of unconscious fantasy.*"

"Hm. That sounds like a Jungian archetype. And what's your definition of unconscious fantasy?"

"*Unconscious fantasy is an interpersonal, emotionally charged, goal-directed scenario that a person is driven to enact behaviorally, while remaining unaware of it as a conscious feeling state or motivation.* You could think of a drive as a kind of psychobiological template for an unconscious fantasy. The drives embody the basic organization of human nature. They determine the emotional charge, the motivational goals, and the adaptive purposes of unconscious fantasies and of the unconsciously driven behavior these fantasies generate."

"This is really interesting. And where does your notion of unconscious fantasy come from? Because it sounds just like what Jung called a complex."

"Well, the concept originated when Freud (1897a) concluded that his patients were suffering from repressed fantasies rather than repressed memories. He thought of unconscious fantasies as individual variations on the theme of the Oedipus complex. The concept was much more extensively developed by object-relations theorists, Melanie Klein and her followers (1948, 1952, 1957), Fairbairn (1954), and more recently Kernberg (1980) and Ogden (1990), who emphasize that the inner world is entirely structured in terms of fantasy configurations, not only the Oedipus complex, but the paranoid-schizoid position and the depressive position. I also like the writings of Arlow (1963, 1969), Lichtenstein (1961), and Stoller (1979, 1985) on unconscious fantasy, but I don't know how relevant they are to Jung. You know, it's embarrassing but I've read very little Jung since those introductory lectures you gave when you first joined the study group. I really have no business writing about Jung for the *Cambridge Companion*."

"Oh stop it, Elio. Even before you had read any Jung at all I told you you were more Jungian in your thinking than I was."

"Hey, is it my fault that when I got in touch with my inner experience it resembled what Jung wrote about? Anyway, I did that in a completely orthodox Freudian analysis, while training in an institute known for its orthodoxy."

"Oh sure, but you also said you chose that institute because you wanted to be sure you knew the classical theory really well before you rebelled against it. You knew you would end up rebelling so you wanted your rebellion to be an informed one, right? That's why your understanding of the psychoanalytic process is so much like mine, because you rebelled, as Jung did, against the narrow Freudian model. There's simply no way you can call yourself an orthodox Freudian, whatever your training was like!"

"Not if you define orthodoxy in terms of the psychoanalysis of the 1950s. But there's been a lot of evolution in the field since then. The definition of drive and unconscious fantasy I just gave you would be recognized as pristine in its orthodoxy today, even by older analysts who would have considered it alien forty years ago. As far as what I said about my need to rebel, that was my bitchy anima talking, before I recognized and reclaimed it in my personal analysis."

"You reclaimed your anima in an orthodox Freudian analysis?"

"Well, I didn't call it that. I called it getting in touch with my envy of femininity and my desire to be a woman. I recognized that my need to rebel was compulsive, based on the fact that embracing orthodoxy had the unconscious meaning to me of being a submissive woman."

"I don't know, Elio. Considering that yours is always the loudest dissenting voice in the study group, I don't see you as having outgrown your compulsive need to rebel, or your defensive male sexism."

"So I haven't achieved perfect enlightenment. So sue me! . . . 'said the poor misunderstood doctor amiably.' "

"Did you learn disavowal in your orthodox analysis too?"

"Yes, but I haven't perfected it yet. Seriously Polly, I don't think a person ever outgrows the tendency to feel driven, or stops acting out unconscious fantasies. Especially not under the kind of relentless provocation I get from you people in the study group! The goal of psychological integration should be that you notice yourself feeling driven, that you can catch yourself in the enactment of a fantasy. You can then recognize that there is another way of inner being, a disposition to a different sort of action, that you are fighting against even as you fight your apparently external dragon. But that doesn't mean you should necessarily stop fighting the dragon. You know what William Blake said: 'Without contraries is no progression.' "

"Yes, in *The Marriage of Heaven and Hell*. And that's just the kind of contrariness I want for *The Cambridge Companion*, Elio. You know what Heraclitus said: 'War is the father of all.' That was one of Jung's favorite aphorisms."

"Whoa, duelling allusions! Well then, if I'm really such a closet Jungian, why am I so uncertain whether I understand even basic terms like *anima*? I tried to read about it once but I couldn't take all the mythology and decided I was better off consulting my own inner experience of femaleness. I understand that the mythology is actually supposed to represent inner experience, but it didn't work that way for me. You know what Keats wrote about negative capability, 'when man is capable of being in uncertainties, mysteries and doubts without any irritable reaching after fact and reason'? Well I think Jung was sometimes guilty of an irritable reaching after myth!"

"Actually, if you're in the right frame of mind, with a little 'willing suspension of disbelief' [*touché*], all those mythical references from different ages and cultures really can help expand your awareness of inner experience. On the other hand, I do think Jung sometimes piles on mythological references to make a point, to prove that certain experiences are universal, archetypal."

"Right. So tell me again, what are archetypes and complexes?"

"*Archetypes are basic organizing forms for expression of human instinctual-emotional responses in relationship. Complexes are integrated configurations of personal images, ideas, feelings and actions that are organized around archetypes.* I think of complexes as 'affective schemata,' similar to what you have just described as emotionally charged scenarios, that are habitually enacted in relationships and in dreams. They can be experienced as moods or fantasies or projections, and can also be expressed in symptoms."

"Sounds pretty much like drives and unconscious fantasies to me. Is that the way Jung talked about them?"

"Well, I don't think he would have disagreed with the way I said it, but he put much more emphasis on the 'image,' the mythic symbol that comes into consciousness through the work of active imagination. He thought of an archetype as an archaic image from the collective unconscious, and a complex as an individualized version of that primordial image, from the personal unconscious. But you have to understand that for Jung a mythological image, even when it came in the form of a picture like the mandala, was not just a pictorial representation. It had all the connotations of drivenness you were ascribing to a compelling, powerfully emotional, unconscious fantasy."

"Like the Oedipus complex. That's certainly a mythological image. In fact, don't you think it was probably Freud's discussion of Oedipus that got Jung interested in mythology in the first place?"

"Sure. Jung was only twenty-five and just graduating from medical school in 1900 when he first read *The Interpretation of Dreams*, and he didn't seriously begin to study mythology until 1909. By that time he was a key figure in Freud's inner circle, and they were all writing about mythology."

"Yeah, I guess Otto Rank's *The Myth of the Birth of the Hero* came out in 1909. You know, although Freud had developed the Oedipal theory of neurosis as far back as an 1897 letter to Fliess (1897b), he didn't officially call it the Oedipus *complex* until 1910, when his romance with Jung was at its peak. He must have decided to call it a complex in honor of Jung."

"Could be. Of course you know that the two men ultimately split over their differing interpretations of the Oedipus complex and the meaning of incest."

"Well, I know what Freud wrote about the split, which is that Jung denied the central importance of infantile sexuality."

"Right. Jung believed in an expanded concept of libido as life energy, somewhat the way you described Freud's concept of Eros as a life force. To Jung, the Oedipal desire of a five-year-old boy, while it does contain a current of infantile sexuality, is mostly about his dependence and his desire to possess the mother for her powerful protective factor. It is not a desire for actual incest, but for mother's nurturing love and the sense of security that comes with it. Jung felt that this infantile dependency became sexualized only sometimes, and only much later, in the course of post-pubertal neurotic conflict. In adult neuroses, incestuous impulses do become activated, as a regressive retreat from the demand that mature sexual desire puts on the growing individual to break out of the parental orbit. But Jung argued that these incestuous impulses represent not only a pathological retreat from conflict but also an adaptive 'falling back and regrouping,' a necessary step toward resolving the conflict. Contrasting his position with Freud's, Jung emphasized that neurosis embodies not only a regressive sexual purpose but a progressive developmental and spiritual one."

"Well, the general idea that neurotic symptoms represent a progressive as well as a regressive purpose is quintessentially Freudian. And the idea of a developmental and spiritual progression, I would argue, is also very much Freudian. As you know, I have written (1991) about psychoanalysis as a philosophy of the quest, which I think of in both developmental and spiritual terms. Libido theory notwithstanding, there was always a strong but implicit spiritual dimension in Freud's theorizing. It became almost explicit in his concepts of Eros and of the superego."

"That's certainly not the way I've ever understood the superego, Elio. Didn't Freud describe it as the internalization of parental restrictions and prohibitions? As I've understood it, Freud saw neurosis as an expression of the conflict between instinct and culture, with the superego representing culture; whereas Jung saw the conflict as an inherent tension between opposing forces within the self. Not instinct versus culture, but instinct versus spirit."

"You're only describing one aspect of the superego, what you might call a 'superego complex' as opposed to the *I that stands above* as an archetype. You should really read Waelder (1930, 1960, 1965) on the superego, or my (1990) paper on *Hamlet* where I discuss Waelder's approach. The idea of an *Über-Ich*, an *I that stands above*, originated in Freud's thinking about psychotic delusions of being observed, which he took as a kind of perception of a self-observing agency within the self. Along with the *I* and the *It*, he then incorporated this agency into his tripartite model of the psyche, a modern counterpart to the rational/spiritual element in Plato's tripartite soul (reason, will, appetite). So this instinct-versus-culture view of neurosis really represents a serious misunderstanding of the Freudian superego. The whole idea of the Oedipus complex is that conflict over sexual and aggressive strivings is inherent in human nature, not a function of cultural values. Sure Freud talked about the clash between instinct and culture, and the internalization of parental and cultural prohibitions, but why would anyone who was purely motivated by blind instinct bother to internalize something he or she was blindly opposed to? The 'I that stands above' is the part of the self that agrees with culture. It's the part of the self that made culture in the first place!"

"Elio, when was the last time you read *Civilization and its Discontents* (1930)? What in the world is it about if not the conflict between instinct and culture? You know, Jung isn't the only person to reject Freudian theory as a philosophy of hedonism. You can hardly deny that Freud described human beings as infantile pleasure-seeking machines, programmed to seek immediate gratification of every impulse unless forced to delay, divert or sublimate by the demands of a hostile and punitive society."

"Polly, when was the last time *you* read *Civilization and its Discontents*? Yes, I know it contains many references to the conflict between instinct and culture. But in the end Freud does a very Jungian thing and uses a myth to express the essence of that conflict in the origin of the superego. It's the myth he made up himself in *Totem and Taboo* (1913), about the primal brothers killing the primal father. Freud says that in that timeless epoch of the primal imagination there was as yet no individual superego and no cultural prohibition against killing the father. Both came into being at the same time through the great *remorse* the brothers felt after the deed. Freud states unequivocally that this remorse stemmed from the innate, unconditioned love of the sons for the father, just as the murder stemmed from their innate hatred, the other half of an archaic ambivalence. For Freud, the sense of guilt which is the foundation of civilization is an expression of that same ambivalence, the eternal struggle between the instinct of destruction and Eros. He didn't go quite so far as to call that a conflict between instinct and spirit, but it amounts to the same thing."

"You're right, I had forgotten that part of his argument. So sue me! [with a real smile!] But still, would you really deny that the overwhelming impression Freud leaves you with is that of the irreconcilable opposition of instinct and culture?"

"Well no. That's what everyone comes away with when they read *Civilization and its Discontents*. And I'll tell you why. That particular book is a good example of Freud's own unresolved ambivalence between his old libido theory and his new dual-instinct theory. He keeps going back and forth between the old model and the new, mixing formulations about the economics of libidinal energy with discussions of Eros as if they belonged together. But the fact is the libido theory was based on the constancy principle, which is antithetical to Eros. In fact, it is identical to the Nirvana principle of the death instinct – the idea that the organism seeks the lowest energy state through immediate discharge of all drive energy. That's your Freudian philosophy of hedonism. Eros, on the other hand, belongs to Freud's philosophy of the quest."

"The death instinct is based on the same principle as the old libido theory!?"

"You got it. Somewhere or other Freud even acknowledges that the constancy principle and the Nirvana principle are one and the same, but he never acknowledged the uncomfortable implication that libido would then really belong under the sign of the death instinct, not under the sign of Eros. It takes a very subtle and careful reading to detect how this confusion runs through *Civilization and its Discontents*, as it does through all Freud's major works, even early ones, like Chapter 7 of the *Interpretation of Dreams.*"

"Wait. How could he have confused the two models at a time when only one of them existed?"

"Well during the first phase of his thinking the confusion was between two different senses he gave to the concept of libido, the one I've emphasized – a dammed-up sexual energy looking for a path to hedonistic discharge – and a more experience-near sense, as the force behind wishing, or an expanded sexuality that was a way of talking about love without admitting it – basically an early version of Eros."

"That's really Jung's idea of libido."

"Maybe so, but he could have gotten the idea from Freud, simply by distilling out half of Freud's ambivalent usage of the term. You know I believe that with Freud, as with any great thinker, there was a creative tension between two poles in his thinking: the *regressive* pole, in which he was constrained by familial attitudes and the dominating cultural assumptions he grew up with, and the *progressive* pole of his authentically original, 'counter-cultural' contribution. True creativity in general depends on the progressive, 'antithetical' element being strong enough to transcend the limitations of the old paradigm, but the process is never a clean one. In the end the great thinkers are all like Michelangelo's 'Prisoners,' struggling nobly to break free from the constraining, inarticulate marble, but only partly succeeding. Freud is no exception."

"Oh Elio, you're such a romantic! But you have to admit you had to chip away a lot of inarticulate marble to find a quest philosophy in Freudian psychoanalysis!"

"Well actually, psychoanalysis contains two conflicting but complementary philosophies, one the quest philosophy of Eros, and the other the egoistic, hedonistic pleasure/pain philosophy of the libido theory. But I didn't really come to the idea of the quest through reading Freud. It was much more my personal experience of the psychoanalytic process, which I then took back to my reading of Freud and Waelder. Well, no. I'm forgetting my years teaching at Bruno Bettelheim's Orthogenic School (Frattaroli, 1992, 1994). Bettelheim regularly talked and wrote (1967) about life as a kind of a quest, a continual striving for ever higher levels of integration through resolving inner conflicts. The first chapter of *The*

*Informed Heart* (1960) is titled 'The Concordance of Opposites,' by which he means the pursuit of self-realization through a continual process of psychological integration within a basically irreconcilable conflict."

"But that's Jung's idea. Sometimes he called it the *complexio oppositorum*, sometimes the *coniunctio oppositorum*, but he was talking about exactly the same thing as Bettelheim."

"Well maybe so, but Bettelheim certainly thought of it as Freud's idea. His psychoanalytic background was strictly Freudian, and I don't think he knew much about Jung until he reviewed Carotenuto's book on Jung and Sabina Spielrein in 1983. Erikson is also a Freudian, and he had basically the same idea of the quest as well. He described the life cycle as a progressive struggle toward wisdom and virtue, through a series of developmental crises organized around sets of oppositions: trust versus mistrust; autonomy versus shame and doubt; initiative versus guilt; industry versus inferiority; identity versus diffusion; intimacy versus isolation; generativity versus stagnation; integrity versus despair. I think that both Bettelheim and Erikson got their ideas of self-realization through integration of opposites from Freud, not Jung. Freud may never have used the term *coniunctio oppositorum*, but his dual-instinct theory strongly suggests the idea. It posits a conflicting combination of Eros and the death instinct in every piece of psychic life. By the way, Freud recognized that his theory had ancient philosophical parallels, not only with Plato's Eros but with Empedocles' universal dialectic of Love and Strife. I guess that's a kind of archetype for the interpersonal dialectic of the psychoanalytic process. So the quest philosophy is implicit in the goal of the psychoanalytic process, to integrate the opposing, ambivalent tendencies of Love and Strife through the ongoing dialectical experience of transference. That is the work of Eros: bringing together, integration, synthesis, love in the full Platonic sense of the term. So you could say that the spiritual source for Freud's quest philosophy was in the original Greek quest philosophies, the Eros of Plato's *Symposium* and the dialectical dualism of Empedocles' Love and Strife."

"Which was very similar to the spiritual source for Jung's philosophy of individuation, in Heraclitus. He too posited an eternally creative dialectic, in which the war of opposites is resolved in the transcendent function."

"Then there really is a strong common theme between Freud and Jung. Think about Freud's famous epigram for the psychoanalytic process: 'Where id was there ego shall be.' *Wo Es war, da soll Ich werden.* Then think about the proper translation: 'Where It was there shall I become.' If you take Freud's *It* as the psychobiological unknown, the unconscious realm of the drives, and the *I*, along with the *I that stands above*, as the self-reflective integrated self, evolving through its perpetual clash with the *It*, then don't you come out with the same thing Heraclitus said? Clearly I didn't get that idea from Jung, but from what you have said it sounds like that was pretty much his idea too."

"That's an understatement! It was the essence of his life's work, starting well before he met Freud. That's what his seminal concept of individuation is all about. He saw individuation as the process of becoming an authentic integrated person, through a synthesis of opposites in the personality. It is the work of the transcendent function, which he wrote about first in 1916, and I think of as somewhat similar to Winnicott's (1971) idea of 'potential space' – holding the tension of opposites until a new discovery or perspective emerges. And by the way, that's where Jung's different view of incest comes in. Like everything else, Jung understood individuation in terms of a symbol, in this case a symbolic internal 'marriage' between the conscious ego complex and the unconscious complexes, the undiscovered self, especially the anima or animus. Well, a marriage with your own anima or animus is like incest, a marriage within the inner nuclear (Oedipal) family, so to speak. So ultimately Jung came to see incestuous desires not as primarily sexual but as spiritual, a longing for inner unity, and he began to understand incest as a mystical symbol for the process of individuation."

"And that idea of individuation is the cornerstone of Jung's psychology?"

"Absolutely."

"So in the end Jung really agreed with Freud that the Oedipus complex, at least the incestuous part of it, is the key to neurosis?"

"Well that's certainly a Freudian way of putting it, emphasizing pathology rather than adaptation. Jung would have called it the key to growth. But it is absolutely true that he remained quite preoccupied with the issue of incest throughout his life. Incestuous images were central in his quasi-psychotic, quasi-mystical visions in the years immediately following his breakup with Freud, and in his mystical visions after his 1944 heart attack. In important works after 1944, Jung's explicit program was a revisioning of Freud's Oedipal complex as an archetype for the process of individuation. I'm thinking specifically of *The Psychology of the Transference* and his last major work, *Mysterium Coniunctionis*, subtitled *An Inquiry into the Separation and Synthesis of Psychic Opposites in Alchemy*. Actually all Jung's obscure works on alchemy which people find so alienating and intimidating are really about symbolic incest. Although, as we've been saying, the synthesis of psychic opposites is a valid and powerful concept even without alchemy, Jung had a strong need to conceptualize it as an alchemical incestuous union, producing an integrated self the way the 'chemical marriage' of the alchemists was supposed to produce gold. He also conceptualized the psychoanalytic relationship as a kind of symbolically enacted incestuous union, viewing the transference as an alchemical crucible from which the gold of individuation would emerge."

"Yeah, well, considering his relationships with Sabina Spielrein and Toni Wolff, it looks like Jung had a bit of trouble discriminating where symbolism ends and sexual intercourse begins. Which, as a Freudian, I would argue proves pretty convincingly that he never really dealt with his down-and-dirty infantile sexual Oedipus complex. Instead he acted it out, all the while denying that the Oedipus complex in that sense even existed. Didn't Jung use against Freud the idea that any psychological theory is limited by the theorist's particular personality limitations? How about applying it to him? As a feminist, don't you think that all those grandiose ideas about alchemical incestuous symbolism begin to sound suspiciously like a callow rationalization, an erudite excuse for Jung's unconscionable boundary violations as a therapist?"

"Well frankly, yes. But you know, Jung didn't really deny the infantile sexual version of the Oedipus complex. He only insisted that it was a regressive sexualization of a complex that was not primarily sexual in its origin, similar to what Heinz Kohut thought. With that proviso, he did consider the Oedipus complex an important and necessary focus for the analysis of people in the first half of life. Still, I agree that Jung's therapeutic misconduct and his lack of respect for women were connected to a poorly analyzed Oedipus complex – and to a powerful mother complex, and to an unintegrated anima."

"Would you agree too that his failure to come to terms with his Freudian Oedipus complex would have necessarily put a serious limitation on the degree of Jungian individuation he could achieve?"

"Sure, but Jung never denied that he had limitations. And let's not get carried away. You obviously agree with what is essential in Jung's theory of individuation. The fact that some aspects of that theory may have consti-tuted a rationalization for him doesn't make the theory incorrect."

"Well, there must be something wrong with it! If his theory, like anybody else's theory, inevitably expresses his psychic blind spots, then it must at the very least be missing something. And what about the issue of his anti-Semitism?"

"Well that's complicated. The C. G. Jung Foundation held a conference on the subject in 1989, and the proceedings have been published (Maiden-baum and Martin, 1991). The overall consensus was that despite many examples of his non-prejudicial and empathic dealings with Jewish friends, colleagues, and patients, Jung's thought and actions did contain a current of anti-Semitism, reflecting his own shadow, his religious upbringing, and the pervasive cultural climate of anti-Semitism that prevailed everywhere up until the Holocaust. I guess that was part of Jung's inarticulate marble that he couldn't fully free himself from. There was an important unresolved difference of opinion at the conference, though, about whether this personal failing in Jung translates to a deficiency in Jungian theory."

"How could it not? Like I said, there has to be something missing!"

"And Freud's isn't missing something?"

"Of course it is. As Jung pointed out many times, Freud was missing an appreciation of the spiritual dimension of experience. He admitted openly in the first section of *Civilization and its Discontents* that he had never experienced anything resembling the oceanic feeling of spiritual sensibility. That was definitely an area of unresolved neurotic conflict for him. I think the spiritual fascinated him, but he was terrified of it, especially Jung's occult mystical-psychotic version. I'm sure he would have objected to the spiritual meaning I give to Eros and to his dictum 'Where It was there shall I become.' To me these meanings are obvious, but to Freud they would have been disowned meanings. And in spite of what I have said about Eros and the quest philosophy, you're right that Freud never really established it as the psychoanalytic paradigm. So I'd be willing to say, Bettelheim and Erikson notwithstanding, that Freud's theory was missing the concept of individuation. It was always implicit, it became partly visible, but in the end remained fairly stuck in that marble. So then what is Jungian theory missing? The concept of the drives?"

"Well, yes and no. The archetypes are certainly related to the drives, but they don't have the experience-near quality you claim drives do. The archetypes, like the drives, are the carriers of powerful emotion, but then Jung's idea about powerful emotions was a bit dissociative. He argued that emotions, unlike feelings, literally put you beside yourself, as if you were possessed by another personality."

"That *is* dissociative. How did he understand the feeling of anxiety that gets activated when a strong emotion threatens to assert itself?"

"He didn't. Jung really had very little to say about anxiety."

"Really!! Well maybe that's what's missing. You know, anxiety was Freud's central lifelong preoccupation, the way individuation was Jung's. So maybe Jung's mysticism was never a fully integrated experience. Maybe the reason it always had a near-psychotic edge to it was because it also represented a flight from profound anxiety which he didn't recognize as such. Probably anxiety about his own destructiveness more than his own sexuality. He certainly never dealt with the destructive aspects of the Oedipus complex that he acted out in his exploitation of patients and in his anti-Semitism, both of which he then tried to rationalize through theoretical disputes with Freud."

"Very plausible, but I must tell you that in daring to penetrate Jung's shortcomings through a Freudian analysis, you've claimed mastery of several theories and proven yourself capable of writing the essay!"

"No way! I was just following your lead. So why don't you write the essay! You've already written about Jung's self psychology, and its parallels to Sullivan, Piaget, and object relations theory (Young-Eisendrath and Hall, 1991)."

"Yes, but I can't write about Freud the way you can. Although I *was* thinking that maybe the progressive elements in Freud that you, Bettelheim, and Erikson have elaborated into a quest philosophy really got into his theory primarily through Jung's influence. They all came after 1920, which would have given Freud five years to emotionally process the breakup with Jung and then use it to energize a major leap forward in his thinking. Certainly that's what Jung did. He was pretty crazy for about four years processing the breakup with Freud, but came out of it with *Psychological Types* (1921), which began the most creative phase of his thinking. So maybe both Freud and Jung went through parallel mirror-image versions of the same process. Even though neither gave the other an ounce of credit for anything they wrote after 1913, maybe each spent the rest of his life trying to integrate the other's contribution into his own new and improved theory."

"Wow. War is the father of all indeed! But if the main task of individuation for a man is to integrate his anima, does that mean that Freud and Jung were anima figures for each other, even though both were men?"

"Well, probably. Men do tend to project their anima on any number of people, as needed, in their lives. And that combination of charismatic attraction and compulsive antagonism is pretty typical of a man's struggle with his projected unintegrated anima."

"So that's what Heraclitus was talking about. But if war was the father, who was the mother?"

"Hmm. Are you thinking what I'm thinking?"

"Yes, but I don't want to be. Sabina Spielrein."

"Why, does it bother you that a woman might have been responsible for both Freud's and Jung's most creative ideas?"

"No, that was Bettelheim's (1983) idea, and I rather like it. What bothers me is John Kerr (1993), who proved Bettelheim's thesis without intending to. He presented new material from Spielrein's 'transformation journal,' a long 1907 letter to Jung in which she proposes that all mental life is governed by two fundamental tendencies, the power of the persistence of the complexes, and an instinct of transformation which seeks to transform the complexes. Spielrein reframed the idea in a 1912 publication, arguing that the sexual drive contains both an instinct of destruction and an instinct of transformation. There's the origin of the psychoanalytic quest philosophy, both Freud's dual-instinct theory *and* Jung's theory of individuation! But Kerr doesn't appreciate that evolution, so he misses the real importance of Spielrein's idea. His not-too-hidden agenda is to discredit Jung, Freud, and the whole psychoanalytic method, which, unfortunately, he doesn't understand either. He thinks that unless the method can be formulated in some kind of manual of interpretation, it shouldn't be taken seriously. But the psychoanalytic method was never a technique of interpretation! It's a technique of self-reflective awareness, a mode of attention to inner experience, within a relationship, in which the unconscious can become conscious with such clarity that it often requires very little interpretation. Kerr has no appreciation of this, or of the psychoanalytic process as a quest for self-realization. He thinks psychoanalysis is a hermeneutic exercise of theoretical interpretation. By the way, I won't write about hermeneutics. I hate drifting on a sea of self-referential signifiers with no hope of ever seeing the solid land of the signified. *Psychoanalysis is not about hermeneutics.* It's about putting felt experience into words."

"So say that in the essay! Look, Elio, I *need* an author for this chapter. I understand that you refuse to do anything resembling what I had in mind, and I can live with that – just as long as you're somewhere in the vicinity of the topic. Believe me, I racked my brains for a week trying to think of *anyone* who could write this essay, and you were the only person I could think of."

I was captured, tantalized by the thought that I was the last person in the world Polly would have considered, but the only person in the world she could think of to do the job. "That's how women have always had their way with men," I vaguely thought as I submitted to my fate. "OK, I'll do it. I have no idea what, but I'm sure I'll dream up something."

## NOTE

1   Transference is an important concept in both Jungian and Freudian psychoanalysis. It is a pattern of reacting to another person as if that person were an emotionally important figure from childhood (the idea being that feelings about a person from the past are "transferred" onto a person in the present). At the same time, it is a pattern of reacting to the other person as if they were an emotionally important but unconscious part of ourself – attributing to the other person feelings, attitudes and motives that are active but unconscious within us (the idea being that feelings about something internal are "transferred" onto someone external), so that we can recognize in the other person what we cannot tolerate recognizing in ourselves.

# REFERENCES

Apfelbaum, B. (1965). "Ego Psychology, Psychic Energy, and the Hazards of Quantitative Explanation." *International Journal of Psychoanalysis*, 46, pp. 168–182.

Arlow, J. (1963). "Conflict, Regression, and Symptom Formation." *International Journal of Psycho-analysis*, 44, pp. 12–22.

(1969). "Unconscious Fantasy and Disturbances of Conscious Experience." *Psychoanalytic Quarterly*, 38, pp. 1–27.

Bettelheim, B. (1960). *The Informed Heart: Autonomy in a Mass Age.* Glencoe, Ill.: Free Press.

(1967). *The Empty Fortress: Infantile Autism and the Birth of the Self.* New York: Free Press.

(1983). "A Secret Asymmetry." In *Freud's Vienna & Other Essays.* New York: Alfred A. Knopf, 1990, pp. 57–81.

Erikson, E. (1950). *Childhood and Society.* New York: W. W. Norton.

(1959). *Identity and the Life Cycle: Selected Papers.* New York: International Universities Press.

Fairbairn, W. R. D. (1954). *An Object Relations Theory of the Personality.* New York: Basic Books.

Frattaroli, E. (1990). "A New Look at *Hamlet*: Aesthetic Response and Shakespeare's Meaning." *International Journal of Psycho-Analysis*, 17, pp. 269–285.

(1991). "Psychotherapy and Medication: The Mind–Body Problem and the Choice of Intervention." In *The Psychiatric Times*, November, pp. 73ff.

(1992). "Orthodoxy and Heresy in the History of Psychoanalysis." In N. Szajnberg (ed.), *Educating the Emotions: Bruno Bettelheim and Psychoanalytic Development.* New York: Plenum Press, pp. 121–150.

(1994). "Bruno Bettelheim's Unrecognized Contribution to Psychoanalytic Thought." *The Psychoanalytic Review*, 81, pp. 379–409.

Freud, S. (1897a). Letter of 21 September. In J. Masson (tr. and ed.), *The Complete Letters of Sigmund Freud to Wilhelm Fliess, 1887–1904.* Cambridge, Mass.: Harvard University Press, 1985, pp. 264–266.

(1897b). Letter of 15 October, *ibid.* pp. 270–273.

(1900). *The Interpretation of Dreams.* In *The Standard Edition of the Complete Psychological Works of Sigmund Freud* (hereafter *SE*), vols. 4 and 5, ed. and tr. J. Strachey. London: Hogarth Press, 1953.

(1910). "A Special Type of Choice of Object Made by Men." *SE* 11, 1957, pp. 165–175.

(1913). *Totem and Taboo. SE* 13, 1953, pp. 1–161.

(1920). "Beyond the Pleasure Principle." *SE* 18, 1953, pp. 7–64.

(1923). "The Ego and the Id." *SE* 9, 1961, pp. 12–66.

(1926). "Inhibitions, Symptoms and Anxiety." *SE* 20, 1959, pp. 77–174.

(1930). *Civilization and its Discontents. SE* 21, 1961, pp. 64–145.

Holt, R. R. (1976). "Drive or Wish? A Reconsideration of the Psychoanalytic Theory of Motivation." In M. Gill, and P. Holzman (eds.), *Psychology versus Metapsychology: Psychoanalytic Essays in Memory of George S. Klein.* New York: International Universities Press, pp. 158–197.

Jung, C. G. (1916). "The Transcendent Function." CW 8 (*The Structure and Dynamics of the Psyche*), 1969.
(1921). *Psychological Types. CW* 6, 1971.
(1946). "The Psychology of the Transference." In CW 16 (*The Practice of Psychotherapy*), 1969.
(1955–56). *Mysterium Coniunctionis: An Inquiry into the Separation and Synthesis of Psychic Opposites in Alchemy.* CW 14, 1970.
(1975). *Critique of Psychoanalysis.* Princeton: Bollingen.
Kernberg, O. (1980). *Internal World and External Reality.* New York: Jason Aronson.
Kerr, J. (1993). *A Most Dangerous Method: The Story of Jung, Freud, and Sabina Spielrein.* New York: Alfred A. Knopf.
Klein, G. (1969). "Freud's Two Theories of Sexuality." In M. Gill, and P. Holzman (eds.), *Psychology versus Metapsychology: Psychoanalytic Essays in Memory of George S. Klein.* New York: International Universities Press, 1976, pp. 14–70.
Klein, M. (1948). *Contributions to Psychoanalysis: 1921–1945.* London: Hogarth Press.
(1957). *Envy and Gratitude and Other Works: 1946–1963.* New York: Delacorte.
Klein, M., Heimann, P., Isaacs, S., Riviere, J. (1952). *Developments in Psychoanalysis.* London: Hogarth Press.
Lichtenstein, H. (1961). "Identity and Sexuality." *Journal of the American Psychoanalytic Association,* 9, pp. 179–260. Also in *The Dilemma of Human Identity.* New York: Jason Aronson, 1977.
Maidenbaum, A. and Martin, S. (eds.) (1991). *Lingering Shadows: Jungians, Freudians, and Anti-Semitism.* Boston: Shambhala.
Ogden, T. (1990). *The Matrix of the Mind. Object Relations and the Psychoanalytic Dialogue.* Northvale, N.J.: Jason Aronson.
Stoller, R. (1979). *Sexual Excitement: Dynamics of Erotic Life.* New York: Pantheon Books.
(1985). *Observing the Erotic Imagination.* New Haven: Yale University Press.
Waelder, R. (1930). "The Principle of Multiple Function: Observations on Overdetermination." In *Psychoanalysis: Observation, Theory, Application. Selected Papers of Robert Waelder.* New York: International Universities Press, pp. 68–83.
(1960). *Basic Theory of Pychoanalysis.* New York: International Universities Press.
(1965). *Psychoanalytic Avenues to Art.* New York: International Universities Press.
(1967). "Inhibitions, Symptoms, and Anxiety: Forty Years Later." In *Psychoanalysis: Observation, Theory, Application. Selected Papers of Robert Waelder.* New York: International Universities Press, pp. 338–360.
Winnicott, D. W. (1960). "The Theory of the Parent–Child Relationship." In *The Maturational Processes and the Facilitating Environment.* New York: International Universities Press, pp. 37–55.
(1971). *Playing and Reality.* New York: Basic Books.
Young-Eisendrath, P. and Hall, J. (1991). *Jung's Self Psychology: A Constructivist Perspective.* New York: Guilford Press.

# 10

# The case of Joan: classical, archetypal, and developmental approaches

In the following pages, three experienced and accomplished Jungian analysts comment on where they would focus, what they would do, and what they imagine to be the course of treatment for "Joan." Joan is a pseudonym for a patient whose printed case material each analyst received and read closely before writing a response. Each received the same case report, summarized from the actual records of a forty-four-year-old female patient at the Renfrew Center for Eating Disorders, a private hospital in the Philadelphia area. Renfrew generously made available this material, which had previously been used in the public domain at a national conference on eating disorders.

Each analyst was asked to see things primarily from the perspective of her or his "school," each one being a prominent representative of that approach. Dr. Beebe writes from the classical approach, Dr. McNeely from the archetypal, and Dr. Gordon from the developmental. The analysts did not consult with each other on the case. As you read their responses, you may note how they highlight the model sketched out by Andrew Samuels in the Introduction in which he weighs the importance of the archetype, Self, and the development of personality as well as the clinical issues of the transferential field, symbolic experience of Self, and the phenomenology of imagery for each of the Jungian schools. What he has sketched as an interpretive model for the three schools of analytical psychology (see Introduction, pp. 8–11) works very well in understanding the interpretations of these authors. It must be remembered that none of the three analysts ever met the patient and, consequently, their essays should not be seen as comparing therapeutic practice. Rather, they are designed to illustrate different *approaches* to a real case. Apart from a few necessary instructions for thinking about the case, the following is all the information the authors received.

## Joan

Referred to Renfrew by her primary-care physician because he was concerned that she had an eating disorder, Joan weighed 144 pounds at 5′ 6″ at the time of admission to the hospital. She was bingeing and vomiting at least three times a day.

Six weeks prior to admission, Joan was extremely depressed and anxious. She said "I'd like to jump in a river." She also reported waking in the early morning hours, full of anxiety. She reported hitting herself in the head or stomach or biting her fingers in episodes of emotional pain.

During the admissions interview, Joan expressed a desire to "work with the feelings I've been stuffing down." She described herself as "really fat" and worried that her husband would leave her, wondering why he had even married her. Recently she had become more acutely aware of memories of incest with her father, something she had known continuously, never having sucessfully addressed it. She wanted to address it in treatment now. She also expressed the desire to eat properly, to stop her bingeing/purging addiction, and to improve her communications with her husband of four months.

Joan lives with her third husband, "Sam" (all names used in this report are pseudonyms), whom she married just four months before entering the hospital. She had become friends with Sam and then lived with him for two years prior to marriage. The couple currently live with Joan's daughter Amy, age twenty-six, and Sam's son David, age fifteen. David's mother died of diabetes when he was three years old. David is a source of conflict in their marriage because he gets into trouble at school and threatens to leave home.

Joan is employed full-time as a cashier and food service attendant in a local convenience store where she has multiple duties and responsibilities. In addition to her work, she has recently organized a women's self-help group for eating disorders and is very enthusiastic about it. Her long-term goal is to become an addictions counselor. She has plans to begin studies when she finishes treatment.

While Joan was at Renfrew, her mother, age eighty-one, became seriously ill with kidney failure. Even so, Joan found it difficult to discuss her anger at her mother's failure to protect her from an abusive father in the past. Joan's mother lived with her briefly, but Joan found it so stressful that she advised her mother to return to her home, which, being in a different state, was distant from her.

At the time of admission, Joan complained of heavy menstrual bleeding, usually every three weeks. Although she has a gynecologist, she had not scheduled an examination with him, claiming that she didn't consider her condition to be "serious enough" to warrant a doctor's help. Often when she was ill or injured, Joan would hesitate to take time off work and/or to seek the medical help she needed.

At the age of eighteen, Joan left home to marry her first husband. She had one daughter, Amy, in this marriage. Joan described the marriage as "painful and abusive." Amy has a history of chronic depression and has been diagnosed as having bipolar disorder. Joan left the marriage after two years. In her second marriage she had two more children, a son, Jack (now seventeen), and a daughter, Lynn (now twenty-one). Both Amy and Lynn were sexually abused by Joan's second husband, for which Joan feels very guilty. "I wish I could have protected my daughters, but I just didn't see the signs."

When Joan was five months pregnant with Jack, she took in a foster child named Johnnie, sixteen months old and afflicted with cerebral palsy. Eventually she adopted him.

Her second husband was unfaithful and abusive, one day abandoning the family without explanation. Because Joan was unemployed and unprepared for this sudden loss, she lost everything at the time: her home and all of her children except Lynn. Joan and Lynn lived in and out of a shelter for a year. During this time, Joan acquired a position as a waitress and prepared to reunite her family.

When she met Sam, her current husband, she found it extremely difficult to trust him, but things have ultimately worked out well.

Joan grew up in a four-room wooden house in rural Arkansas (USA). Her parents and only sibling, a sister eleven years older, lived at home. Her father was a "sanitary engineer" and was strict and emotionally distant. Most of the time, food was scarce and comfort was unavailable. Joan recalls her father being absorbed in repairing his automobile when he was at home and commented "it was more important to him than we were." Her mother was "always depressed" and very obese. Joan recalls feeling ashamed of her mother, who weighed over 300 pounds.

Joan reported that she had been sexually abused by her father, beginning in early childhood. She usually slept in the same bedroom with her mother and father, while her older sister slept in another. Her father would fondle her genitals in the morning before he left for work and when Joan complained to her mother, her mother did nothing. She also had some memories of being urged to fondle her mother's breasts during this time when they shared a bedroom. In general, Joan describes her childhood as "unsafe and full of fear."

# A classical approach

The first thing I would ask myself in approaching the case of "Joan" is what I think I know about the patient. That is, I have to discover what my own more conscious fantasies and expectations are, then inquire, more deeply, as to what my unconscious may have already done with the imminence of her upon my psychological scene. And, because I am about to function as Joan's psychotherapist, I shall be looking for what I can relate to naturally in her – what I can immediately gravitate to in her from my own center.

Let's start with a shared interest. Reading the case, I was not feeling anything in particular, beyond a certain drabness, until I noticed that Joan is "employed full-time as a cashier and food service attendant." Somehow this detail grabbed me. I have a long-standing interest in the ways in which food is implicated in the activities of our culture, and particularly in how food may serve as a medium for interpersonal communication. I enjoy getting to know people who sell, prepare, and serve food. And I love to eat, and even to diet, which gives me a new relation to the pleasures of food selection.

In the "classical approach" the analyst's lead is the Self's; that is, one trusts one's psyche to provide the libido – the energy – for relating to the patient – and brackets off considerations of "narcissism" or "appropriateness," letting fantasy toward the patient run its course until a pattern is established which can then be scrutinized. The classical Jungian tradition of analysis of the transference is by way of permitting the countertransference of the analyst its say, and this the analyst does primarily by attending to spontaneous reactions to the client, and only secondarily subjecting them to evaluative self-analysis. It is this approach I am following here.

That Joan has an eating disorder had started to turn me off, but that she works in a food-related employment piques my interest in her: perhaps she values food positively, or at least can relate positively to my instinctive interest in food, and this might form the basis of a spontaneous connection between us – provide a sort of glue, based on a shared mystery, a secret pleasure and passion between us. (At a more thought-out level, I recognize Joan's perhaps affirmative connection to food as the potentially creative side of her neurosis: the resourcefulness that accompanies her oral problem, the "purposiveness," in Jung's sense, that would give her symptoms meaning.)

I find myself also taken with the statement Joan made during the admission interview, expressing her desire to "work with the feelings I've been stuffing down." I like the way her mind moved to this metaphor –

although I recognize she may have been echoing the rhetoric of her self-help group for eating disorders. On the hopeful side, it was she who formed the group, and her having done so is another sign of her resourcefulness in the face of her adverse and regressive "oral" symptomatology.

I think I like Joan's energy; I feel that it augurs well for the psychotherapy. It's important, in the classical approach, that the analyst be able to find something to like in the patient, or else one has to conclude that the energy won't be there in the analysis to affirm the emerging selfhood of the client. In that event the client would be far better off – and safer – in another analyst's hands.

For me, as I read Joan's case, it is a particular plus that her memories of incest have become more available to her recently. The classical analyst "likes" signs that the personal self is taken seriously, as something to be honored and not violated – for this little "s" self is the core of integrity upon which analytical psychotherapy will build in reaching out to the wider Self to integrate the personality. (This honored personal core is sometimes referred to in the psychoanalytic self psychology that has so many resemblances to the classical Jungian approach as the "self that knows what's good for itself.") It is as if Joan's sense of the worth of her self is heightened just now and her imagination is working, ready to tackle the violations of integrity that have compromised its functioning in the past. Perhaps this is part of the honeymoon glow from marrying Sam.

I imagine Sam to be a positive figure for her, yet when she reports that she wonders why he'd even married her, I think she is expressing her difficulty accepting that she deserves the caring of another. In more classical Jungian language, Sam – with whom "things have worked out well" – would represent, or evoke within Joan, the image of the caring animus, the inner "husband" of her life resources. He would open her up to the possibilities of a more focused connection with herself, aimed at taking better care of the person she is.

At this point I would begin to criticize the fantasy I have so far simply allowed. I am trained to reflect on the assumptions I have been making: such *reflexio* is a critical next step in the classical Jungian handling of countertransference fantasy if inappropriate action is to be avoided (*CW* 8, p. 117).[1] I notice that the fantasy that has developed so far imagines Joan at a positive turning point in her life, having married Sam. It has given me hope that a therapy undertaken at this time will be more fruitful than the long history of dysfunctional living and repeated disappointment in relations with others would seem to predict. I have to admit to myself that in taking up the positive, I have, in terms of Jung's theory of psychological types, revealed my own characteristic attitude toward a new situation. A classical Jungian would not fail to note that I have moved toward the case in accord with my extraverted intuitive nature – that is, sensing the long-shot possibility at the expense of a more realistic focus upon the client's limitations, which are everywhere underscored in the facts of the bleak case history. Nevertheless, I trust my intuition and feel ready to go out on a limb and tell myself that, despite appearances, this is a therapy that can work.

Joan will soon, however, be a real person talking to me in my office. I wonder how much to share with her of my experience reading the intake summary. Usually, I like to begin a therapy by telling the patient what I know of her and by letting my own reactions to what I have heard and read about her case come through. But should I tell Joan about my liking for food or speak of my respect for what sounds healthy in her marriage to Sam? Jung is clear that he gave himself permission to tell a number of patients how he felt about them, as early as the first session. He found it particularly important to share his unbidden reactions, since in his view these were governed by the unconscious itself. "[M]y reaction is the only thing with which I as an individual can legitimately confront my patient" (CW 16, p. 5). So, early self-disclosure would be an option for me in building the transference relationship with Joan. But even as my fantasy runs toward how to create a relationship to this new client, I begin to recognize a certain seductiveness in the way I have imagined an easy merger of our natures around a shared, unambivalent aspiration for her betterment, as if there could be no problem between us in the psychotherapeutic collaboration.

It dawns on me, as I examine my initial fantasy more critically, how much my connection to her – so far – is on a narcissistic basis. I have no fantasy as to what she is really like. Am I already behaving like the incestuous father, who must have related to her almost exclusively through his own needs and preoccupations? I recall what a long time it took Joan to trust Sam. I realize that Joan will not trust me if I make a series of moves to "merge with" her – even (or especially) if she initially complies with them. Probably she would defend against my extraverted enthusiasm with increasing messages of discouragement. Even if I succeeded in becoming a good object to her – that is, someone whom she perceives as ideally positioned to foster the emergence of a potentially healthy self in her – there is no evidence that Joan will be unambivalent about merging herself with such a good object. From the number of self-defeating choices that pervade her reported history, I suspect that Joan may suffer from what I have elsewhere termed "primary ambivalence toward the Self," and I realize that I am going to have to make room for her ambivalence toward people who might be able to help her to thrive if I am going to function effectively as her "selfobject" (Beebe 1988, pp. 97–127).

Interpolating from the history both of parental neglect and abuse and, later, of self-destructive behaviors, it is likely that in her own fantasy life part of her is still identified with parental figures who did not always want what was best for her and that she therefore will find it hard to embrace wholeheartedly a program for self-improvement. Further, even if she has already decided that she wants to be helped, this choice could only be accompanied by an uncertainty as to whether any caretaker she might find could fully share her purpose. I know, therefore, that I will be tested to see if I can be a good doctor who doesn't put his own needs ahead of hers.

I also realize that, although Joan has the goal of becoming a therapist and will sometimes enjoy seeing how I go about doing my work, she is more than just another adult caretaker in the making, who might learn by merging with me in an apprentice mode. In that mode, I could talk to her continuously, instructing the therapist in her as I would do with a junior colleague in supervision. With Joan, I think such an approach would backfire. There is a far more fundamental need to be cared for that shows through her history, which particularly suggests maternal abandonment. I could not indefinitely adopt the mode of even a good father without recapitulating this maternal abandonment: after a period of compliance with my guidance of her conscious efforts toward self-betterment, Joan would probably begin to get severely depressed.

Probably she would not ask for relief of the depression within the therapy sessions themselves, but would signal her need more indirectly, possibly through canceled appointments or intercurrent illnesses of a physical nature. I have noted that she has characteristically had difficulty asking for help directly. (She did not think her heavy menstrual bleeding was serious enough to warrant a doctor's visit.) It may be hard to get to the abandoned child in Joan. I will have to be careful not to ally so directly with the seemingly adult part of Joan that the child in her continues to starve and to feel abandoned. Were I to ignore the child, she would be forced to ask for help in symptomatic ways, including perhaps a return to the suicidal behaviors mentioned in her history.

For a therapist working in the classical Jungian tradition, the habit of trusting the psyche to shape an attitude toward a client means allowing one's clinical fantasy to develop its own tension of opposites. If one lets the natural ambivalence about how to approach a treatment emerge, one avoids the danger of a one-sided countertransference stance. Here, my initial identification with the good father role gives way, spontaneously, to a maternal anxiety. This tension of opposites is a sign of the analyst's self-regulation, which will operate reliably if the analyst has been analyzed sufficiently to be comfortable in allowing the compensatory function of the unconscious to do its work, and if the analyst has learned to bear the conflicts that emerge. Thus, even when one starts as I did, to shape a stance toward Joan by trying to transcend her deep mother problem and to encourage the "flight into health" represented by merger with a progressive analyst-father, if the clinical rumination is allowed to proceed, a maternal anxiety for the abandoned child in this client will eventually surface in the fantasizing therapist.

Finding myself now thinking about Joan's mother problem, I begin to focus more consciously on the signs of the wounded child. I immediately see, along classical Jungian lines, the prospective meaning – the value – of the child image. Could the child be the way to the maturity that I sense is possible for Joan? Joan's desire to jump in a river, the closest to archetypal imagery we are given, could be heard as her desire to reenter the intrauterine condition, to be reborn in the mother's bloodstream, through what Jung calls the "night sea journey." Perhaps I can help her realize this ambition in the therapy through an immersion in the unconscious. This would mean attention to her dreams and fantasies, but not in too verbal a mode, which would again be meeting her prematurely at the level of the father and the patriarchal order of words.

Here I have made use of the classical Jungian method of amplification in attending to Joan's stated wish to drown herself, taking this alarming threat as an archetypal motif, scanning it, with the image taken less literally and more symbolically, for a clue to what her own psyche may think is necessary to heal her. But again the clinician in me rises up in opposition to the archetypalist: I realize that her immersion in the river, even if indicative of a baptism into a new being, is more likely to be accomplished if I accept a period of regression in which a less organized, maybe less verbal, Joan appears as a precursor of her transformation. I may have to contain her through a period in the therapy in which she can't say much. It occurs to me that she might like to draw, or at least be shown where I keep crayons and paper so that a way of communicating in a fluid medium while she is "underwater" in the unconscious is made available to her. Above all, I can't expect her to be conscious of what she's doing in therapy. She may for a long time need just to be safely there in my restrained presence. An underappreciated strength of the classical Jungian position – exemplified by Jung himself, who maintained his strong grounding in psychiatry alongside his interest in "religious" healing through traditional symbolism – is its ability to straddle clinical and symbolic modes in the service of fostering a patient's recovery.

Whatever the process that eventually turns out to help Joan most, I know that I will have to respect my own nature in following it: classical Jungian analysis conceives itself as a dialectical procedure, a meeting of two souls, each of which must be respected if the exchange is truly to be therapeutic. As Jung says, the analyst is "as much 'in the analysis' as the patient" (*CW* 16, p. 72). There is no way for an extraverted analyst like me to participate in a client's period of maternal regression except interactively. In the classical approach, this can occur in a verbal, face-to-face mode simply by listening to the practical particulars of the patient's day-to-day life – her struggles paying her bills, finding the energy to keep the house clean, and dealing with her relatives. It is classically Jungian to take patients where they are. If as therapist I submit to the mundane reality of Joan's situation and respond without attempting to make interpretations that force her into a higher symbolic understanding at a psychological level, I may succeed in getting into the healing river with her. There, I will have to stay with the current of her affects, mostly mirroring them back to her and rarely pushing for their illumination. I will have to say very simple things back to her like, "That's particularly hard," or "that's lonely" or "that's scary," to go through the river which in her suicidal fantasy she imagined as the way to bring her chronic dysphoria to an end.

As this second wave in my fantasy of what it would be like to work with Joan overtakes me, I realize that I am trying to will myself into becoming the accompanying mother Joan never had. Once again, I am led to reflect on what I have imagined. I realize that by colluding in principle with Joan's imagined wish for this kind of mother, I have entered another trap, fallen into a subtler failure to accept Joan as my patient than my earlier attempt to be her good father. For it is not possible simply to undo the wounds of the past by compensating for them now with a corrective regressive experience in the present. Indeed, I suddenly get the feeling that Sam, her good husband, may be trying to do just this: he sounds to me very much like a maternal caretaker, who saw his last wife through diabetes and is now carrying Joan through her ambivalence about deserving his help. Or maybe that's a projection onto him of the maternal role I now fear falling into.

In any case, I realize what I am going to have to do is harder than being Joan's good-enough mother. It is to help Joan grieve over the fact that she didn't have this kind of mother and, in a definite sense, never will – certainly not at the developmental stage when a mother like that would have been most needed. I have to let Joan grieve the lack of that needed mother, and rage at the lack of the needed father too.

Suddenly I see the way (and now it feels like the only way) to work analytically with this wounded woman. I will make a space in which she can tell me or not how it has felt to be her – as a person whose father and mother were both inadequate to the task of taking care of her needs – and in which she can begin to articulate how she proposes to go about being her own mother and father. At this point I feel suddenly released from my own fantasies and ready to hear from Joan's psyche in an unprejudiced way. This emergence of a new attitude out of a tension of opposite, incomplete solutions was called the transcendent function by Jung (*CW* 8, pp. 67–91) and it is this function the classical analyst relies upon in developing a sound approach to a client. The appearance of the transcendent function is signaled by a release of creative energy for the therapeutic work itself.

Sooner or later, Joan will tell me a dream. Without a need to make that dream a transcending symbolic solution to all her difficulties, or the occasion to foster a regression into a less conscious state in which I can nurture her back to greater psychic health, I may be able to hear it as the authentic statement of Joan's psychic position toward the person she has been and the possibility of the person she may yet be. My job will be to hear that dream, to take it in. It will be the authentic vision of who she is, not the fantasies I can't help bringing to that lacuna in the case, which is only a report of successive abandonments and partial restitutions, not the authentic vision yet of the psyche, which can only be supplied by the patient herself. In classical Jungian analysis, the treatment plan is dictated by the patient's psyche. Any real planning for Joan's treatment will have to be shaped by us on the basis of what her dream suggests is possible, and I would expect the dream to create an unconscious role for me in her life which will have a most inductive effect on my unconscious attitude toward the treatment and a major effect, therefore, on the treatment planning. In the absence of that dream, I can only supply a very approximate guess as to the course of treatment with Joan.

I imagine that I will offer Joan once-a-week psychotherapy, explaining that this is a place where she may come to say what she would like to about her life. I might explain that I have no fixed way of working, but that I too will say what I want to say as we go along, and also that I am open to her comments and questions about what we are doing as we proceed. I would let her sit either on a chair facing mine or on the two-seater couch at right angles to me. My expectation is that she would be sitting up. For the time being, I probably would not show her the drawer with paper and crayons nor would I suggest that she might like to lie down on the little couch, as I feel either of those behaviors, upon reflection, would be to encourage a regression I have not established is fully in her interest. Equally, I would not make too much of the fact that I listen to dreams and fantasies as well as to more consciously produced communications and associations, because this could commit me to making more interpretive commentary than I might like to get into at this early stage. Mostly, I will try to make room for this woman to tell me what she wants to and for me to respond out of my sense of what I would really like to say in return.

I would predict that Joan spends most of the first hour communicating her shame at having to seek treatment for herself once again, and that she guesses that it's just a case of like mother like daughter, she just can't lick being fat. And I think I would say that it sounds as if, along with the self-hate, she has a lot of energy toward doing something to get past this problem – even that it seems to be her task at this time to solve many of the problems her mother left behind. I would try to convey that I could accept Joan's sense of having inherited the weight problem, even though she is not literally as fat as her mother was. If I felt a glimmer of interest in me, I would probably say that I know what it feels like to be engaged with food and that there are worse things to be occupied with. If she asked me what I meant, I would say that a struggle with food can be creative, in addition to being a pathological problem. I would hope in this way to provide a kind of inclusive context for ongoing discussion at the very beginning, indicating that my office could be a place of creative ambivalence.

I would expect Joan to feel held by this approach, and to engage in a committed way with the work. I would expect treatment to go on for a number of years. I imagine at the start that there would be many tests of my ability to accept her ambivalence toward treatment, mostly in the form of suddenly canceled appointments following the more "integrative" sessions (on the model of bingeing and purging). My main response would be to continue to "be there," to accept the cancellations calmly and to say to her at the next meeting, I think it's clear that you are still trying to figure out if there is anything nourishing here and if you can truly accept the feelings associated with the therapy as meaningful parts of yourself.

Gradually, as she begins to understand her ambivalence, she would, I imagine, come more regularly. Then it might be possible to identify more specifically the ways in which I seemed to her like an unresponsive mother or like a frightening, intimate, too-good father. I might be able to facilitate some recognition of how she needed to distance herself from me when I was in the overly enthusiastic father role, and how, when I assumed the role of a more distant mother for her, it plunged her into a sense of despair over felt abandonment. In this way, we might "work through," over a very long time, the transference to earlier self-objects.

But I would also be watching for moments when I seem to her to be interesting in a new way, for those would be times in which I am incarnating the person she might be in the process of becoming. I would particularly look for stretches of untense "meeting" between us, in which I feel naturally accepted for being the therapist I am and I can glimpse a part of her that hadn't lived much anywhere else. (At those times she might look like a "new face" in a movie, and I would be experiencing the unique dimension of her personhood.) At those moments I would not be afraid to laugh with her or to respond with enthusiasm toward her developing sense of psychological life.

I will not know for a long time in this therapy whether I am taking care of the mirroring needs of the very young one- or two-year-old self or supplying a measure of Oedipal (and therefore erotic) appreciation to a five-year-old self who can also feel safe that I will not preempt its sexual development to gratify my own need for intimacy. In short, I would not know if, in the transference, I was an appropriately interested mother or father, and I would not be surprised if instead I turn out to be neither, but rather a kind of transference brother, a fellow sufferer enjoying a respite from the arduousness of adulthood, and a model for the animus that will relate to some creative aspect of her personhood. For at those moments Joan and I would be experiencing the Self in its function as what Edward Edinger (1973, p. 40) calls an "organ of acceptance." These would be times at which we transcended ambivalence toward the Self in favor of simple gratitude for the possibilities of being human. It is my belief that such moments can provide the glue for the many years we would be working together, which would very likely include suicidal periods, times when I would hate her for her stubbornness or lack of movement, and periods when she would experience contempt for my limitations in understanding or accepting the inevitable slowness of her path to healing.

Letting fantasy help to structure the treatment planning, as a classical Jungian analyst does, inevitably means experiencing the problem of opposites, and in practical terms, a refusal to embrace either artificially curtailed forms of treatment, such as time-limited brief psychotherapy, or rigorous prescriptions to guarantee depth, such as insistence on multiple-sessions-a-week on the couch. In classical Jungian analysis, the frequency is dictated by the analyst's experience of the tension between too little and too much. Probably with Joan I would not increase the frequency of sessions, as that would upset the balance between promising too much and offering enough. I would feel compelled to hold this tension for the work to have sufficient integrity; and so I would resist trying to force a deepening of the work. What would increase would be my depth of commitment to the work and my availability to Joan as someone who could engage with her personhood each time we met, regardless of the level of her distress.

Jung says (CW 16) that the doctor "is equally a part of the psychic process of treatment and therefore equally exposed to the transforming influences." I would anticipate that my own relation to food would become more conscious during the period of my work with Joan. For Joan to complete her analysis with me, I will have to make a space in myself to examine my own ambivalence toward food, perhaps getting in touch with a part of myself that is suspicious, controlling, and devouring in relation to sources of nurture. This self-analysis might free Joan from the necessity of having to carry that for me as an eternal patient.

I hope Joan will realize her goal of becoming an effective counselor to people with eating disorders. I imagine her becoming a pillar of her particular self-help food-community, maybe even starting a business like a health food store. As she becomes less dependent on Sam and thus less the carrier of the wounded anima for him, I imagine Sam will eventually have a serious depression, but that Joan will see him through it, and that he will begin to get in better conscious touch with the needy side of himself. I predict she will have made reparative connections with all her children by the end of her treatment, and that she will value her contacts with them and will discover that she can be nurturing.

## NOTE

1 "*Reflexio* is a turning inwards, with the result that, instead of an instinctive action, there ensues a succession of derivative contents or states which may be termed reflection or deliberation. Thus in place of the compulsive act there appears a certain degree of freedom, and in place of predictability a relative unpredictability as to the effect of the impulse" (CW 8, p. 117).

## REFERENCES

Beebe, John (1988). "Primary Ambivalence toward the Self: Its Nature and Treatment." In *The Borderline Personality in Analysis*, ed. Nathan Schwarz-Salant and Murray Stein. Wilmette, Ill.: Chiron Publications.

Edinger, Edward (1973). *Ego and Archetype*. Baltimore: Penguin Books.

Jung, C. G. (1960a). "The Transcendent Function." CW 8, pp. 67–91.

(1960b). "Psychological Factors Determining Human Behavior." CW 8, pp. 114–128.

(1966a). "Principles of Practical Psychotherapy." CW 16, pp. 3–20.

(1966b). "Problems of Modern Psychotherapy." CW 16, pp. 53–75.

DELDON McNEELY

# An archetypal approach

Here I am asked to demonstrate how one person applies an archetypal orientation. At the risk of oversimplification, I would isolate three definitive marks of that orientation as I see it playing out in my clinical work. One is that I regard the patient's relationship to the archetypal material selected by the psyche as having priority over transference considerations. This is not to underestimate the essential value of intimate relatedness as a transforming crucible, but to acknowledge that the therapeutic relationship is one arena of several in which the archetypes can be met face to face. Whether the patient invests in symptom, struggle, social functioning, dreams, etc., I am inclined to see myself in a role of fellow-explorer and witness, unless the role of representative of some powerful inner figure is clearly projected onto me.

Secondly, the range of behavior that I consider "human" and soulful rather than pathological is wider than that of many of my colleagues of non-archetypal approaches. And when pathology is obvious, my first intention is to explore and understand the meaning of the pathology for the patient's individuation. I am dismayed at how quickly medications, hospitalizations, and direction are dispensed in today's psychological milieu, and appalled by the pressure that even I feel from every corner to do something to fix the situation, promise redemption, resolve the conflict, end the impasse, take away the pain, by some heroic intrusion on a natural process, as if there are no inner resources to be encouraged and fanned to life in the patient. I stake my purpose on the wisdom of the psyche, and trust that attention to the archetypal sources of distress will enable the psyche to align itself without strong-armed interventions. I encourage focusing on soul-searching rather than improving.

Thirdly, focusing on archetypal themes brings the analytic process through a gamut of possibilites via the imagination from the densest physiological impulses to the most ethereal psychic experiences, without any preconceived order or expectation of stages, except as determined by the flow and direction from within the patient's psyche. Theoretically we mature through developmental levels, but seldom do we as therapists see a straightforward progression through stages of growth or integration when we are very close to the patient's world; only with hindsight do we see how seemingly disparate or irrelevant experiences are linked to a larger picture. Archetypes manifest through the instinctual life of the body, its revulsions, impasses, and attractions, as well as through ideational content and spiritual inclinations. I am wary of imposing probables and shoulds into the patient's psyche.

Archetypal psychology speaks of "psyche" or "soul" with respect for the mysteriousness of human nature, which can never be reduced to simple determinants. In soul is implied a depth of association to life and death that leads beyond our personal histories and connects us with the intensity of the transpersonal – not a transpersonal that is remote, but one which is always present, the other side of everything ordinary. I imagine the analytic journey to be accompanied by Mercurius, whom Jung (CW 13, para. 284) designated "archetype of individuation"; also, I imagine the presence of the goddess of the hearth, Hestia, as the principle of centering and grounding that keeps the process in focus and creates a balance to the hermetic energy.

Leaving the abstract,[1] let us speak about the coagulation of theory in terms of Joan's story. To some extent, having a bit of history of Joan as we do deprives me of the kind of initial impact that I look forward to with a new patient. For the benefit of new therapists who might be reading this, I want to admit that the looking-forward-to is not entirely comfortable, as I always experience anxiety before meeting a new patient. The anxiety may last a few minutes or weeks before something in the relationship gels. Initially uncomfortable feelings on the part of either person do not mean that the therapy is unworkable, but only that deep personal material is potentially engaged.

Despite anxiety, I do anticipate the first meeting as an exceptional encounter. First impressions, gleaned through a primal animal scent, bring essential information which is soon enough overridden by words and conscious intents. Later these first glimpses into the interaction can be compared with further data to provide insight into the unconscious dynamics of the relationship, and into my shadow projections – that is, what this other person enables me to see about my own discarded selves.

Now the fact that we readers have this history about Joan has certain advantages, too, even though it diminishes my initial whole-Joan-phenomenon by coloring the encounter with prior information. Only when I meet Joan will I put these already coded impressions from others together with her physiognomic presentation and respond to her voice, gestures, postures, eye contact, odors, dress and ornamentation, etc., and only as she eventually unveils herself will I see whether the historical facts we have been given are authentic and relevant.

The difference between meeting the patient for the first time without prior information and meeting the patient within the context of her history is an important one, and is one of the issues that separates the experience of private practice from most agency work. I personally like to work with ambiguity, and as much spontaneity as possible, and do not ordinarily take any history in or before the first session with adult patients. Usually I let the story slowly unfold, trusting that the facts are less important than what has been made of them by the patient's inner storyteller. This is a point on which analysts differ, and where each must find his/her own comfort zone.

Another thing about the initial meeting: the referral person plays a significant emotional role. The patient transfers a preconception of being received to the first professional contact; whether that first person contacted is conceived of as savior, confessor, judge, healer, parent, or servant, the "fit" between the actual reception and the patient's image of therapy strongly colors the beginning work. Sometimes such a strong attachment is made by the patient to a professional person who has seen the patient first, that the fear and grief about leaving that person must be acknowledged and dealt with before anything further can be done.

All of this has bearing on Joan. What has her referring physician inferred about therapy, and what is her attachment to that physician? What is her image of psychotherapy, and what does she expect of me and of herself? Will I work with her during her hospitalization, and will I be able to continue seeing her as an outpatient, or will she then have to see a new therapist? Joan's leaving the hospital with its twenty-four-hour-a-day in-utero containment may involve a period of grief or separation anxiety to which is added the experience of loss of the first therapist. In some unfortunate treatment settings, the follow-up after inpatient treatment is scanty and takes little notice of these very powerful dynamics. Patients then experience abandonment. In any case, I would recommend intense after-care, including long-term therapy, even after successful treatment as an inpatient.

Before making recommendations, however, let me note my initial reactions to the verbal portrait we've been given of Joan. My first impression is that Joan possesses such a stalwart spirit and an embodiment of hope that I find myself strongly in her corner, wishing her the best. After much pain and failure she actualizes her hope with a new attempt at healing, a new marriage, a new career. I respect her steadfast commitment to life, to Eros, which she demonstrates by taking the initiative to start a self-help group, to want to care for others, to continue to expect to change things for the better, even while feeling hopelessly suicidal at times. I expect to meet a strong, earthy woman, full of vitality, much of that vibrance perhaps beyond her awareness and maybe very different from her self-perceptions. If she is able to choose long-term therapy, my positive response to Joan will lubricate our work. Still, as a countertransference attitude, this positive feeling must be objectified. I cannot let my respect and admiration color my behavior so overtly as to give her a false sense of security or an impression of my seeming manipulative or condescending, nor do I wish to create in her unnecessary dependence upon me, or to expect too much of her too soon, or to covertly promise too much, or to be blind to her darker aspects.

Regarding the dark, I wonder what appeals to her about "jumping into a river," a transforming image of quite different quality than, say, strangling herself with a rope, or blowing herself to bits. Is she so hot and pliable that she needs to be plunged into water to cool and harden, or does she yearn to be dissolved into some greater flowing substance, swallowed, returned to the amniotic container? Perhaps I can plunge with her through some combination of curiosity and compassion to learn what her fantasies of transformation would be, to see what essential ingredients of Joan would survive a dissolution. Joan's image, an invocation of the alchemical process of *solutio*, deserves serious care. The fantasy of death by water on ego's terms carries a wish from the Self for renewal, for a spiritual baptism. In analysis we will explore this wish rather than concretize it as "nothing more than" a suicidal impulse.[2] But the dangers of coming too close to Joan! Would she allow me to collaborate with her in this exploration? Would she swallow me in and vomit me out in disgust?

Behind the initial impressions await crowds of questions like this, the answers to which I expect to learn if Joan comes to trust me. I welcome my curiosity as evidence that her story has touched me, but I will refrain from asking these questions. I will usually allow Joan to decide what we will discuss, and in what order. Once the content is chosen I may become active in eliciting more associations, pursuing and amplifying themes, confronting inconsistencies, and so on, but I like to make it clear early in the work that the patient takes primary responsibility for the stuff of therapy if she can possibly do so.

Meanwhile, those questions crowd around. Will Joan reject me as she is rejecting her new husband (through projective identification, i.e. setting him up to leave her)? Is there something too dangerous in Joan to be able to hold onto what she loves? The feminine principle seems vividly present in Joan in all of its primary ambivalence, and not refined into some harmonious self-image (such as nurturant mother, artistic medium, sex-goddess, devoted wife, inspiratrice, etc.). Can she include under her warm, earthy cloak her husband's grieving son, or will her unconscious sadism feast on a vulnerable young male? For, as the bulimic symptom demonstrates, the need to gather into herself and the need to expel from herself coexist in contention, a theme that seems to have been with her since she struggled to survive in the hungry family of origin.

I am curious about that early family life, and the mysteries performed in those small bedrooms of her infancy and childhood. What was given to and what received from the silent, frustrated parents unable to fill the hunger in each other? What forces kept Joan's parents together, kept father rising daily and going to his arduous job, kept mother alive for eighty-plus years? I want to know mother's story, too. Was she desperate for touch, trying to elicit some gratification from her baby? If we examine our fantasies and cultural myths truthfully we cannot deny the sensual pleasure to be derived from closeness to the child's body; it is not denial that protects adults from exploiting children sexually in the face of such pleasure, but the capacity to contain and redirect the desires. What prevented these parents from managing their sensuality? What anxieties lay drowned beneath mother's fat globules, and why were her anxieties not allayed with her man? The man, pouring all of his attention into the machine, avoided some essential contact with his women in the daylight; a machine is predictable, will not bleed, gain weight, run away, insist, or dissolve in tears, but will stand firm to his ministrations and attempts at mastery. We are given a picture of this couple, seemingly trapped in mutual disappointment and resignation, with a life task to send two reasonably hopeful girls out into the world. Why couldn't the two adults sleep together and comfort each other, enjoy lust, give mutual attention? Were they afraid of having more children? Were they frustrated in some way by sexual inadequacy? Was one or both too frightened of the intimacy of being seen and known? Did they find the natural irritations and anger of everyday accommodation to another too frightening? Were they impeded by family myths and ancestral ghosts in the form of crippling self-images and unreasonable constraints?

We can only speculate about what went wrong in that little house which could have glowed with human warmth and laughter, but instead took a dark turn toward secrecy, scarcity, perversity, and fear. I try to imagine the atmosphere in that little house, and Joan's response to it. I do this because it is interesting and I am curious, but also because the information will be helpful when she inevitably tries to recreate the atmosphere in our relationship, as some part of her seems to be doing in her relationship with Sam. My sense of the ambience in that household is so sad and cold, but the confusion in our professional field about incest and false memories underlines how careful one must be about allowing the patient to expose her interpretations about her early life, and not suggesting how it was with pointed questions or inferences.

Living in such a circumscribed world as those four did certainly must have played a powerful role in shaping Joan's images and expectations of life, men, motherhood. However, it did not determine what Joan would become, as her psyche made its selections and expressed its inclinations. She was able to take from that world some essential satisfaction, emerging with a body whose desire for intimacy and generativity propelled her out of the house and into a life rich with experience. I think of the feminine principle in her as prodding her to such instinctual interests, for instance, as enjoying emotion in relatedness, mating with a man, creating a baby, giving birth to some generative project, contributing to some communal or aesthetic enterprise; and I imagine the masculine principle in her as engaging the world, determined that these interests become articulated and actualized beyond the plane of fantasy. At eighteen Joan demonstrated sufficient impetus from her masculine principle, or animus, to assert her independence from her parents and to find a partner to help her expand and differentiate her image of masculinity from the father complex. Unfortunately, as is often the case in women deprived of the experience of a wholesome father who encourages self-love and good judgment in his daughter, her way out was not to become self-sufficient, but to enter a different dependency situation, probably projecting the good and powerful father onto her young husband.

Joan's first two choices of partners reflect a lack of judgment and an unconscious attraction to the kind of dangerous atmosphere she had left behind. Only now, in mid-life, does she seem to have acquired – not by early preparation and good models, but by experience, trial, error, and suffering – a strength within herself which I think of as masculine: that is, the strength to assert her choices, to make realistic plans, to criticize and be willing to detach herself from wrong judgments, to seek out and think through beneficent experiences rather than letting herself follow only her heart's desires and intuitive choices. These functions begin to balance her strong feminine need for nurturance, attachment, and emotional intensity. Joan may now be more capable of internalizing the tensions between what attracts her to a man initially and what benefits her in the long run; and she may be more able to resolve those tensions intrapsychically instead of acting them out in relationship to actual men. I should add that not all archetypal psychologists find the gender differentiation of psychological functions useful. Some Jungians of all schools feel that the anima/animus concept is more disruptive than heuristic, for reasons beyond my scope to elucidate here. But for me the concept of feminine and masculine principles is valuable in helping me organize my perceptions of personality.

Joan may have acquired some healthy animus qualities by this time in her life, but as a young adult her life was colored more by the mother-complex as she lived and moved in a soup of concerns with dependency which overpowered discerning the personality characteristics of her husbands, or finding her niche in the world of work and independence, or developing her mind and talents. Imagine a twenty-eight-year-old pregnant woman with two young children and a troublesome husband taking on a fourth, handicapped child. What on earth was she trying to do? I can only guess it was something psychically related to weighing over 300 pounds, expressing something akin to her mother's hunger. . .nurturing gone wild, nurturing taken to such excess that inevitably it must collapse, and then comes the other side: she loses it all and becomes the helpless victim. Her children are removed and she has to depend on the state to sustain herself and one child. Such powerful nurturant instincts reveal creative energy which, if submitted to processes of reflection, can serve and gratify Joan and others touched by her.

Joan's story evokes so many images of ravenous hunger that I wonder how I will react to such stimulation over a period of exposure. Surely I can expect, in addition to my initial admiration of its heroic flavor, a counter-transference that is breast-dominated – whether by a need to care for, or by a tendency toward stingy withholding remains to be seen. I should watch for both these reactions, and also for the invitation from Joan to be pulled in as her adversary against perceived wrongs by the men in her life. Now that she has the protection of a husband and a therapist, I would expect her to begin to feel safe enough to allow her young needs to be felt, and that unfulfilled need for a mother to align with her against the exploitative principle (whether in mother or father, but certainly now incorporated into her own character structure) warrants repetition. Although she was strong enough to extricate herself from two arduous marriages, it sounds as if she did not meet her husbands' aggression with much potency of her own. Now she meets Sam with more self-determination, even though it seems to frighten her. I want to allow her to feel the strength of her need to make mother her savior without playing that out with her and prolonging unnecessarily that image as reality. I imagine holding and keeping in check the starving, devouring, exploitative parent, while the sacred space of the therapeutic vessel creates an opportunity for the generous, full mother to flourish in Joan.

So many alimentary images evoke and want a timeless quality that promises to allow all necessary functions of introjection and absorption to mature according to their proper schedules. Ideally I would want unlimited time with Joan, because my experience of working with such fundamental contradictions as her life exemplifies is that, despite good motivation, change is very slow and tenuous. On the level of the digestive system we meet primitive monsters of the brainstem and basic cell structures, where insight is virtually useless, so that the same ground must be taken and retaken from insidiously monstrous greed. By this I mean that the same issues and incidents must be talked about again and again, the same affects expressed, the same misunderstandings unraveled in the relationship with the therapist more than once. I would hope she could be seen daily as an inpatient until the suicidal purging was able to be contained and curtailed. Then, as an outpatient ideally I would plan to see her for one to three hours per week for several years. Provided her strength and motivation met my initial expectations, I would expect a good prognosis with this schedule.

Under the present circumstances she may not be able to afford the usual fee. This we would have to discuss thoroughly, for working out a feasible financial contract is an essential factor of the therapeutic process, setting the scene for the adult-to-adult nature of a relationship which is at the same time allowed to be infantile and regressive. In her case the financial issue could become a way of falling into the starving-mother complex with one of us feeling deprived, if money is not dealt with straightforwardly. I want Joan to consider our work together as valuable and mutually purposive, requiring of her an input of energy, financial and emotional, which I will meet with a like input of psychological sustenance and reliability, and ideally, some wisdom about the psyche which will be useful to her. If we cannot establish such a timeless mother-world in which she has frequent, reliable access to a safe, permissive therapy setting, I would have to consider a more guarded prognosis in terms of substantial change. In that case I would direct Joan to set up for herself a strong support system, including, for example, her self-help group, perhaps an educational program with access to college counselors, perhaps a twelve-step program, perhaps brief marital or family counseling, and periodic follow-ups with me or someone else in which I would attempt to support her continued interest in the meaning of her problems. The periodic follow-ups ideally would continue as long as we both deem necessary.

But suppose that an unlimited duration of treatment is possible. I know of no substitute for the kind of self-reflection that is possible only with the intimate support established by enduring contact. Anyone who has experienced this therapeutically knows the indescribable moments of transformation. Transformative happenings (which I can only call "moments" though years may be represented by the moment) hold an integration that may be most easily conveyed in images – chemical images, as the thickening of a sauce or fusion of metals or moment of crystallization; physical images, as the coming together of coordination in learning to drive a machine or a potter's wheel; mental images of "getting" the meaning behind the formula, or having the foreign language become automatic. Something like this happens in therapy when a place of readiness is reached, but it does not happen overnight. It is not the flash of insight of a breakthrough or peak experience, but is something quiet and abiding. As a therapist I have my personal image for fostering this happening, which is to follow the "aha's" which reflect the mobility and excitement of Mercurius, while remaining steadily settled before the warm hearth of Hestia, where all the flashes of brilliance come to the integrity of repose.

In Jung's theory, the language to be mastered is the communication between the conscious ego and its archetypal source in the Self, the archetype of wholeness that is being's circumference, source, and power, and manifests as an experience of being contained, centered, or guided.

Natural adaptation to society requires defensive postures that cannot be felt consciously and cannot be unloosened quickly, postures which diminish the ego's awareness of its archetypal source and keep us searching for completion in the world of conscious events. Complexes outside the ego's conscious sphere of influence, however, do maintain their numinous connection with the Self, which is why they have such power over us and cannot be "controlled" by the ego's will-power. Therapies which rely on ego-strength, as all short-term and cognitive therapies do, ignore this fact that is the foundation of depth psychology. Patients may accept suggestions and interpretations in a desire for health, but eventually these cognitions are reabsorbed by the dominant complexes, unless a dialectical relationship with the complex occurs which allows it to be accepted more or less comfortably into ego-awareness. Eating disorders reflect complexes which dominate the ego and are often not able to be contained by will-power alone. In discovering the archetypal source of the complex we hope to find the key to transformation. What gods or demons in the patient drive the hunger, who is represented in the irresistible food, who withholds a sense of safety, satiety, and fulfillment? What is being compensated, and what avoided?

In the short-term therapies, patient and therapist do not stay in relationship long enough to get to the problems of trust which are the inevitable fate of any long relationship and which reflect the power of autonomous complexes to undermine our love and determination. The honeymoon of complete trust eventually must give way to doubt, and then transformation processes begin. Romantic relationships falter at this point, and the personality's true colors come forth. Similarly, in therapy, the hardest and most potentially rewarding work begins when the patient begins to question the value of the work, or the integrity of the therapist.

Let us assume that Joan has elected to participate in unlimited psychotherapy. In addition to noting my first impressions, I will want to try to establish a sense of how she perceives her situation at the moment. Of what feelings is she most aware? To what are her attention and affect being drawn? Is she able to think symbolically, and is she able to feel symbolically? The former requires an intellectual capacity to abstract an essence or universal quality from the concrete event, and is a minimal requirement for depth psychotherapy, obviously. The capacity to feel symbolically is more nebulous: to be able to hold within the accessible psyche a gratifying image which enables one to postpone impulsive, immediate satisfaction of one's tensions and desires is an asset but not a requirement for depth psychotherapy. In fact, it is often one of the weak or absent capacities that we hope will come to fruition in successful psychotherapy. In psyche are included not only mental contents and visual images, but physiological and transcendental contents and experiences. Jung referred to these as the psychoid events, those experiences on the edge of consciousness at the level of instinctual and spiritual awarenesses. Imagining is not just visual, but also kinesthetic and auditory.

Freudian, neo-Freudian, and neo-Jungian psychoanalytic theorists have given exquisite attention to the developing infant in attempting to understand how this capacity for symbolic gratification becomes part of a human being's psychological equipment, for all communal life depends on the ability of most of its members to postpone physiological gratification through symbolism. The infant who negotiates successfully the substitution of a transitional object for the incomplete and inconstant mother has acquired one of the magical tools which will make the journey of individuation possible. However, patients seeking individuation often come to us without having ever developed this capacity for symbolizing feeling, this tool or ability which will allow them to relativize and objectify their emotional needs. In such cases we hope to recreate in the therapy vessel the archetypal context in which can occur the leap of trust that allows a relatively undifferentiated psyche to anticipate and await gratification with some degree of self-reflection. This theme can be found in countless fairy-tales in the form of the hero's or heroine's convoluted journey toward patience and self-containment until the time for just the appropriate action is propitious.

I predict Joan to be a person who will remain long in the non-symbolic mother-world, and who will have some difficulty in translating her symptoms into psychological meanings, but who will bring an enlivening energy to her work which will gradually become more symbolic and open to creative uses of unconscious material. If she remembers dreams, can learn to do active imagination, can put her feelings into some form of symbolic process – imagining, drawing, painting, dancing, writing, or translating into music – then these psychic conduits will become rituals to channel the mythic world into the significant emotional events of everyday life and ordinary relationships. Imbued with meaning and the primal dimensions of archetypal events, everyday life and ordinary relationships become filled with spirit, passion is allowed to enter everyday life instead of stagnating in emotional impasses, and there is no reason to hide from reality behind fears and inhibited desires. We look forward, then, to encounters with both material and spiritual worlds for whatever those encounters offer, for richer, for poorer, till death do us part.

Inevitably an interplay between levels of integration occurs throughout life and within the analytic session. Patient and therapist both dip into early infantile, child, and adolescent states if the process is moving. Also, even patients with fragile integrity may move into highly differentiated or enlightened states, which could pass unnoticed if we are conditioned to expect less of that person. It is important, then, that the therapist see and recognize these enlightened states by being open to them. I am afraid that if we define or diagnose too well, we may be closed to such recognitions. Consequently, I look at each session as a potential adventure, and try not to be bogged down in expectations and predictions based on diagnoses and prognoses. Sometimes the adventure feels more like being hindered by leaden weights or buried in earth … hardly open to the influence of Mercurius the Holy Journeyer. Still, a journey it is, and subject to change at any bend in the road.

In her family of origin Joan learned an attitude of abuse toward herself, probably through a contemptuous relationship between masculine and feminine principles modeled in the family, which now manifests in a cavalier attitude toward the unusual menstrual bleeding, as well as in her forcing her body to compete with its own digestive processes. Such obstinate refusal to submit to the fundamental processes of nutrition reflects a deep fury toward her body and its wants. In whatever way the body's wants are imaged, whether as the devouring mother, poisonous breast, insatiably greedy child, implacable father, we want to discover and bring to light that image. I reject the notion that there is a universal dynamic underlying all bulimias (such as anger toward father). Such an assumption is no more valid than saying that a particular dream symbol has the same meaning for everyone. While there would appear to the observer to be a conflict between uncontrollable hunger and a repudiation of that impulse to devour, we cannot assume what the bulimic's underlying conflict consists of until her images tell us about her relationship to the symptom.

It is fashionable to treat the eating disorders with anti-depressants and anti-anxiety drugs. I am wary of medications, which may interfere with the coming to light of the images, our clues to the archetypal meaning underlying the symptoms, those very meanings which will unlock the compulsive nature of the symptoms. Some anxiety is required for the individuation process to unfold and for the kind of plodding, trial-and-error work of plowing over the same soul-sod repeatedly until it is pulverized to the point where something new can be planted. But repetition is two-faced. How do we know when we are in a pattern of futile cyclical compulsion, and when inching our way to individuation? Here therapy furthers self-reflection that enables a patient to ask the right question, examine the dream, notice the inner experience, or single out the authentic voice, that tells that ground is being broken, however slowly. Despite the evidence of self-contempt in

Joan's symptoms and her disgust at her body's demands, a counter-movement toward self-care is bringing about constructive changes in Joan. I would hope that both the disgust and the self-care will have time to be explored, and that those seemingly dualistic alternatives can be reconciled.

Therapy feels most successful to me when it ends by mutual agreement of patient and therapist at a point of completion of some significant integration of complex contents. Ideally, there is a consideration of ending, perhaps dreams that confirm the decision, and an opportunity to review the process, particularly the relationship which has imparted its mark on therapist and patient to be remembered as a connection of soul.

## NOTES

1   In addition to theoretical discussion in chapter 6 (above), see also Hillman, 1975, pp. 170–195.
2   Images of alchemical operations are elucidated in many sources. One comprehensive overview is given in Edinger, 1985.

## REFERENCES

Edinger, Edward (1985). *Anatomy of the Psyche: Alchemical Symbolism in Psychotherapy.* La Salle, Ill.: Open Court Publishing Company.
Hillman, James (1975). "Archetypal Theory." In *Loose Ends: Primary Papers in Archetypal Psychology.* Dallas: Spring Publications.
Jung, C. G. (1967). *Alchemical Studies.* CW 13.

ROSEMARY GORDON

# A developmental approach

When I first read Joan's history, as described by the Renfrew Center, I felt shocked by the bleakness of her story. Her whole life seemed to have been devoid of any experience of love, support, concern, or of somebody or anybody who might have been able to hold her, contain her, or encourage her to value herself, to care for herself and to protect herself. Such a case history can provoke despair, pessimism, pity, and discouragement.

Yet there were just one or two features in her history that were like points of light blinking like small stars in a very dark space. Their very presence provokes a question. To what extent is Joan really only the victim of fate; or is she, or has she been, also, the maker of her fate?

Before I attempt to deal with such questions I want to digress briefly in order to survey both theory and clinical practice that characterize the developmental school. I will also try to describe the use I make of it, though restricting myself to only a few points.

Andrew Samuels (1985) in his book *Jung and the Post-Jungians* described how the various analytical psychologists became differentiated into three schools, the "classical," the "archetypal," and the "developmental." Until then we used to think of a London versus a Zurich school, which gave it a tribal, chauvinistic, or even jingoistic air. Samuels introduced a more meaningful classification, based primarily on the predominance or the neglect of one or other of Jung's theoretical concepts or clinical practices. When I found myself placed by him into the developmental school I had really no difficulty in recognizing and accepting this attribution.

Now, ten years later, I want to examine whether I am still thinking and working as a "developmental" Jungian analyst, and whether I still value this approach. In other words whether I still believe:

1.  that development is, could or should be, a life-long process, beginning from birth – or even from before birth – and hopefully continuing to the very end of life (Fordham's seminal work and the recent researches by Daniel Stern have led us to recognize that individuation does indeed start unbelievably early);

2.  that it is helpful and growth-producing for a person – or a person's therapist – to be in touch with and take account of the important events, developmental stages, and experiences in his or her life and personal history;

3.  that men and women (i) have physical bodies and therefore have physical or sensory experiences; (ii) are social beings with emotional and social needs, having been thrust into the emotional and social context of parents, families and communities; and (iii) experience an inner world of internalized personages and relationships and of images and phantasies that carry both remembered and also innovative, unfamiliar, or numinous features;

4.  that exploration and use of the transference and the countertransference is central to analytic work, because through it are set in motion valuable bridging processes – bridgings between oneself and the other, bridgings between the different parts and tendencies within the psyche, and bridging between the basic desire for fusion or union and the opposing wish for identity and separateness; furthermore, that it is through the transference that events or conflicts experienced in the past can become a "present past," experienced and lived now, but perhaps in a somewhat new and different way; that as for the analyst's countertransference, this may help to recover what had seemed lost,

and it may even assist in its potential transformation; but, finally and importantly, that transference and countertransference can serve to potentiate the evolution of the symbolizing function.

Now to return to the case of Joan. There have been many adverse conditions in her history, much early damage, and clearly her images and symptoms belonged to a pre-Oedipal stage. But signs of a nascent capacity to experience and to communicate through metaphors and symbols, and a potential identification with the wounded healer – all this triggered in me interest and some optimism. It led me to sense that the outcome of her development and therapy may show that men and women are not inevitably passive bystanders of their fate. They are not necessarily just an arena in which biological, instinctual, or even archetypal forces disport themselves.

I believe I feel comfortable in the developmental school because due value is given there to both analysis and synthesis and to the psychological processes of both differentiation and integration.

Taking a cool clinical look at Joan, I believe that she is a depressive person with quite marked masochistic tendencies which are often enacted in a compulsive way. Again and again she has managed to get herself into situations in which she is exposed to conditions that are revealingly similar to some of her earlier painful childhood experiences. This creates the suspicion that there is in her an unconscious need to repeat what has been; that she can't let go of the past. Is it that she dare not risk meeting the new? Her unconscious repetition compulsion is neatly disguised and over-compensated by her behavior and her conscious thoughts: she appears to move swiftly and frequently from one sexual partner to another and from one childbirth to the next one and from one job or occupation to another.

There seems to be in Joan, as a result of a nature–nurture combination, a predisposition to depression and to eating disorders. She has described her mother as being "always depressed" and weighing a quite unbelievable 300 pounds; and her own eldest daughter, Amy, has been diagnosed as having a "bipolar disorder."

Apparently both parents, father and mother, have abused her. Her father, although strict and emotionally distant, abused her sexually from when she was about five years old onwards, while her mother wanted Joan to "fondle her breasts." In other words all the potentially pleasant, nourishing, and enriching stuffs, experiences, and feelings were forced on her, rather than offered as gifts; they were not allowed to develop naturally and organically out of meaningful, relevant, and emotionally matching relationships. It is easy to empathize and to believe that she remembers her childhood as "unsafe and full of fears."

When Joan was admitted to Renfrew she was bulimic, "bingeing and vomiting (purging) at least three times a day." Her bulimia, I think, is undoubtedly linked to a powerful body image distortion. She weighed a normal 144 pounds, being 5′ 6″ high, but she thinks of herself as fat; this suggests to me that there is an unconscious identification with her obese, her grossly overweight, mother. This must be quite particularly painful, given that she is likely to experience a near-explosive cocktail of ambivalence in relation to her mother. She probably longed for this mother to transform herself into a loving, caring one, but primarily and more realistically, she feels an intense hatred and distrust for her who, instead of protecting her against her father's abuse, had actually organized their living arrangements for it to happen, once her older sister had left and escaped from their parents' manipulation and collusive betrayal.

Just knowing about her history and before I have actually seen her or worked with her tempts me to suspect that her bingeing and vomiting is a caricaturing dramatization, an enactment of what her parents have done to her. After all, mother forced her to attend to her breast, the breast that is associated with food, that is, with milk and the oral pleasures that are linked to sucking. And father forced on her a premature experience of the excitement and pleasures linked to and derived from the genitals.

Thus what could and should be potentially satisfying and fulfilling is lost, is perverted, if the stimulations of the body organs are forced upon one, and are out of one's own control. Has Joan's compulsive bingeing not just this very effect of making her feel humiliated if not de-personalized, turning pleasure into intense displeasure?

The bulimic person's body experience, it seems to me, is thrust from states of feeling that his or her inside is uncomfortably over-full to states of feeling the insides as a gaping emptiness. In Joan's case what she vomits and expels represents, symbolically, I suspect, mother's unwanted milk and father's unwanted semen.

The powerlessness and the victim role that Joan had experienced as a child, particularly in relation to her parents, could perhaps be understood as having been transmuted in the adult Joan into compulsions and addictions which then continued to make her feel helpless and impotent.

The fact that Joan had failed to "see the signs" when her second husband sexually abused her two small daughters shows how very deeply she had repressed and split off her own experience of abuse from her father. Indeed very complex and ambivalent feelings must have got associated with the theme of father–daughter incest, which then left her insensitive, blind, and deaf and cut off from her children; and possibly here too is some sort of identification with her own mother.

Joan's masochistic tendencies seem to have taken her into two marriages in and through which she repeated and relived all the hurts and dramas of her childhood. Her first two husbands were cruel, abusive, unfaithful, and ruthless; the second one abandoned her and the three children suddenly without preparation, warning, or explanation. When she came to Renfrew she was in her third marriage, but there was yet no information and no way of knowing how that one might develop.

She also reported to Renfrew that she would, at times, when particularly anxious and in emotional pain, hit herself either on the head or in the stomach. I wonder if this might not show that there is something of a split in her ego consciousness, because by hitting herself she gives vent not only to her masochism, that is her addiction to pain, but also to her sadism, for this activity involves not only a victim, but also a perpetrator.

Adopting another baby, a damaged baby, a baby with cerebral palsy while she was in her third pregnancy strikes me as another acting out of masochism, although I just wonder whether this could perhaps also be understood as expressing an unconscious striving toward an almost heroic caring and healing.

This brings me back to my initial impression that in spite of the general adverse features of her relationships in childhood and also later, there were some glimmers of light. I am thinking of the fact that she had "recently organized a women's self-help group for eating disorders," or that after having "lost everything" when her second husband had deserted her, she managed in the end to find a job as a "cashier and food service attendant" and succeeded in keeping it. But even more encouraging for any possible psychotherapeutic venture are some signs that Joan may be capable of using and thinking and expressing herself in and through metaphors and symbols, as when she asked at Renfrew that she wanted to be helped to "work with the feelings I've been stuffing down." Her long-term goal to become an addiction counselor also supports my hunch, my vague suspicion, that there is in her, linked to her experience of pain, distrust, and impotence, an opposite force, a drive to heal herself and others.

Thus, as I studied and immersed myself longer and more deeply into the descriptions of Joan's history and her presenting problems, my original gloomy forebodings were shot through by some shafts of light; that is, I could see one or two possibly hopeful signs that encouraged me to think that some analytic work might be possible and prove to be helpful.

Let me now suppose or guess how I might proceed, given my theoretical and clinical experience and point of view, and given what I have by now learned about Joan.

Having seen Joan for an initial interview and assessment I might decide to offer to take her on for analytic psychotherapy. I might have liked her; I might have seen her as a woman who had been badly damaged, and who had a very poor sense of her own value and who was very unsure of who she is and what she is; yet I would have sensed an unexpected but deeply buried core of toughness and tenacity. This impression would have led me to feel that she and I might be able to establish enough rapport between us to weather the storms as well as the periods of becalmment, of hatred and love, of feelings of persecution and feelings of trust, of longing for and of angry rejection of dependence, closeness, intimacy.

I would also have realized that we would have to begin very slowly the analytic work, that is, the exploration of her conscious and unconscious experiences, of her history, her memories, her phantasies, and her dreams, and also of the present-day frustrations, satisfactions, events, conflicts, hopes, and fears. Above all it would be most important to respect her privacy and her boundaries and avoid anything that could rouse the suspicion that I might try to intrude with my own thoughts and speculations by making and giving interpretations. Joan having been so much abused, both sexually and as a person, my function as her therapist would be to guide her, slowly, toward her own possible insights. Consequently whatever I said to her would have to be said in the form of a question, except, of course, when I might want to express and tell her something about my own feelings and reactions.

Expressing myself in the form of questions rather than in statements, which I consider to be particularly important in working with Joan, is actually something I tend to use with most of my patients, because questioning involves the patient in taking an active part in the analytic work rather than remain a passive recipient of whatever the therapist produces. In other words the patient must examine whether or not what has been offered seems to fit and make some sense; and if distortions have crept in, they can give a clue and reveal what is happening in the patient–therapist relationship and/or what kind of intrapsychic complex dominates the functioning of perception, thinking, feeling, and intuition.

On taking Joan into therapy I would certainly suggest a face-to-face encounter. The couch would be quite inappropriate for someone so fettered and abused by both parents. Should she, at a much later date, having worked through the traumas of her childhood – and her two marriages – and become herself interested and absorbed in the deeply unconscious inner world inside her, the world of phantasies and symbols, then a move to the couch might be entertained and tried. But the idea of such a change would then need to come from her, by being verbalized, or by the occasional, apparently inadvertent, glance at the couch.

As regards the frequency of her analytic sessions, I would, to start with, see her twice a week. One has to strike a fine balance, in making decisions: a fine balance between on the one hand containing her and making the depression bearable, and on the other hand precipitating the collapse of her defenses and the external structures she has managed to make and keep. I am thinking of work, family, children, and the third marriage. But I would also keep in mind that she is liable to addictions: admittedly addiction to therapy or her therapist may be less harmful than her bulimic addictions, but in the long run such addiction may sap the transformative potential of the therapy.

As in all analytic therapy, the most important function is the transference and countertransference, that is, everything felt, believed, projected, and introjected that happens between patient and therapist. As I have said elsewhere, "Transference is a 'lived bridge' between the I and the other, between past, present and future, between the unconscious that is the split-off parts of the psyche on the one hand, and between the conscious and the rational on the other hand" (Gordon, 1993, p. 235). In other words the transference creates "a present past." Through the process of projection the persons and personages, real, historical, phantasized, or archetypal, that had furnished the patient's inner world in the past, are put onto or into the therapist. Thus, through the transference the fears, hopes, longings, moods and feelings that had been experienced but were then lost – repressed, denied – are reevoked, rediscovered and reexperienced.

Were I to read Joan's case notes, I would, in real life, now want to see the patient myself and so explore my own reactions, intuitive understanding, and expectations. I would try to suspend my memories of the assessor's report, in order to make myself empty enough to receive my own impressions of her. For we know there are no unbiased, pure, and neutral observations; every assessor's interest and personal characteristics inevitably affect his or her view of a patient, quite apart from the fact that a person will react and bring along different parts of him- or herself to different interviewers. If I were to be Joan's psychotherapist then I would have to get to know and to experience her as early and as uninfluencedly as possible.

I would now start to wonder what sort of Joan I would meet in our first interview. She is forty-four years old. Amy, her first child from her first marriage, is twenty-six years old. So Joan was eighteen years old when she first got married. I imagine her to be slightly plump and of low average height.

I expect that her approach and attitude to me in this our first contact would show conflict and ambivalence. She wants to be helped and cared for, but she wouldn't easily be able to trust me: to trust that I wouldn't abuse her need for help. She resents it if and when she recognizes that she depends on someone else – on me, the therapist in this situation. She is actually ashamed of her neediness and fears that she might be considered a nuisance, a nuisance who does not really merit professional attention. (I am thinking here of her hesitation to consult her gynecologist when she suffered from heavy menstrual bleeding, and that she hesitated to take time off from work. Of course, fear of losing her job or the cost of medical attention may be other reasons, other considerations to take into account.)

If I suspected that these internal contradictions prevented her from using this first encounter and making some sort of contact with me, leaving her excessively tense and anxious and unable to speak or look, then I would try to convey to her that I understood something of this inner turmoil. I would also suspect that Joan probably knew that I might be her therapist, which meant that she would see me regularly for quite a long time. Knowing this might be reassuring; but it might also make her more reluctant to speak to me because she might fear that whatever she told me I would remember, I would hold on to it; and if that happened then she would not be able to re-bury it, to forget it, to repress it once more, or to deny it; for I would then be able to push it back into consciousness and confront her with those memories and feelings that she had – and still has – experienced as being too painful, too shameful or too guilt-laden.

Before ending this first meeting I would discuss with Joan some of the practical arrangements – number of sessions per week, the times and dates I would offer her, fees, length of sessions, holidays, etc. But finally I would ask her if she did want to embark on this therapeutic venture, and embark on it with me.

Her masochistic tendencies and her compulsion to repeat the early abuse from both her parents could also hinder, or even sabotage, the analytic work. Masochism can indeed obstruct therapy because it carries with it a denial of one's own responsibilities and the experience of guilt. Nor can discomfort and/or pain act as incentive to change, to develop, to grow, since pain and discomfort are in fact sought out and desired. And if masochism is actually the object of a repetition compulsion – as it is in Joan – then the therapy's effectiveness is likely to be obstructed. As I have already mentioned at the beginning of this chapter, the presence of a repetition compulsion points to a person's need to hold on to the past, the familiar – however bad or painful this past has been – rather than step into the new, the relatively unknown. "The devil you know is better than the devil you don't know" is a folksy word of advice or wisdom one hears occasionally.

I can imagine that on meeting Joan I might come to feel that, in spite of the rather pessimistic case notes, in spite of the severe damage she has suffered in early childhood and later, and in spite of the various psycho-pathological features in her make-up – in spite of all this, I might feel inclined to offer her psychotherapy. In fact, I might find myself actually liking her. I might see in her something touching, perhaps because she gives the impression of a vulnerability against which she has not erected impene-trable defenses. It is true she seems to look at one with a watchful suspiciousness, yet I sense that there is inside her a stubborn tenacity which I would find encouraging.

Obviously she would not be easy to work with; I would expect crises and rages and also periods of clinging to me and anger and despair when the inevitable occasions of separation loom, for instance, at weekends and holidays. But I might be persuaded – or seduced? – to trust that her tenacity could and would in the end rescue her and our work together in her therapy.

But what might prove to be even more important and encouraging are the various signs that there is in her a quite active archetypal image of the wounded healer; she might be drawn to identify herself with this intra-psychic personage and let herself be guided or inspired by it. The adoption of a brain-damaged infant, her ambition to become an addiction counselor, and having already succeeded in setting up a women's self-help group for eating disorders – all this suggests to me that a wounded healer archetype is present and functions; this bodes well, I think, for a psychotherapeutic venture.

I expect that Joan's feelings for me, that is, her transference, would swing wildly and frequently between hate and love, between a demand for total availability, total provisioning, and total rejection of anything I offer her, or between almost blind trust and deep distrust. Particularly at the beginning of our work together she would not be able to trust me, would not be able to believe that I would willingly give her something good and nourishing, such as my caring for her, or my being there for her, or my interpretations to help her find meaning – all this without demanding in return her submission to me or the surrender of her selfhood, of her own sensuous pleasures, of her instinctive needs.

In view of her experiences of abuse – abuse of her body, her feelings, or her identity – I realize that I would have to be particularly careful in doing or saying anything that could trigger further the projection onto me of the abusing parents.

But having to restrain myself and thwart my wish to make her a gift of some of my insights, my understanding, my discoveries of some of her unconscious forces or personalities – all this would at times leave me angry, frustrated, and impatient. Even in retrospect I would not always know whether these almost hostile reactions to Joan issued from a counter-transference illusion or from a countertransference syntony (in which case they would inform me via projective identification of what was experienced unconsciously by Joan). But at other times I might feel myself as if infected by sadness and despair and a fear that I was useless and that nothing could get better. When that particular mood invaded me I would experience a sort of impotent compassion for Joan that would make me imagine myself stroking her cheeks and reassuring her that there was value in her, that she had already achieved much, and that she could become more attractive and lovable. Like many bulimic patients, Joan has very little self-respect and fears that she might rouse in people disgust and repulsion. The fact that her self-attacks are so intense and pervasive might tempt one to counter them occasionally with some simple and straightforward reassurance. Such improved self-valuation might help her when she had to confront and deal with some of the impulses and experiences which, I suspect, exist and are active inside Joan, but had been relegated to the shadow – impulses and experiences such as, for instance, anger, hatred and resentment, or phantasies of violence, of murder, of revenge, or even of furtive sexual pleasure.

One would obviously have to work hard with Joan on the bulimia and on the theme of the conversion of and interdependence and interaction of body and psyche, and on the displacement of genital experience to oral experience and on the whole symbolism that is involved here. Joan herself seemed to be ready to tackle this, to judge by the comment she made in her Renfrew interview when she expressed a desire to "work with the feelings I've been stuffing down." This remark would be particularly significant when I had to decide on whether to take Joan into analytic psychotherapy.

There seems to be an inverse correlation between the tendency to develop psychosomatic symptoms or even actual illness and the capacity to symbolize. Awareness of this fact would determine one's therapeutic strategy and would be particularly important for work with Joan.

So far there is little known of Joan's early infancy, of her pre-Oedipal impulses and phantasies. Her experiences from age five onwards when she felt – and was – abused by her parents were obviously so painful, so intense, so frightening and conflictual that their darkness, their shadow obscured earlier as well as later events in her life. I suspect that some of these events would be revealed in and through the transference and countertransference. And in and through the transference–countertransference we might haul up not only memories of what happened to her, but we might also facilitate the reexperiencing, here and now, of the affects that accompanied those events. It is in this reexperiencing in the new, the present-day context, and the present-day relationships that change and healing may happen. And the present-day relationship to her analyst might help increase trust, trust in the "other" and trust in herself, in her own resources and capacities. And it might help release her from the dark and sinister parts of her own psycho-history in which she had felt trapped and condemned to repeat it again and again.

## REFERENCES

Gordon, R. (1993). *Bridges: Metaphor for Psychic Processes*. London: Karnac Books.
Samuels, A. (1985). *Jung and the Post-Jungians*. London: Routledge and Kegan Paul.

# III
# ANALYTICAL PSYCHOLOGY IN SOCIETY

# 11

## POLLY YOUNG-EISENDRATH

# Gender and contrasexuality: Jung's contribution and beyond

> Sexuality belongs in this area of instability played out in the register of demand and desire, each sex coming to stand, mythically and exclusively, for that which could satisfy and complete the other. It is when the categories "male" and "female" are seen to represent an absolute and complementary division that they fall prey to a mystification in which the difficulty of sexuality instantly disappears.
>
> (Jacqueline Rose, Introduction to J. Lacan, *Feminine Sexuality*, 1982, p. 33)

### Gender and difference

The universal division of the human community into two sexes, marked by signs and symbols of gender, has enduring and powerful effects on our psychological functioning as individuals, couples, and groups. Not only are we born into on-going stories about our own and the opposite sex, stories that constrain and engender possibilities for action and identity, but also we form strong internal images of femininity and masculinity. While we identify with one, we develop an unconscious complex around the Other (I capitalize the subjective Other to distinguish it from the interpersonal other).

Gender is a central organizer of interpersonal reality. It carries so much meaning that we feel compelled to get it established quickly, both at the birth of an infant and in any instance in which we encounter a stranger. "What is this person's sex?" is a question that opens the way to fantasy, symbol, and speech. Any confusion or obscuration of a person's gender creates anxiety. How can I address, act, or engage this person unless I am sure about the category that will determine so much of what I shall expect and perceive?

There are many fertile conscious and unconscious consequences of the division into two genders. Rarely have they been treated seriously within depth psychology without being tied to some biological and/or essentialist argument that women and men are "born that way." Then the mysteries of sexuality are reduced to formulas about differences that should be or just are. This leads to psychological theories about what is missing, left out, or diminished in one or the other sex. Since most theorists of depth psychology have been androcentric (taking male people to be the standard for health and success), most theories of gender and sex have described female people in terms of deficits – *lack* of penis, power, moral fiber, cultural strivings, or intelligence – and have assumed that female people are "naturally" depressed, narcissistic, envious. Although there have been exceptions to this, particularly among object relations theorists and feminist psychoanalysts who may see envy belonging to both sexes, most psychodynamic theorizing about gender has been flawed by reducing sex differences to a formula that imitates stereotypes.

Jung's psychology is in some ways an exception to this. Jung loudly calls our attention to one important theme in regard to sex differences: the opposite sex as a projection-making factor. He invites us to see aspects of ourselves that are denied to consciousness (because they are intolerably awful or idealized) through our projections into others. His theory of contrasexuality, that everyone has a biologically based opposite-sexed personality derived from genetic traces of the other sex (hormonal, morphological, and the like), *is* tainted by essentialism but clear about its psychological domain. This condition creates an Other within, an unconscious subpersonality. That subpersonality has a life of its own, usually dissociated, and often projected onto the opposite sex, a fetish, or an aspect of the world, in order to defend the self against anxiety and conflict.

Jung's theory of anima and animus (the Latin names he gave to these subpersonalities) as archetypes is both a cultural analysis of universal opposites, and a psychological theory of "projection-making factors." The anima of Jung's theory, the feminine subpersonality of a male person, and the animus, the masculine subpersonalty of a female person, are biologically driven natural evolutions of contrasexuality. Although they develop throughout life, they come into play especially at mid-life because of the shifting nature of identity development in that era. Expressed as emotionally laden images, these archetypes structure what is latent of the opposite sex in each of us, a sort of soul-mate of both ideal and devalued potentials. Jung's contrasexuality is a contribution to depth psychology that problematizes the "opposite sex," tracing the shadow of Otherness back to its owner. In contrast to Freud's narrowly focused theories of castration anxiety and penis envy (which centralize the penis, the phallus, and the power of the male) Jung's gender theory is fluid and expansive in its potential uses in a post-modern, decentered world. Long before object relations theorists (such as Melanie Klein, Ronald Fairbairn, or Wilfred Bion in the earlier group, or Thomas Ogden, James Grotstein, or Stephen Mitchell among contemporaries) conceived of personality as decentered into autonomous suborganizations, Jung had developed a dissociative model of personality with a major emphasis on the split in identity between the conscious gendered self and the less conscious (or unconscious) constrasexual Other.

In my practice and theorizing (Young-Eisendrath, 1993; Young-Eisendrath and Wiedemann, 1987) of analytical psychology, I have revised the definitions of contrasexuality and anima/animus in response to contemporary critiques of feminism and constructivism. In my view, as in the view of many other psychoanalysts, these critiques have effectively undermined beliefs in universal gender differences, in ways of being that are biologically "masculine" or "feminine." Instead of archetypes of masculine, feminine, anima or animus, I focus on the universal opposition or dichotomy of a split-gender world. The two sexes imagined as opposites, as carrying complementary potentials, are spun out into many psychological, cultural, and social fantasies and symbols. As psychologist Gisela Labouvie-Vief (1994) says of the cultural constructs of gender:

> They not only *reflect* certain inner self-identifications and outer social realities, but they also come to *create* those very inner and outer realities. Thus, the resulting language of gender attributions becomes a framework within which developing selves define themselves, attempting to validate their "appropriateness" as men and women in culture. (p. 29)

Before exploring some cultural and clinical applications of this revised Jungian theory of gender and contrasexuality, it's useful to specify some definitions.

I differentiate between sex (as in sex differences) and gender. The "sex" we are born as and the "gender" we are assigned at birth do not add up to being the same thing, although one flows from the other. Sex is the difference of embodiment, the structural and functional properties of the human body (including hormones and brain structure) that provide both possibilities for and constraints on who we can be. Most of these relate to reproductive life in some way, although there are biological differences between the sexes – such as mortality differences at birth and longevity – that stand outside our reproductive period.

Gender is the identity club, the social category, that we are assigned at birth (and now sometimes sooner, thanks to ultrasound tests) based on the sex of the body. Whereas sex is inflexible, gender identities vary from culture to culture, even from family to family. In some societies, for example, men are expected to be more nurturant and home-oriented than women, taking care of the young (see Sanday, 1981, for examples). In our North American and European societies, men are usually expected to be more autonomous than nurturant, but in some subcultures in North

America that may vary. Young Iranian males (even in America), for example, as anthropologist Mary Catherine Bateson (1994) describes them, separate from their parents much more gradually than Americans, are often expected to sacrifice for their mothers' care, and are respected by older males for doing so. As Bateson puts it,

> American culture has gone further than most in valuing the autonomous self, downplaying the importance of relationship. It was once virtually unique, for instance, in the preference for having infants sleep alone. (p. 60)

The way a culture plays out the opposition of autonomy and dependence is often reflected in the roles expected of the two sexes. When the arenas of nurturance and relationship are not highly valued, they tend to be assigned to female people. When they are more valued they belong to both sexes and individuality is often downplayed (see Sanday, 1981, for a full discussion of this).

There is also evidence that people may have different gender expectations in different contexts, depending on whether they are making judgments about themselves or others (Spence and Sawin, 1985). North American men, for example, tend to use categories of strength or size to evaluate their own gender whereas women use roles, such as mother or wife, to evaluate theirs. And yet both sexes tend to regard gender as a "fact of life" – not as a construction based on their socialization. Most of us confuse the immutability of sexual characteristics with the variability of gender. From all available studies of sex and gender differences, it appears that *no* long-standing personality traits are connected to any consistent differences between female and male people (Maccoby, 1990; Unger, 1989, p. 22).

Once we see gender as culturally constructed – as female and male people assigned into roles, identities, and status – biological explanations of sex differences lose their explanatory force. Not only are we not "born that way" but roles and identities of women and men are shifting almost by the moment in all major societies – with one exception. Men continue to have more power than women, both status and decision-making power, in all major societies. To threaten this power dichotomy (that men are more powerful and women less) is to threaten the fabric of civilized life. Major economic systems of the world depend on the unpaid and underpaid labor of female people (see Young-Eisendrath, 1993, Chs. 1–3 for a full discussion). Most of us, both women and men, feel uncomfortable about women out-earning men in the workplace, women playing major political roles, and females being the majority (as they are) in today's world. The relative flexibility of gender roles and the power difference between the sexes have to be acknowledged in any contemporary account of gender, inside or outside the therapeutic consulting room. The changing meanings of gender, the recognition that it's constructed, and the enduring effects of male dominance are as significant in doing Jungian analysis as they are in revising Jung's theory to be applicable to contemporary life.

When people insist on a strong division between the sexes, and assume that women are naturally more relational and men naturally more autonomous, they risk losing parts of themselves forever. Externalization of these parts through projection, envy, and idealization can become a way of life. Romantic partners may be consciously or unconsciously chosen because of their willingness to carry idealized or devalued parts of the self. As psychoanalyst Evelyn Cleavely (1993) says,

> In . . . choosing a partner who for reasons of his own is willing to receive certain projections, it is possible to have unwanted aspects projected outside oneself and at the same time remain in vital contact with them in the other. What is projected into and rediscovered in the partner is then treated in the same way as it was treated in the self. What you cannot stand in yourself, you locate and attack (or nurture) in the other. (p. 65)

Projections into those close at hand are played out through the internal theater of projective identification, an unconscious *participation mystique* as Jung aptly called it. The mystique of projective identification is its uncanny capacity to evoke in another, often an intimate other, the most dreaded or idealized aspects of the self.

## Projection, projective identification and splitting

Although Jung did not fully understand projective identification, he noted the powerful mixing up of two people's unconscious dynamics in analysis, psychotherapy, and marriage. Using the anthropological term coined by Lévy-Bruhl, *participation mystique*, to name the condition, he was undoubtedly referring to the same phenomenon that was later called "projective identification" by object relations theorists from Klein to Ogden. Bion (1952) was probably the first to emphasize the interpersonal component of projective identification. He described the feelings of the recipient of the projection as "being manipulated so as to be playing a part, no matter how difficult to recognize, in somebody else's phantasy" (p. 149). The recipient feels almost kidnapped or coerced into carrying out the unconscious fantasy of the projector. Only through a struggle to be conscious and differentiated can the recipient resist the pull and symbolize the experience, essentially making the projection available to be recognized by the projector.

When gender is strongly dichotomized, in an individual or a group, people lose parts of themselves by "proving" that the others are exclusive owners. For example, if I see myself simply as a giving, feminine person, then I am likely to project my more demanding and aggressive aspects into others, especially men if I believe stereotypes about men being naturally aggressive and self-interested. By implying that my motives are *never* self-interested, I can evoke in my male partner an annoyed or aggressive statement, "showing" myself that *he's* the aggressive one.

Men may fail to recognize their own nurturant and relational capacities if they "see" them as merely natural to women. Women may silence the voice of their own authority if they assume that men are more rational, decisive, or objective by nature. And so on. The effect of projection is to externalize aspects of oneself and "meet" them in other people, animals, or things. The effect of projective identification is to evoke in another what has been externalized from the self, and then to "prove" that the quality or aspect belongs to the other and not to the self. As psychoanalyst Jacqueline Rose says in the opening quotation, the mystery of sexuality, as a contrapuntal play of opposites, is obscured and even lost when the two sexes are seen as absolute and complementary divisions. Then the content is set and nothing new can be evoked, nothing new can be discovered, and aspects of both sexes are forever lost to themselves.

Too often Jungian theory has portrayed the sexes as a complementary division of the Masculine and the Feminine. This has led to a defensive splitting of interpersonal and intrapsychic worlds, both in theorizing and in practice. Each sex then seems to represent a preset part of the human experience. The meaning of Masculinity, men and maleness in this kind of theory is Logos, rationality, independence, and objectivity. The meaning of Femininity, women and femaleness is Eros, connectedness, and subjectivism. This is the picture of the two sexes that Jung painted, reflecting the biases of his cultural era.

Stretching beyond those biases, though, he added the concept of contra-sexuality, the potential of each sex to develop the qualities and aspects of its opposite in the second half of life, through the process of individuation, the completion of the self. Accordingly, each sex could integrate its opposite at a time in life when reflection and personal creativity might be enhanced, after one had taken one's place in society and attained one's "appropriate" gender development. Critiques of Jungian gender splitting have been written by many Jungian theorists: Demaris Wehr (1987), Polly Young-Eisendrath and Florence Wiedemann (1987), Mary Ann Mattoon and Jennifer Jones (1987), Andrew Samuels (1989), Claire Douglas (1990), Deldon McNeely (1991), and Polly Young-Eisendrath (1993), among others. Several strategies have been proposed for revising Jung's theory of anima and animus: (1)

assume that gender identity is flexible and that everyone, male and female, has both anima and animus, recognized as unconscious prototypical femininity and masculinity; (2) assume that gender identity is flexible, but that biology is the greater determinant of sex differences, and that anima and animus are archetypes related to biological substrata of sexuality, leaving males exclusively with anima, and females with animus; and (3) assume that gender is flexible but that the division into two sexes is not, and hence keep the idea of anima and animus as unconscious *complexes* of the "opposite sex," affectively charged images of the Other(s) as they arise in an individual, family, or society.

I subscribe to the third strategy. Because of its yield of theoretical richness in considering the effects of projection and projective identification, and its clinical usefulness in helping individuals and couples change, I use Jung's concepts of anima/animus as a theory of contrasexuality: psychological complexes of the opposite sex in each of us. This theory includes accounts of sex differences in embodiment (inherent possibilities and limitations) that lead to envy and idealization of the opposite; of the universal division into opposites; and of gender as fluid constructions that change over time and contexts. In my approach, the term "animus" refers exclusively to the contrasexual complex of a woman, and "anima" to that of a man, highlighting the exclusive nature of gender and sex: no one can be *both* genders or sexes, and there is no third possibility.

The division of the symbolic order (that is, language, image, and expression) into opposites leads to an intrapsychic division between a conscious identity of female or male, and a contrasexual complex of its opposite. Both ego and Other are emotionally charged psychological complexes organized around archetypes. The core of ego is the archetype of Self; the core of Other is the archetype of contrasexuality (opposite sex). Ego and Other are expressed in images, habits, thoughts, actions, and meanings that arise and are sustained in a matrix of relationships. Ogden (1994) in depicting Fairbairn's theory of "internal objects" describes the way in which psychological complexes (internal objects, in his language) operate within the overall personality:

> When Fairbairn says that internal objects are not "mere objects" but dynamic structures, he seems to mean that . . . internal figures are not simply mental representations of objects, but are active agencies whose activity is perceived by itself and by other dynamic structures to have specific characteristics . . .
>
> (p. 95)

These characteristics are easily ascertained in regard to the ego complex, the most conscious subpersonality, but recognizing the "active agency" of animus or anima is difficult. It usually requires self-awareness and a psychological understanding – the capacity to recognize and claim what has been projected into a partner, lover, friend, parent, child, or therapist.

What makes contrasexuality such a powerful emotional determinant of development is its unique relationship to the ego: the contrasexual Other constrains and defines what the ego can be. The way I act and imagine myself as a woman carries with it a limitation in terms of what I consider to be "not-woman" – male, masculine, not-self. The contrasexual complex is paradoxically the product of a gendered self. What for a man is anima, or (in the term I have used elsewhere, 1993) his feminine "dream lover" – in its positive or negative aspects – is the product of that man's masculinity, what he permits himself to be as a man. What for a woman is animus, her masculine dream lover, is similarly a product of her femininity. Our fantasies of the opposite sex are based on what is excluded, often absolutely excluded, from the self.

When gender is strongly dichotomized and the world is split into two, masculine and feminine, then an individual is likely to defend the self by splitting off the contrasexual complex entirely, seeing it exclusively in others. There are many symptoms of this on a broad cultural level. Witness fiction, movies, and visual arts in which female people are portrayed as powerful madonnas, whores, overwhelmingly seductive or destructive mothers, bitches, witches, hag mothers-in-law, and so on. These images are legion and they are mostly the product of male contrasexuality, the emotionally charged images, habits, thoughts, actions, and meanings that arise from being a male in a society that fears female power. They depict little about what it means to be female, and yet they may be internalized by female people through a kind of cultural introjection. Female identity has been culturally created as emotionally powerful (often in a negative way), while female people are expected to lack authority and decision-making power. Images of men's dream lovers tap into familiar feelings and identity issues in female people, but they are not authentic portraits of female lives.

What about female dream lovers? Because women's impact on culture has burgeoned in the last twenty-five years, we now have access to female contrasexual complexes in movies, fiction, and art. Witness demonic and overpowering bully men, developmentally and relationally incompetent lost boys, sensitive erotic heroes, and androgynous lovers. To some extent men are internalizing these projections of female contrasexuality, especially the "they just don't get it" component of the incompetent lost boy. Many adult men come to couples therapy with the complaint that they "just don't get it" and can't seem to figure out why their partners are complaining and/or why their (the men's) methods of communication fail. When contrasexuality remains projected, it permeates the world around and creates barriers to further development, barriers that may never be crossed if strong dichotomizing of the sexes persists over a lifetime.

## Individuation, self-awareness, transcendent function

Jung described individuation as a recognition and integration of inner conflicts, conscious and unconscious complexes, including contrasexuality. This awareness of self-division brings with it a new kind of freedom, a knowledge of the complexity of one's own nature, and an ability to "disidentify" with aspects of it. By disidentify, I mean to see, label, and acknowledge aspects of personality *without* enacting them. This involves developing self-reflection to include both knowledge and choice about one's motives. Although everyone has the potential to develop self-awareness, and to become relatively freed up from childhood and other complexes, only some people actually do. Everyone's invited, but few arrive at individuation – the experience of "psychic totality," in Jung's words.

The door to individuation often opens through the experience of neurosis: self-dividedness in its first bold sweep. Relational disillusionment, lack of agency, the inability to meet one's goals no matter how hard one tries, and painful enactments of negative complexes (for example, acting like your aggressive father, your depressed mother, or the child who was victim) are the usual wake-up calls. Our wishes and fantasies depose realistic goals and our decision-making seems impossibly impeded. So long as our childhood complexes are the structures on which "reality" rests, either by unconsciously identifying with being children and projecting the parental image, or by identifying with being the aggressive parent and projecting the powerless child, then we are unable to feel our own dividedness.

A person unable to feel self-division is not a "psychological individual," in Jung's terms, not capable of self-reflection and personal meaning. Such a person believes that meaning comes entirely from "the way things are" and "the way we were born." Ask such a person, even a symptomatic person (an addict or an eating-disordered person, for instance), why she believes what she does when the belief seems patently irrational, and you will hear "because it's true." There's no awareness of the frame of reference, the assumptions, the emotions that color the "truth."

Many adults in North America and Europe live without self-awareness; they are not psychological individuals. They develop instead through tradition and ritual. Although it's possible to become a psychological individual on the path of tradition and ritual (certainly in some traditions, such as Buddhism, this is a part of the design), many who conform to traditions remain as psychological children throughout adulthood. They are not aware of the subjective factors of their experience, nor do they feel responsible for the lives they've lived.

Some cultures seem to invite neurosis. They value diversity and individuality, rather than homogeneity or community. The individual code is more salient than the collective and people are likely to encounter a lot of conflict about what is ideal, true, and desirable. This kind of society – such as North American democracies – produces social chaos and hierarchical individualism, but it also engenders individual freedoms and felt inner conflict. People are regularly confronted by *differences* of ideals, desires, and the like, and those differences are validated by the culture. By contrast, other societies value sharing and non-competitive community in such a way that neurosis is less likely to develop. There may be no acute awareness of self, self-division, individual needs and truths in such a communal society. Collective traditions provide the means for orderly development across the lifespan. Perhaps the only readily available means of development for those of us without clear traditions is psychological awareness. Through such awareness, we gradually create order from inner chaos and come to take responsibility for our own subjective states.

What happens to people who never fall into self-dividedness or never resolve it? According to Jung, identification with the "persona" both precedes experience of self-dividedness and may prevent the experience altogether. Jung's persona, the defensive mask that presents oneself in a role or "social look," comes into being with identity formation in childhood. One appears as one is "supposed to act." In adolescence, among those in cultures of individuality, the persona takes on the function of *appearing* as a psychological individual, at a time when *uniqueness* is hypervalued but as yet a complete mystery to the individual. The persona then functions as a pretend-individuality, as a posture of uniqueness that has been imitated. Psychoanalyst D. W. Winnicott's concept of a "false self" (defense of a true self core) is comparable in many ways to Jung's persona, but the false self is originally and primarily pathological. The persona is originally adaptive, a function of imitating or enacting a way of being prior to understanding it. The persona only *becomes* pathological if it prevents the development of self-awareness, authenticity, and other capacities after early adulthood.

When self-searching adolescents ask themselves the question "Who am I?," they answer in terms of the persona: either imitating or opposing received values and ideals. Under ordinary conditions, without childhood trauma, the persona of late adolescence is "only a mask of the collective psyche, a mask that *feigns individuality*, making others and oneself believe that one is individual" (Jung, CW 7, p. 157, italics in original).

In order to become self-aware, a person must break the identification with the persona and take responsibility for the multiple voices of subjectivity in the self. As Jung sees it, neurosis is often the first opportunity to make this developmental move:

> Neurosis is self-division. In most people the cause of the division is that the conscious mind wants to hang on to its moral ideal, while the unconscious strives after its . . . unmoral ideal which the conscious mind tries to deny.
>
> (Jung, CW 7, p. 20)

Neurotic conflict leads to loss of self-control, and this loss often brings the individual to question her or his motives or ideals.

The goal of individuation is the power to draw on the transcendent function, the tension and interplay of opposites, in everyday life. In order to reach this goal, one must develop "metacognitive processes" – the capacity to think about and entertain one's own subjective states from different perspectives. To do this, one comes to see oneself not merely from the perspective of the conscious ego complex, nor merely from a complex-related hyper-emotional ("gut feelings") perspective. Instead one can find a "third" point of view from which both of the others can be entertained and looked at without impulsively enacting them. This third perspective is the transcendent function (comparable to Winnicott's "potential space") from which one can engage in a dialectical relationship with aspects of oneself. Theoretically, Jung believes that this function illustrates the existence of an underlying Self that is a "supraordinate subject" (Jung, CW 7, p. 240). Experientially, one comes to witness and accept a range of subjective states without blame and with a certain playfulness or lightness of being. The usual outcome of this process is greater courage, insight, empathy, and creativity – means for uniting the opposites, as Jung would say.

### Gender and contrasexuality in neurosis and individuation

> Just as early development is experienced in terms of different primary paths for boys and girls, so later development is experienced differently for men and women. The primary issues of identity and development for men revolve around a sense of loss and disempowerment as they upgrade modes of knowing and ways of being that they previously experienced as "feminine." In contrast, the main focus for women's development is a deidealization of the "masculine" as they struggle with issues of personal empowerment.
>
> (Labouvie-Vief, 1994, p. 18)

The all-important persona of adolescence includes roles and identities of masculinity and femininity that are powerful and often consuming for young people.

Female people are encouraged to evaluate their worth in terms of appearance, and to believe that they are secondary to male people in strength and intelligence. Even these days, when some young women may be encouraged to see themselves as "equals," they are still more fully rewarded for their appearances (slenderness and beauty) than for their performances in athletics, academia or human service.

Journalist and author Naomi Wolf (1991) calls our contemporary demands on the female body a "beauty myth." She reminds us that adolescent girls are socialized to become objects of desire, rather than subjects of their own desires. In the midst of the gains women have made in claiming and developing their own authority, the beauty myth is still recited as an essential "truth" based on biological ideology, as Wolf describes it:

> The quality "beauty" objectively and universally exists. Women must want to embody it and men must want to possess women who embody it. This embodiment is an imperative for women and not for men . . . because it is biological, sexual, and evolutionary: Strong men battle for beautiful women, and beautiful women are more reproductively successful . . .    (Wolf, p. 12)

This mystifying gender dichotomy of "strong" men and "beautiful" women holds sway over adolescence, and carries major implications for later developments in neurosis and individuation.

The "double bind" of female authority comes into play for the first time in adolescence. If young women claim their authority too directly they will be regarded as "too much" – too emotional, too pushy, too intellectual, too aggressive, or too masculine. If they disclaim their authority, on the other hand, they will be treated as "too little" – too dependent, weak, immature, or even emotionally disordered. No matter how a woman deals with her authority, she will inevitably get it "wrong" because the whole issue is a double bind (for a fuller discussion, see Young-Eisendrath and Wiedemann, 1987). As female people are socialized to be marginal or secondary to men, the contrasexual complex of strengths, intelligence, and competence is dissociated, or projected into male people and institutions. Then young women identify themselves as being flawed, problematic, weak, or incompetent. Overall, adolescent women underestimate their strengths and abilities, and rely for self-esteem on the resources of their appearances (if they feel the resources aren't there, then their self-esteem drops).

Adolescent boys, on the other hand, are encouraged to overestimate their abilities and possibilities. They tend to see the world as "a man's world," and often fall into an inflation of the persona based on an identification with being uniquely athletic, strong, intelligent, or creative. Discouraged in feeling their weakness or failures, young males may believe they are exempt from the ordinary constraints of life and pursue activities that are obviously dangerous or foolhardy. The persona of a young white male is shaped around themes of success, competition, strength, and independence. The dissociated contrasexual complex of weakness, limitation, dependence, personal need, and vulnerability is viewed as "feminine" and often thought to belong exclusively to females. Even when young men see themselves as sensitive, creative, and expressive, they tend to believe that these qualities are powerful and unique, in a way that reflects their differential privilege and status in the symbolic order.

Often it takes a decade or two of adult life before the male persona begins to erode. In mid-life especially, many men become painfully disappointed in what they have not achieved: the recognition and friends they have not amassed, the status and power they have failed to collect, the money and material goods that have slipped through their fingers. Some men are confronted by family members at this point about what is missing in their relationships.

In otherwise healthy men, the neurotic breakdown of the persona usually includes depression in the face of what seems to be missing in the self. Men who earlier fell prey to an inflation of the persona will have become narcissistic, defending themselves absolutely against feeling their dependence on others. Other men may have experienced an inflation of the ego, and suffered manic, compulsive, or anxiety states in demanding success from themselves. When the youthful persona cracks, most men experience a profound despair about ever finding the missing qualities or abilities in themselves because of the adolescent inflation of the persona or ego. Rather than *blaming* themselves (as women will do, as I discuss in a moment), they feel helpless. The gap between the previously inflated persona or ego and the current recognition seems impossibly large.

For women, the situation is usually quite different. Because women have so many confrontations with the double bind of female authority and the impossibility of "getting things right," they often come to neurosis earlier as a kind of identity crisis precipitated by problems at work, in child-rearing, in romance. They see themselves as the reason things have gone awry. Self-blame and feelings of inferiority are the two most common neurotic symptoms I see in women who come for psychotherapy. In the case of otherwise healthy women, without childhood trauma, the double bind of female authority is often the door leading to neurosis.

The developmental tasks for a woman are to recognize the disclaimed and dissociated authority, competence, goodness and/or power that she has seen as belonging to others, and to dissolve the persona of adolescent femininity. Although the traditional psychoanalytic jargon is "increasing ego strength," I find the Jungian concepts more useful clinically. The persona of appearance-as-worth (or the "unattractive" self as inferior), the contrasexual complex of disclaimed abilities, and the mother complex are – more often than ego strength – the issues of psychotherapy with adult women in my practice. Such a woman has often justified and defended her feelings of inferiority and self-blame through an unconscious identification with a depressed or unfulfilled mother, and the projection of her own (the woman's) strengths into others. She cannot use her own aggression, anger, or authority confidently on her own behalf, nor can she count on her intelligence or knowledge. A typical example is a woman in her early thirties with a college degree, rearing two children, working in a profession, who finds herself to be completely devoid of abilities and unable to make decisions for herself. She often feels dissatisfied or angry, but cannot decide what she wants. The integration into conscious subjectivity of the dis-claimed contrasexual complex, the dissolution of the adolescent persona of female inferiority and the analysis of the depressed, resentful mother complex clear the path for individuation. The goal is to be able to recognize the various subjective complexes of her personality, to know something of the biography of each one, and to keep a perspective that is flexible and creative.

What happens in psychotherapy with a despairing mid-life man? Often the experience of depression and loss must first be encountered in terms of the projected and dissociated feminine complex. Being able to feel and see one's dependence, personal needs, and weaknesses is a liberating but not uplifting experience. In recognizing and expressing these, though, a man is gradually able to find in himself the missing parts or resources that originally seemed impossible to envision. Often these resources lie within his relationships with others, as well as in his ability to treat himself more gently – with less expectation to be perfect, successful, ambitious, constantly able, and the like.

Accurate empathy and mirroring of vulnerability and need are especially important for allowing the contrasexual complex to emerge in psy-chotherapy with mid-life men. The mother complex may have colored a man's experience of his contrasexuality for the years he's been identified with the persona. A great sensitivity to male experience is required of the female therapist who is likely to be seen as a powerful (either seductive or punitive) Mother within the transference. One man I saw for some years, who was reworking his narcissistic, demanding, but indulgent mother complex was startled when I said something about the *difference* between admiration and love. "Are they really different?" he asked innocently. I quickly alerted myself to hear this question, not as defensive, but from a person who had deeply and genuinely confused the two. He'd been greatly admired for his athletic and intellectual abilities in adolescence, and had identified with an invulnerability to failure or defeat. He was now facing open-heart surgery at a relatively young age, and couldn't imagine how this had come about. He distrusted any statement of affection if it sounded too close to sympathy, and he frequently echoed his mother complex in saying he couldn't tolerate incompetence. His contrasexuality was split between a "beautiful, but demanding" bitch and a "feminine, admiring" young woman whom he found erotic. The integration of the contrasexual complex in this case included his ability to feel his own dependency needs, to express his weaknesses and fears, and to sense very clearly how emotionally powerful he was in his relation to his wife and children.

Encounters with the contrasexual are the stuff of couples psychotherapy, especially with heterosexual couples, where projective identification is frequently the major suffering of a wounded couple. Each member enacts the most ideal, dreaded, and primitive aspects of the other in a way that drives both partners crazy. With the knowledge of contrasexual complexes, especially their social and cultural connections to gender, a psychotherapist is able to assist couples in transforming deadening antagonisms and painful attacks into effective dialogue (see Young-Eisendrath, 1993, for a full discussion).

A Jungian approach to psychotherapy with couples is an unusually rich psychoanalytic approach to resistant unconscious dynamics between partners. Lifting into consciousness the Others within, Jungian therapy with couples creates a space, a dialogical space, in which partners can encounter the transcendent function in conflicts. By containing the tensions of projected "opposites" and reflecting their meanings to each other, partners discover that their "marriage" is a "psychological relationship," as Jung (CW 17, p. 187) called it in an essay published in 1925. By this he meant *not* a therapeutic relationship, but a sacred space in which each partner encounters both the dreaded and the ideal through the other's reflections. Then an intimate relationship is a place of individuation for both partners as they reflect each other through mirroring transformations, and discover a playful attitude for dealing with the demons and whores of contrasexuality. The goal is to protect the safe, committed space of an intimate friendship while taking responsibility for primitive destructive and creative demands of contrasexuality. Although conflict and difference are always components of any intimate friendship, especially a marriage or committed partnership, they take on new meaning when they become a progressive uncovering of truths about oneself.

## Concluding remarks

In this chapter, I have tried to show how Jung's theory of contrasexuality can be expanded by contemporary understandings of gender and projective identification. I have touched on only a few of many ways in which sex, gender, and contrasexuality mark our development.

In the first section of the chapter, I discuss why the division into two genders is such a powerful psychological organizer of conscious and unconscious identities. Recognizing that the experience of being a person consists of multiple subjectivities, Jung has been prescient in providing contemporary psychoanalysis with an understanding of the projection-making factors of oppositeness in sex and gender. Still, Jung's cultural biases and tendencies to universalize gender differences need to be revised in the light of contemporary findings of developmental and anthropological research on the sexes.

With this revision, his theory is freed to be more fluid and to move beyond the stereotyping of the sexes according to Jung's own cultural norms. This stereotyping has sometimes led Jungian therapists and theorists to assign preset formulas of Masculine and Feminine to people's experiences in place of discovering the meanings actual people have assigned to gender.

While theories are themselves only stories, and never more than particular stories, the theory of contrasexuality is particularly rich and fluid for understanding how people play out in their erotic relationships and fantasies what is most dreaded, desired, idealized – and excluded from the self. Integrating the meanings of contrasexuality, drawing on them for creative development and responsible partnership, is a major component of life-long individuation.

REFERENCES

Bateson, M. C. (1994). *Peripheral Visions: Learning along the Way*. New York: Harper-Collins.

Bion, W. (1952). "Group Dynamics: A Review." In *Experiences in Groups*. New York: Basic Books, pp. 141–192.

Cleavely, E. (1993). "Relationships: Interaction, Defense and Transformation." In *Psychotherapy with Couples: Theory and Practice at the Tavistock Institute of Marital Studies*. London: Karnac.

Douglas, C. (1990). *The Woman in the Mirror: Analytical Psychology and the Feminine*. Boston: Sigo.

Jung, C. G. (1966). *Two Essays on Analytical Psychology*. CW 7.

Labouvie-Vief, G. (1994). *Psyche and Eros: Mind and Gender in the Life Course*. Cambridge: Cambridge University Press.

Lacan, J. (1982). *Feminine Sexuality*, ed. J. Mitchell, ed. and tr. J. Rose. New York: W. W. Norton.

Maccoby, E. E. (1990). "Gender and Relationships: A Developmental Account." *American Psychologist*, 45/4, pp. 513–520.

Mattoon, M. and Jones, J. (1987). "Is the Animus Obsolete?" *Quadrant*, 20/1, pp. 5–22.

McNeely, D. (1992). *Animus Aeternus: Exploring the Inner Masculine*. Toronto, Canada: Inner City.

Ogden, T. (1994). "The Concept of Internal Object Relations." In *Fairbairn and the Origins of Object Relations*, ed. J. S. Grotstein and D. Rinsky. New York: Guilford.

Samuels, A. (1989). *The Plural Psyche: Personality, Morality and the Father*. New York: Routledge.

Sanday, P. (1981). *Female Power and Male Dominance: On the Origins of Sexual Inequality*. Cambridge: Cambridge University Press.

Spence, J. T. and Sawin, L. L. (1985). "Images of Masculinity and Femininity: A Reconceptualization." In V. E. O'Leary, R. K. Unger and B. S. Wallston (eds.), *Women, Gender and Social Psychology*. Hillsdale, N.J.: Erlbaum, pp. 35–66.

Unger, R. (1989). "Sex, Gender and Epistemology." In M. Crawford and M. Gentry (eds.), *Gender and Thought*. New York: Springer-Verlag.

Wehr, D. (1987). *Jung and Feminism: Liberating Archetypes*. Boston: Beacon.

Wolf, N. (1991). *The Beauty Myth: How Images of Beauty Are Used against Women*. New York: William Morrow.

Young-Eisendrath, P. (1993). *You're Not What I Expected: Learning to Love the Opposite Sex*. New York: William Morrow.

Young-Eisendrath, P. and Wiedemann, F. (1987). *Female Authority: Empowering Women through Psychotherapy*. New York: Guilford.

# 12

JOSEPH RUSSO

# A Jungian analysis of Homer's Odysseus

## I

We often employ symbolic thinking in our quest to represent some of the mystery and power that we feel in the world around us. Such symbol-making can be unconscious as well as conscious, and finds especially congenial vehicles for its expression and artistic elaboration in dreams, myths, and storytelling. Hence it is no surprise that literature in general, and in particular those literary genres that are closest to the fantasy structures of myths and dreams – i.e. folktale and epic – yield themselves easily and successfully to symbolic readings.

Psychology and anthropology (with its offshoot in folklore) are the two disciplines that have most systematically offered us both theories and methodologies for making sense of the elaborate symbol systems that individuals and societies employ for their visions of what is most vital in life. I hope to demonstrate how the archetypal theory of Jungian psychology, supported with insights derived from folklore and anthropology, can illuminate a significant aspect of one of the cornerstones of the Western literary tradition, Homer's *Odyssey*.

Much of the distinctive complexity of this epic poem is generated by the moral ambiguity of its hero Odysseus, commonly acknowledged by critics but never fully explained. I believe that this quality in the hero strikes us and disturbs us deeply because it draws its energy from a major universal archetype, that of the Trickster.

Of all Carl Gustav Jung's contributions to the world of ideas, his theory of archetypes of the collective unconscious is doubtless the best known and most important to both psychologists and laypersons. The concept of the archetype has undergone many redefinitions since Jung first introduced it, including several by Jung himself. His conception at times suggests something akin to Plato's ideal forms (CW 9.i, paras. 5 and 149), entities that exist beyond the world of particular sensory phenomena and offer perfect

240

and timeless paradigms to which individual items can be referred. At other times, he distinguishes clearly between these more abstract and "irrepresentable" archetypes "as such" and the multiple archetypal images and ideas that belong to individuals and which, we may infer, can represent the experiences of a particular time and place (*CW* 8, para. 417). Recent Jungian scholarship, to avoid the high degree of abstraction and separation implied by some of Jung's formulations, has continued to emphasize the archetypes' *immanence* in the individual unconscious and their *responsiveness* to specific social-historical contexts (Wehr, 1987, esp. pp. 93–97; and for an overview of recent critiques of archetype theory, Samuels, 1985, pp. 24–47). Archetypes are best conceived of as patterns of energy with image-making potential, and may be compared to the Innate Releasing Mechanisms discovered by ethologists to be part of the physiological structure and thus the biological inheritance of the animal brain (Storr, 1973, p. 43; Stevens, 1990, pp. 37 and 59, following Tinbergen, 1963). It is this potential for organizing perception around certain key ideas and images, and infusing such perception with exceptional energy, that makes archetypes highly important for the interpretation of literature. Literary artists instinctively mold their narratives around characters, situations, and dramatic sequences that carry a high "payload" of emotional or spiritual impact. We may well say, in fact, that the greatest creators of literature are those who have the best combination of intuition for invoking major archetypes and skill in manipulating them effectively.

Homer's *Odyssey* has captivated the minds of listeners and readers for millennia, and much of its power is due to its archetypes. Let me pass by the Devouring and Swallowing Monsters (Cyclops, Laestrygonians, Charybdis), the Powerful Hindering/Helpful Witches (Calypso, Circe), the driving force of Homecoming, the Descent to the Underworld, the Wise Old Man (Tiresias), and the Reunions of Son and Father, and center my attention on the singular hero who experiences all of these and gives the poem its name.

Odysseus is, undoubtedly, a strange kind of epic hero, as was well noted by W. B. Stanford (1963) in two chapters of his important book, *The Ulysses Theme*, called "The son of Autolycus" and "The untypical hero." Stanford's intuition was excellent as he detailed many negative and ambivalent attributes of this untypical hero; but he made no attempt to connect the complex figure that emerged from his analysis to any larger pattern or explanatory theory, a deficit which the present chapter seeks to remedy.

My own preference is to connect Odysseus by lineage to the archetypal trickster figure of world mythology, a claim which no scholar seems yet to have pursued in its full implications. The one fleeting identification of Odysseus as a trickster that I have found in Jungian literature comes from

Anthony Storr (1973, pp. 33–34), introducing the concept of archetype in the second chapter of his introductory study. Storr invokes Odysseus in the course of giving an excellent explanation of how the archetype is a "flexible matrix" that will allow different cultures to place their distinctive or local stamp on a universal figure. Citing the example of the Hero Archetype he points out that in English culture the hero will be a model of self-control, a "perfect gentle knight," whereas in another culture, such as Greek, the hero will be a master of guile and deception, a trickster like Odysseus.

In my view, Storr's interpretation of Greek heroes in general, and of Odysseus in particular, needs a slight correction. First, it is wrong to imply that because guile is an admirable trait for the Greeks it is a natural expectation that their heroes will be paradigms of wiliness. Greek literature and mythology consistently present Odysseus as an *exception* to the heroic norm, which is clearly embodied in the more or less "perfect knights" like Achilles, Diomedes, Ajax, and the Trojan Hector.[1] Second, and more to the point, Storr has missed what I see as the true archetypal nature of Odysseus: he is not the universal *hero archetype* colored locally, in Greek terms, as a trickster, but is rather a particular Greek embodiment of Jung's universal *trickster archetype* itself.[2] In the creation of the *Odyssey*, I shall argue, a figure of trickster lineage has been adapted to the needs of traditional heroic epic, which required that certain negative qualities be muted while others be transformed to a more "civilized" form. The result is a composite figure – Stanford's "untypical hero" – who balances with some unsteadiness between an aristocratic Trojan War hero and an unreliable leader with a dangerous shadow side.

## II

As one of the few truly universal figures in world mythology, the trickster deserves a theory that can adequately explain his omnipresence and significance. Jung conceived the trickster as an archetype embodying the unsocialized, infantile, and unacceptable aspects of the self. This figure symbolizes the psychological infancy of the individual and is in some sense his "Shadow." The anthropologist Paul Radin's (1956) description of Wakdjunkaga, trickster of the Winnebago Sioux and perhaps the most fully documented trickster in North American mythology, is as follows:

> Trickster is at one and the same time creator and destroyer, giver and negator, he who dupes others and is always duped himself. He wills nothing consciously. At all times he is constrained to behave as he does from impulses over which he has no control. He knows neither good nor evil yet he is responsible

for both. He possesses no values, social or moral, is at the mercy of his passions and appetites, yet through his actions all values come into being.

(p. xxiii)

In other words, trickster represents an archaic level of consciousness, an "animal" or primitive self given to intense expressions of libido, gluttony, and physical abuse. His presence is seen in perhaps its purest form in the Native American tricksters Wakdjunkaga, Raven, and Coyote (who still lives on in Hollywood's Roadrunner and Coyote cartoons), and in the African figures of Ananse, Eshu, and Legba.[3] Although in essence mischief-makers, these trickster gods are at the same time great benefactors, and in Native American mythology the trickster is often the main culture-hero.

The major trickster gods of archaic Europe are Loki, Hermes, and Prometheus. Because they were reworked several times over in various literary genres, they have attained more complex personalities than the Native American or the African tricksters. The Norse Loki, for instance, begins as one of the enemy giants (*jotnar*) who has been "adopted" by the gods (*aesir*) and seems happily integrated into the society of Asgard. He affords Thor companionship and aid on his adventures, his playfulness frequently entertains the gods, and his cleverness helps them as often as he causes them distress through his trickery. On the other hand, as "father of monsters," a role apparently influenced by the Medieval learned tradition (Roothe, 1861, pp. 162–175), Loki is the source of the greatest threats to the stability of the gods' world. And ultimately this dark side prevails as he evolves downward into a rather diabolical figure, a pattern which may well be due to the distorting influence of Christianity, which had an interest in "satanizing" Loki (Davidson, 1964, p. 176; Roothe, 1861, pp. 82–88).

In extant records of Greek mythology, the two divine trickster-figures, Prometheus and Hermes, lack the emphatically troublemaking character we see in Wakdjunkaga or Loki.[4] The Greek attitude toward both is consistently positive. Prometheus is a great founder of culture, the bringer of fire and subsequent technologies, whose trickiness is exercised only at the expense of Zeus and on behalf of humankind. Hermes, in spite of his fundamental association with thievery and stealth – Brown, 1947 emphasizes how the two concepts are closely related, as seen in the cognate English words "steal" and "stealth" (both expressed by the Greek root *klept-*) – is most commonly felt as a benign presence in human affairs. It seems almost paradoxical that a "god of thieves" should be one of the most genuinely popular of all Greek deities. Clearly, for the Greeks, his numerous "helper" attributes outweighed his negative trickster associations.

To understand how the heterogeneous mixture of attributes seen in these various divinities not only coexists in one figure but can cohere so success-fully as to be a universal mythological presence, it may be fruitful to combine Jungian archetypal theory with other theories, developed from anthropological, folkloric, and religious perspectives, that say more about the texture of socio-cultural reality and its spiritual needs. An idealist or essentialist model like Jung's, applied simplistically, runs the risk of reductionism, assigning all cross-cultural manifestations to a common underlying essence and thereby undervaluing the distinctiveness and value of their local adaptation. The best application of Jung's archetypal theory will follow Storr's vision of a mold flexible enough to permit context and local culture to refract the original image into its specific and distinctive variants, which should be the true objects of our study.

Thus we can can combine the truth of Jung's psychological archetypes with anthropologist Laura Makarius's (1965) view that sees trickster as the spirit of the possibility of violating taboos, functioning in social contexts as a highly valued positive, liberating, life-enhancing spirit. Closely related is folklorist Barbara Babcock's (1975) interpretation of trickster as a spirit of necessary disorder, the "tolerated margin of mess" needed to keep off the entropy that is always threatened by too much order and too much control. The joy of release and freedom from the confines of order becomes trickster's gift of laughter. By his parodies of social forms and structures, his inversion of roles, hierarchies, and values, trickster offers us the excitement of seeing that any established social pattern has ultimately no necessity; that all finalities are in doubt, and all possibilities are open. Or, as Jesuit scholar Robert Pelton (1980) puts it,

> more than just a symbol of liminal man, the trickster is a symbol of the liminal state itself and of its permanent accessibility as a source of recreative power. . .He can disregard truth, or better still, the social requirement that words and deeds be in some sort of rough harmony, just as he can overlook the requirements of biology, economics, family loyalty, and even metaphysical possibility. He can show disrespect for sacred powers, sacred beings, and the center of sacredness itself, the High God, not so much in defiance as in a new ordering of their limits. (p. 35)

This composite and complex portrait allows us better to understand the strange need the Norse gods have for Loki's entertaining, provocative company, even though he harms them constantly and will become their ultimate betrayer, reverting to the side of his fellow giants and monsters in the final battle at Ragnarok. It allows us to understand why the tricksters of Amerindian and African mythology are simultaneously figures of fun, even ridicule, and of great reverence. And it may help us understand why Greek mythology needed not only to split the archetype but to split it on each of two levels, represented by the archaic Titan-benefactor Prometheus and the young Olympian god Hermes. Each divinity is in turn divided: Prometheus is fundamentally helpful but his alter ego Epimetheus carries his negative aspects, as Kerényi points out (in Radin, 1956, pp. 180–181); and Hermes carries both positive and negative aspects in simultaneous contradiction, being a god of good luck and a god of thieves.

The classic statement in Greek myth of Hermes' contradictory capacities is the story told in the Homeric Hymn "To Hermes" of the infant Hermes who steals Apollo's cattle and then skillfully reverses their tracks (by making them march backwards), invents sandals (a gift to humans) to cover up his own tracks, and then cleverly lies to Apollo. The newborn god is already proficient in the violation of rules, boundaries, signs, and truthful speech, much like the human hero Odysseus. We might therefore expect Odysseus' patron deity to be Hermes, rather than Athena, as in the *Odyssey*. In the following pages, then, my aim is to argue that Homer's *Odyssey* represents a deliberate attempt to re-fashion an *earlier* Greek tradition and to replace Hermes, in this role, with Athena.

First, let us conclude this section on the mythological trickster by summing up the archetypal figure by arranging representative characters from a few well-studied mythologies in a chart (p. 246). The left-hand column lists qualities that define the trickster as seen in native North American and African mythology. Corresponding attributes are noted for three major figures from European mythology, the Norse Loki and the Greek Prometheus and Hermes. The specific details listed will be meaningful to readers who know these traditions.

## III

The scholars whose work we have reviewed and attempted to synthesize have analyzed trickster tales and myths. But the goal of my investigation is the understanding of a trickster-like presence intruded, as it were, into a different genre with a different purpose, heroic epic. My specific concern is with the process by which mythological material is bent to the purposes of literature, in the hope of identifying what is changed and what is kept, and the reasons why. Obviously these reasons have to do with the nature of the genre that is appropriating the mythology.

Let us return to the difference between Homer's Odysseus and other heroic figures of Greek epic and legend, and delve more deeply. Achilles, Ajax, Herakles, Perseus, Theseus, Jason, and the like face enormous human and super-human obstacles and win through by courage and strength,

## Characteristics of the trickster: a comparative chart

| WAKDJUNKAGA, ANANSE | LOKI | PROMETHEUS | HERMES |
|---|---|---|---|
| unsocialized spirit of anarchy & mischief; violates rules; reverses social values | mischief, both harmless & serious (Balder's death); changes sides | defies Zeus & the Olympian order | mischief against fellow gods; kills Argos |
| receives & gives hurt; paradoxical double nature | offends & is punished (lips sewn, tied to rock, snake drips venom) | offends and is punished (nailed to rock, eagle eats liver) | offends Apollo who threatens punishment |
| culture-creator: benefactor & facilitator; inventor of important "firsts," both positive & negative | helps gods against giants, helps build Asgard, steals back Thor's hammer; gives birth to Sleipnir, Hel, Midgard Serpent | gives fire and technology; makes first humans; invents sacrifice; brings Pandora's ills to men | invents lyre, firesticks, sandals; helps Odysseus & Priam; friendliest god; helps thieves |
| shape-change & disguise | takes form of salmon, hawk, fly, giantess, etc. | | disguises cattle-prints & footprints; appears to Priam in disguise |
| primitive level of body functions; involvement with anus & phallus | seducer of goddesses | [creates seductress Pandora] | phallic aspect in herm; seduces nymphs; patron (with Aphrodite) of seduction |
| steals | steals Sif's hair, Freya's necklace, etc. | steals fire from gods | patron of thieves; steals cattle; gives Pandora "thieving" ethos |
| tells lies | constantly lies | cheats Zeus | lies to Apollo; gives Pandora "lies & cajoling speeches" |
| greedy | gluttonous | | "common Hermes," proverbial phrase expressing greedy impulse |

sometimes abetted by a little clever maneuvering and a magical or divine helper. Odysseus, by contrast, is the very embodiment of clever maneuvering, abetted by a little courage and strength. He also has significant divine help, usually in the form of Athena, traditionally labeled the goddess of wisdom but more accurately the goddess of cunning intelligence – the Greek word is *metis*, which is the name both of the quality *and* of the Titaness mother whom Zeus swallowed to bring about the birth of Athena from his head. If the protecting deity is the daughter of Cunning and embodies the quality of cunning, small wonder that Odysseus wins his successes by his innate cunning resourcefulness.

But anyone familiar with ancient Greek thought will note that cunning resourcefulness is a talent widely admired throughout Greek culture (Vernant and Detienne, 1978) and not one that belongs exclusively or primarily to a trickster. Why then should Odysseus' embodiment of this quality make him not merely an "untypical" hero but specifically a trickster and the refraction of an archetype? There are two reasons. The first is the way he combines cunning resourcefulness with significant traces of other essential trickster qualities. The second is his connection to Hermes.

To unravel Odysseus' link to Hermes, we must go back to the figure of Athena and see her as a kind of positive alternative to the highly ambivalent Hermes. She is the perfect "good" goddess, too above-board and thoroughly respectable to be the patron of a trickster. I think it likely that this goddess is only a later adjunct to Odysseus' career as a clever strategist, and is in essence a replacement. Odysseus' grandfather was Autolykos, whose "speaking name" means "the Very Wolf"; and his grandfather's father – a parentage deliberately suppressed in the key passage in Book 19 on Odysseus' origins – was Hermes, the god of thievery and stealth. In *Odyssey* 19, lines 396–398, we learn that Autolykos got his tricky disposition from Hermes, "who accompanied him with kindly intent," but Homer omits to say what Greek tradition elsewhere says clearly: that the *father* of Autolykos – and therefore Odysseus' great-grandfather – was Hermes.

If we look outside of Homer's literary working over (or "cover-up") of tradition, and go to some fragments of the equally early poet Hesiod (frags. 64, 66, 67) and combine them with other details from such sources as the Homeric hymn to Hermes and the late writers Apollodorus (I.9.16) and Pausanias (ii.3.4, vi.26.5, vii.27.1), we can put together the following composite picture. Hermes was the trickster-god whose chief attributes included craftiness and theft (especially cattle-stealing); disguise, invisibility and shape-changing; clever and useful inventions; fertility, the protection of flocks, and luck and the ever-present potential to be helpful to human society (when he wasn't helping thieves); a phallic representation in sculpture; and finally the more general but crucially important principle of mobility and exchange between zones – as patron deity of transactions and interchange he is the god of travelers, crossroads, traders, and interpreters (the Greek verb made from Hermes' name, *hermeneuein*, means "to translate between languages," hence modern hermeneutics means interpretation).[5] Also as god of special and liminal space his statue stood in public places and at entryways to private homes, presumably for his protective powers in general and protection against thieves in particular.

Hermes had a son called Autolykos who inherited the more negative of his father's qualities but none of the more positive ones. He was a cattle thief who succeeded by virtue of his ability to make things invisible, and he was widely disliked as a deceiver and, more specifically, as someone who deceitfully manipulated oaths in order to get the better of people with whom he dealt.

His grandson, Odysseus, inherited these negative "Autolykan" qualities – as well as his negative Autolykan name, which suggests "causer of pain/grief (*odyne*)" – but in a milder form, mixed with some of the more positive qualities of his great-grandfather Hermes. Inheriting Autolykos' skill at "stealth and oath" (19.396), Odysseus knows well how cleverly oaths can be administered, and in the *Odyssey* shows himself extremely wary as he applies the strongest possible oaths to bind others from deceiving him. He is greedy and mistrustful, fearing that others will steal from him. On the other hand Odysseus' shape-changing, although in one case magically imposed by Athena, is not normally magical but reduced to a human and realistic level: he is an absolute master of disguise, the only Greek hero who is famous for it. His craftiness is usually positive whereas his grandfather's was negative; thus it endows him with a resourcefulness that saves his men from danger again and again. And yet it may on occasion – as befits a trickster – flip over and lead to wholesale destruction of these same men, as almost happens in the adventures with the Cyclops and the Winds of Aeolus, and finally *does* happen in the Laestrygonian episode.

Odysseus' ability to meet and mediate new situations and people, along with his constant mobility and search for the next encounter, remind us of Hermes as god of travelers, crossroads, and the good luck that attends such interchange; and his eventual restoration to his kingdom is described as a return to legitimacy and good order under a beneficent ruler. But the several reminders that Odysseus once ruled Ithaca as a benign and beloved king contrast oddly with his powerful capacity for causing pain, loss and/or death to a surprisingly large number of people. He brings death to his crew after they eat the Cattle of the Sun God, and to the one hundred and eight Suitors of Penelope, who are seen as parallel to the crew (both are called "fools who perished by their own reckless behavior"); he causes the helpful Phaeacians who bring him home the loss of their ship; he causes the Cyclops great pain and the loss of an eye; and in the final book of the poem he subjects his father to unnecessary mental torment before dropping his disguise and revealing that he is the long-lost son returned. This last episode has struck some critics as so irrational that they have assumed it was not composed by Homer but is part of a spurious late addition to the poem. But according to the views we have been developing, this gratuitous pain-giving is exactly right for a trickster and is a legitimate part of Odysseus' archetypal legacy.

In this scene of Odysseus' seemingly irrational desire to play callously with his father's feelings, we find an interesting play on significant names. He introduces himself as a stranger named Eperitos, which could mean "object of contention or strife." This fits well in its negative connotation with his real name Odysseus, which is the object of significant etymological play in Book 19, where it is derived from Autolykos' career as "causer of resentment to many people." "I therefore name this grandchild Odysseus," he says, underscoring the name's etymological transparency as "man of resentment" (19.407–9). The very form of the verb from which the name Odysseus is derived is suggestive in its indeterminacy: it may have an active or a middle-passive meaning, denoting either the man who actively hates or he who is recipient of others' hatred (see Stanford, 1952, p. 209; Clay, 1983, pp. 59–62; and Russo *et al.*, 1992, p. 97).

There are other negative trickster qualities that do not seem apparent in Odysseus, but may be brought to the surface with a little searching. He seems, for example, to lack the requisite lechery and gluttony, the phallic qualities and human–animal dualism that often characterize the mythological trickster. But note that lechery or sexuality can be discerned in his involvements with Circe and Calypso and his evident sexual appeal to Nausicaa. Gluttony may be seen in the recurrent theme that symbolically identifies this hero with a belly (Greek *gaster*), and is also represented by the widespread use of excessive or transgressive eating throughout the *Odyssey*.[6]

We have, then, in Homer's Odysseus a figure containing many contradictions: savior and destroyer of people; devoted son who nonetheless causes his father gratuitous pain; intrepid hero who nevertheless sends others out to face the danger first (in both the Lotus Eaters episode and the Circe episode, and in the Laestrygonian episode he causes the loss of eleven of his twelve ships by sending them to dangerous moorings within range of these cannibalistic giants' weapons, while keeping his own flagship moored safely *outside* of range); a man praised by Athena and Zeus for exceptional piety, who nevertheless can ask a friend for poison for his arrowtips and is *denied it* on the grounds that it would offend the gods to resort to such unheroic tactics. A hero of contradictions indeed.

And overarching the whole structure of the epic is the apparent contradiction between the centrifugal and the centripetal impulses of the poem: Odysseus' constant tendency to seek out new encounters and wander further from home, in conflict with his avowed purpose of returning home to the wife and child he is so eager to see again. Stanford (1963, pp. 50–51; 180–183; 211–240) notes that this contradiction is successfully, almost miraculously balanced in the *Odyssey* so that it is not strongly felt as a contradiction; but in later literature in the Odyssean tradition it tends to simplify itself into one direction or the other. The Ulysses of Dante's *Inferno*, for example, surrenders to the pure, centrifugal impulse, and destroys himself and his crew while declaiming grandly "You were not born to live as animals, but to follow virtue and knowledge": "fatti non foste a viver come bruti, / ma per seguir virtute e conoscenza" (*Inferno* 26, lines 119–120). The only works complex enough to be able to re-mount the edifice in its full contradictory grandeur, centripetal and centrifugal at once, Stanford shows, are Kazantzakis' *Odyssey* and Joyce's *Ulysses*.


## IV

My reading of the *Odyssey* shows that Homer's Odysseus, the hero of Bronze Age epic tradition, masks a more shadowy figure, Odysseus the descendant of the trickster god Hermes. Homer surely had some awareness of his hero's complexity, and seems to have consciously striven to elevate him to epic standards. Siberian epics can have shaman heroes and folktales can have trickster heroes, but heroic epic must have mortal heroes who are warriors and kings, successful adventurers and leaders of men. Homer therefore had to avoid direct association of Odysseus with his great-grandfather Hermes and any outright portrayal of this Trojan War hero as a scaled-down human version of a divine trickster (whereas in the *Iliad* he could frequently portray Achilles directly appealing to his goddess mother Thetis for help, because the divine lineage did not imply un-heroic qualities). A new divine protector for Odysseus had to be found, and the goddess Athena was the perfect choice.

While a thoroughly respectable goddess with no trace of trickster ambivalence about her, Athena *is* the goddess of *metis*, the cunning intelligence that overcomes obstacles in ingenious fashion, an intelligence broadly based and widely admired in Greek culture, and not confined merely to the ambivalently helpful/harmful cunning of the trickster. The study of *metis* by Detienne and Vernant offers a nice distinction between the positive *metis* of Athena and Hephaistos, one of strategy and craftsmanship, and the ambivalent *metis* of Hermes and Aphrodite, one of thieves and lovers. It is the patronage of Athena, replacing that of Hermes, that allows Odysseus to be a favorite in Olympus (as seen in the divine councils of *Odyssey* Books 1 and 5) while still retaining a distinct trace of that irregularity or impropriety that gives away his trickster genealogy. In Book 10, for example, Odysseus returns to the god of the winds Aeolus to ask him to collect and tie up the winds again for him, because his men have ruined his homecoming by letting the winds out of Aeolus' bag. Aeolus rejects his request and sends him away angrily, calling him "most shameful of men, a man hated by the blessed gods." And he adds, "Go, since you come here hateful to the immortals" (10.72–75) – a characterization that the action of the poem itself does not bear out. We catch the scent here of a tradition that Homer has partially suppressed.

In Book 13 when the disguised Athena is lied to by a clever Odysseus who is *not* clever enough to know whom he is trying to fool, she is amused, and says "this is why I can never abandon you, you are always so fluent and fixed-minded and tenacious" (331–332). With the final two adjectives her praise emphasizes not his tricky cleverness but his prudence and careful planning – qualities of Athena not of Hermes. When Homer gives us the one scene (Book 10) where Odysseus and Hermes *actually do meet*, there is no shock of recognition as there should have been between a man and the god who tradition said was his grandfather's father. Homer has again done a successful make-over. Hermes in this scene gives Odysseus a charm that will protect him from Circe. The protection that confers immunity from her magic comes from a little plant that Hermes plucks from the ground in front of them, the moly plant that is "black at the root and white at the flower" (304). As it joins opposites in a successful, organic union, so it has the power to prevent the unnatural splitting of man's mixed nature into the extreme polarity of human and bestial, and will be the effective counter-charm to Circe's magic. Thus Hermes as the god who controls shape-change and crossing over will use his power to preserve Odysseus his great-grandson from undergoing those transitions adversely. This is a short and undramatic scene, but we have seen that it has a great deal compressed into it and can be unraveled only by knowledge that we are dealing with a classic trickster god who is extending his characteristic magical protection to a favorite mortal descendant. The archaic folk tradition preceding Homer's creation of the *Odyssey* by centuries would have understood Hermes the trickster god to be the divine patron of Odysseus; Athena at that time had no connection with this disreputable hero.[7] But in the creation of heroic epic poetry to be sung at a royal court, new paradigms were needed that embodied the more dignified ethos that went with Trojan War legends and their claims to ground the present in a glorious past, and so to ground present-day heroes in prestigious divine lineages and connect them with divine protectors. Thus Odysseus lost his special connection to his great-grandfather Hermes, the god of tricky inventiveness, and gained in his place, as a kind of foster parent, Athena the "good" goddess of civilizing intelligence.

Despite Homer's careful re-shaping of tradition, Odysseus' very name, and the contradictions inherent in his character and actions, reveal the archetype underneath the mortal hero. He is a more fascinating, more mysterious figure than anyone else in Greek heroic tradition precisely because the trickster archetype is more unfathomable, its paradoxes more ultimately irreconcilable, than the archetypes of hero, warrior or king. The vision afforded us by Jung's theory of archetypes thus permits us to begin to understand the limitless appeal of Homer's extraordinary epic.

## NOTES

1   *Iliad* iv. 339–48, the earliest portrait of Odysseus, presents him as a dubious representative of the hero archetype. Agamemnon, reviewing his chieftains, specifically praises Diomedes as his perfect knight and condemns Odysseus as a crafty fellow forever seeking personal advantage and reluctant to face the dangers of battle. Odysseus' fullest portrayal after Homeric epic (late eighth century) is in Sophocles' two plays *Ajax* and *Philoctetes* (second half of the fifth century). In the first he is a cunning and skillful adversary, a pragmatic hero contrasted with a self-destructive one (Ajax), but not without some measure of nobility – in other words, more or less the same complex figure we know from Homer. In the second play, however, he has devolved into a creature of pure guile and opportunism, as if the trickster component has largely taken over and tilted the balance decisively toward the negative or "shadow" side. By the fourth century, in the supposedly spurious Platonic dialogue *Hippias Minor*, the opening discussion turns on the contrast commonly perceived between the two heroes, Achilles being brave, simple, and true and Odysseus wily and false.

2   Jung, *CW* 9.1, paras. 456–488 discusses the trickster archetype in detail, a discussion reprinted in Radin, 1956.

3   Detailed discussion of these African trickster deities can be found in Pelton, 1980; see also Gates, 1988, who describes their assimilation into African-American literature.

4   Studies of Hermes that attempt to establish an original, primitive core for this complex deity's multiple characteristics have been consistently unconvincing. Arguments for an original Hermes as god of the stone-heap (*herma*) or as Master of the Animals (Chittenden, 1947) were successfully refuted by Herter, 1976. See also Kahn, 1978, pp. 9–19 for a review of earlier theories with further bibliography.

5   The more closely we look at the earliest representations of Hermes in early Greek literature, the more details we see that suit his status as that most mysterious, multiform, and elusive of divinities, the archetypal trickster. For example, of all the gods named in early Greek poetry (Homer, Hesiod, and the Homeric Hymns), where standard descriptive epithets are the norm for human and divine characters, Hermes is the only god whose epithets remain largely opaque and resistant to the interpretations of the most brilliant and ingenious modern linguists. He has six commonly used epithets. Of these only two have clear, undisputed meanings, *chrysorrapis* ("golden-wanded") and *Kyllenios* ("of Cyllene"). The familiar *Argeiphontes*, conventionally translated as "slayer of Argos," has been seriously contested recently by three eminent philologists, none of whom thinks it means "slayer of Argos." Of the remaining three, we have no clear sense of the real meaning of *diaktoros*, *eriounios*, or *akaketa*. In addition there is the mysterious and untranslatable *sokos*, used of him only once at *Iliad* 20.72. Passing from authors of the archaic period to the later classical period, we find Hermes given the adjective *dolios* ("tricky") by Aeschylus, Sophocles, and Euripides, and much later, in Pausanias (7.21.1) we find reference to a cult of "Hermes dolios."

6   Pucci, 1987, pp. 157–172, 181–187 traces a suggestive thematic pattern in both Homeric epics whereby "heart" (*thymos*) is emblematic of the *Iliad*'s emphasis on courage, and "belly" (*gaster*) is emblematic of the *Odyssey*'s emphasis on instinct, hunger, and sexual need. Simon, 1974 sees the Odyssey's plot structured by an unconscious fantasy of male sibling rivalry, progressing from an oral stage (in which eating takes excessive forms) to an Oedipal stage (the competition for Penelope).

7   Several interesting details in the epics suggest the usurpation by Athena of attributes originally and more properly belonging to Hermes. Both gods use the cap of invisibility, and the sandals that speed divine travel. Stanford, 1965, commenting on *Odyssey* 1.96ff. actually suggests that Homer has here transferred to Athena one of the main characteristics of Hermes, the divine sandals that carry him over land and sea. Their interchangeability as helpful divinities is also apparent in the two Olympian councils of Books 1 and 5, in which Athena and Hermes are dispatched in parallel fashion as conveyors of Zeus' benign dispensation for Odysseus. A similar equation of the two may be implied elsewhere in myth, e.g. by their shared role in equipping the hero Perseus for his successful encounter with the Gorgon (Apollodorus 2.4.2–3). In his recent *Odyssey* commentary (Hainsworth *et al.*, 1988), J. B. Hainsworth at 6.329 and 8.7 characterizes Athena as "the symbol of fortune and success," qualities that scholars of Greek tradition normally reserve specifically for Hermes, e.g. Burkert, 1985, pp. 158–159.

## REFERENCES

Apollodorus (1921). *The Library*, vol. I, tr. J. G. Frazer. London: W. Heinemann.

Babcock, B. (1975). "A Tolerated Margin of Mess: The Trickster and His Tales Reconsidered." *Journal of the Folklore Institute*, 11, pp. 147–186.

Brown, N. O. (1947). *Hermes the Thief*. Madison, Wis.: University of Wisconsin Press.

Burkert, W. (1985). *Greek Religion*, tr. J. Raffan. Cambridge, Mass.: Harvard University Press.

Carpenter, Rhys (1946). *Folktale, Fiction, and Saga in the Homeric Epics.* Los Angeles and Berkeley: University of California Press.

Chittenden, J. (1947). "Master of the Animals." *Hesperia*, 16, pp. 69–114.

Clay, J. S. (1983). *The Wrath of Athena.* Princeton: Princeton University Press.

Davidson, H. R. E. (1964). *Gods and Myths of Northern Europe.* Harmondsworth, Middlesex: Penguin.

Gates, H. L. (1988). *The Signifying Monkey.* New York: Oxford University Press.

Hainsworth, J. B., *et al.* (1988). *A Commentary on Homer's "Odyssey".* Oxford: Clarendon Press.

Herter, H. (1976). "Hermes: Ursprung und Wesen eines griechischen Gottes." *Rheinisches Museum*, 119, pp. 193–241.

Hesiod (1967). *Fragmenta Hesiodea*, ed. R. Merkelbach and M. L. West. Oxford: Clarendon Press.

Jung, C. G. (1934). "Archetypes of the Collective Unconscious." *CW* 9.1.

(1946). "On the Nature of the Psyche." *CW* 8.

(1954). "On the Psychology of the Trickster-Figure." *CW* 9.1.

Kahn, L. (1979). *Hermes Passe, ou les ambiguités de la communication.* Paris: Maspéro.

Makarius, L. (1965). "Le mythe du trickster." *Revue de l'Histoire des Religions*, 175, pp. 17–46.

Pausanias (1971). *Guide to Greece*, vol. I, tr. P. Levi. Harmondsworth, Middlesex: Penguin.

Pelton, R. (1980). *The Trickster in West Africa.* Berkeley and Los Angeles: University of California Press.

Pucci, P. (1987). *Odysseus Polytropos.* Ithaca, N.Y.: Cornell University Press.

Radin, P. (1956). *The Trickster: A Study in American Indian Mythology.* With contributions by K. Kerényi and C. G. Jung. New York: Schocken Books.

Roothe, A. B. (1861). *Loki in Scandinavian Mythology.* Lund: C. W. K. Gleerup.

Russo, J., *et al.* (1992). *A Commentary on Homer's "Odyssey"*, vol. III. Oxford: Clarendon Press.

Samuels, A. (1985). *Jung and the Post-Jungians.* London and Boston: Routledge & Kegan Paul.

Simon, B. (1974). "The Hero as Only Child." *International Journal of Psycho-Analysis*, 55/4, pp. 552–562.

Stanford, W. B. (1952). "The Homeric Etymology of the Name Odysseus." *Classical Philology*, 47, pp. 209–213.

(1963). *The Ulysses Theme: A Study in the Adaptability of a Traditional Hero*, 2nd rev. ed. Ann Arbor: University of Michigan Press.

(1965). *The "Odyssey" of Homer*, 2nd rev. ed. New York: St. Martin's Press.

Stevens, A. (1990). *On Jung.* London: Routledge.

Storr, A. (1973). *C. G. Jung.* New York: Viking.

Tinbergen, N. (1963). "On Aims and Methods of Ethology." *Zeitschrift für Tierpsychologie*, 20/4, pp. 410–433.

Vernant, J-P. and Detienne, M. (1978). *Cunning Intelligence in Greek Culture and Society*, tr. J. Lloyd. Atlantic Highlands, N.J.: Humanities Press.

Wehr, D. (1987). *Liberating Archetypes.* Boston: Beacon Press.

# 13

TERENCE DAWSON

# Jung, literature, and literary criticism

What part of me, unknown to myself, is it that guides me?
(Fernando Pessoa, 1917)

Every artist is a mediator for all others.
(Friedrich Schlegel, late 1790s)[1]

Jung would often insist he was an "empiricist."[2] So one might expect his work to have been based on the analysis of his clients' case histories. Instead, one finds that many of his major ideas were derived from his interpretation of a remarkable range of *texts* – from an account of a young woman's fantasies (as published in a clinical journal) to the Book of Job, and from spiritual texts of the East to the writings of Western alchemists.[3] Thus it is somewhat disappointing to discover that his three essays on the psychology of specifically *literary* texts are amongst his least successful work (CW 15, pp. 65–134). His essay on James Joyce's *Ulysses* (1932) is embarrassingly vague and the distinction he made in 1930 between two modes of artistic creation – between "psychological" works (whose psychological implications are fully explained by the author) and "visionary" works (which, confusingly, "demand" a psychological commentary) – is neither convincing nor useful.

A great deal of Jungian literary criticism has appeared in the last sixty years: some of it is excellent.[4] Many studies, however, especially studies written in the 1960s and 1970s, suffer from very dubious premises. They treat Jung's concepts as proven entities and either impose these concepts in a schematic fashion onto the text in question or else interpret a text by way of its affinity with an archetypal interaction whose meaning is assumed. Whilst such methodological naïvety is largely a thing of the past, Jungian criticism has suffered the consequences: it still remains very much on the margins of contemporary debate.

One of the strongest merits of a Jungian approach stems from Jung's basic attitude toward his patients. Although psychotherapy is inescapably "theory-driven," Jung claimed that he always began a clinical encounter by reminding himself not to have any preconceptions about the nature of his patient's dilemma. Moreover, he often cautioned his followers against regarding his ideas as a finished theory to be "imposed" onto either a dream or a situation. Contemporary literary criticism is also theory-driven. Critics tend to "project" their preconceived assumptions into the texts they read, thereby stifling their ability to perceive the unexpected possibility. A text is an autonomous product and must be respected as such.

Interpretation is always tentative. Jung never intended his concepts to be regarded as proven entities. He thought of them only as auxiliary "tools."[5] Just as analytical psychology was evolved in order to explore the possible significance of individual experience, so Jungian literary criticism seeks to explore the *possible* psychological implications of a literary text. The first part of this chapter argues for the need (a) to establish "whose" experience is reflected in a narrative fiction, and (b) to view *all* of its events as a representation of a dilemma facing this character. The second part outlines a theory of literary history which underlines the interrelationship between the two defining characteristics of modern literature: its simultaneous engagement with personal *and* social issues.

## Approaching the individual text: a reading of *Pamela*

Any methodology for analyzing the psychological implications of a text will provoke questions about the psychology of the author. We must therefore be clear from the outset what is meant by this "author." I do not mean the sum of everything that is known about the historical author in question. Depth psychology does not argue *from* biographical event *to* a text, but *from* a text *to* its psychological implications, i.e. to the way in which a text reveals a specific complex of problems pertinent to a "presumed author" at the time of writing. One will inevitably want to refer to biographical material in order to corroborate a claim and so affirm its pertinence to the historical author – but the analysis itself must be derived entirely from the text.

Many contemporary analysts (especially of the archetypal school) would argue that *all* personifications encountered in a dream have an equal status and that one can relate a dream to any of them. Such a view has the merit of "opening up" a large number of interpretive possibilities. In contrast, this essay subscribes to the view that the events of a dream must be related either to the dreamer (i.e. a specific individual) *or* to the character whom Jung described as the "dream-ego" (i.e. to a single dream-figure that can be defined as the "primary carrier" of the dreamer's unconscious personality). As literary criticism should be wary of introducing biographical material into a literary analysis, this essay will seek to argue that the psychological interpretation of a literary text rests on the relation between its events and the character who can best be described as the "primary carrier" of the author's unconscious personality. It cannot however be assumed that such a character in a novel functions in the same way as the "dream-ego" in a dream. In the following pages, I define the "primary carrier" of the author's unconscious personality in a narrative fiction as the *effective protagonist*.

In order to identify the "effective protagonist" of a novel, one needs (1) to compare the situation at the outset of the work with the situation at its conclusion and (2) to ask which of the characters is most radically *changed* by the events described (see Franz, 1982). If this is the obvious hero, there may be no need to inquire any further. But very often one finds that another character – and this might indeed be an *apparently* minor character – undergoes an even more significant change. If *all* the events of the novel can be convincingly related to this apparently less central character, then he or she will be its effective protagonist.

To inquire into the possible psychological implications of a literary text is to consider its "surface structure" (i.e. the story told) as a projected representation of a "deep structure."[6] I understand the deep structure to mean the events described in the surface structure *when viewed in relation to the effective protagonist*. My aim is to explore and test two claims:

1. that the events described in the "surface structure" of a novel offer a projected representation of a dilemma confronting the effective protagonist at the outset, and
2. that the events of a narrative fiction describe how this character deals with the challenge implicit in this dilemma.

In other words, my contention is that a novel is conditioned by, and also offers a projected representation of, *an implicit challenge facing the effective protagonist throughout the events*.

The following reading will explore this hypothesis: it is an experiment in methodology. I have chosen to examine Samuel Richardson's *Pamela* (1740), the first "bestseller" in English literature, partly because it might seem an improbable choice for a "post-Jungian" analysis and partly because it prepares the ground for a claim that I shall advance in the second half of this essay. The novel consists, almost exclusively, of letters written by a fifteen-year-old maidservant to her parents:

In the first letter, Pamela Andrews informs her parents that the "lady" she has been serving has died and that, just before she died, she exhorted her son to take care of "poor Pamela." Pamela's new "master" is called Mr. B. (an eighteenth-century convention to give an appearance of realism). In spite of his gestures of good will toward her, she quickly begins to suspect

his intentions on her "virtue." Unknown to her, he coerces one of her fellow
servants into showing him all her letters, many of which have to do with her
fears about his conduct. Whilst protesting that his interest in her is honest,
he repeatedly tries to take advantage of her. She always manages to escape,
either by slipping out of his arms or by falling into "fits." Mrs. Jervis, the
housekeeper, tries to help her, but to no avail. He eventually accepts her
resignation and tells her that his coachman will drive her back to her home.
Robin drives her instead to Mr. B.'s Lincolnshire house, where she is, in
effect, held prisoner. During this time, her letters, which she cannot send,
take the form of a journal.

Although Mr. B. promises Pamela that he will not set foot in his
Lincolnshire house without first obtaining her permission, he still continues
to importune her. Her new housekeeper, Mrs. Jewkes, does everything she
can to forward his purpose. Pamela appeals for help to Mr. Williams, her
master's chaplain, but Mrs. Jewkes quickly thwarts their plans. Then,
unexpectedly and without having obtained her consent, Mr. B. arrives. One
night, disguised (somewhat improbably) as one of his other maids, he slips
into her bedroom. While Mrs. Jewkes holds her down, he attempts to rape
her, but she has another fit and the worst is once again avoided. Following
this scene, Mrs. Jewkes steals Pamela's journal and presents it to Mr. B. In
spite of Pamela's protestations, he reads it. This is the turning point. He
begins to show her more consideration and eventually allows her to return
to her parents. No sooner has she left, however, than he discovers that he
cannot live without her. He sends her a letter. She relents and returns to his
house. Mr. B. tells her that his sister, Lady Davers, has threatened to
renounce all relation with him if he should marry a maidservant. But
Pamela's absolute refusal to become his mistress compels him at last to
propose. She is thereupon visited by the neighboring gentry, all of whom are
delighted with her. The wedding is soon celebrated. The final test comes
when she has to overcome her jealousy upon learning, from Lady Davers,
that Mr. B. once had an affair with Miss Sally Godfrey. But the end is in
sight. All is resolved, even Mrs. Jewkes is forgiven, and Pamela resolves to
take care of Miss Goodwin (Mr. B.'s daughter by Sally Godfrey) at the
earliest opportunity.

*Pamela* is a long novel: almost five hundred pages in the Penguin edition.[7] A
complete analysis would examine all the major encounters and so require
infinitely more space than is here available. In these pages, I can only
indicate some of the ways in which Jung's "auxiliary tools" might serve to
explain and specify various interrelated features of the central relationship.
My primary aim is to illustrate a possible methodology.

Most readers, and also most literary critics, assume that a narrative fiction is about the experiences that befall the main character in the "surface structure." In literary terms, this may be adequate, but if one is seeking to discover the *psychological* significance of a text, the apparent "main character" of the work may not be its effective protagonist. Our first task, then, is to identify the novel's "effective protagonist."

The novel consists mainly of letters written by Pamela: there is no question that the "surface structure" is seen from *her* point of view. She appears to be the main protagonist – until one notes that she changes remarkably little in the course of the novel. Even more significantly, she never determines the events. She only responds to them: her resistance is passive. The sub-title – *Virtue Rewarded* – suggests that she is "rewarded" by the prestige of greater social status and, we are led to believe, the permanent possession of Mr. B.'s affection. But, in spite of Fielding's parodies,[8] the novel is *not* (at least, not primarily) concerned with her ambitions for either of these.

In contrast, Mr. B. is considerably changed by the events of the novel. He used to be "wildish" and in the course of the novel he undergoes a radical (even if not altogether convincing) character transformation. The novel is about his fascination by – and his desire to "possess" – a model of unimpeachable "virtue." By reading Pamela's journal, he learns that she really is that rare creature that he has always desired, a "virgin" in mind and body. At the end, he wins himself the wife that he has wanted all along. It is Mr. B.'s obsession with Pamela that determines the shape of the narrative: he creates the events. He makes all the significant decisions and all the events, without exception, are related (directly or indirectly) to him.[9] He is the effective protagonist.

My claim, then, is that if one is interested in the novel's psychological implications, one must view *all* the interactions that are ostensibly described by Pamela in relation to Mr. B. The "surface structure" tells Pamela's story; the "deep structure" is composed of the same events, but seen from Mr. B.'s point of view.

Critics such as Morris Golden (1963), W. B. Warner (1979), Roy Roussel (1986), and others have long been aware of Mr. B.'s centrality.[10] Even so, there are three fundamental differences between their analyses and this "Jungian" approach. In the first place, I wish to argue not that some, but that *all* the events – *including* Pamela's own desires – must be seen in relation to Mr. B. Secondly, Roussel (1986, p. 78), for example, categorically asserts that the situation between Mr. B. and Pamela is "not primarily psychological." My aim is to argue that this situation *is* primarily psychological. And thirdly, whilst all of these critics make parallels between Mr. B.

and Richardson, these parallels make little or no distinction between the part and the whole. This chapter subscribes to the view that the individual is composed of numerous splinter personalities and that we cannot confuse the "whole" personality with what is only an "aspect" of this personality. In the following pages, it will be argued that Jung's terms provide a possible way in which to *specify* both the nature of the dilemma that conditions the fictional events and the nature of the parallels that can be drawn between Mr. B. and his author.

My premise is that all our ideas about society represent a "projection" of our own concerns into the world around us.[11] *Pamela* has often been defined as an early example of a novel with a realistic social background – and so it is. But this needs to be qualified: the novel is built upon the assumption that a woman "true and fair" cannot be found in Mr. B.'s social class. We remember that Mr. B. has had an illegitimate child by Miss Sally Godfrey, who belongs to the privileged (albeit only minorly privileged) classes. Moreover, we note that Mr. B. has no further interest in young women from the privileged classes: having been a bit "wildish" and seduced several members of the privileged classes – and had a child by one – he imagines that *all* young women belonging to "his" class are careless of their virtue. In other words, his ideas about society are inseparably connected with his instinctive attitude toward women. Mr. B.'s portrait of society is a "projection" of his own way of seeing the world. The laxity of morals that he ascribes to society is a reflection of his own "repressed" desires: that he *conceals* his affair with Sally Godfrey corroborates this hypothesis. In similar fashion, at the end of the novel, Pamela's desire to do good reflects Mr. B.'s unconscious desire to become a better integrated and more useful member of society. The social theme – the desire to improve society – may therefore also be seen as a projected metaphor for his unconscious desire for personal development.

We have to assume that Mr. B. is a likeable young man – the sense of the novel's ending depends on this – and yet, in the course of the novel, he neither behaves as if he is nor recognizes to what extent his behavior toward Pamela is reprehensible. Thus, in effect, there are *two* Mr. B.s in the novel. One is "the best of gentlemen" by whom Pamela is attracted and whom she finally agrees to marry. The reiterated idealization suggests that this Mr. B. is not so much a carrier of the authentic – albeit only hypothetical – center of consciousness (the ego) as a *persona*, i.e. a representation of the way in which an individual likes to imagine himself.

The "other" Mr. B. is the brutal master, i.e. the personification of everything that the first Mr. B. fails to recognize about himself. This may be understood in the light of Jung's concept of the *shadow*. Jung used this term to describe two related but nonetheless different phenomena: (1) the entirety of the unconscious: i.e. everything that we fail to recognize about ourselves; and (2) a specific personification of what a person "has no wish to be" (*CW* 16, para. 470), "the sum of all those unpleasant qualities" a person likes to hide: *CW* 7, p. 65n). The shadow is thus a personification of an aspect of one's personality *as it really is*. Because the ego tends to repress such aspects of its personality, the shadow often manifests itself compulsively. In the course of the first two thirds of the novel, the first Mr. B. is "possessed" by the second Mr. B., i.e. by the "best" of gentlemen's own shadow-tendencies. After reading Pamela's journal, the first Mr. B. at last understands *her* merit: in other words, he reads the story he wants to read. But he fails to read the story it really tells: that of his own sexually aggressive and even violent behavior. In other words, Mr. B. is reluctant to acknowledge his own shadow-tendencies or, to borrow Pamela's words, how he is "in his true colours" (p. 54).

The intensity of his desire for Pamela suggests that he unwittingly invests her with archetypal attributes. Now, literary critics interested in applying Jung's ideas to a text are very often primarily concerned with trying to establish its governing archetypal image or pattern. I question this approach for two reasons: it assumes that the significance of archetypal material is always essentially the same, and it assumes that apparently similar narrative structures have a similar psychological significance.

Mythic patterns are not static, but evolving structures. Sometimes the significance of a motif will diminish. In classical times, the battle between the Lapiths and the Centaurs had sufficient importance for it to be chosen as the theme for the metopes on the south side of the Athenian Parthenon but, in time, this story gradually ceased to feature in art. In other cases, a myth will develop new layers of meaning. The myth of Narcissus is perhaps the most obvious example. Although of relatively minor importance in classical times, from the Renaissance onwards, its importance gradually increased until by the early nineteenth century it had become one of the dominant myths of the Romantic period. There are, for example, striking parallels between Ovid's version of the story of Narcissus and Alexander Pushkin's verse-novel *Eugene Onegin* (1823–31). But it is unlikely that even an elaborate expansion on these parallels will be able to illuminate more than one aspect (albeit perhaps an important aspect) of the novel. The significance of archetypal material is forever changing and every new formulation of a basic pattern *modifies* the existent implications of the pattern.

There are clear parallels between the "surface structures" of the myth of Daphne and Apollo and *Pamela*, but these parallels fall apart when we consider the events in relation to the effective protagonist. A Greek myth about a young *woman* fleeing from the brightest of the gods and an eighteenth-century English novel about a young *man* obsessed with an archetypal image of virginity have very different psychological implications.[12] In other words, if one wants to explore an archetypal pattern, one must first ascertain the point of view from which it is being perceived: i.e. identify the effective protagonist.

Pamela exists only in relation to Mr. B., who cannot understand why she should not surrender to his advances. When she repulses him, his desire for her increases. He wants her *because* she is a virgin; had he been able to gratify his wishes, she would no longer have been a virgin and (one can assume) he would have rejected her just as he did Sally Godfrey. Pamela's continued rejection of him feeds his desire for her. Since he is the novel's effective protagonist (i.e. its actions correspond to *his* desire), sending her away to Lincolnshire represents a wish to be freed not only of the irritation she causes him, but also of his own desire. His sexual violence toward her can thus be seen as a representation of a compulsion to put an end to his own desire because he cannot control it.

Over the last thirty years, criticism has shown considerable interest in the way in which Pamela stands up to Mr. B. and answers him back. She displays remarkable strength of character both in rebutting Mr. B.'s unwelcome advances and, later, in assuming responsibility for his shortcomings.[13] But this strength of character also raises a question: "Why should Pamela be invested with characteristics so entirely at odds with those of the effective protagonist?" Two of Jung's concepts provide a way in which to explain this.

The first is his view that the figures encountered in the unconscious *compensate* a one-sided conscious attitude (see *CW* 7, pp. 171–185). Jung held that the psyche has a self-regulating function: i.e. that the unconscious expresses an instinctive urge to "correct" any misguided one-sidedness in a person's conscious orientation. One can identify at least three ways in which Pamela embodies qualities that Mr. B. "lacks."

1. She embodies moral rectitude, which "compensates" his view that *society* is morally lax. If he is to recover a sense of his own moral worth, he must be "redeemed" by a very strong-minded young woman from outside his own social class. Pamela comes from the respectable yeoman class, a social class below his own, but into which it would not be unthinkable for him to marry.

2. She embodies fidelity to her own authentic being, which compensates the loss of his *own* authentic identity. If he is to become once again "the best of gentlemen," he must be redeemed by a woman who personifies being "true to herself."

3. She embodies the conviction that the only kind of relationship between a man and a woman is a lasting one, which compensates his inability to form a lasting relationship. This may be explained by reference to Jung's concept of Eros, a term he used to describe a principle of psychic "relatedness" (CW 13, para. 60). Mr. B. can feel powerfully drawn to a woman (e.g. Sally Godfrey, Pamela), but he cannot bring himself to enter into a long-term relationship with her. He wanders from one relationship to another without ever developing any sense of commitment. His unconscious "compensates" this tendency by facing him with an irresistible compulsion to possess an archetypal embodiment of Eros. Pamela thus faces Mr. B. with a challenge to come to terms with his fear of Eros as relatedness. One notes that she only consents to marry him when *he* finally demonstrates his desire for a long-term relationship.

At the outset of the novel, the death of his mother releases Mr. B. from the moral constraint that she represents and he thinks himself free to do as he likes. Instead, he discovers himself "captivated" not only by a model of unimpeachable "virtue," but also by the intensity of his own desire for Pamela. The literal imprisonment that he imposes on Pamela can thus be envisioned as a symbolic representation of the way in which his own better nature is imprisoned by his shadow, i.e. his "inferior" nature.[14]

The dilemma facing him can be defined as a twofold challenge: (1) to come to terms with his own shadow-tendencies; and (2) to come to terms with the *values* that Pamela personifies. The novel traces the process by which she compels Mr. B. not only to come to terms with qualities that he lacks, but also, at the end, to become a more useful member of society. Mr. B.'s fascination with her is bound up with the question of class difference. Previous idealized female figures in literature (e.g. Virgil's Dido, Isolde, or Milton's Eve) have little or no connection with a *social* reality (as we would understand this phrase today): they exist as archetypal images operating within archetypal interactions. Pamela challenges Mr. B. to connect with the society in which he lives. The novel has very evident social concerns. The personal and the social themes are different aspects of the same problem. The challenge facing Mr. B. is to acknowledge and confront aspects of his own personality and social responsibility that he does not even recognize either as part of his own psychological make-up or as his concern.[15]

Everything so far has been deduced from an analysis of the *text*. It is time to test our hypothesis against what we know of its author.

The question whether we can identify Mr. B. with Samuel Richardson presupposes that one has a theory about the nature of literary production. One can readily understand why so much literary criticism inspired by Jung has been devoted to narrative fictions, especially to nineteenth- and twentieth-century novels. A great many novelists have described the way in which their basic idea for a work originated in a dream and how their novel came about from consciously "reactivating" the scenario encountered in a dream.[16] This is very similar to what Jung called *active imagination*, the process of consciously inducing a waking dream in order to experience the workings of one's own unmediated fantasy life.[17]

*Pamela* originated in the author's commission to produce a so-called "letter-writer," a series of "model letters" designed to help young women express themselves elegantly in their correspondence. Richardson became so absorbed by the question of what an innocent young maidservant might write to her parents about the difficulties facing her in her job, that he quickly laid his "letter-writer" aside in order to write a novel about such a maidservant.[18] After a long day's work as a printer, he wrote his novel at night and it took him only two months to complete the very long manuscript. Thinking about a maidservant's possible difficulties clearly activated an "inner image" of a woman that had a high emotional charge for him: i.e. his *anima*. Just as Mr. B. speaks of being "bewitched" by Pamela, so the novel provides a clear instance of a man coming under the spell of his "anima." Pamela may be defined as Richardson's *anima*. The novel grew from an experience that may be compared with active imagination. Thus Mr. B. can be regarded as a personification of the author's *unconscious desires* when confronted by an anima-figure that exercised a powerful fascination on him.

In psychological terms, the entire action may be described as a *projected* representation of a dilemma facing Samuel Richardson at the time of writing. Even so, our reading has suggested that one must *specify* the nature of any parallels one wishes to make between Mr. B. and Richardson. Mr. B. as "the best of gentlemen" represents his "persona." The other Mr. B., the protagonist of the fictional events, is a "shadow-figure." The shadow is only a part of the personality. It cannot be equated with the whole and, by definition, it is "unconscious." This suggests that Richardson, in spite of hinting at certain parallels in his letters, was largely unconscious of the psychological implications of his own novel.

This conclusion is lent some weight by the tentative nature of the novel's ending. Mr. B. finally overcomes the pride that has prevented him from contemplating marriage with a maidservant. It is a first step and clears the way for the happy, but nonetheless only *tentative* resolution. After his marriage, Pamela accepts responsibility for his illegitimate child (i.e. for *Mr. B.*'s shortcomings) and makes him do so too. The past is thereby integrated, suggestive that Mr. B. has at least come to partial terms with his "inferior" nature. But that Mr. B. never really acknowledges how badly he has behaved tells us that there is a great deal more to be worked through. It prepares the way for the domestic upsets that provide the grist for Richardson's "sequel," *Pamela: Part Two* (1741). And that Richardson continued to remain obtuse to the implications of his own fictions is implied by the fact that his next novel, *Clarissa* (1747–48) – a much longer and better novel – expands on very much the same theme. Only, in *Clarissa*, the heroine is a much more rounded character drawn from the middle classes.

This brings us to the crux of the novel. In psychological terms, perhaps its most striking feature is that the effective protagonist cannot be defined as any kind of "ego" figure. On the one hand, Mr. B. is an idealized persona; on the other, he is a representation of the shadow. By definition, the shadow is an archetypal image. Mr. B. is related to Satan, the dominant archetypal image of the shadow in Western literature: he is "as cunning as Lucifer" (p. 89) and his purpose is to "tempt" Pamela (pp. 116–117).[19] Even so, he clearly cannot be seen as an eighteenth-century "variant" of the devil. He is an archetypal image (in the sense that he shares some of the attributes of the collective shadow) but, in relation to the novel, he is only a personification of Mr. B.'s shadow-tendencies. In *Pamela*, there is no "ego-figure." The novel illustrates a phase in the evolution of consciousness immediately prior to the differentiation of the shadow as separate from the "ego," a perception necessary if an individual is to become conscious of his or her *individual* identity.

It would be difficult to exaggerate the importance of *Pamela*. Mr. B.'s wrestle with his shadow-tendencies and his compulsion to possess a girl from a lower social class anticipate the two great themes of Goethe's *Faust* (1808). Pamela also served as a "model" for innumerable later images of women whose strength of character can be boiled down to their ability to bear with an intolerable husband and make themselves useful by their good deeds. Such women became a stock type of Victorian fiction, especially in novels by women.[20] Pamela's characteristics thus provided a pattern of behavior that was to be enormously detrimental to the personal fulfillment of several generations of women. Clearly, we need to better understand not only *how* such "stereotypes" came about, but also *why*. For, although there is no space in which to explore this question here, implicit to our argument is the view that the psychological implications that a work once had either for the society that produced it or for its author are equivalent to a major aspect of its continuing significance for the reader today.

It has long been recognized that preoccupations with class conflict, gender stereotyping, and sexual power lie at the centre of *Pamela* and that they meet in the figure of Mr. B. Our reading confirms these, but it also expands on them. Of course the social issues contained in the novel will require examination *as* social issues. My aim is only to insist that the questions of class difference, gender stereotyping, and sexual power are also – and *inherently* – aspects of a psychological "complex." Our reading of *Pamela* has drawn attention to a dilemma-cum-challenge that is at once *unique*, in the sense that it relates to a specific text (and, by extension, a specific author), and yet also of *collective* interest, in the sense that the dilemma facing Mr. B. is a variant of a widespread psychological "complex" of continuing relevance.

*Pamela* is one of the earliest novels in the English tradition that has a well-developed sense of social reality, and perhaps the earliest in which the events can be seen as a "projection" of the personal concerns of its author. Given our findings about Mr. B., this suggests that one's consciousness of reality is inseparably related to one's consciousness of one's shadow-tendencies. In other words, that it is only after one has come to tentative terms with one's shadow that one can begin to have either a notion of oneself as "ego" (distinct from the collective consciousness of one's society), or a *conscious* awareness of one's place in a social reality. The second part of this essay will explore this hypothesis.

## Toward a theory of literary consciousness

According to the eighteenth-century Italian philosopher Giambattista Vico, it is a manifest error to assume that people have always thought as we do today (Pompa, 1990). And yet almost all criticism written today – including Jungian literary criticism – does just this. In spite of the sophistication of its rhetoric, post-modern debate is steeped in what Vico called the "conceit of scholars," i.e. the intellectual error of assuming that people have always thought in the same way. Critics approach texts written a hundred, four hundred, or even two thousand four hundred years ago as if they were written by people with the same basic psychology as their own. This is inadmissible: one cannot *assume* that people in the past thought – or even *could* have thought – in the same way as we do today: to do so will produce bad literary criticism and worse psychology.

That it is notoriously difficult to define the gradual evolution of consciousness is no reason to doubt that it has occurred. All cultural products bear witness to it, especially all kinds of written texts. Whilst any attempt to specify the nature of consciousness can only be tentative, we must continue to explore possible ways in which to describe and measure both consciousness in itself *and* the evolution of consciousness.

In the course of two lectures on alchemy delivered in the summer of 1942, Jung outlined a theory explaining how we gradually "withdraw" our various projections, i.e. integrate the nature of the dilemma implicit in the projection (*CW* 13, pp. 199–201; Franz, 1980, pp. 9–19). Each stage corresponds to a different kind of consciousness.

The first stage describes a state in which people are utterly unconscious of any distinction between themselves and the world in which they live. They have little or no concept of themselves as beings distinct from what society expects of them. Their ideas are entirely in accord with societal expectations of them.

The second stage consists of a long and sometimes painful separation of a person from the "other." It describes the process whereby a person gradually explores his or her own identity, usually by way of a dialectic with different facets of the "other" (e.g. figures representing authority or "difference").

The third stage concerns the differentiation of moral properties. In this stage, a person is constantly engaged in testing the collective morality of his or her society in order to ascertain and frame his or her own ethical code.

A fourth stage begins with the realization that the aura and authority with which one has invested all the collective norms and expectations within which one lives are of one's own making. The "projection" is thereby broken and the world is seen as it really is, thereby freeing the person to become the specific human being that he or she is. This stage might seem to be the goal of the process but, according to Jung, it is not. For, divested of all its mana, the world can seem utterly devoid of either certainty or meaning and such a perception very quickly leads to feelings of alienation. This, self-evidently, cannot be described as any kind of goal.

Thus, according to Jung, a fifth stage begins when we initiate a fresh dialectic with ourselves, a conscious questioning of our innate tendencies, especially those of which we are least aware and which are revealed to us only through a searching analysis of our dreams and waking fantasies. The end of this long process is to know oneself *not* as a rebel or outsider, but as the *specific* human being that one is within one's own society. In this way, the process comes full circle, for the goal is a new integration with society, utterly different from the first stage by virtue of one's full *consciousness* of one's individual nature, function, and limitations.

These five stages are not intended to be seen as a "fixed scale" of exclusive distinctions. One does not leave the first stage entirely behind when one moves onto the second, or the second when one moves onto the third. Different parts of oneself very often "inhabit" different stages. One part of oneself might be relatively independent, another utterly unable to break free from either the expectations of one's immediate family or one's own immature longings. Similarly, people who live in the *first* stage must have some kind of consciousness about the reality of the world in which they live, i.e. of Jung's *fourth* stage.

Jung's scheme rests on the definition of the fourth stage: i.e. on how one understands "reality." The phrase "as it is" is not meant to imply that reality is an absolute. Reality is defined by one's need to adapt to it. A tribesperson from the interior of Brazil requires just as strong a sense of reality as a New Yorker, but their respective definitions of reality will be radically different. This explains the inter-related aspects of the fourth stage. One aspect describes the ability to see the world as it is for oneself – but one cannot even begin to understand the world as it is (in relation to one's immediate needs) until one has at least begun to understand oneself as the specific being that one is (i.e. come to at least tentative terms with one's own shadow). Because reality is relative, the scheme applies to every individual in a different fashion. In other words, each of Jung's five stages are *relative*: they measure adaptation only in relation to a given point of view that itself implies a particular kind and degree of self-awareness.

I would like to suggest that Jung's five stages in the withdrawal of projections can serve the literary critic in two ways: (1) they can help to identify various aspects of the conscious awareness shown by the effective protagonist of any given fiction, and (2) they provide a frame by which to understand the evolution of literary concerns.

I  Identifying the dominant psychological concern of a text

Just as different parts of each individual inhabit different stages of development, so one can invariably ascribe the different aspects of the conscious awareness shown by the effective protagonist of a narrative fiction to each of Jung's five stages.[21] Let us test this possibility against *Pamela*, retaining only our identification of Mr. B. as the effective protagonist.

1. There is nothing "individual" about Mr. B.: he is simply a handsome young gentleman who is almost entirely contained, and thus "defined," by societal expectations of him. This aspect of Mr. B. may be explored by reference to Jung's first stage.

2. The novel consists of various confrontations with an "other": Pamela with Mr. B., Mr. B. with Pamela and, crucially, Mr. B. as persona with his own shadow-qualities.[22] These confrontations may be examined in the light of the second stage.

3. Whilst the entire novel revolves around the various moral dilemmas that these confrontations represent, Mr. B. stops short of recognizing his

own shadow-tendencies. Jung's third stage offers a way in which to explore these various dilemmas.

4. Mr. B.'s notions about society are determined by his notions about women. The only *decision* he makes that could be ascribed to an "ego" (as opposed to a persona) is his decision to brave Lady Davers and marry Pamela – but one notes that he is only able to do this because his neighbors have been very liberal in their praise of Pamela. The tension between the social and the personal can be understood in terms of Jung's fourth stage.

5. Mr. B. is reluctant to acknowledge and thus come to terms with his own shadow-tendencies, which means that he cannot "integrate" the challenge that Pamela faces him with. As a result, his intimation of his "ego" has no substance: he remains imprisoned in his persona, which means that his shadow-tendencies will inevitably manifest themselves again: hence the sequel to *Pamela* and, in *Clarissa*, the nature of Lovelace, an even more duplicitous rake than Mr. B. Jung's fifth stage provides a way of understanding Mr. B.'s lack of confidence.

As each stage serves to reveal a different facet of the dilemma confronting Mr. B., each could be said to represent a different challenge facing him. Each identifies a major aspect of his psychological development and thus a distinct line of possible literary investigation. Considering the action of a text against each of Jung's five stages in turn therefore serves to highlight the different aspects of a psychological dilemma. This inevitably provokes the question: Can a work of literature be said to have a *dominant psychological concern*?

One notes that consideration of the final stage reveals the degree to which the effective protagonist is able to "integrate" the content of his or her projections: i.e. the nature and limitations of his or her "consciousness" which, by extension, can usually also be ascribed either to the author or "presumed author." Even so, the absence of an ego-figure can hardly be regarded as the dominant psychological concern in *Pamela*. A brief consideration of our findings will suggest that the *dominant* psychological concern of the novel lies somewhere on the boundary between the third and fourth stages: i.e. it concerns the tension between the various aspects of the moral dilemma and the intimation of an individuality that is distinct from collective expectations.

This, however, will not always be the case: different literary fictions will almost certainly have different dominant concerns. Thus a further way in which Jung's scheme might help the literary critic is as a template for discussing and comparing the psychological concerns of *different* works.

II    Toward a psychological history of literature

If Jung's five stages can serve to specify the dominant psychological concern in any given literary work, the question arises: Might they also provide the basis for a way in which to understand the *evolution* of literary concerns?

Any theory about the psychological interpretation of an individual literary text must be allied to a broader theory of literary history. Thus it is somewhat surprising to note that critics have been applying psychoanalytic theory to literary texts for the best part of a century without having any clearly defined theory about the evolution of literary expression. So too have Jungian critics: without a blush, they describe *all* works produced between the earliest recorded myths and a twentieth-century fiction as "archetypal." Now whatever parallels we might wish to make between a Babylonian myth and a twentieth-century American novel, there is a self-evident need to distinguish "difference": i.e. for the Jungian critic to distinguish between the products of one literary period and another.

Clearly, a major proviso must be made at the outset. Even if Jung's theory about the withdrawal of projections can be found useful for considering individual texts, one should be cautious about using an ontogenetic model as a basis for a phylogenetic theory. It is likely that we shall find even more overlapping between the different stages at a phylogenetic level. Even so, I would like to suggest that Jung's five stages in the withdrawal of projections can provide a possible way of understanding the *evolution* of the dominant psychological concerns in literary artifacts.

My contention is that the "dominant concern" of the most basic oral traditions and very early myths is *identity in itself*. One thinks, in the first instance, of the products of tribal societies in which people are entirely "at one" with their collective traditions, unable to differentiate between themselves and the world in which they live. They enjoy a greater sense of wholeness than their modern counterpart, but it is an undifferentiated and unconscious form of wholeness, utterly without individuality as we understand this term. Even so, this "stage" should not be thought of as only pertinent to primitive societies: it applies to all writing where there is little or no distinction between the personal and the collective.

In similar fashion, I would suggest that specific adaptations of oral culture are primarily concerned with issues of *identity in relation to an "other."* The extant myths and literature of the Middle East and ancient Greece provide perhaps the most obvious examples. Both the surviving epics about the Trojan War present a hero in confrontation with an "other" or "others" (Achilles vs. Hector; Odysseus vs. Polyphemos, Circe, Scylla, the suitors, etc.). If the *Iliad* is centrally concerned with the differentiation of *cultural* – not to be confused with "national" – identity, the dominant concern of the *Odyssey*, as of the great classical tragedies, is the differentiation of *personal* – not to be confused with "individual" – identity (e.g. Oedipus, in Sophocles' best-known play).[23]

One can see intimations of a predominant concern with *moral conflicts* in the Greek tragedies, but the clearest examples of this are provided by the literature of the late Middle Ages and the Renaissance. One thinks of the moral imperatives that underlie St. Augustine's *Confessions* (c. 400), Dante's *Divine Comedy* (c. 1300), morality plays such as *Everyman* (c. 1512), or, of course, Shakespeare's plays (written between 1588 and 1613), almost all of which are centrally concerned with a moral dilemma. One notes that such literature is invariably related to the moral tenets of a dominant religious ideology: i.e. in the Western tradition, this stage embraces the classical period, when the Olympians were the more or less unquestioned divinities of the Greco-Roman Empire, as well as almost all works produced while Christianity was the unchallenged religion of Europe.

The emergence of a literature which is predominantly concerned with the exploration of both a *social reality* and *individual consciousness* is a relatively recent phenomenon. Its first clear manifestations date from about the third quarter of the seventeenth century when the collective projection represented by the Christian "worldview" gradually began to break apart. Inevitably, this occasioned a radical shift in consciousness. It compelled individuals to make sense of their own reality *and* identity. For the first time in history, writers began to see a much fuller social spectrum than had ever been noticed before and to explore the implications of this for the individual: i.e. to explore both a social reality and a sense of individual consciousness that are recognizably related to our own concerns at the turn of the twenty-first century. The apparently conflicting aspects of this fourth stage are perhaps best illustrated by the works of the French philosopher Jean-Jacques Rousseau. His *Social Contract* (1762) begins with the words "Man is born free, but everywhere he is in chains," and his *Confessions* (written in the 1760s; published 1782 and 1789) begins with the assertion, "I may not be worth any more than my fellow men, but at least I am different." In these two phrases we can see the seeds of modern sociopolitical consciousness *and* modern individualism.[24]

Just as Jung's theory about the withdrawal of projections rests on assumptions about the nature of the fourth stage, so too does the scheme outlined above. We need, therefore, to further explain *why* one might consider the period 1675–1800 as a watershed in both literary and psychological history.

First, there is a fundamental difference between the social reality expressed in literary works prior to the eighteenth century and those published since. The "reality" implicit in Western literature from the *Iliad* (*c.* 725 BCE) to *Paradise Lost* (1667) is an essentially idealized "reality" reflecting only the changing interests of a privileged class. The emergence of a new and well-educated middle class in the course of the seventeenth century gradually resulted in the formulation of new ideas about the distribution of wealth and social responsibility. The beginnings of what we can loosely describe as "socialism" radically altered the way in which social reality was perceived.[25] Defoe's *Moll Flanders* (1722) is one of the first novels to show an evident concern with a *broad-based* social reality, a concern which gradually came to dominate not only the English novel, but also Western consciousness.

The dilemmas and challenges implicit in the "deep structures" of literary texts written prior to the eighteenth century are "collective": they reflect "collective" concerns, *not* the "personal" concerns of their authors. The great tragedies of Shakespeare do not reflect his personal anxieties and concerns. This is not to say that people had no concept of their "individuality" prior to the eighteenth century. They did: the surviving works of Sappho, St. Augustine, Petrarch, and Cellini all manifest a consciousness of their writer's distinct personality. But their mode of self-inquiry is *philosophical* rather than *psychological*. St. Augustine, for example, may have been able to claim that his "inner being was a house divided against itself" (*Confessions*, viii, 8), but he had no means to analyze this insight outside the terms offered him by his religious convictions. Although his experience was clearly autonomous, he could only interpret it in the light of a collective view. His consciousness – like that of Sappho, Petrarch, Cellini, and even Shakespeare – was confined by his assumptions about a theocentric universe and a "pyramidal" social structure. Only when these began to collapse in the course of the eighteenth century were writers free to explore the reality of their inner experiences: i.e. their individuality.

In *Paradise Lost*, whilst one might be able to relate *some* of Satan's attributes to Milton, one could hardly define Satan as Milton's personal shadow. In contrast, although the psychological implications of Richardson's novel are of collective interest, Mr. B. himself can hardly be defined as a collective image of the shadow: only in relation to the *reader today* might he be described as such. In relation to the *novel*, he personifies Richardson's "personal shadow." Which brings us to the second reason why the period 1675–1800 is such a turning point.

Mme de Lafayette's *Princesse de Clèves* (1678) and Richardson's *Pamela* (1740) are the first major works in their respective traditions to reflect the personal concerns of their authors. And, significantly, both works consist of a persona's confrontation with a character that can be defined as the author's *personal* shadow.[26] In the same way as one cannot move from "collective" to "individual" consciousness without confronting one's shadow, so the *first* literary works to reflect the personal concerns of their respective authors represent a confrontation with the shadow. For the first time in the history of literature, writers began to "project" into their works a personal dilemma facing them at the time of writing – and the nature of these dilemmas are recognizably related to those that still confront individuals today. From this time on, literary narratives became increasingly autobiographical.

Modern socio-political consciousness and individualism are often regarded as opposites. Jung, Paulo Freire (see Ch. 14), and Andrew Samuels (e.g. Samuels, 1993) have all shown that they are not. They are inseparable aspects of a sea change in consciousness that took place between 1675 and 1800 and which radically transformed the nature both of socio-political debate and of the individual's sense of his or her identity. The ability to question and, by questioning, come to terms with one's own reality is an inseparable aspect of one's ability to question and come to terms with oneself as one really is. In other words, in psychological terms, this change came about when individuals began to explore their own *personal shadow*. Our scheme thus illustrates how more and more of what was once imagined as "other" was gradually assimilated until it became part of modern consciousness.

We are still caught in the tangles of this "fourth stage." We now acknowledge that we have only just begun to see the world around us "as it is" and have barely begun to understand even our most basic psychological needs and drives. Only dreamers can think that either science or political leaders will soon discover a panacea for all our ills. Our anxieties and our dilemmas stem from ourselves. The world we see is of our own making. We *cannot* completely free ourselves of our projections and, in all likelihood, never will be able to. All we can do is strive to understand them so as to better understand the implications of our own conflicting tendencies and so better integrate ourselves with the world. The fifth stage begins when one determines to become more conscious of the nature and extent of one's own projections. It is a path, or goal, or ideal rather than a stage in the same sense as the others; even so, it could be argued that it has a literature of its own.

It is from our own time and place in history that we respond to the literary works of the past. We must therefore make a distinction between works that show little or no concept of what we mean by "reality" today and those that are concerned with examining facets of social reality and individual consciousness that are evidently related to the ways in which we understand these terms. There is nothing new in suggesting that the period

1675–1800 witnessed the beginnings of the modern world: much has been written about the social changes engendered by this age of revolution. My contention here is that we cannot fully understand the import of these changes without better understanding the nature of the massive shift in individual consciousness that made them possible. And this is perhaps most clearly revealed in literature.

Clearly, there isn't space in these pages to explore these hypotheses in full. My aim here is only to propose a way in which to identify the evolution of the dominant concerns in literary narratives. Jungian literary criticism has been too dependent on the notion of archetypal images. There is a pressing need for Jungian psychology to find a way to distinguish different *kinds* of archetypal imagery. I would suggest that Jung's five stages in the withdrawal of projections provides a way to distinguish between archetypal material that is predominantly concerned with

1. identity in itself
2. identity in relation to an "other"/"others"
3. moral or ethical dilemmas
4. social reality/individual consciousness
5. individual identity

Literary history is not only a question of changing literary styles or of evolving social interactions: it is also an expression of the evolution of human consciousness. The great works of literature are landmarks along the road toward the manifestation of *individual consciousness*.[27]

Bearing our reading of *Pamela* in mind, the proposed scheme suggests that Jung's concepts of specific archetypal images requires further specification. Jung referred only to *the* shadow. It has long been recognized that he meant at least two very different things by this term (the totality of the unconscious *and* a specific personification of all those characteristics that one conceals so well from others that one is usually unaware of them oneself). A further distinction is needed, for there is a radical difference between the *collective* shadow-figures of pre-eighteenth-century texts and the *personal* shadow-figures of post-Enlightenment works. It is in this "fourth stage" that writers began to be aware of their own *personal* shadow and thus to explore their own "ego" in the contemporary sense of this term. In similar fashion, there is also a need to distinguish between the *collective* anima/animus-figures of pre-eighteenth-century fictions and the *personal* anima/animus-figures that become more and more prominent in subsequent narrative fictions.

There can be no doubt that notions about both "social reality" and "individual consciousness" have undergone a radical evolution in the last three thousand years. Changes in society and in the individual's relation to society have been documented from any number of positions. A great deal has been written on the evolution of socio-cultural attitudes and psychohistory has opened up new paths of historical inquiry. But we still do not have any well-developed theories about how *literary* consciousness has evolved over the same period.[28] The fascination of contemporary debate with sociopolitical ideology has led to an emphasis on the "social history" of literature. But the social domain is only *one* aspect of our reality: the other is the personal. Social and personal consciousness are two sides of the same coin. In order to understand the evolution of psychological concerns we have to understand changing socio-historical conditions. The corollary is *equally* true: in order to better understand the evolution and direction of socio-political conditions we must *also* be aware of changes in collective and individual consciousness. It is time for criticism to develop and engage with a "psychological history" of literature.

## Conclusions

The purpose of regarding a narrative fiction as a projection of a dilemma facing the author at the time of writing is *not* to "restrict" the reading to exclusively psychological considerations, but to "open it up" so as to reveal the interrelationship that exists between apparently disparate elements. We have seen how an archetypal image of a "virgin" lies at the heart of *Pamela*, but there is more to the novel than this image alone can reveal. It is often thought that Jung was so emphatically concerned with psychological processes that he had little notion about culture beyond a somewhat simplistic distinction between East and West. This may have been true of him as an individual, but it is not an intrinsic limitation of the views he formulated. Any application of Jung's various theories to literature will reveal the need for individuals to engage with their own cultural tradition. A Jungian reading of a work of literature is one that, whilst rooted in the exploration of ordinary human dilemmas, *also* engages with social, political, national, and cultural realities.

- My reading of *Pamela* emphasizes the need to establish *whose* experience is really being described in any given text. Literary critics often explore the psychology of a main character without any regard for the role of this character in relation to the text as a whole. This chapter argues that, if one is interested in the psychological implications of the *text*, one must identify the "effective protagonist" and relate *all* its events to this character.

- Jung's "auxiliary tools" provide a way of defining the nature of the dilemma confronting the effective protagonist.
- The dilemma facing the effective protagonist very often manifests itself as an implicit "challenge." In *Pamela*, this was defined as Mr. B.'s need to confront his shadow-tendencies and come to terms with his problematic "Eros." Nonetheless, it must be insisted that one of the defining characteristics of a Jungian approach is that every text examined will reveal a different dilemma conditioning it.
- One must always *specify* the nature of any parallels between the protagonist of a literary work and its author. Jung's concepts were called upon in order to demonstrate that Mr. B. represents two different *aspects* of Richardson's personality (his persona and his shadow).
- Literary criticism of all persuasions ought to become more aware of what I have called the "psychological history of literature." I have proposed two ways in which Jung's theory about the withdrawal of projections might help –
  (1) to specify the nature and degree of consciousness implicit in any given work and so identify its "dominant concern," and
  (2) to trace the evolution of *literary* consciousness.
- Jung's five stages in the withdrawal of projections provide a way in which to distinguish between different *kinds* of archetypal images and interactions.
- Jungian literary criticism needs to distinguish between collective archetypal images (i.e. *the* shadow) and archetypal figures with a more specific relation to the individual (i.e. the "personal" shadow).
- Contemporary socio-political reality and individual consciousness are inseparable aspects of an upheaval in consciousness that began in the late seventeenth century/early eighteenth century and which still characterizes our own time: to explore either one, the critic must also take account of the other.

## NOTES

1 Schlegel, 1790s/1991, p. 98 (translation slightly modified).
2 For example, in his letter of 7 September 1935, to Pastor Ernst Jahn, Jung, 1973, 1976, vol. I, pp. 195–197, and his "Reply to Martin Buber," written February 1952, in CW 18, pp. 663–670.
3 For Jung's analysis of Miss Frank Miller (pseud.), "Some Instances of Subconscious Creative Imagination" [1906], see *Psychology of the Unconscious* (CW B, rev. as *Symbols of Transformation*, CW 5); for his essay "Answer to Job" and *The Tibetan Book of the Dead*, see CW 11; for "Western" alchemy, see CW 12, 13, 14.

4  Two recently published volumes now form an indispensable introduction to Jungian approaches to literature: Van Meurs and Kidd, 1988, whose introduction offers a brief critical survey of the field, and Sugg (ed.), 1992, an anthology of some of the best work in the field. An example of an influential work by a therapist is Marie-Louise von Franz's study of Saint-Exupéry's *The Little Prince* in *Puer Aeternus* (Franz, 1981). For a well-received book-length study by a literary critic, see Tacey, 1988.

5  See Jung's claim, advanced in 1952: "I have set up neither a system nor a general theory, but have merely formulated auxiliary concepts to serve me as tools, as is customary in every branch of science" (*CW* 18, p. 666).

6  The phrases are borrowed from structural anthropology: see, for example, Lévi-Strauss, 1968. Not only will a structuralist, a Freudian, and a Jungian each understand the phrase "deep structure" differently, but even amongst critics from the same "school," significant differences will arise.

7  The edition used in preparing this essay was Richardson, 1980; page references in the text are to this edition.

8  *Pamela: or, Virtue Rewarded* was published in November 1740; Henry Fielding, writing under the pseudonym "Mr Conny Keyber," quickly responded with a parody of it called *An Apology for the Life of Mrs. Shamela Andrews*: it was published on 4 April 1741. In December 1741, Richardson brought out his "sequel," *Pamela: Part Two*. Two months later, on 22 February 1742, Fielding published, anonymously, *The History of the Adventures of Joseph Andrews*, in which the "hero" is presented as Pamela's brother: Joseph is a footman to Lady Booby, and his "virtue" is threatened, first by Lady Booby and then by her chambermaid, Mrs. Slipslop.

9  Interestingly, this can be noted even in the plot-outline: it would be difficult to summarize the action without making Mr. B. appear as the effective protagonist.

10 See also Kinkead-Weekes, 1973; Doody, 1974; Miller, 1980. For a reading inspired by Michel Foucault, see Armstrong, 1987.

11 For an account of projection, see Franz, 1980.

12 For a discussion of the "virgin" as archetypal image, see Layard, 1972.

13 This aspect of Pamela corresponds to the moral authority often invested in the anima. This raises the interesting question, is the moral authority invested in women primarily a male projection? And if so, what is the nature of the "hook" on which it rests?

14 Jung uses the word "inferior" to describe those functions of the personality that, for one reason or another, have been either *repressed* or left *undeveloped*; consequently, when they do manifest themselves, they often do so with irrational compulsion: see Franz, 1971.

15 A great many literary fictions can be seen as originating in a similar attempt to escape from a condition envisioned as "imprisoning": see Dawson, 1989a, 1989b, and 1993.

16 For example, Mary Shelley, in her vivid description of how the idea for her first novel came to her in the summer of 1816: see the "Author's Introduction to the Standard Novels Edition" (1831), in Mary Shelley, 1992 (reprinted in most modern editions).

17 For an account of active imagination, see Watkins, 1984; Hannah, 1981.

18 The "letter-writer" was eventually completed and published a year after *Pamela*,

as *Letters written to and for Particular Friends, on the most important Occasions, Directing not only the requisite Style and Forms to be observed in writing Familiar Letters; but how to think and act justly and prudently, in the common Concerns of Human Life* (1741).

19 This is even more obviously true of Lovelace in *Clarissa*.

20 The clearest examples are the heroines of novels by George Eliot, especially Romola and Dorothea Brooke, both of whom portray women who had to suffer the consequences of a predominantly male, but nonetheless collective (and thus *also* female), projected expectation: see *Romola* (1863) and *Middlemarch* (1871–72). A further parallel with George Eliot is Pamela's assuming responsibility for Miss Sally Godfrey: compare Nancy Lammeter's willingness to adopt Eppie at the end of *Silas Marner*: see Terence Dawson, 1993.

21 I am grateful to Andrew Samuels for having suggested I explore this possibility.

22 I use the word "other" here more loosely than Papadopoulos, 1984: in particular, I see the "other" as an aspect of the "shadow" rather than the "self."

23 This is not a quibble: *personal* is used in the sense that Oedipus and other Greek heroes are different from the "crowd": but they remain "types." That we can speak of an "Oedipus complex" is evidence enough that we are not dealing with an "individual." In contrast, *individual* is used to describe someone who is consciously wrestling with the dilemmas presented by the fourth and fifth stages identified in Jung's scheme: i.e. someone who is manifestly "conscious" of the implications of his or her actions.

24 There are clear parallels between the scheme outlined and the interest shown by Foucault in the period of the French Revolution: see O'Farrell, 1989; Cutting (ed.), 1994.

25 I use "socialism" here not to indicate an ideology in opposition to either bourgeois liberalism or capitalism, or to indicate a workers' movement: I use it here only to indicate new ideas about the responsibilities of the privileged toward the less privileged that came into being in the course of the eighteenth century.

26 For Mme de Lafayette, see Dawson, 1992.

27 A major proviso needs to be made about the scheme outlined: the examples I have chosen are all from the Western literary tradition. It cannot be assumed that it applies to all cultures in the same way. Indeed, the differences in the way in which different societies have stressed one element or another in any given phase would certainly provide a key to better understanding and so responding to cultural differences.

28 For a provocative theory about the origins of consciousness, see Jaynes, 1982. Interestingly, philosophers have also shown a keen interest in this question: e.g. Taylor, 1989.

## REFERENCES

Armstrong, Nancy (1987). *Desire and Domestic Fiction: A Political History of the Novel*. New York: Oxford University Press.

Cutting, Gary (ed.) (1994). *The Cambridge Companion to Foucault*. Cambridge: Cambridge University Press.

Dawson, Terence (1989a). "The Struggle for Deliverance from the Father: The Structural Principle of *Wuthering Heights.*" *Modern Language Review*, 84, pp. 289–304.

(1989b). "An Oppression Past Explaining: The Structures of *Wuthering Heights.*" *Orbis Litterarum*, 44, pp. 48–68.

(1992). "Catherine de Médicis and *La princesse de Clèves.*" *Seventeenth-Century French Studies*, 14, pp. 191–210.

(1993). "'Light Enough to Trusten By': Structure and Experience in *Silas Marner.*" *Modern Language Review*, 88, pp. 26–45.

Doody, Margaret A. (1974). *A Natural Passion.* Oxford: Clarendon Press.

Franz, Marie-Louise von (1971). "The Inferior Function." In Marie-Louise von Franz and James Hillman, *Lectures on Jung's Typology.* Zurich: Spring Publications, pp. 1–72.

(1980). *Projection and Recollection in Jungian Psychology: Reflections of the Soul.* La Salle, Ill. and London: Open Court.

(1981). *Puer Aeternus* [1970]. Santa Monica, Calif.: Sigo Press.

(1982). *An Introduction to the Interpretation of Fairy Tales* [1970]. Dallas: Spring Publications, pp. 27–28.

Golden, Morris (1963). *Richardson's Characters.* Ann Arbor: University of Michigan Press.

Hannah, Barbara (1981). *Encounters with the Soul: Active Imagination as Developed by C. G. Jung.* Santa Monica, Calif.: Sigo Press.

Jaynes, Julian (1982). *The Origin of Consciousness in the Breakdown of the Bicameral Mind.* Harmondsworth: Penguin.

Jung, C. G. (1922). "On the Relation of Analytical Psychology to Poetry." *CW* 15, pp. 65–83.

(1930). "Psychology and Literature." *CW* 15, pp. 84–105.

(1932). "*Ulysses*: A Monologue." *CW* 15, pp. 109–134.

(1952a). "Reply to Martin Buber." *CW* 18, pp. 663–670.

(1952b). "Answer to Job." *CW* 11, pp. 355–470.

(1956). *Symbols of Transformation. CW* 5.

(1967). *Alchemical Studies. CW* 13.

(1968). *Psychology and Alchemy*, 2nd ed. *CW* 12.

(1970). *Mysterium Coniunctionis*, 2nd ed. *CW* 14.

(1973, 1976). *Letters.* Ed. G. Adler and A. Jaffé, tr. R. F. C. Hull, 2 vols. London: Routledge & Kegan Paul.

(1991). *Psychology of the Unconscious* [1912]. Ed. W. McGuire, *CW* B.

Kinkead-Weekes, Mark (1973). *Samuel Richardson: Dramatic Novelist.* London: Methuen.

Layard, John (1972). *The Virgin Archetype: Two Essays.* Zurich: Spring Publications.

Lévi-Strauss, Claude (1968). *Structural Anthropology* [1955], tr. C. Jacobson and B. Grundfest Schoepf. London: Allen Lane.

Meurs, Jos Van, with John Kidd (1988). *Jungian Literary Criticism: 1920–1980: An Annotated, Critical Bibliography of Works in English.* Metuchen, N.J. and London: The Scarecrow Press.

Miller, Frank (Miss). *pseud.* (1906). "Some Instances of Subconscious Creative Imagination." In C. G. Jung, *CW* 5, pp. 445–462.

Miller, Nancy K. (1980). *The Heroine's Text: The French and English Novel, 1722–1782*. New York: Columbia University Press.

O'Farrell, Clare (1989). *Foucault: Historian or Philosopher?* Basingstoke: Macmillan.

Papadopoulos, Renos (1984). "Jung and the Concept of the Other." In R. K. Papadopoulos and G. S. Saayman (eds.), *Jung in a Modern Perspective*. London: Wildwood House, pp. 54–88 and 290–294.

Pessoa, Fernando (1917/1990). *Obra poética*, ed. Maria A. Galhoz, Rio de Janeiro: Editora Nova Aguilar, pp. 129–130.

Pompa, Leon (1990). *Vico: A Study of the "New Science,"* 2nd ed. Cambridge: Cambridge University Press, pp. 7–14.

Richardson, Samuel (1980). *Pamela: Or, Virtue Rewarded*, ed. Peter Sabor, with an Introduction by Margaret A. Doody. Harmondsworth: Penguin.

Roussel, Roy (1986). *Conversation of the Sexes*. New York: Oxford University Press.

Schlegel, Friedrich (1790s/1991). *Philosophical Fragments*, tr. Peter Firchow. Minneapolis: University of Minnesota Press.

Shelley, Mary (1992). *Frankenstein*. London: Penguin.

Sugg, Richard P. (ed.) (1992). *Jungian Literary Criticism*. Evanston, Ill.: Northwestern University Press.

Tacey, David (1988). *Patrick White: Fiction and the Unconscious*. Melbourne and New York: Oxford University Press.

Taylor, Charles (1989). *Sources of the Self: The Making of the Modern Identity*. Cambridge, Mass.: Harvard University Press.

Warner, William B. (1979). *Reading "Clarissa": The Struggles of Interpretation*. New Haven: Yale University Press.

Watkins, Mary (1984). *Waking Dreams* [c. 1976] Dallas: Spring Publications.

# 14

## LAWRENCE R. ALSCHULER

# Jung and politics

Jung sometimes described the relationship between the ego and the unconscious as a *power struggle* (CW 9.i, paras. 522–523; CW 7, paras. 342 and 381). In this struggle, when an unconscious complex *takes over* the ego, there is "possession" (see Sandner and Beebe, 1984, p. 310; CW 7, p. 224). When the ego *takes over* from the unconscious certain attributes which belong to the Self, there is "inflation" (CW 7, pp. 228–229). Jung compared the progressive transformation of this power struggle in the individuation process to a sequence of political regimes. He described the initial unconscious unity of the psyche as the "tyranny of the unconscious." The situation in which the ego is predominant he described as "a tyrannical one-party system." And when the ego and the unconscious "negotiate" on the basis of "equal rights," the relation resembles a "parliamentary democracy" (CW 18, p. 621).

This apt political metaphor for the individuation process points to the larger issues of the relationship of Jungian psychology to politics. Three such issues to be discussed in this chapter are: (1) the relationship between "the political development of the person and the psychological development of the person" (Samuels, 1993, p. 4), (2) the relationship between the psychological development of the person and democracy (Odajnyk, 1976, pp. 182–187), and (3) the contribution of Jungian psychology to the study of politics (Samuels, 1993, p. 14). The attempts to address these three issues may be grouped into two categories. The first revolves around Jung's own political thought. Several of Jung's writings deal directly with politics: *Essays on Contemporary Events, The Undiscovered Self.* Among the outstanding analyses of Jung's *political thought* are those by Odajnyk (1976), D'Lugin (1981), and Samuels (1993, esp. Chs. 12, 13). The second category of scholarship addressing these issues revolves around Jung's *psychological theories* as applied by others to the study of politics. Applications include those by Jungian analysts: Stevens (1989), Bernstein (1989), Stewart (1992); and by political scientists: Steiner (1983), Alschuler (1992, 1996).

The present chapter stands in the second category and focuses on the issue of the relationship between the psychological development and the political development of the person. My resources extend from Jung's theories of the psyche to those of the post-Jungians. My approach will be to describe first the individuation process, which I consider to be the *psychological* development of the person. Then I will compare this to what the Brazilian educator Paulo Freire defined as the process of "conscientization," which I consider to be an excellent formulation of the *political* development of the person. To anticipate my conclusions from this comparison, there are solid grounds for believing that individuation supports, though does not determine, conscientization. If conscientization contributes to democracy, then individuation provides a psychological basis for democracy.

## A critique of Jung's political thought

My essay stands in the second category of scholarship rather than the first because, as a political scientist, I am troubled by Jung's political thought. Here, in brief, are three of the reasons for my discomfort, based on Jung's last major writing on politics, *The Undiscovered Self* (CW 10).

1. The overstatement of the psychological causes of political phenomena (pp. 60–61). According to Jung, political problems have mainly psychological causes and solutions (p. 45). Refering to the Cold War, Jung states that the splitting of opposites in the psyche has caused the division of the world into the opposing mass movements of the East and the West (pp. 53, 55, and 124–125). As for the solution to these same problems, Jung states that the individual's spontaneous religious experience will keep the individual "from dissolving into the crowd" (p. 48). Healing the split in the human psyche comes from the withdrawal of shadow projections (pp. 55–56). In recognizing our shadow we become immune to "moral and mental infection" (p. 125) which accounts for mass movements and the world political division.

2. The over-emphasis of the reality of the psyche (inner) and the de-emphasis of the reality of politics (outer). Jung views political conflicts as mainly the outer manifestation of (inner) psychic conflicts (von Franz, 1976, p. x). Jung states that the only carrier of life is the individual personality and that society and the State are ideas which can claim reality only as conglomerations of individuals (p. 42).

3. Pathologizing politics. Jung considers political mass movements to result from the pathological split between the conscious and the uncon-

scious. He states that when human beings lose contact with their instinctual nature, consciousness and the unconscious must come into conflict. This split becomes pathological when consciousness is unable to suppress the instinctual side. He explains, "The accumulation of individuals who have got into this critical state starts off a mass movement purporting to be the champion of the suppressed" (p. 45).

What I find troubling about these three points is that throughout his political analyses Jung focuses on the role of the individual, either the individual in mass movements or the individual political leader. He seems unable to grasp the ways in which the political system operates both in generating and in managing social conflicts. Further, it is troubling to find Jung categorizing mass political movements as pathological when such movements also include the American, the French, and the Russian revolutions, not to mention those movements which ended the Soviet empire. There is a one-sidedness in Jung's political thought, emphasizing the pathological more than the normal and emphasizing the individual more than systemic political behavior. A more holistic application of Jungian psychology to the study of politics would transcend these opposites.

## The psychological development of the person: individuation

My aim in this section is to select from the writings on individuation those elements that will enable us to discern its parallels with and its relations to the political development of the person (in the following section). To begin, individuation includes the expansion of ego consciousness. More conscious-ness means more individuation, almost in the quantitative sense described as "increments of consciousness" that raise the level of consciousness. Yet when we ask, "consciousness of what?," we encounter qualitative differ-ences in the level of consciousness. Self-awareness marks the second stage of individuation while awareness of powers in the psyche greater than oneself marks stage three.

My description of the stages of individuation adopts a usual Jungian view that there are three such stages (Whitmont, 1978, p. 266; Edinger, 1972, p. 186). The first stage is "the emergence of ego consciousness" from the unconscious unity of the psyche, followed by the stage of "the alienation of the ego." The third stage, "the relativization of the ego," moves toward conscious wholeness (Sandner and Beebe, 1984, p. 298). There are many potentially useful analogies and images to elucidate these stages. Jung, himself, often likened individuation to the stages in alchemical transformation of base metals into the "uncommon gold." Jacobi describes

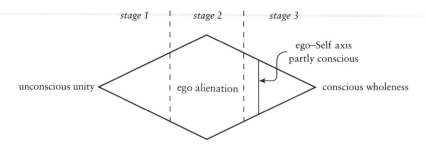

Fig. 3. The "diamond": stages of individuation

individuation as a recurring "night sea journey" of the soul (Jacobi, 1967, pp. 68–70). Whitmont refers to the image of a "labyrinthine spiral" with the Self at the center and the ego passing through recurring phases in the direction of wholeness (Whitmont, 1978, pp. 93 and 309).

The particular image I find most suitable for our purposes does incorporate many elements in the analogies used by others. This is the image of a diamond (Fig. 3) in which the process of individuation proceeds from left to right, from the initial point of "unconscious unity" through "ego aliena-tion" in the middle, toward the point at the right, "conscious wholeness." The upper line traces the path of consciousness while the lower line traces the path of the unconscious. The varying vertical distance between the lines represents the relationship between consciousness and the unconscious, the ego–Self axis.

It is as if Neumann had this diamond image in mind when he described the individuation process:

> We speak of an ego–self axis because the processes occurring between the systems of consciousness and the unconscious and their corresponding centers seem to show that the two systems and their centers, the ego and the self, move toward and away from each other. The filiation of the ego means the establishment of the ego–self axis and a "distancing" of the ego from the self which reaches its high point in the first half of life, when the systems divide and the ego is apparently autonomous. In the individuation of the second part of life the movement is reversed and the ego comes closer to the self again. But aside from this reversal due to age, the ego-self axis is normally in flux; every change in consciousness is at the same time a change in the ego–self axis.
>
> (1966, p. 85)

In the above diamond image I have added two vertical dotted lines that separate the individuation process into three stages. Now we can refer to the diamond in presenting the events which mark the qualitative differences between the three stages. This pattern for the first half of life may not be universal since a number of women Jungians consider this to be more typical of male psychological development.

Two key concepts already mentioned require clarification. The Self may be understood *both* as the archetypal urge toward the integration of the conscious and unconscious parts of the psyche *and* as the archetypal image of this integrated personality. The ego–Self axis is Neumann's term for describing the two-way communication between the ego and the Self which is essential for personality integration. A succession of one's prayers and one's dreams exemplifies this two-way communication.

### Stage one: the emergence of ego consciousness

The ego begins to emerge from its origin in the matrix of the unconscious during infancy. An urge to individuation establishes an initial tension of opposites: between the primary unity (identity) of ego with the Self, and the separation of ego from the Self. An infant's sense of omnipotence (primary inflation) stems from this ego–Self identity. The lack of differentiation between inner and outer results in a magical rapport with persons and objects, a "knowing" what they feel and think. Jung likened this latter experience to *participation mystique*, what most psychoanalysts now call projective identification (Samuels, 1986, p. 152). The gradual dissolution of the original ego–Self identity produces increments of consciousness (Edinger, 1972, pp. 21 and 23). The ego complex begins to form, involving a sense of "continuity of body and mind in relation to space, time and causality" and a sense of unity by means of memory and rationality (Whitmont, 1978, p. 232). As the ego emerges from the unconscious it becomes the center of personal identity and personal choices.

The emergence of ego consciousness necessarily involves a polarization of the opposites as the ego makes choices between what is good and bad in reference to the value system of society, as mediated by the parents:

> Duality, dissociation and repression have been born in the human psyche simultaneously with the birth of consciousness . . . The innate and necessary stages of psychic development require a polarization of the opposites, conscious vs. unconscious, spirit vs. nature. (Edinger, 1972, p. 20)

In more clinical terms, dissociation is a normal unconscious process of splitting the psyche into complexes, each personified and carrying an image and an emotion. The splitting occurs, according to Jung, because the image and emotion are incompatible with the habitual attitude of consciousness. Jung believed that the feeling-toned complexes were "living units of the unconscious psyche" which give the psyche its structure (1934, pp. 96, 101,

104). The ego shapes its identity by aligning itself with what is compatible with habitual attitudes, and by splitting off and repressing that which is incompatible (Sandner and Beebe, 1984, p. 299).

Sandner and Beebe place the stage of the emergence of ego consciousness within the overall process of individuation. The nucleus of every complex is connected to the Self, the center of the collective unconscious. The Self produces complexes, splits them off, and reintegrates them in a new way. In doing so the Self guides the process of individuation away from an original state of unconscious unity toward a state of conscious wholeness (*ibid.*, p. 298; see also Alschuler, 1995).

### Stage two: the alienation of the ego

The task in the first half of life, according to Jung, is to consolidate one's ego identity and to construct a persona as an adaptation to the external standards of society, the workplace, and the family. According to Whitmont, those innate dispositions which do not correspond to society's standards are split off from the ego's image of itself and form the shadow. In this way, ego, persona, and shadow develop in step with each other under the influence of societal and parental values (Whitmont, 1978, p. 247). This splitting and formation of unconscious complexes, as noted earlier, are necessary aspects of the individuation process. In the second stage of individuation this splitting reaches its limit, as shown in the "diamond image," where the vertical distance separating ego consciousness from the unconscious is at its maximum. The one-sidedness of the personality, so often mentioned by Jung, refers to this extreme separation.

The one-sidedness of the personality takes its toll in mid-life. The mid-life crisis is often experienced as meaninglessness, despair, emptiness, and a lack of purpose. This experience corresponds to the ego's alienation (disconnection) from the Self (the unconscious). As Edinger tells us, the connection between the ego and the Self is essential for psychic health, giving the ego foundation, security, energy, meaning, and purpose (Edinger, 1972, p. 43). The disconnection of ego consciousness from the unconscious, encountered especially in the mid-life crisis, epitomizes the stage of ego–Self alienation. According to Edinger, problems of alienation between ego and parental figures, between ego and shadow, and between ego and animus (or anima) are forms of alienation between ego and Self (*ibid.*, p. 39).

The ego generally endures its alienation in a cycle of inflation and depression, producing increments of consciousness. In the inflated phase, the ego experiences power, responsibility, high self-esteem, and superiority, all of which enable the maturing ego to carry out the tasks of the first half of life. In the depressive phase, the ego experiences guilt, low self-esteem, and inferiority, all of which counterbalance inflation and prepare the ego for a greater awareness of the Self (*ibid.*, pp. 15, 36, 40, 42, 48, 50, 52, 56).

### Stage three: the relativization of the ego

The qualitative change marking the third stage of individuation is a partial consciousness of the ego–Self axis. This change has been prepared in the stage of ego alienation where inflation and depression alternate in cycles (*ibid.*, p. 103). The diamond diagram shows the reconnection of the ego to the Self in the reduced distance between the top and bottom lines. The solid vertical line represents the partially conscious ego–Self axis.

In this stage of individuation the ego integrates many unconscious complexes and acquires a "religious attitude." These experiences will be described in turn. The emerging ego in the first stage of individuation began its awareness of the opposites and made its choices in accordance with social values in order to form an acceptable self-image. Unacceptable aspects of the personality were repressed, falling into the unconscious and forming the complexes. In the stage of alienation the ego separated even further from the unconscious through dissociation, resulting in the further growth of complexes and the ego's one-sidedness. Activated complexes are met in projection and, of course, in dreams (Jung, CW 8, p. 97). While the first two stages of individuation saw the formation of complexes and the multiplication of projections, in the third stage the ego's main task is the withdrawal of projections through the integration of complexes:[1]

> Only when one's self-image has developed to a sufficient degree can one be in a position to perceive other people's selves as they actually are. If one is not in this happier state, one is inclined to experience people through the veil of one's own imagery, in positive and negative emotional projections . . .
>
> (Perry, 1970, p. 6)

The growth of consciousness, through the withdrawal of projections, removes this "veil" and permits genuine human relationships (*ibid.*, p. 7).

The second qualitative change characterizing this stage of individuation is the development of a "religious attitude." This attitude is called "religious" because it entails a realization that there is an autonomous inner directive power supraordinate to the ego, which is the Self (Edinger, 1972, p. 97). The ego experiences itself as the center of consciousness, but no longer as the center of the entire personality (conscious and unconscious). The ego's new awareness of its subordination to the Self constitutes its "relativization." The ego–Self axis, which was always unconscious before, sometimes even disconnected, now is reconnected and partially conscious. When this occurs suddenly as a breakthrough following a period of depression, it may feel like a religious experience (*ibid.*, p. 69, also pp. 48–52). To conclude, the individuation process describes the movement of the psyche from the initial condition of unconscious unity toward the goal of conscious wholeness.

## The political development of the person: conscientization

My aims in this section are to present an example of the "political development of the person," a concept offered by Samuels (1993, p. 53), and to compare this with the "psychological development of person" which we have just described as the individuation process (see Alschuler, 1992). The question to be kept in mind is: does the psychological development of the person contribute to the political development of the person?

The most advanced formulation of "the political development of the person," in my view, is Paulo Freire's concept of "conscientization" (Freire, 1972 and 1974). This Brazilian educator has formulated his theories out of the adult literacy programs he has directed in South America, North America, and Africa since the 1960s. Through these programs Freire seeks to further the process of humanization among oppressed peoples by raising their political consciousness (1972, p. 28). The goal of humanization is in many ways compatible with the goal of wholeness in the individuation process. Now we must ask, "raising political consciousness of what?" Given the poverty, violent repression, economic exploitation, and social injustice of oppressed peoples, the task is to raise their consciousness of the problems of oppression. Conscientization progresses through three stages, each of which is characterized by the way in which a person (1) *names* the problems, (2) *reflects* on the causes of the problems, and (3) *acts* to resolve the problems of oppression (Smith, 1976, p. 42).

### Stage one: magical consciousness

Freire calls this stage "magical" because people feel powerless before an awful reality and an awe-inspiring powerful, irresistible force which changes or maintains things according to its will. A person with magical consciousness will *name* problems in terms of physical survival, including poor health and poverty, or will simply deny that these conditions constitute "problems" since they are seen as normal facts of existence. When one *reflects* on the causes of these problems one attributes responsibility to factors beyond one's control, supernatural powers such as fate, God, or the boss . . . or simplistically to natural conditions (e.g. one is poor because the land is poor). *Acting* to solve problems is considered futile since the causes are uncontrollable, leading to resignation and waiting for "luck" to change.

*Comparison.* When comparing "magical consciousness" to the stage of ego emergence, we should remember that conscientization is an adult process. In adults, nevertheless, there are vestiges from earlier stages of individuation. The residual ego–Self identity (Edinger, 1972, p. 6) blurs the distinction between inner and outer, between willing and causation. The ego–Self identity also produces archetypal projections onto people and events, endowing them with a numinous quality. The autonomous and emotional nature of these projections evokes fear and fatalism (Whitmont, 1978, p. 273), for spontaneously they overwhelm the ego independently of its will. Authority figures, including political and religious leaders, as carriers of these projections will have an aura of supernatural power.

## Stage two: naive consciousness

In contrast with the conforming nature of magical consciousness, naive consciousness is reforming. At this stage people readily *name* problems, but only in terms of "problem" individuals. Individual oppressors are named because they deviate from the social norms and rules to which they are expected to adhere. A lawyer may cheat a client or a boss may fail to provide medical assistance for sick employees, for example. Alternatively, the "problem" individual named may be oneself, the oppressed individual who fails to live up to the oppressor's expectations. One may believe that one does not work as hard as the "norm" requires or that one is not smart enough to perform well. At this stage one has at best a fragmented understanding of the causes. One is unable to understand the actions of individual oppressors and the problems of oppressed persons as consequences of the normal functioning of an oppressive and unjust social system. Thus, when one *reflects* on the causes of problems, one tends to blame oneself in accordance with the oppressor's ideology which one has internalized as one's own. Or, if one names as a problem an individual oppressor's violation of a norm, one will understand the oppressor's evil or selfish intentions as the causes.

*Acting* at this stage corresponds to the manner of naming. Those who blame themselves for not living up to the oppressor's expectations will reform themselves and attempt to become more like the oppressor (e.g. imitate the oppressor's manner of dress, speech, work). Having internalized the ideology of those who oppress, containing beliefs in one's own inferiority and of the benevolence of the oppressors, one may view one's own peers pejoratively as inferiors, leading to "horizontal aggression" against them. Or, if one has identified the problem as the individual oppressor, one will seek to restrain or remove the people who oppress and to restore the rules to their normal functioning.

*Comparison.* In the individuation process, at the stage of ego alienation, no power appears superior to that of personal will-power. Those who identify with this will-power experience psychological inflation enabling them to undertake the tasks of the first half of life. At the naive stage of conscientization, in the absence of systemic understanding, problems appear to derive from the will of individuals. When an oppressed person blames an oppressor's ill will for a problem, he/she asserts his/her own will-power in order to oppose the oppressor. The oppressed person constructs a persona which corresponds to the value standards in the ideology of those who oppress. This ideology deems as "good" all that resembles the oppressor and as "bad" all the inherent traits of the oppressed people. Also at the naive stage is the oppressed person who, in accordance with the oppressors' ideology he/she has internalized, views him/herself as inferior and holds him/herself responsible for his/her problems. This corresponds to the depressive phase of the cycle alternating with inflation at the stage of ego alienation. Individual will-power is essential, yet unavailable to the depressive who experiences guilt and inferiority.

### Stage three: critical consciousness

At this stage the individual has an integrated understanding of the socio-political system, enabling him/her to relate the instances of oppression to the *normal* functioning of an unjust and oppressive system. An individual *names* as problems the failure of his/her self-affirmation (collective), sometimes expressed in terms of his/her ethnic or gender identity. These problems tend to be viewed as community problems rather than as personal problems. In addition, the individual may *name* the socio-political system as the problem. "They see specific rules, events, relationships, and procedures as merely examples of systemic institutionalized injustice" (Smith, 1976, p. 63). When *reflecting* on the causes, the oppressed person understands how he/she colludes to make the unjust system work (by believing the oppressors' ideology and by aggressing other oppressed people, for example). Becoming demystified, he/she rejects the oppressors' ideology and develops a more realistic view of him/herself, of his/her peers, and of the oppressors. While recognizing weaknesses in self and peers, he/she abandons self-pity in favor of empathy, solidarity, and collective (ethnic) self-esteem. While recognizing evil in individual oppressors, he/she understands that the problem involves a history of vested interests and political power (*ibid.*).

At the critical stage, *acting* takes two forms: self-actualization and transformation of the system. Collaboration, cooperation, and collective self-reliance replace aggression against one's peers (other oppressed people). Personal and ethnic collective identity fill the void left by the oppressors' ideology which has been rejected. Collective actions to transform the socio-political system replace isolated actions against individual oppressors. These actions aim at creating a society where truly human relationships are possible. In summary, the process of conscientization describes the movement of the political consciousness of the oppressed from dehumanization to humanization while the objective conditions of oppression, deriving from the socio-political system, are gradually eliminated, a goal never fully attained.

*Comparison.* The relativization of the ego in the third stage of individuation, as we have seen, means that the ego becomes aware of its subordination to the Self, the center of the entire psyche, while retaining its place as the center of consciousness. This change of attitude is so basic that it is often compared to a religious conversion. Similarly, at the critical stage of conscientization, the oppressed become aware of the roles they play within a socio-political system which serves the interests of those who oppress. This sudden political awakening comes for some oppressed people as "revolutionary consciousness." The Self and the political system occupy analogous places in two processes of personal development: psychological and political. In these processes both the ego and the oppressed person are able to exert some influence on this superordinate power. However, at the critical stage of conscientization, for the oppressed person this influence is far more extensive, capable of transforming the political system into a less oppressive one guided by rules and institutions which reduce injustice and exploitation.

In both processes, the major transformations just described depend on a prior "demystification" of the ego. The alienated ego lives in a one-sided world largely experienced "through the veil of [her/his] . . . emotional projections" (Perry, 1970, p. 6). The initial task in the third stage of individuation is the withdrawal of projections, especially the integration of the shadow. Similarly, in the stage of critical consciousness, the oppressed person must become aware of the oppressors' ideology through which the oppressed have internalized their own inferiority (low self-worth and powerlessness) and the superiority (prestige and power) of the oppressors. As long as this ideological mystification prevails, critical consciousness cannot emerge, for the oppressed person will lack the self-esteem and the trust necessary for collective political action. And as long as the ego remains one-sided and mystified, it will not acquire the ego-strength it requires to "negotiate" with the Self on the basis of "equal rights" (*CW* 18, p. 621; also *CW* 9.i, p. 288).

## Psychological and political development of the person: implications for democracy

From the comparison I conclude that individuation supports conscientization in a movement toward the compatible goals of wholeness and humanization. Despite their striking parallels neither process can be reduced to the other, for they describe two distinct but related worlds: the political development of the person in essence concerns the "outer" world while the psychological development of the person concerns the "inner" world. The relationship between these two worlds is a topic for future research, one which I would like to approach by asking what might be the implications of individuation for democracy.[2] My line of reasoning builds upon the conclusion that individuation supports conscientization. If I argue convincingly that conscientization contributes to democracy, then I will be in a position to conclude further that individuation contributes indirectly to democracy.

In the stage of "critical consciousness," conscientization – the process chosen to exemplify the political development of the person – *empowers* the oppressed classes. Their collective self-affirmation and self-reliance, solidarity, and understanding of systemic causes enable them to form political organizations and to transform the political system in order to further their interests. The empowerment of subordinate classes, according to a recent political theory, is the *sine qua non* of democracy (Rueschemeyer, Stephens, and Stephens, 1992, pp. 270 and 282). This conclusion is based on comparative historical evidence from Europe, Latin America, and the Caribbean. According to this theory,

> if the struggle for democracy is a struggle for power, it is contingent on the complex conditions of subordinate class organization, on the chances of forging alliances, on the reactions of dominant interests to the threats and opportunities of democratization, on the role of the state, and on transnational structures of power. *(ibid.*, pp. 77–78)

Two key conditions for the empowerment of the subordinate classes are their ideological and organizational autonomy (*ibid.*, p. 50). In the process of conscientization, as we have seen, those at the stage of "critical consciousness" both reject the oppressors' ideology and become collectively self-reliant. Even without elaborating further the many causal conditions for democracy presented in this theory, I may safely conclude that conscientization contributes to democracy. This means that there is a causal linkage between individuation, conscientization, and democracy. I believe that this causal linkage invites further research and promises to make Jungian psychology even more relevant to the study of politics.

### Conclusion: the prospects for Jungian psycho-political analysis

My attempt to relate individuation, conscientization, and democracy is an example of Jungian psycho-political analysis. Jung pioneered this field, defined by the intersection of the inner world of the psyche, including the unconscious, and the outer world of politics. My analysis suggests ways in which Jungian (not only Jung's) *psychological* theories may be applied effectively to the study of politics. While writing this conclusion, I reflected further on the reasons why I have been uneasy with Jung's *political* thought and asked myself at what stage of conscientization would Jung be located. Then the reasons for my uneasiness became apparent: Jung's political thought would locate him at the stage of "naive consciousness." Throughout his political essays Jung focuses on the role of the individual, either the individual in mass movements or the individual political leader. This is characteristic of "naive consciousness." Jung *names* political problems in terms of charismatic political leaders who impose dictatorships, *reflects* on the causes in terms of their psychological disturbances, and *acts* in terms of verbal opposition to these leaders. When Jung turns to the individual in mass movements, he *names* the problem as one's vulnerability to psychic infection and one's submersion in a mass movement. Jung *reflects* on the causes in terms of one-sidedness and the loss of individualism and *acts* in terms of promoting a religious attitude in the individual as a protection against psychic infection. In other words, as is typical of the naive stage of consciousness, Jung emphasizes the individual, either the oppressor or the oppressed.

Jung insisted that in psychoanalysis the patient could progress no further than the analyst had progressed in his or her psychological development (CW 16, para. 545). If one applies this same idea to political analysis, one will conclude that the student of politics will progress no further than the political analyst has progressed in his personal political development. When I consider Jung as a *political* analyst whose political thought progressed only to the stage of "naive consciousness," I must encourage the student of politics to turn elsewhere. My critical views on the limitations of Jung's political thought are offered here in order to persuade those now engaging in Jungian psycho-political analysis to turn away from Jung's own political thought and toward the rich resources of Jungian psychological theory.

### NOTES

1 In fact, the cycle of complex formation and integration extends as well to the third stage.

2  An earlier attempt to link Jungian psychology to democracy is that of Odajnyk, 1976, Ch. 10.

# REFERENCES

Alschuler, Lawrence (1992). "Oppression and Liberation: A Psycho-Political Analysis According to Freire and Jung." *Journal of Humanistic Psychology*, 32/2, pp. 8–31.

(1995). "Re-psychling: the Archetypal Image of Asklepios, the Wounded Healer." *International Journal of Comparative Religion and Philosophy*, 1/2.

(1996). "Oppression, Liberation, and Narcissism: A Jungian Psycho-political Analysis of the Ideas of Albert Memmi." *Alternatives*, 21/4.

Bernstein, Jerome (1989). *Power and Politics: The Psychology of Soviet-American Partnership*. Boston: Shambala Publications.

D'Lugin, Victor (1981). "C. G. Jung and Political Theory: An Examination of the Ideas of Carl Gustav Jung showing their Relationship to Political Theory." Doctoral Thesis. Ann Arbor, Mich.: University Microfilms.

Edinger, Edward F. (1972). *Ego and Archetype: Individuation and the Religious Function of the Psyche*. New York: Penguin.

Franz, Marie-Louise von (1976). "Preface." In V. W. Odajnyk, *Jung and Politics*. New York: New York University Press, pp. xiii–xv.

Freire, Paulo (1972). *Pedagogy of the Oppressed*. New York: Herder and Herder.

(1974). *Education for Critical Consciousness*. New York: Seabury Press.

Jacobi, Jolande (1967). *The Way of Individuation*. New York: Meridian.

Jung, C. G. (1934). "A Review of Complex Theory." *CW* 8, 1966, pp. 92–104.

(1937). "The Realities of Practical Psychotherapy." *CW* 16, pp. 327–338.

(1939). "Conscious, Unconscious, and Individuation." *CW* 9.i, 1980, pp. 275–289.

(1946). "Preface and Epilogue" to *Essays on Contemporary Events*. *CW* 10, 1966.

(1949) Foreword to Erich Neumann, *Depth Psychology and a New Ethic*. *CW* 18, pp. 616–622.

(1951). "Fundamental Questions of Psychotherapy." *CW* 16, 1966, pp. 111–125.

(1953). *Two Essays on Analytical Psychology*. *CW* 7, 1972.

(1957). *The Undiscovered Self*. *CW* 10, 1990.

Neumann, Erich (1966). "Narcissism, Normal Self-formation, and the Primary Relation to the Mother." *Spring*, pp. 81–106.

Odajnyk, Walter (1976). *Jung and Politics: The Political and Social Ideas of C. G. Jung*. New York: New York University Press.

Perry, John W. (1970) "Emotions and Object Relations." *Journal of Analytical Psychology*, 15/1, pp. 1–12.

Rueschemeyer, Dietrich, Evelyne H. Stephens, and John D. Stephens (1992). *Capitalist Development and Democracy*. Chicago: University of Chicago Press.

Samuels, Andrew (1986). *Jung and the Post-Jungians*. London: Routledge & Kegan Paul.

(1993). *The Political Psyche*. London: Routledge.

Sandner, Donald F. and John Beebe (1984). "Psychopathology and Analysis." In

Murray Stein (ed.), *Jungian Analysis*. Boulder and London: Shambala, pp. 294–334.

Smith, William A. (1976). *The Meaning of Conscientização: the Goal of Paulo Freire's Pedagogy*. Amherst, Mass.: Center for International Education, University of Massachusetts.

Steiner, Miriam (1983). "The Search for Order in a Disorderly World: Worldviews and Prescriptive Decision Paradigms." *International Organization*, 37/3, pp. 373–414.

Stevens, Anthony (1989). *The Roots of War: A Jungian Perspective*. New York: Paragon House.

Stewart, Louis H. (1992). *The Changemakers: A Depth Psychological Study of the Individual, Family and Society*. London: Routledge.

Whitmont, Edward C. (1978). *The Symbolic Quest: Basic Concepts of Analytical Psychology*. Princeton: Princeton University Press.

# 15

ANN ULANOV

# Jung and religion: the opposing Self

## Why Jung on religion?

How are we to respond to the twentieth-century phenomenon, which Jung noted with such alarm: that the collective containers of religious symbolism are weak, if not altogether gone? For centuries the symbols, rituals, and dogmas of religions, East and West, gathered the psychic energy of individuals and nations alike into traditions that bore witness to life's meaning and acted as underground springs nourishing different civilizations. Jung saw our century as one no longer in daily touch with the meaning of being which lies at the center of life. We have plumbed the resources of consciousness as best we could in our efforts to fathom and to control the contradictions and paradoxes of spirit that have remained to us, but we have lost touch with our roots and the symbolic life that they support and nourish.

Where are we now? What has happened to all the energy that is no longer channeled into religious containers? According to Jung, it has poured back into the human psyche with disastrous effect. Deprived of its proper outlet in religious experience, it assumes negative forms. For the individual, this misplaced energy can lead to neurosis or psychosis; in society, it can lead to all kinds of horrors, genocide, holocaust, and gulags. It can give rise to ideologies whose potential good is soured by the bullying of adherents into frightened compliance. Afraid of being swamped, we erect barriers of rigid rules and compartments against the negative barrages of psychic energy, creating religious, political, and sexual fundamentalisms that trap us in unyielding certainties. And what happens then? We live high and dry, far away from the life-giving waters of religious experience, confined to routines of a humdrum carrying on, without joy or meaning. In such a society we feel afflicted by a deadening malaise, unable to effect healing measures against rising crime, ecological depredation, and mental illness. A sense of hopelessness seeps into all, like a rotting damp. These sufferings, as Jung sees them, can be traced to the failure to secure any reliable connection to the psychic reality that religion once supplied by virtue of its various symbol systems.

There is also, however, a positive effect in the pouring back of all this psychic energy into human beings. It is nothing less than the emergence of a new discipline, that of depth psychology, which is a new collective way of exploring and acknowledging the fact that the nature of our access to God has fundamentally changed. Our own psyche, which is a part of the collective psyche, is now a medium through which we can experience the divine. Jung saw the purpose of his analytical psychology as helping us re-establish connection to the truths contained in religious symbols by finding their equivalents in our own psychic experience (CW 12, paras. 13, 14, 15).

## Immediate experience and psychic reality

The new discipline of depth psychology enables us to study the importance of our immediate experience of the divine which comes to us through dream, symptom, autonomous fantasy, all the many moments of primordial communication (CW, paras. 6, 31, 37; Ulanov and Ulanov, 1975, Ch. 1). People have had, and continue to have, revelatory experiences of God. But in earlier times such encounters were contained by the mainstream of religious tradition and translated into the terms of familiar and accepted religious ritual and doctrine. In our time, Jung believes, these various systems of belief have lost their power for a great many people (see Ulanov, 1971, Ch. 6). For them religious symbols no longer function effectively as communicators of divine presence. Individual men and women are left alone, quite on their own, to face the blast of divine otherness in whatever form it takes. How are we to respond to such a summons? How are we to find a way to build a relationship to the divine? Jung responds to this challenge by marking the emergence into collective discourse of the new vocabulary of psychic reality.

By psychic reality, Jung means our experience of our own unconscious, that is to say, of all those processes of instinct, imagery, affect, and energy that go on in us, between us, among us, without our knowledge, all the time, from birth until death, and maybe, he speculated, even after death (Jung, 1963, Ch. 11; see also Jaffé, 1989, pp. 109–113). Coming into conscious relation with the unconscious, knowing that it is there in us and that it affects all that we think and do, alone and together, in small groups and as nations, radically changes every aspect of life.

By observing the effects of unconscious motivations on our thoughts and actions, our ego – the center of our conscious sense of I-ness, of identity – is introduced to another world with different laws that govern its operations. In our dreams, time and space collapse into an ever-present now. We can be our five-year-old self at the same time in the dream that we are our present age, and find ourselves in a distant land that is also our familiar backyard. Our slips of tongue, where wrong words jump out of our mouths as if propelled by some secret power, our projections onto people, places, and social causes, where we feel gripped by outsized emotions and compulsions to act, our moments of creative living where we perceive freshly, bring a new attitude into being, craft original projects, attest to the constant presence of unconscious mental processes. Something is there that we did not know was there. Something is happening inside us and we must come to terms with it.

If we pay attention to this unconscious dimension of mental life, it will gather itself into a presence that will become increasingly familiar. For example, just recording our dreams over a period of time will show us recurrent motifs, personages, and images that seem to demand a response from us, as if to engage us in conversation around central themes or conflicts. These dominant patterns impress us as if they came from an other objectively there inside us. Jung calls this ordering force in the unconscious the Self.

The Self exists in us as a predisposition to be oriented around a center. It is the archetype of the center, a primordial image similar to images that have fascinated disparate societies throughout history. It is, like all the archetypes, part of the deepest layers of our unconscious which Jung calls "collective" or "objective" to indicate that they exceed our personal experience. We experience the Self existing within our subjectivity, but it is not our property, nor have we originated it; it possesses its own independent life.

For example, some aboriginal tribes in Australia pay homage to Oneness. They know its presence in themselves yet they speak of it not as my Oneness or our Oneness but as the Oneness at the heart of all life. When we respond to the predisposition of the Self we, each of us, experience it as the center of our own psyche and more, of life itself. Our particular pictures of the Self will draw on images from our personal biography, what in the jargon of depth psychologists we call our relations with "objects" – with parents and all other persons who significantly influence us. And what we do in this theater of relations will depend on how we have been conditioned by collective images of the center dominant in our particular culture and era of history, including especially our religious education or lack thereof. But our images of the Self will not be limited to these personal and cultural influences. They will also include such primordial universal images of the Self as may confront us from the deep layers of our own unconscious life.

The Self is neither wholly conscious or unconscious but orders our whole psyche, with itself as the mid-point or axis around which everything else revolves. We experience it as the source of life for the whole psyche, which means it comes into relationship with our center of consciousness in the ego as a bigger or more authoritative presence than we have known before (*CW* 9.ii, paras. 9 and 57). If in our ego-life – what we ordinarily call "life," the ideas and feelings and culture of which we are strongly aware – we cooperate with the approaches of the Self, it feels as if we are connecting with a process of a centering, not only for our deepest self but for something that extends well beyond us, beyond our psyche into the center of reality. If we remain unconscious, or actively resist the signs the Self sends us, we experience the process as altogether ego-defeating, crushing our plans and purposes with its large-scale aims.

## Ego and Self, the gap and God-images

A gap always remains between ego and Self, for they speak different languages. One is known, the other unknown. One is personal, the other impersonal. One uses feelings and words, the other instincts, affects, and images. One offers a sense of belonging to community, the other a sense of belonging to the ages. They never merge completely, except in illness (as in mania or an inflated state for example), but merely approach each other as if coming from two quite different worlds, and yet, even so, they are still somehow intimately related. The gap between them can be a place of madness where the ego falls in and loses its foothold in reality, or where the unconscious can be so invaded by conscious ambition and expediency that it seems to withdraw from contact forever, leaving the ego functioning mechanically but juiceless and joyless.

If we really become aware of and accept the gap between ego and Self it transforms itself into a space of conversation between the worlds. We experience the connecting going on in us and in all aspects of our lives. A sense of engagement follows that leads us into a life at once exciting and reverent. For it is precisely in that gap that we discover our images for God. Such images point in two directions: to the purposiveness hidden in our ego-life, and across the gap into the unknown God (Ulanov and Ulanov, 1991, Ch. 2).

Jung talks about God-images as inseparable from those images of the Self that express its function as center, source, point of origin, and container. Empirically, Self and God-images are indistinguishable (*CW* 8, para. 231). This has led Jung's theological critics to accuse him of reductionism, and of bringing down the transcendent God to become a mere factor in the psyche.

But Jung defends himself hotly by attacking the argument as nonsense (CW 11, paras. 13–21; Jung, 1975, p. 377). Can we ever experience anything except through the medium of the psyche? The psyche exists. We cannot get around it. It subtly influences everything we see or know of "objective" reality with our own individual colorations – of physical constitution, family, culture, history, symbol system. Of course our images of God reflect such conditioning.

But do our God-images tell us something else? Yes, Jung answers. These are the pictures through which we glimpse the Almighty (Ulanov, 1986, pp. 164–178). Who knows what God is objectively? How can we ever tell? Only through our own experience of God addressing us, and through other people's experiences reported throughout history. The unconscious is not itself God, but it is a medium through which God speaks (CW 10, para. 565). God addresses us through images from the deep unconscious just as much as through the witness of historical events, other people, scriptures, and worshiping communities.

Jung thus provides another method of interpretation of religious tradition to the familiar ones of historical, literary, and socio-political criticism. When we acknowledge psychic reality, we must add, to all the others, a method for the psychological interpretation of religious materials. Jung's ideas provide a method for investigating recurrent archetypal symbols that specific religious rituals or doctrines embody and employ, by means of linking them to equivalent experiences in our psyches. He applies this method to Eastern as well as Western religious traditions (CW 11). This method no more reduces revelation to psychology than other methods of, for example, historical or literary or sociological criticism reduce God to historical event, literary metaphor, or sociological sampling.

The transcendent God speaks to us through our God-images and at the same time smashes them, for no human image can take in the incomprehensible divine except in such words and images as the divine shares with us. The images, when they arrive, may evoke in us a negative feeling of such power that we feel invaded and overrun by an alien force, or a positive feeling of being healed or blessed by a life-changing vision.

Jung speaks about religion, its images and symbols, from both sides of the gap between ego and Self. His contribution to religion focuses on bringing unconscious psychic reality into relation to our conscious avowals of faith. He explicitly states that a major function of his psychology is to make connections between the truths contained in traditional religious symbols and our psychic experience. Religious life involves us in ongoing, scrupulous attention to what makes itself known in those moments of numinous experience that occur when ego and Self address each other. We do not control such primordial moments, but rather place our confidence in their meaning for our life. This kind of trustful observance forms the essence of the attitude Jung calls religious (CW 11, paras. 2, 6, 8–9). Our ego acts as both receiver and transmitter of what the Self reveals (Jung, 1973 [22 December 1942], p. 326), which does not mean that we always simply fall in placidly and passively with what comes to us. The conversation with the divine can grow noisy indeed. Like Jonah we may protest our fate, or like Abraham defending Sodom, we can try to argue Yahweh out of his pledge of destruction. Our proper ego attitude in the face of the Self and what it reveals is a willing engagement. A process of sustained communication develops, out of which both ego and Self emerge as more significant and conscious partners. No one else can engage in this process for us. Society cannot give it to us. In immediate confrontation with the mysterious other who seizes our consciousness grows the root of our personal self and our heartfelt connection to the meaning of reality.

## Official religion

Religious dogma and creeds, for Jung, stand in vivid contrast to such immediate experiences, and he always values the latter over the former. Jung does see great value in dogma and creed, however, as long as we do not substitute them for direct experience of the divine. Dogma and creed function as shared dreams of humanity and offer us valuable protection against the searing nature of firsthand knowledge of the ultimate. They offer us different ways to house our individual experiences of these puzzling or disturbing numinous events. Like Nicholas von der Flüe, we may find refuge in the doctrine of the trinity as the means of translating into bearable form a theophany so powerful that the experience was said to have changed his saintly face forever, into a frightening visage (CW 11, para. 474; Jung, 1975 [June 1957], p. 377).

By connecting our immediate psychic encounters with the numinous to the collective knowledge of God contained in humanity's creeds and dogmas, we fulfill what Jung emphasized as the root meaning of religion (CW 11, para. 8; Jung, 1975 [12 February 1959], p. 482). *Religio* and *religere* mean we must bind our individual experience back into the common possession of religious tradition. That protects us from too great a blast of the Almighty by offering us the softening containers of humanity's collective symbols. To the ongoing life of inherited symbols we contribute our own personal instances of what they represent collectively, thus helping to keep tradition from ossifying. If we do not live the tradition in this way, it falls into disuse, becoming a mere relic. We may give it lip-service, but it no longer quickens our hearts. In our personal experience of the timeless symbols of tradition, we are lifted beyond ourselves to partake of the ancient mysteries while at the same time living our ordinary ego-lives, of paying taxes, voting, making meals, cleaning out closets, fetching the children from school, holding down jobs.

Bound up in tradition in such lively ways, we participate in our own special groups and join the whole of humanity. Our secret numinous experience, now shared, brings us into the community upon which we depend to digest whatever the experience represents. Not only are we part of the human family, but by bringing to it our own personal experiences of the transpersonal, our unconscious flows together with everyone else's and we join in the attempts of the unconscious to create a new basis of community. Our immediate experiences of the divine revivify tradition and remind us in fresh ways that our shared life together depends upon a very deep source of what we love in common.

Religion also means that as individuals we must be bound back to the pivotal numinous experiences that mark our lives, because they establish, in full consciousness, our particular idiosyncratic roots in transcendence. According to Jung, forgetting such experiences, or worse, perjuring them by acting as if they make no difference, exposes us to the risk of insanity. Encounters with the holy are like flames. They must be shared, to keep light alive, or they will burn us up or burn us out. The religious life is one of increased alertness, of keen watchfulness of what goes on between this mysterious Thee and me (Jung, 1973 [10 September 1943], p. 338).

For Jung, religion is inescapable. We may reject it, revile it, revise it, but we cannot get rid of it. This early discovery by Jung has been reaffirmed recently in the research of Rizzuto (1979). When he was accused of being a mystic, Jung objected that he did not invent this idea of *homo religiosus* but only put into words what everyone knows. His vast clinical experience with people afflicted with neurosis or psychosis impressed upon him the fact that half of his patients fell ill because they had lost hold of the meaning of life (CW 11, para. 497). Healing means revivifying connection to the transcendent which brings with it the ability to get up and walk to our fate instead of being dragged there by a neurosis. Thus Jung saw the numinous even in pathology; it expresses how we have fallen out of the Tao, the center of life. Recovery requires remythologization (Ulanov, 1971, pp. 127–136).

## Religious instinct and society

Our instinct for religion consists in our being endowed with and conscious of relation to deity (CW 12, para. 11). If we repress or suppress this instinct, we can fall ill just as surely as we do when we interfere with our physical appetite for food, or with our sexual instinct (A. Ulanov, 1994). Many of the substance-abuse disorders to which we fall prey can be traced, *au fond*, to displacement onto chocolate, cocaine, valium, liquor, or whatever, of our appetitive need for connection to the power and source of being beyond us. We can understand this displacement operating in all of our addictions – even the ones that surprise us – such as to a lover or to a child, to becoming pregnant, or to health or diet routines, to money or power, to a political cause or a psychological theory, or even to a religious discipline. The energy that our instinct for religion brings must go somewhere. If it is not directed to the ultimate, it will turn manic or make idols out of finite goods. Jung reminds us "It is not a matter of indifference whether one calls something a 'mania' or a 'god' . . . When the god is not acknowledged, ego mania develops and out of this mania comes sickness" (*CW* 13, para. 55).

Our religious instinct also possesses a social function. Our connection to transpersonal authority keeps us from being swept away into mass movements (*CW* 10, paras. 506–508). It offers us a point of reference outside family, class conventions, cultural mores, even the long reach into our private lives of totalitarian governments. Because we feel seen and known by God, however dimly and inarticulately we may express this, we can find the power, when necessary, to stand against the pressures of collectivities for the sake of truth, our soul, our faith. This capacity in individuals offers society a bulwark against movements that can dominate it and destroy it like out-of-control brush fires. Having such a reference point beyond personal whims and needs, and beyond dependence on others' approval, makes us sturdy citizens, capable of contributing to group life in fresh and sustained ways. This furthers the health of society and our enjoyment of its community life. Knowing a connection to the author of life, we feel a mysterious binding force in our own authority as persons, which we come to respect in our neighbor as much as in ourselves. The sense of being a person who matters combats at a deep level any loss of confidence and hope in our society to facilitate an environment where we all can thrive.

In clinical situations, acknowledging the force of religious instinct may save us from abysmal humiliation and depression. When the majority of the world's people are starving, it is morally embarrassing to be afflicted with obsession over one's weight. To see the larger context of this suffering – that it stems from misdirection of soul hunger, twisting the hunger for connection to ultimate purpose – can release a person from self-revilement in order to pay trustful attention to what the Self is engineering through vexatious symptoms.

The religious instinct may lurk in any of our disturbances, from the extreme of homicidal urges to get even with those who threaten and hurt us unbearably to the seemingly mild but actually lethal affliction of the chronic boredom that results from the suffocation of our inner life. In every case, an impulse toward the ultimate, toward expression of what really matters, mixes in with early childhood hurt and distorted relations with other people. Our energy to live from and toward the center has lost its way, or we have lost touch with it. We are out of sorts. We need help. Part of the help, in Jung's view, means feeling emboldened enough to risk again immediate experience of the numinous (Jung, 1973 [26 May 1945], p. 41).

## Individuation

In our experience of the numinous, according to Jung, what we feel is its effects on our ego (CW 17, para. 300). We feel summoned by something beyond ourselves to become all of ourselves. We sense the Self, "heavy as lead," calling us out of unconscious identification with social convention (the persona or "mask" we adopt for social functioning), pushing us to recognize even those parts of ourselves that we would rather deny and disown, those that lie in what Jung calls the shadow (CW 17, para. 303). These parts confront us with evil. If we open to awareness of our shadow, we know firsthand the agony of St. Paul when he says "the good I would, I do not, and the evil I would not, that I do." Becoming ourselves also means encompassing what ordinarily we think of as opposite to us, to claim as part of us a departure point so different from our conscious gender identity that it symbolizes itself in our dreams, for example, as figures of the opposite sex. Jung calls these figures the anima in man and the animus in women. To be wholly who we are means including as part of our ego identity what these contrasexual parts bring into our consciousness (Ulanov and Ulanov, 1994). They open us sexually as well as spiritually to conversation with the mysterious center of the whole psyche that Jung calls the Self, and through it to the reality the Self symbolizes. In sum, the call to live and integrate into a vibrant whole all the parts of us greatly enlarges our ego-identity, making us much more vividly the unique individuals we are.

This is not individualism. For the Self brings with it the bigger center that exceeds our limited ego needs and aims. Jung says:

> the self is like a crowd . . . being oneself, one is also like many. One cannot individuate without being with other human beings . . . Being an individual is

always a link in a chain . . . how little you can exist . . . without responsibilities and duties and the relation of other people to yourself . . . The Self . . . plants us in otherness – of other people, and of the transcendent.

(Jung, 1988, p. 102)

The Self acts as an unconscious source of community. Awareness of the Self shifts our focus from the private to the shared, or to put it more accurately, to the inevitable mixture of the public in the private, of the collective in the individual, of the universal in the idiosyncratic.

The task of individuation makes us appreciate the world around us with renewed interest and gratitude. For we see that we are continually offered objects with which to find and release our own particular personality. We come to understand that we are objects with whom others can create and unfold their lives. Issues of injustice and oppression are thus brought right into our hearts, as we recognize that in addition to all the rest of the deprivations they effect, they can keep the heart from loving and unfolding, whether in ourselves or in our neighbor, and most often in both of us. When that happens we cease to see in each other the mutual opportunities that are there to become our true self in company with others. Another whole dynamic substitutes for this life-giving one. Now we feel pushed to discover, however sneakily, who has more and who less, who does what to whom, and how we can wreak revenge. "More" for us now seems possible only as a result of someone else's "less." The interest in each other's unique and secret response to the mysterious call of life is eclipsed, as envious combat takes over.

If, however, we are embarked on our own individuation, we see this process going on in others too, and we gain a whole new sense of community. We recognize how much we need each other to accomplish the tasks of facing our shadows as our own, of encountering otherness as embodied in the opposite sex, of gathering the courage to respond wholeheartedly to the summons of the Self. We connect with each other at a new depth, equivalent to what Jung calls kinship.

## The archetypal and the body

Awareness of the Self deeply affects the clinical situation. Analyst and analysand are rearranged around the call to answer the Self. In the midst of working with the most vexing problems – urges to suicide and homicide, depression and anxiety, schizoid splitting, narcissistic wounding and borderline fragmenting, and the ways these psychic conditions complicate our relating with spouse, parent, or child, interfere with our jobs, and can reduce us to despair – analyst and analysand now look directly to see what the Self may be bringing us through all these difficulties.

Jung defines the personal layer of the unconscious as a gathering of complexes, clusters of energy, affect, and image that reflect the conditioning of our early life. There, drawn well down into us, we find all those who have had formative effects on us, parents, friends, lovers, of whatever age or place in our lives. Our complexes show the influence of our cultural milieu, the colorations of class, race, sex, religion, politics, education. At the heart of each complex an archetypal image dwells. Engaging that image takes us through the personal unconscious into a still deeper layer that Jung calls the objective psyche. The archetypes compose its contents, and deep analysis means identifying and dealing with the particular sets of primordial images that operate in us.

My mother complex, for instance, will show the influence of my own mother's conscious and unconscious personality, her style of relating to me and making the world available to me. The cultural images of motherhood dominant in my childhood, and the particular archetypal image of the Mother that arises from the objective layer of my psyche will also shape the mother complex in me. If I see my mother as malign and depriving, and jump from this judgment to a condemnation of Western society for generating a culture that is antagonistic to all women who do not conform to the stereotype of the sacrifical mother, I may find, rising in me from the unconscious, fantasy and dream images of an ideal mother whose abundant goodness compensates for my conscious, negative experience of motherhood. Another person who has suffered at the hands of a negative mother, but who fell into self-blame instead of blaming her parent, may find pictures of a dread witch or a stone-making gorgon sent by the unconscious in order to convince the ego that the problem is not hers – but, rather, it stems from the witch-like constellation that surrounds her mother (Ulanov and Ulanov, 1987, Ch. 2).

Breaking through to the archetypal layer of the unconscious, and finding ways to sustain conversation across the gap between ego and Self, relieves us from the ardors of blaming, either of ourselves or others. We are confronted with life right before us and its blunt questions. How are we to bring together conscious suffering and unconscious compensations for it? How are we to make sense of the ancient truth that parents visit their sins on their children? How are we to reconcile our suffering with the understanding that our parents did their best given their own problems and illnesses? We enter a larger space of human discussion and meditation on the hardships of life, but we are not glued to hardship. Life is addressing us here; it wants to be lived in us and through us. We feel this on a deep body level. Our spirit quickens.

Jung talks about the instinctual and spiritual poles that characterize every archetype (*CW* 8, paras. 417–420). His best definition of the archetype is as our instinct's image of itself (*CW* 8, para. 277). Instinct is body-backed, the body originating energy, life-energy. The image is its self-portrait that expresses how we experience it. And so every archetype has a spiritual facet which explains the "incorrigibly plural" quality of human beings' numinous experiences, to borrow Louis MacNeice's wonderful phrase (see B. Ulanov, 1992, and Ulanov and Ulanov, 1994, for examples). Some of us feel the spirit touch us through the Great Mother archetype. Others feel it through feminine wisdom figures; still others through a wondrous child, a compelling quest, and so forth. The unconscious is not creedal, but compensatory. It dishes up the images needed to balance our conscious one-sidedness so that we can include all sides of ourselves as we become ourselves.

In investigating our God-images, we must examine their personal and archetypal bases. Personal factors will include details from our special upbringing and culture. Archetypal aspects will show which of the fund of primordial human images have been constellated in us. Our God-image may be communism because our parents were devout revolutionaries, an image that may collapse with the fall of communism in the late 1980s. Our image of the divine may be scripture-based – the Yahweh who woos his people, sews garments for them when they are naked, and designs ephods for them to wear when they lead worship. Whatever they are, our God-images show a definiteness, and through their distinct idiosyncratic qualities we feel the God beyond us touching us in the flesh.

The body means specific form, it means boundedness, not generality or shifting shadows. The body is life in the concrete. Our body restricts us to a certain place and time and thus permits us to focus on what is right there, in front of us. We are thus protected from "the elemental quality of cosmic indistinctness." The body with its definitive finiteness is "the guarantee of consciousness, and consciousness is the instrument by which the meaning is created" (Jung, 1988, pp. 349–350). Without the body, we can easily float off into the timeless quality of the archetypal, lured by no longer having to be ourselves:

> You cease to think and are acted upon as though carried by a great river with no end. You are suddenly eternal . . . liberated from sitting up and paying attention, doubting, and concentrating upon things . . . you don't want to disturb it by asking foolish questions – it is too nice.     (Jung, 1988, p. 240)

This drifting as if "one with the universe" is not, however, the life of the spirit, for it is no longer life in the body. We need both body and spirit or we forfeit both. We possess both or neither. For there to be life in the spirit, we need life in the body. For contact with the unconscious, we need consciousness. Otherwise the unconscious, like the waves of the ocean, wells up, comes forward, builds toward a climax, and then pulls downward, retreats, and disintegrates. For something to happen, consciousness must interfere, "grasp the treasure," make something of what is offered (ibid., p. 237). We need the ego as the center of consciousness to know the Self as the center of the whole, the conscious and the unconscious psyche. We need to enter the conversation that fills the gap between them. That process of conversation constructs the Self that claims us, and builds up an ego that becomes decentered. If we fail to engage in that process, our ego can easily be taken over by archetypal contents, as we see to our horror in any kind of religious or political fanaticism. Under such pressures, we rush out against others, compelled by the force of the archetypal. Convinced we alone possess the truth, we know no bounds in dealing with others who may disagree with, or even defy, us; segregating, maligning, oppressing, imprisoning, murdering others are crimes we can commit in the name of our twisted version of truth and salvation.

If we do engage in ego–Self conversation we come to know archetypal images inhabiting our very own bodies. This feels like energy, sometimes in greater amounts than we think we can handle. Then our bodies stretch, both physically and psychologically, into new postures and new attitudes of acceptance and celebration. We might, for example, finally lay to rest a lifelong addiction to a substance, or a drink, or a special kind of food. We might find our blood-pressure lowering after many years. We might find back pain dispersing, or our power to endure it increasing. We might feel ushered into sexual ecstasy for the first time after many years. We feel we live in our finite form, in touch with something infinite.

## God-images and evil

To enter conversation with our God-image is not an easy task. The partial nature of this dialogue, its basis in small individual experience and its all too limited human perspective soon become only too clear. The conversation begins to crumble. We realize with unerring certainty that we are not reaching God or the transcendent, or whatever we choose to call it, from our side. We cannot cross the gap: we can only receive what comes from the other side, from the mysterious center of reality that our all-too-human symbols point to. Jung's image of the Self, for example, cannot be taken as God in us, let alone the transcendent God, because it too is a product of a merely human theory. It cannot substitute for the reality to which it points, the reality to which the Self – i.e. that within the psyche that knows about the transcendent – is trying to lead us.

Attempting to engage our God-image in serious conversation and meditation is to face its inadequacy to cover the complexity of human life. For example, Jung asks, "What about evil? The suffering of the innocent?" Jung is distinguished among depth psychologists for his preoccupation with finding answers to these questions (CW 11). They are not questions we can avoid, for our own shadow natures throw us right into them. Terrible things happen all around us, to ourselves and others. We lose our minds. Human rights disappear. Bodies are born crippled and we are maimed. Storms and floods destroy our world. We murder each other. How can there be a just, powerful, and merciful God when so much suffering exists?

Jung's answer places evil, finally, in God directly. God's nature is complex and bears its own shadow side. It needs human beings, with their focused body-based consciousness, to incarnate these opposites in divine life and thus help in their transformation. In considering the book of Job, Jung surmises that Yahweh suffers from unconsciousness, himself forgetting to consult his own divine omniscience. Job's protests against his unmerited suffering make Yahweh aware of his own shadow dealings with Satan and finally he can answer Job with the figure of Christ, who takes the sufferings of human beings into his own life and pays for them himself.

Jung considers the Christ figure the most complete Self symbol we have known in human history, but he is aware that the Christian myth must be lived onward still farther (Jung, 1963, pp. 337–338). Christ, unlike the rest of us, is without sin. Evil splits off into the opposing figure of the Devil or the Antichrist. Christianity, Jung says, thus leaves no place for the evil side of the human person (CW 8, para. 232). For him, the doctrine of evil as the privation of good fails to recognize the actual existence of evil as a force to be contended with. The doctrine of God as the *summum bonum* lifts God to impossible heights, while crushing humans under the weight of sin.

Critics of Jung question his reading of the Christ figure as separated from evil. In fact, they say, Christ lives his whole life on the frontiers of evil. Christ is no stranger to evil and sin, from his birth as an outcast in poverty, his occasioning Herod's murder of innocent babies, to facing the demons of mental illness, righteous rule-keeping, scapegoating judgments, abandonment by his friends and neighbors, the refusal of the good, not to speak of his own fate, suffering betrayal, abandonment, and death (A. Ulanov, 1987, pp. 46–54, and B. Ulanov, 1992, Ch. 5).

Jung works out a solution that is satisfactory to himself. We can read this as the fruit of his engagement with his own God-image. He sees God as both good and evil. Some critics of Jung surmise he projected his own unintegrated aggression onto the Godhead (Redfearn, 1977; Winnicott, 1964). We serve God, in this reading, by accepting the opposing elements in ourselves – conscious and unconscious, ego and shadow, persona and anima or animus, finally ego and Self. These opposites are best symbolized by masculine and feminine and thus Jung brings into religious discussion the body-based sexuality and contrasexuality of the human person (*CW* 12, para. 192). This inclusion goes a long way toward recovering the inescapable importance of the feminine mode of being, so long neglected in patriarchal history (see *CW* 11, paras. 107, 619–620, 625; and Ulanov, 1971, pp. 291–292). By struggling to integrate the opposites, we incarnate God's struggle. The solutions we achieve, however small, contribute to divine life. Thus we participate in Christ's suffering and serve God by becoming the selves God created us to be. We fulfill our vocation, redeeming our own pain from meaninglessness and partcipating in the life of God.

## The transcendent function and synchronicity

Jung demonstrates in reaching his own working solution to problems he knew directly what is in some ways his most daring method, that of the transcendent function. He enters the conversation of opposites, lets each side have its say, endures the struggle between the opposing points of view, suffers the anguish of being strung out between them, and greets the resolving symbol with gratitude. The psyche, says Jung, possesses this function to overcome opposition through arriving at a third point of view that includes the essence of each conflicting perspective while at the same time combining them into a symbol of the new.

We must enter this process and cooperate with it if we are to be fully – and ethically – engaged in living, says Jung (*CW* 8, paras. 181–183 and Jung 1963, paras. 753–755). It is not enough just to appreciate the transcendent function and marvel at the new symbols that arise with it. We must live them, use them, bind them back into personal and communal life if we are to submit to the religious attitude. The transcendent function is the process through which the new comes about in us. This is a costly undertaking, for we feel our egos losing their grip on secure frames of reference. We float and drift and seem to know nothing. We hover over the gap between ego process and Self process. When the new begins to show itself in image form, we pause, look, contemplate, in order to integrate into a new level of unity parts of ourselves and of life outside us that were hitherto unknown to us (Ulanov and Ulanov, 1991). But to reach that precious ego capacity to reflect and respond to the creating of the new, we must renounce the certainties we have so long depended upon.

The religious attitude, therefore, involves sacrifice (*CW* 11, para. 390). We offer up our identification with our ego's point of view as the best and only authority. We surrrender what we identify with as "mine" or "ours," sacrificing our ego-claims without expectation of payment. We do this because we recognize a higher claim, that of the Self. It offers itself to us, making its own sacrifice of relinquishing its status as the all and the vast, to take up residence in the stuff of our everyday lives. The conversation between ego and Self becomes our daily meditation.

When this happens, reality seems to reform itself. Odd coincidences of events that are not causally related occur, impressing us with their large and immediate meaning: what Jung called synchronicity (*CW* 8, para. 840). Outer and inner events collide in significant ways that open us to perceive what Jung calls the *unus mundus*, a wholeness where matter and psyche are revealed to be but two aspects of the same reality. Clinically, I have seen striking examples of this. A man struggled in conversation with a childhood terror of being locked in a dark attic as punishment for crying out too often to his parents when he was put to bed at night. Eventually, he reached the key to unlock a compulsive fetish that he now saw had functioned as the symbol to bridge the gap between his adult personality and his abject childhood terror in the locked attic. When this new attitude emerged out of his struggling back and forth with the fascination of the fetish on the one hand and his conscious humiliation and wish to rid himself of this compulsion on the other, an outer event synchronistically occurred. The attic room in the house of his childhood was struck by lightning and destroyed – but only the attic part of the house!

Jung's theory links such outer and inner happenings through his theory of the archetype as psychoid, as possessed of the body and spirit poles (*CW* 8, paras. 368ff, 380). When we engage in the conversation between the ego point of view and the Self's, we touch both poles of the Self archetype, which opens us to what is going on all the time in the interweaving of physical and spiritual events. When our conversation grows deep enough to show us that the Self not only is a center of the psyche but symbolizes the center of all of the life that lies outside our psyche, we become open to the interdependent reality of the whole, not only of all that is human, but of all other animate and inanimate life (Aziz, 1990, pp. 85, 111, 137, 167, 1990).

## Method

Jung gives us a method to approach religious documents of all kinds, which he demonstrates by his attention not only to materials of the Judeo-Christian tradition, but also to those of alchemy, Zen Buddhism, Tibetan

Buddhism, Taoism, Confucianism, and Hinduism, to elements of African and Native American religions, and to the mythologies of many times and cultures (*CW* 11, 12, 13). We must ask, How does a given document reflect the conversation of ego and Self? What dogmas and rituals from the ego side collect and contain immediate numinous experiences that give rise to Self symbols? What are the dominant Self symbols that point to a reality beyond the psyche? What are the main archetypal images employed to do such symbol-forming activity? Is the dominant archetype the transformation of father and son, as in the Christian eucharist, or is it the transformation of mother and daughter, as in the ancient Eleusinian mysteries? Jung saw alchemy, for example, as taking up the problem of the spiritualization of matter which Christianity did not adequately solve (Jung, 1975, p. 401). In alchemy the Self symbol is the *lapis* or "stone," which, unlike the Christ symbol, combines good and evil, and matter and spirit; it is the end-purpose of all the alchemical operations which symbolize all our attitudes.

Jung leaves us ways that are practical and spiritual, hard-headed and open-hearted, to connect with the archaic roots of our religion, whatever this may be, and with the necessary clinical methods to give full measure to include our experience of the numinous in the enterprise of healing.

## REFERENCES

Aziz, R. (1990). *C. G. Jung's Psychology of Religion and Synchronicity.* Albany, N.Y.: State University of New York Press.
Jaffé, A. (1989). *Was C. G. Jung a Mystic?* Einsiedeln: Daimon Verlag.
Jung, C. G. (1916). "The Transcendent Function." *CW* 8, 1960.
    (1919). "Instinct and the Unconscious." *CW* 8, 1960.
    (1929). "Commentary on the Secret of the Golden Flower." *CW* 13, 1967.
    (1932). "Psychotherapists or Clergy." *CW* 11, 1958.
    (1933). "Brother Klaus." *CW* 11, 1958.
    (1934). "The Development of the Personality." *CW* 17, 1954.
    (1938). "Psychology and Religion." *CW* 11, 1958.
    (1942). "A Psychological Approach to the Trinity." *CW* 8, 1958.
    (1947). "On the Nature of the Psyche." *CW* 8, 1960.
    (1952a). "Answer to Job." *CW* 11, 1958.
    (1952b). "Synchronicity: An Acausal Connecting Principle." *CW* 8, 1960.
    (1953). *Psychology and Alchemy* [1935, 1946, 1944]. *CW* 12.
    (1954). "The Transformation Symbolism of the Mass." *CW* 11, 1958.
    (1956). "The Undiscovered Self." *CW* 10, 1964.
    (1958). *Psychology and Religion: West and East. CW* 11, 1958.
    (1959). *Aion. CW* 9.ii.
    (1963). *Memories, Dreams, Reflections.* New York: Pantheon.
    (1967). *Alchemical Studies. CW* 13.
    (1973). *Letters*, vol. 1. Princeton: Princeton University Press.

(1975). *Letters*, vol. II. Princeton: Princeton University Press.

(1988). *Nietzsche's "Zarathustra"*, 2 vols. Princeton: Princeton University Press.

Redfearn, J. (1977). "The Self and Individuation." *Journal of Analytical Psychology*, 22/2.

Rizzuto, A.-M. (1979). *The Birth of the Living God.* Chicago: Chicago University Press.

Ulanov, A. (1971). *The Feminine in Christian Theology and in Jungian Psychology.* Evanston, Ill.: Northwestern University Press.

(1986). *Picturing God.* Cambridge, Mass.: Cowley Press.

(1987). *The Wisdom of the Psyche.* Cambridge, Mass.: Cowley Press.

(1992). "The Holding Self: Jung and the Search for Being." In *The Fires of Desire: Erotic Energies and the Spiritual Quest*, ed. F. Halligan and J. Shea. New York: Crossroads.

(1994). "Jung and prayer." *Jung and the Monotheisms.* New York: Routledge.

Ulanov, A. and Ulanov, B. (1975). *Religion and the Unconscious.* Louisville, Ky.: Westminster.

(1987). *The Witch and the Clown: Two Archetypes of Human Sexuality.* Wilmette, Ill.: Chiron.

(1991). *The Healing Imagination.* Mahwah, N.J.: Paulist Press.

(1994). *Transforming Sexuality: The Inner World of Anima and Animus.* Boston: Shambhala.

Ulanov, B. (1992). *Jung and the Outside World.* Wilmette, Ill.: Chiron.

Winnicott, D. W. (1964). Review of C. G. Jung, *Memories, Dreams, Reflections.* In *Psycho-analytic Explorations*, ed. C. Winnicott, R. Shepherd, M. Davis. London: Karnac, 1989.

# GLOSSARY

**Active imagination**    A method Jung developed to induce an active dialogue with the unconscious while in a waking state. In a relaxed, trance-like state, one holds in mind an image (e.g. from a dream) and inquires of the image its origins, meaning, etc. as if it were another person.

**Alchemy**    From the late 1920s until his death, Jung was fascinated by the writings of major alchemical theorists such as Paracelsus. He held that their writings reflect the projected expression of unconscious (or only half-conscious) psychological processes and that the terms and phases of alchemy correspond with imagery and stages encountered in psychotherapy: common to both are notions of joint work, transformation, and a goal. Jung often used alchemy as a metaphor to describe tension between opposites and the resolution of opposites by way of the transcendent function (see Projection and Transcendent function).

**Amplification**    The process by which an analyst or analysand expands the meaning of an unconscious image or dream-figure by connecting it with an existing mythology, religion, literary motif, or other metaphorical system. Jung saw this as the opposite of "reductive analysis" (i.e. the breaking down of an image into its possible causes).

**Anima**    (Latin = "soul"). The image of a woman or feminine figure in a man's dreams or fantasies. Related to his "eros" principle (see Eros), it reflects the nature of his relationships, especially with women. Described by Jung as "the archetype of life". Problematic relationship is often caused by unconscious identification with the anima or projection of the anima into a partner resulting in a feeling of disappointment with the real person (see Possession). By extension, also used to describe the unconscious, feminine side of a man's personality. Anima figures are not depictions of actual women but are fantasies colored by emotional needs and experiences. Characteristic anima figures: goddesses, famous women, mother-figures, young girls, prostitutes, witches, and female creatures (e.g. a siren-figure).

**Animus** (Latin = "spirit"). The image of a man or masculine figure in a woman's dreams or fantasies. Related to her "logos" principle (see Logos), it reflects the nature of her connection to ideas and spirit. Described by Jung as "the archetype of meaning". A woman's difficulties are often caused by unconscious identification with the animus (see Possession). By extension, also used to describe the unconscious, masculine side of a woman's personality. Animus figures are not depictions of actual men, but are fantasies coloured by emotional needs and experiences. Characteristic animus figures: father-figures, famous men, religious figures, idealized figures, boys, and morally dubious figures (such as criminals).

**Archetype/Archetypal images** The "archetype" is a hypothetical construct posited by Jung to explain the manifestation of "archetypal images," i.e. all images that appear in dreams and fantasies that bear a striking similarity to universal motifs found in religions, myths, legends, etc. (see Unconscious). Archetypes are universal because human emotions are universal. Whilst the most characteristic archetypal figures might be the persona, the anima, animus, shadow, and self, other images encountered in dreams and waking fantasy may be imbued with archetypal meaning if they carry a powerful emotional meaning (e.g. numerical groupings, a mountain, a clock, a dominant father, a treacherous friend). In his last version of "archetype," Jung described it as an innate tendency to form emotionally powerful images that express the relational primacy of human life.

**Association** An idea or image spontaneously suggested by a trigger word or image. Associations are related through common emotional themes that comprise psychological complexes, driven by archetypes (see Complex).

**Collective unconscious** See Unconscious.

**Compensation** Consciousness and unconsciousness are in a relationship of compensation, in which only part of the meaning or motive is in awareness. Our inflations and deflations have their opposites in the unconscious. Jung held that unconscious images and products show us what is compensating our conscious one-sidedness. Normally, people instinctively adjust to such compensatory material: e.g. a man who is unaware that he often acts like a bully might dream of his house being invaded by a bully. The dream "compensates" his misguided ideas about himself, thus providing the man with the opportunity to come to terms with his unconscious tendencies. Problems arise when the ego *resists* such adjustment: this often results in identification (see Identification).

**Complex** An emotionally charged cluster of notions or images that acts as if it were an autonomous "splinter" personality. At its core is an emotionally infused archetype (e.g. the Terrible Mother). Jung, who took the term from his teacher Pierre Janet, regarded the complex as the "*via regia* to the unconscious" (see Word association test).

**Coniunctio**  (Latin = "conjunction") A meeting with the "other," especially of opposites encountered in a dream sequence: usually envisaged as symbolizing a positive development. By extension, also used to describe the therapeutic work between analyst and analysand.

**Constellate**  The activation of a psychological complex, usually owing to an emotionally charged reaction (whether conscious or unconscious), whether to a person or to a situation.

**Depth psychology**  All forms of psychoanalysis in which therapy largely or partly consists in the interpretation of unconscious meanings in action, defenses, transference, and other situations in which such meanings are examined (see Psychoanalysis).

**Ego**  Jung used the word "ego" to describe two significantly different phenomena: (1) to define that complex to which the sense of "I" is attached, at whose core is the archetype of the Self; and (2) as the center of consciousness. Jung inferred a dialectical relationship between the ego and other complexes of the unconscious. This relationship, while depicted in dreams, is unconscious. The relationship of the ego to other complexes is handled differently by the different post-Jungians.

**Eros**  A principle of connectedness or relationship between people, among people and others. As the principle of love and life, Eros was understood as the exact opposite of Thanatos, i.e. death and destruction. Jung contrasted Eros with Logos, the principle of rational discrimination.

**Feeling**  One of four psychic functions (see Typology). It is a rational function which invests relationships and situations with value. It is not to be confused with "emotion," which Jung described as an instinctual energic system. "Feeling types" are characterized by strong personal attachments and preferences.

**Identification**  A defense mechanism in which a person is completely overtaken by an emotional state, such as a complex, refusing to recognize the actual emotions, images, and content of that state (see Possession).

**Individuation**  The process leading to a more conscious awareness of one's specific individuality, including a recognition of both one's strengths and one's limitations. Jung describes this process as emerging in middle and later adulthood, first with the recognition of one's neuroses and shortcomings. It continues as an awakening to one's own divided nature (conscious and unconscious) and the ultimate acceptance of that nature.

**Inferior function** The unconscious function: the one which "compensates" a person's dominant function. Inferior does not mean "weak": the inferior function very often manifests itself with irresistible force: e.g. "intuitive types" are often at a loss how to deal with ordinary sensory experience, which can throw their life into disarray (see Compensation and Typology).

**Inflation** Inflation is an unconscious identification, that may be passing or chronic, with an archetypal image (positive or negative) or an ideal or principle that leads to grandiose and/or manic actions (see Possession).

**Intuition** One of the four psychic functions (see Typology) and one of the two non-rational functions. It is the capacity to apprehend possibilities and tendencies without knowing details and facts. An "intuitive type" will tend to rush ahead with leaps of imagination, but may not be able to execute the final steps necessary to carry out a plan.

**Logos** A principle of rational discrimination. Jung borrowed this principle from classical scholarship and thought it was complemented by Eros (see Eros).

**Mandala** (Sanskrit = "circle") Jung used this word loosely to describe all images of circles, especially symbolic circles such as rose windows or dream images. He believed that the symbolic circle depicted the image of psychic totality, the goal of individuation.

**Numinous** Either a noun or an adjective, used to describe a "dynamic agency or effect not caused by an arbitrary act of will [which] seizes and controls the human subject" (*CW* 6, para. 6).

*Participation mystique* A term borrowed from the anthropologist Lévy-Bruhl, who used it to describe an unconscious psychological identification with objects or other people, resulting in a strong unconscious bond with the "other".

**Persona** (Latin = actor's "mask") The archetype of the mask, the persona was considered by Jung to be a necessary, non-pathological development of the individual, especially in the capacity to assume a social role, such as teacher, parent, student, etc. It could become pathological if, as an adult, one rigidly identified oneself with it.

**Personal unconscious** See Unconscious.

**Possession**   Describes the condition in which a person is dominated by a powerful psychological complex: e.g. a man who is consumed by a fascination with an anima-figure (cf. Keats, *La Belle Dame Sans Merci*), or a woman, by a fascination with an animus-figure (e.g. a celebrity or a priest).

***Privatio boni***   St. Augustine's idea of evil as the privation of good. Jung objected that this view asserted that evil had no existence, to which theologians have objected that Jung misunderstood Augustine.

**Projection**   The situation in which one unconsciously invests another person (or object) with notions or characteristics of one's own: e.g. a man, fascinated by a woman because she corresponds to his anima, falls in love with her. Feelings, images, and thoughts can be projected onto others. One also projects negative feelings: e.g. a woman has a grudge against a friend, so she *imagines* that her friend is angry with her.

**Psyche**   In the English translation of Jung's works, psyche is an all-embracing term used to describe "the totality of *all* psychic processes, conscious as well as unconscious".

**Psychoanalysis**   (1) Theories of unconscious instincts and meanings, originated by Sigmund Freud and his followers, and expanded to include many accounts of unconscious motivations and images, as experienced in relationships, dreams, works of art and other aspects of culture. (2) *All* theories that that seek to understand unconscious processes (see "Depth Psychology").

**Psychological types**   See Types/Typology.

***Puer aeternus***   (Latin = "eternal youth") An archetypal image of a youth reluctant to mature (e.g. Peter Pan). By extension, the term is used to describe a man who identifies with this image: such a man is very often characterized by a strong unconscious attachment to the mother (actual or symbolic) and an unwillingness to forgo adolescence.

   The female counterpart is the *puella*, an archetypal image of eternal girlhood (often expressed in the "child-woman" dynamic such as anorexia nervosa or the perpetual "little girl"). A woman who identifies with being a *puella* may have a strong attachment to an idealized father, have had a premature sexual relationship (as in incest), or be in retreat from an intrusive mother.

**Self**   (1) An archetypal image of "wholeness," experienced as a transpersonal power which invests life with meaning: e.g. Christ, Buddha, mandala-figures. (2) The hypothetical center and totality of the psyche, experienced as that which governs the individual and toward which the individual is unconsciously striving. The principle of coherence, structure, organization that governs balance and integration of psychic contents.

**Sensation**  Sensation is one of the two non-rational psychic functions. Sensation is the capacity of knowing reality or truth through the senses. A "sensation type" is strongly motivated by the sensory world and comfortable in the physical world (see Typology).

**Shadow**  Jung used this term in two very different ways: (1) to describe the entirety of the unconscious, i.e. everything of which the person is not fully conscious; and (2) to mean an unconscious aspect of the personality characterized by traits and attitudes which the conscious ego does not recognize in him- or herself: the shadow is often personified in dreams, usually by persons of the same sex as the dreamer. Because one tends to reject or be ignorant about the least admirable aspects of one's personality, most shadow-figures have negative connotations, but in people with very low self-esteem, the shadow can have positive attributes. Consciously assimilating one's shadow usually results in an increase of energy.

**Symbol**  A symbol can be defined as the best possible expression for something inferred but not directly known or which cannot be adequately defined in words. A symbol should not be confused with a sign. A cross on a church steeple is a "sign," indicating to the passer-by that the building beneath it is used by Christians for worship. For a Christian, the cross on the altar inside the church is a *symbol* expressing the ineffable mystery of Christ's sacrifice, whilst for a Buddhist, it would be a sign: i.e. it is only the individual's perception or interpretation that a symbol exists. One cannot reduce the symbol to any pat definition of its significance.

**Tao**  An image of the center, a symbol of God, and the way to God (*CW* 6, 361–366).

**Teleology**  (from Greek = "end" or "objective") A philosophical system that focuses on the motive or power of a goal or end-point as the process of development – toward an end. Jung conceived of the human personality in both causal and teleological ways, but emphasized the goal of "individuation" as the objective of a human lifetime.

**Thinking**  One of the two rational functions, thinking indicates a preference for logical coherence and facts as the basis of "knowing". A "thinking type" discriminates and evaluates (see Typology).

**Transcendent function**  The tension between opposites in a conflict that, when held in a dialectical relationship of allowing influences from both sides, can resolve into a uniting "third" or new synthesis. Jung saw this function as the center of growth.

**Transference and countertransference**   Describes a kind of projection that usually arises in a therapeutic encounter, resulting from wishes and desires about oneself and the other:

*Transference* names both the psychological complexes enacted by the patient with the therapist (responding to the therapist as though she or he were Mother or Father or sister), and the general feeling of need, idealization, or distrust that the patient irrationally feels for the therapist.

*Countertransference* refers to similar dynamics felt by the therapist toward the patient. The therapist can draw on the countertransference feelings to indicate certain typical patterns of relationship in the patient that have always existed with important figures and many constitute the patient's major problems in life.

**Types/Typology**   Jung distinguished two basic *attitudes* (Extraversion and Introversion) and four *functions*: Thinking, Feeling, Sensation, and Intuition. He described Thinking and Feeling as "rational" (because they involve an act of judgment), and Sensation and Intuition as "non-rational" (because they respond to stimuli without judgment). Thus there are eight basic types: e.g. Extraverted Thinking, Introverted Thinking, etc. Jung's typology has been developed into systems of assessment (e.g. the Myers-Briggs Type Indicator) that have been very successful in assisting people in handling differences in organizations and relationships.

**Unconscious**   That which is unknown, broadly speaking. Jung's theory of a "collective unconscious," innate and already organized in humans, was a contrast with Freud's "repressed unconscious" which was the residue of early relationships. In Jung's early theory of the unconscious, he hypothesized that the collective unconscious was organized by "archetypes," or primary *imagos* – almost inborn images. In his later theory, he believed that archetypes were innate releasing mechanisms (or predispositions) to form coherent images in aroused emotional states. Around these universal images (e.g. Great Mother and Terrible Mother) develop psychological "complexes" (see Complex) that are the primary building blocks of the human personality. Originally Jung believed these complexes formed the structure of a "personal unconscious," but later saw the archetype as the core of the complex, uniting the collective and the personal unconscious in the concept of a highly motivating psychological complex. Everyone's personality is composed of multiple complexes: Ego, Mother, Father, Brother, Anima or Animus, and so on. The integration of these complexes into conscious awareness is one aspect of individuation.

**Uroboros**   The image of a tail-eating dragon or serpent: according to Jung, one of the two fundamental images of alchemy (the other being the circle). The uroboros expresses the primitive self-enclosure of an undifferentiated personality, trapped within itself. It is also the first stage of development.

**Word association test** Early in his career, Jung developed a word association test in which patients were asked to give their immediate "associations" to a list of carefully selected stimulus words. Previous researchers had been interested only in the content of actual responses. Jung was the first to be interested in physiological responses (e.g. sweating) and delays as information about unconscious processes. He held that even slight delays in responding to a particular word reveal an emotionally charged issue pertinent to the patient's current situation: e.g. if "family" were to produce the association "escape," one might infer that the patient had problems with his/her family. The cluster of associations center around a "complex" (see Complex).

# INDEX

active imagination 6, 28, 65, 93, 105,
107–109, 137, 158, 173, 264, 277n
Achilles 242, 246, 250, 252n, 270
Adler, Gerhard 11, 12n, 46, 48
Aeschylus 253n
affect 54, 58, 59, 129, 137, 139, 145, 150,
158, 172, 193, 204, 206, 218, 297, 299,
306
Agamemnon 252n
*agape* 148
aggression 40, 98, 111, 127, 204, 236, 289,
310
AIDS 115
Ajax 242, 246
alchemy 12n, 24, 29, 30, 52, 75, 95, 147,
148, 150, 156, 178, 267, 311, 312
alienation 267, 284, 286, 287
ambivalence 74, 126, 128, 175, 190, 191,
193, 195–197, 201, 212, 215, 250
amplification 63, 121, 137, 147, 192
analysis 5, 6, 26, 89, 91, 96, 104, 105,
107–113, 142, 144, 145, 148, 150, 154,
157, 158, 188, 190, 192, 193, 196, 201,
227, 293, 306
and infancy 132
purpose of 68, 104
training analysis 56
Ananse 243
anima 2, 23, 46, 60, 92–94, 104, 107, 108,
113, 143, 145, 165–167, 171, 172, 178,
179, 181, 197, 203, 224, 225, 228–230,
264, 274, 276, 286, 304, 310
reclaiming the 171
*anima mundi* 113
animus 2, 23, 60, 92–94, 178, 189, 196, 203,
224, 225, 228–230, 274, 286, 304, 310
anthropology 20, 21, 147, 240
anxiety 25, 39, 126–128, 148, 168, 180, 186,

191, 192, 199, 200, 208, 223, 224, 235,
305
Aphrodite 112, 251
Apollodorus of Rhodes 247, 253n
Aquinas, Thomas 74
archetypal image(s) 9, 25, 66, 101–104, 110,
125, 128, 130, 132, 159, 192, 217, 241,
261, 262, 263, 265, 274–276, 285, 306,
308, 312
archetypal psychology 8, 101, 103–105, 115,
116, 198
archetypal school 8, 10, 11, 63, 101,
103–116, 256
archetype(s) 2, 8, 9–10, 23, 54, 58, 59, 71,
73, 80, 82, 90, 92, 101–104, 107, 122,
127, 166, 172, 198, 229, 240–242, 298,
307, 311, 312
and archetypal images 103
and drives 180
and gender 224
and numinosity 59
archetype-as-such 9, 103, 241
as categories of the imagination 102
definition of 9, 57, 101, 102, 166, 172,
173, 241
Great Mother/Goddess 57, 59, 104, 109,
153, 236, 307
hero 242
Jung on 58, 102
mother 90, 306
Terrible Mother 59
theory of 4, 9, 24, 27, 240, 311
trickster 240, 242–252
wise old man 25, 107, 241
wounded healer 157, 159, 211, 217
Ares 112
Aristotle 72, 73, 74, 76
art 112, 261

322

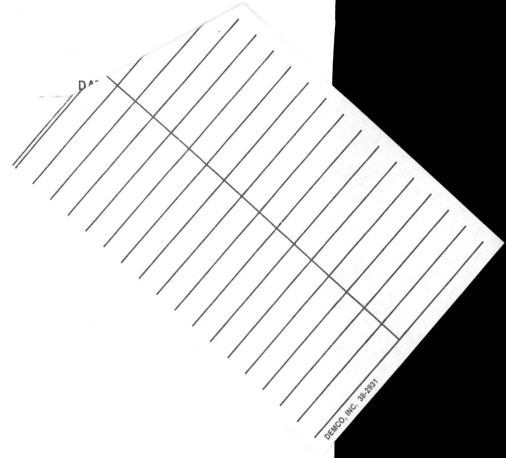

DEMCO, INC. 38-2931